The
Weight
of the
Stars

The Life of Anarchist
Octavio Alberola

The
Weight
of the
Stars

The Life of Anarchist
Octavio Alberola

Agustín Comotto

TRANSLATED BY
Paul Sharkey

ISBN 978-1-84935-408-0
E-ISBN: 978-1-84935-409-7
LCCN: 2021935965

AK Press   AK Press
370 Ryan Avenue #100   33 Tower Street
Chico, CA 95973   Edinburgh, EH6, 7BN
USA   Scotland
www.akpress.org   www.akuk.com
akpress@akpress.org   akuk@akpress.org

Please contact us to request the latest AK Press distribution catalog, which features
books, pamphlets, zines, and stylish apparel published and/or distributed by AK Press.
Alternatively, visit our websites for the complete catalog, latest news, and secure ordering.

Cover and interior illustrations by Agustín Comotto
Cover design by John Yates, www.stealworks.com
Printed in the United States of America on acid-free paper

Contents

Preface: History's Accidents

by Octavio Alberola

IN ONE OF LIFE'S strange coincidences, I was born the very same year as Che Guevara and Noam Chomsky, albeit several thousand kilometers away from them. I was born in Minorca, Spain, on March 4, 1928, Che shortly after that, on May 14 or June 14 (depending on which source one goes by) in Rosario, Argentina, and Noam Chomsky on December 7 in Philadelphia. There was nothing to predict how we would turn out, much less, the meetings of minds and disagreements that we would have.

A lot of years went by and a lot happened around the world before my path crossed with Che's in Mexico in 1956. That was shortly before he set sail on the *Granma* with Fidel Castro to embark upon a guerrilla war in Cuba's Sierra Maestra against General Batista's dictatorship. Later, quite some time after that feat of liberation and its institutionalization as a revolution, after Che's epic demise, and after he had been turned into a revolutionary icon, I met his grandson Canek Sánchez Guevara ... At the beginning of the second millennium, Canek came to Paris intent on helping us with the publication of the *Cuba libertaria* bulletin. When, towards the end of 2015, Canek unexpectedly died in Mexico, it fell to me to write his obituary notice.

As for Noam Chomsky, our paths crossed in Paris in the mid-1970s during one of his lectures at the University of Vincennes, the free university that had arisen out of the May 1968 student unrest (even then it was on its last legs as a libertarian forum). Many years would pass before I took issue with him for having, in 2013 in Caracas, endorsed the socialist rabble-rousing of Colonel Hugo Chávez's "Bolivarian revolution."

I mention those two instances of synchronicity linked to my birth date because, ever since I was very young, I've had the impression that each historical moment shapes the way that each generation sorts out its contradictions and leaves its mark on history. And also because, not only is there a close connection between the individual and his surroundings, but on certain occasions the simultaneity of seemingly unconnected events is not chance but the effect of the causal impact of each age's episteme. In other words, such exceptional events—generally chalked up as "coincidence," luck, and even magic—are the outworking of the historical determinism that governs our lives and triggers the events that amount to human history.

It strikes me, therefore, that in my own case such synchronicities are telling in that they are suggestive, right from the very opening of my autobiography, of the direction that my life was to go through, the upheavals in the history of these past ninety years: both the ones that it fell to me to live through as a more or less consciously implicated witness and the ones I witnessed at some distance and, occasionally, sheltered from their disastrous consequences.

Of course, what such upheavals meant to me during my childhood days and the awareness I acquired of them later, I can only recount on the basis of what I learned from subsequent study or from what I was told by my parents and friends. Broadly speaking, we all have great difficulty remembering the events of our childhood days; this is a phenomenon explained by the unrelenting creation of new neurons, neurogenesis, which enables children to learn more and more things but that wipes away their memories—even their most personal ones. This is all the more true of the memories that might be left behind by the upheavals generated by the class struggle and the survival instinct in childish minds before the onset of adolescence.

Being cognizant of that difficulty, how can I sum up the most important events from my childhood years—after my parents, a father from Aragon and a mother from Catalonia, conceived me on the island of Minorca, where they had set up a year or two before my birth, driven by my father's passion for rationalist education and a sort of an instinctive calling to a social apostolate that my mother shared with him? How am I to explain, from memory, how that "apostolate" was marked throughout by an advocacy of freedom and equality for all?

Later, as an adolescent, as my own conscious life was starting to assert its autonomy, I began to understand that influence on my developing mind, how my thinking and self-awareness and the feelings were shaped by them. Nevertheless, the likeliest thing is that those events and their meaning took shape as recollections in my mind after what I learned later or heard said about my parents, and it was on the basis of such neuronal synthesis that I have been able to "remember them."

There is—no question about it—a passing-on such as occurs between one generation and the next, which also requires a written and oral record before it can constitute a remembrance. Consequently, being certain that anything I might recount from those times would be a construct rather than an authentic memory, it strikes me as more logical to leave the responsibility there up to Agustín ... Not just out of honesty, but also for consideration of coherence, the aim being the sort of transparency that should govern the drafting of an autobiography.

My autobiographical narrative opens, therefore, in my adolescent years, when I was a student at secondary level and at preparatory school in Xalapa, the capital of Veracruz state in the Mexican Republic.

Introduction: Stowaway in a Long Train

by Agustín Comotto

THIS ALL STARTED BACK in the summer of 2014, when I was looking through the Biblioteca Arús in Barcelona for information for the graphic novel I was working on, on the life of Simón Radowitzky. Tracking something down in an old library is no easy matter. I was trying to fathom the modus operandi of the paper files essential for locating the materials one is looking for, when, just as I was floundering among the nineteenth-century arrangements, I received assistance from a stranger. This was Agustín Guillamón. He suggested a search methodology that proved of great assistance. We chatted and swapped email addresses. Agustín is a historian with a prodigious memory when it comes to dredging up seemingly irrelevant facts, dates, and data. That casual encounter brought me a lot of subsequent gratification, which was wholly unexpected. A year later, I received an email from Guillamón in which, in the usual terse manner he always employs in his messages, he stated: "Octavio Alberola was present at Radowitzky's funeral in Mexico in 1956. Here is his email address. He lives in Perpignan."

This is how I came to write to Octavio. A dab hand in the digital world, he didn't take long to respond to my email. This was an extraordinary opportunity as he was a primary source and I was keen to interview and make the acquaintance of (insofar as I was aware) the only person alive who had been acquainted with Simón. The itch I had to learn more about the personality—which had, for years, been costing me so many sleepless nights—was now satisfied. Octavio gave me "pointers" as to the ending of the book and it was thanks to him that I found a way of bringing the writing to fruition. At the time I interviewed him, Octavio had no recollection of the Radowitzky funeral, but did confirm for me that he had known the man. Both my partner, Anna, and I were impressed by his lucidity, serenity, and tremendous humanity. When I met Octavio and his partner, Ariane, I also met a number of exiles who, for a variety of reasons, never went back to Spain after the end of the dictatorship.

Octavio is in all likelihood right when he talks about there being a degree of logic underlying chance. "Look and ye shall find" and, if the lookers are seeking much the same thing, the likelihood is that their paths will cross. Which doesn't, however, make it any less fascinating how a certain gravitational force attracts persons with shared purposes.

Two years on from that meeting in Perpignan, I had the graphic novel about Radowitzky done and dusted and was about to launch it. It had been a protracted and complex process and, given the important part that Octavio had played in it, I wanted him at the launch event. This was asking a lot, because Octavio was up in years and could have told me no. But he said "yes." And, after many years of hard work and striving, the circle came to a natural close.

I can still remember the utter silence that descended upon the launch when Octavio took the microphone and starting speaking about Simón, about the short time when their paths had crossed in Mexico City in 1955. Octavio spoke for around fifteen minutes. When he speaks, Octavio casts a curious spell, a blend of ethical awareness and appreciation of well-being in which the listener is engulfed and carried away. He seems to make everything comprehensible. The unforced silence of the listener on a journey through time and ideas. There we all were, that November day, on a journey back into the past, witnessing the ailing, weary Simón Radowitzky and the youthful Octavio full of energy and chatting with him. By means of the agelessness of the spoken word, a concrete recollection was being conveyed to us. Because when Octavio speaks, I can just imagine the ritual acted out thousands of years ago in some cave, in front of a warming fire, as the tribal elder recounted his tales of the hunt, the gods, or calamities.

Knowing that his own life story deserved to be placed on record, I asked Octavio on several occasions why he hadn't written his autobiography, and his answer to me, every time, was that it had occurred to him but that circumstances had not spurred him into doing it. A month after that, I got a message from him in which he bluntly said that I should help him write his autobiography. According to Octavio, his story was worthy of comment in the sense of "a stroll through the events that shaped his life and the chances of a dialogue about them." Initially, I had the odd misgiving. What right did I have to inject myself into his life? I couldn't come up with an answer that might justify it. I deferred to intuition and to Octavio's tremendous wisdom. "If that's what he wants, he must have his reasons."

Octavio is an anarchist. Meaning what? That I am not quite clear on, as I have known lots of anarchists and each of them possesses a highly personal notion of what anarchy as a modus vivendi and way of thinking ought to be. Octavio is an antiauthoritarian possessed of an ability to communicate, which I have rarely encountered in anyone and, above all else, he is possessed of boundless curiosity. Octavio wonders about life, nature, the cosmos and its laws or the disorderliness of human existence. In that sense, his interest in how life is played out in society has prompted him to construct a life rich in experiences, and through his personal approach and activism, he's tried to influence others in their own pursuit of fairness, harmony, and mutual respect.

I waited for Octavio at the train station in Sants, Barcelona. He was traveling up from Valencia to attend a libertarian festival. I kept my eyes peeled for him as Octavio had no cell phone; if I didn't see him, we would miss each other. In the end, he was the one who spotted me.

"The story begins with my parents. Check them out if you can."

"Of course, Octavio. You want me to start off the book with them?"

"Yes. Strikes me as a good idea; what their beliefs were and what they fought for. My father was an anarchist and I imagine that that had an influence on me. What I like about the project," he remarked, "is that your generation will get a mention in the book too."

We chatted through the two hours we had available to us, and in the end, I saw Octavio to his train. He almost missed it, as we had lost track of time and neither of us was wearing a watch.

MISTY MEMORIES

From Apprentice to Teacher

STUNTED HOLM-OAK TREES, SOIL of greyish hues, blanketed in the dried yellows of winter grass and, here and there, the dusty villages blending in with Aragon's rural landscape. Nothing in the countryside showed any sign of having been changed here, where José Alberola, Octavio's father, was born.

José was born in Ontiñena near Fraga, where Aragon abuts Catalonia and where the different languages play havoc with the traveler who has lost his way. Ontiñena, on the river Alcanadre, is just one of a long list of familiar names, dots on the map: Fraga, Bujaraloz, Mequinenza ... Places that conjure up the utopian dreams that efforts were made to realize during the civil war years. In 1895, the year of José's birth, however, life in Ontiñena was not easy, and for that reason his mother, together with José and his two sisters left the village for Barcelona. Apart from looking for more promising prospects, there was another reason for their departure: José's father had died and left behind a young widow, a mother of three who she would be required to dress in mourning all her life in the backward-looking Bajo Cinca region with its strong religious traditions.

They arrived in Barcelona at the beginning of the 1900s. With its economic growth then at its height, the city boasted two industrial arteries, the rivers Besós and Llobregat, filled with manufacturing activity and smoke, attracting increasing numbers of migrants from different parts of the Peninsula, looking for work and opportunities. By the start of the 1900s and in less than five years, more than 250,000 people arrived in the city.

How did these Aragonese country folk arrive in the city? By cart? By train? What assets might a widowed mother of three have brought with her back then? Naturally, the experience was a rough one for a boy of just five years of age, holding on tight to his older sister's hand as if it was his only salvation.

José would go to school, and his sisters, as was the norm for poor women back then, worked, cleaning bourgeois homes. They were outsiders, poor folk from Aragon.

It was about this time, that Barcelona started to register a few ventures designed to introduce progressive changes to the social order. One of those revolved around schooling. Alfonso XIII's Spain saw an upsurge in conservatism and, in the field of education—under the sway of the Church—those progressive changes had not gone unnoticed.

José started his education under the Salesians in Sarrià, at a religious school in the upper part of the city. Later he attended Francesco Ferrer i Guàrdia's recently founded Modern School, which found itself in the sights of Church and State, in light of the educational innovations introduced by Ferrer i Guàrdia. In the religious and state schools back then, the separation of boys and girls, physical punishment, learning by rote as a teaching method and the instillation of fear and obedience through dogma were common practices. But José had embarked upon a brand-new form of education in accordance with the ideas of Ferrer i Guàrdia, whereby the learning methods were the very opposite of what was practiced by the priests: which is to say, José was learning how to learn.

How could a boy from such poor circumstances possibly have attended the school founded by Ferrer i Guàrdia, a school targeted at the middle class? We don't know that, but clearly Ferrer i Guàrdia's Modern School was one of the keys to understanding why José and then Octavio became anarchists.

We have no hard and fast information about José Alberola back then. Nothing with which we can flesh out his story; just conjectures about a boy whose future path we know. However, it is interesting to note that the fears of the detractors of the Modern School's teaching methods were well founded. Because, at that school, José Alberola learned how to think rather than merely to be obedient. This wrought such a change to his intellect that, added to the flurry of social happenings in the city, by the time he reached his adolescent years he was directing his energies into taking over the baton from Ferrer i Guàrdia (shot by the regime in 1909) and devoting himself to teaching. And so, in the Rosa de Foc (or Fiery Rose), a port city of bourgeois comportment that was packed with proletarians who were forever erupting into social upheaval, José Alberola trained as a rationalist teacher and anarchist.

At the time, combining studies with real life was not such an easy undertaking. Rarely was this humble fourteen-year-old not caught up in the events happening all around him. For instance, there was the order issued by the Antonio Maura government on July 10, 1909 that reserve troops (youngsters aged between seventeen and eighteen) were to be sent off to the war in Morocco. Tensions erupted into what the history books today refer to as the Tragic Week. Yet again, the Rosa de Foc (i.e., Barcelona) went up in flames. On that occasion, José was part of the fire in the city that slowly but inexorably was on the march to anarchosyndicalist revolution. But, as Octavio remembers it, his father was not a young direct actionist but rather enthralled by the anarchist ideas of Elisée Reclus, Piotr Kropotkin, and Pierre-Joseph Proudhon. José must have been sixteen or seventeen when he began teaching. He was deeply influenced by his own experiences as a student of Ferrer i Guàrdia and by what he had read of the most humanistic strand of anarchism. The likelihood is that statements such as the following struck him to the core:

Under the present system of social economics, machines, and likewise the division of labor, are at once the source of wealth and the ongoing, fatal cause of poverty.
—**Pierre-Joseph Proudhon**

The stream that I watched emerge into the daylight, flowing so clear and carefree, is now no more than a sewer into which the entire city dumps its trash.
—**Elisée Reclus**

In the midst of this sea of anxiety, the tide of which is constantly rising all around, in the midst of these folk perishing of hunger, these bodies stacked up in the mines and these mangled corpses sprawled in heaps on the barricades ... You cannot remain neutral: you will come to side with the oppressed because you know that what is fine and what is sublime—as you yourself are—is on the side of those who fight for light, for humanity, for justice.
—**Piotr Kropotkin**

All of this was happening in a city that had a penchant for setting churches on fire or overturning streetcars and mounting strikes in answer to oppression. Octavio recounts how his father had made the trip to Paris in 1918.

There he made the acquaintance of Paul Reclus—nephew of the anarchist geographer Elisée Reclus—and of Renée Lamberet, the like-minded historian and intellectual.

In Octavio's opinion, our parents' experiences of that sort eventually leave their mark on us. And he is right, because this blend of great thinkers and the direct action of Barcelona meet in Octavio.

In Barcelona in 1919, the dynamics of society sped up, just as the machinery in the factories had, and by then, the workers boasted mighty trade unions. With a mere nine years in existence was a trade union confederation, the Confederación Nacional del Trabajo/National Confederation of Labor (CNT) that was planning to do away with the state and install libertarian communism. What is more, it had a large membership, felt a degree of affinity with the socialist Unión General de Trabajadores/Workers' General Union and was counting upon building the future on the basis of Spanish trade unionism. So its main spokesmen decided to foster direct action as a strategy and to shun all compromise with the bourgeoisie and manufacturers. For their part, the bosses, backed by the government, hired gunmen (*pistoleros*) to eliminate the most significant trade union leaders. Unable to bring the situation under control, in 1923 Alfonso XIII backed the coup d'état by Primo de Rivera and withdrew from active politics.

By then, twenty-four-year-old José was a rationalist schoolteacher with some experience under his belt; he was writing for anarchist publications of the day, such as *La Revista Blanca* and *Solidaridad Obrera*. Teaching brought him to a variety of sites such as the CNT-sponsored La Farigola i Natura (Thyme and Nature) rationalist school in El Clot. Eventually, José traveled to the town of Olot, where his sister Florentina lived, to work as a teacher.

Back then, Olot was a small town with industrialization already under way. José taught children's classes by day and adults in the afternoons and nights, which was unremarkable, given the large number of illiterates among the workers. The bosses very soon began to look askance at the anarchist teachers who were "infecting" the workforce with their beliefs.

1919 was the year of the big Barcelona general strike, which was triggered by lay-offs at the Riegos y Fuerza del Ebro S.A. power company, known popularly as La Canadiense. The strike created ripples elsewhere in the region and affected the textile plants in Gerona and Olot. As a member and active member of the CNT, José was familiar with what was going on in Barcelona and was therefore one of the activists behind the strikes in Olot. José used to draft the manifestos and all the propaganda in support of the protest.

Also living in Olot, was the Surinach family, a family of peasant extraction that had come up, and now belonged to the town's well-to-do bourgeoisie. They owned a number of properties and, on one of them, the young Clara Surinach held an informal conversation with the industrial employers, leading businessmen, and members of the clergy. At that meeting there was talk of the strike, anxieties regarding the rebelliousness of the workers, and the overall climate of unease in Olot. It was not long before the guilty parties were being named as those anarchists from the CNT and, in Olot itself, that José Alberola, sowing the seed of defiance with his school.

Clara Surinach had a great vocation as a Samaritan. An austere, practicing Catholic involved in charitable efforts, she felt at home with talk about help for the poor. She took Christ's message deeply to heart. Her religiosity was simple, based on simple values and bereft of clerical artifice. For these reasons she was greatly concerned when her uncle, who was a priest and who had attended her gathering, raised with the other employers the possibility of "getting rid" of the rationalist teacher. Somebody brought up the name of an alcoholic thug nick-named Barretinas: he could "dump José in the river," exploiting the fact that it was Jose's habit to read while strolling through a grove near the riverbank.

The very next day, Clara went to see Florentina, José's sister, to warn her about the plan to take action against him. José and Clara first met that day.

The strike carried on and the bosses in the textile sector threatened to enforce a lockout, or employer boycott, a threat behind which other local branches of industry threw their weight. The workers' response was to lock themselves inside the factories, ignoring the ultimatum.

Following Clara and José's meeting, and against every expectation of the Surinach family, Clara brought food to the workers entrenched in their workplaces.

Some days after that the strike ended; a lockout was enforced and the authorities in Olot adopted a tougher line towards the workers and those sympathetic to the strike and ordered that the teacher be "banished," or be arrested.

José left town at the start of 1920, bound for Barcelona. He passed through a number of schools, stepped up his activism within the CNT, and carried on contributing to anarchist publications. In the midst of all this activity, José and Clara wrote letters to each other, until she joined him in Barcelona and they set up a home together.

Clara's decision was unusual for those times and for the social class to which she belonged. It was a leap in the dark in the direction of anarchist principles and something that her family found very hard to swallow. Octavio remembers hearing talk of Clara's family being outraged because she had to clean house for some Russian emigrés from Odessa living in Barcelona. Furthermore, Clara had four brothers and one of them traveled to Barcelona to talk her into coming back to Olot. He cautioned her about the perils of social struggle and the anarchists, and tried to persuade her that there was a better future waiting for her in Olot, where she could live a different lifestyle alongside her own kind.

"I think it is essential that we talk about the importance of your mother," I told Octavio. "Lots of people talk about your father, José, because in the historical context his name stands out, but it strikes me that your mother made a monumental sacrifice. She was very brave."

"Sure, sure. Tremendously brave. As you will appreciate, back in those days my father was the visible head of the struggle and she was just the '*compañera*,' a partner and no more. Which is why I think it is important that we now rescue my mother's standing."

"As far as I am concerned, the sacrifice made by Clara is crucial. Waking away from one's family, one's religion, everything one had previously believed in is an act of love, an act of an agile mind, and it rarely gets a mention. The *compañeras* are always overlooked, their personalities eclipsed by those of the fighters. What was your mother like, Octavio?"

"She saw religion as a matter of love, love for the human being. She saw that too in my father's trade union struggle. She embraced free love and bearing children outside of wedlock and until her dying day she clung to her break with the Church. But she stuck by the Christian faith's discourse on love too." Octavio paused for thought here, transported back many years into the past. "Oh, and she also clung to a kind of a life-long puritanism. For example, when I was eighteen and living in Mexico, I was very friendly with one girl…" (Octavio is forever referring to "girlfriends.") "My mother called me to one side and remarked that this was a very serious matter. She said that she had not brought children into the world just to 'bring people into this valley of tears,' but because my father 'had wanted that.' And she added, 'The physical act never held any charms for me.'"

"Meaning that the urge to procreate had come, not from her but from your father. For all her Christian background, there is a paradox in her 'breaking' with her duty to procreate..."

"Yes. It was my father that wanted children. She never had any interest in the material, carnal side of things. That was something she had rejected, way back, in her youth, back in the days of her charitable works."

"Maybe she thought of becoming a nun once upon a time," I ventured to suggest.

"Possibly. At the very least, the folks at home thought she would become a nun. To her, charity was everything, up until she met my father."

There is not much question about the menace to the physical integrity of anarchist activists in the 1920s, given the tremendous violence unleashed by gunmen in the hire of the employers, violence that left many dead on the streets. So, the realization that one was a target for the bosses' hired guns, since one's charisma or contributions to newspapers simply added to the personal risks, flew in the face of the rational decision to have children. However, we have to keep in mind that the decision to bring children into this world is a consistent feature of individuals involved in revolutionary processes.

In 1923, one of the bosses' hired guns murdered the anarchist leader Salvador Seguí aka El Noi de Sucre in Barcelona's El Raval quarter. Seguí was thirty-seven and his partner was expecting their baby. José knew El Noi de Sucre, and Octavio has confirmed that he had often chatted with him in his home. Seguí's impact upon José's thinking was palpable. In one of his many talks, Seguí said:

> Granted that anarchy is not an ideal that can be implemented in the short term ... granted that anarchism, through time, might be achievable, have no doubt but that it will first provide scope for the devising of other ideas and other schools of thought springing naturally from the crude version of the idea....
>
> There is no denying that our organization, that syndicalism, is the spiritual progeny of anarchism ... plainly, syndicalism is not anarchism, but it is a measure of anarchism. The distancing of the anarchists from the trades associations is suicide. Everything should and can be done inside the unions.

José went on later to join the Iberian Anarchist Federation (FAI) and his thinking remained Proudhonist. Such anarchist contradictions could be found in José Alberola and in Salvador Seguí alike. Contradictions between direct action, revolutionary violence, and classical anarchism's nonviolent approach.

But the possibilism of the times was vital if one was not to lapse into simplistic thought patterns. Those were not the days of "harmonious living," "breakdown of the ego," "the society of the future," or "naturism." No, the keynotes of the day related to "the unions," "guns," and "general mobilizations."

That said, José's romantic anarchist ideal was not entirely discarded, as we can read in an extract from his report to a CNT congress in Madrid in 1931:

> Those lobbying on behalf of Federations of Industry have lost their faith in the value of man and defer to that of gear mechanisms ... We are not in favor of the retention of capitalism without capitalism ... It is the ideal that sustains our belief. We cannot countenance anything bordering on statism.

In the same year that witnessed the murder of Salvador Seguí, José and Clara's daughter Helie was born. And in the wake of a thwarted experiment with a modern school in Alicante in 1926 (which was shut down due to pressures brought to bear by the catechist nuns who alleged that it was offering "tendentious lessons"), José and his family moved away to Alaior in Minorca.

It was in that little village, basking in the Mediterranean light that can only be appreciated by visitors to the Balearics, that Octavio Alberola was born on May 4, 1928.

Backwater in Cinca

THE ALBEROLAS ARRIVED ON the island of Minorca in 1926 and lived in Alaior in a rented home of Indian construction.

Since the Primo de Rivera coup d'état in 1923, the CNT was outlawed, publications with anarchist leanings were banned, and any dissent from the regime was persecuted. The "class war" (to borrow historian Josep Termes's characterization) between the industrial bourgeoisie and the working class culminated in a dictatorship that formalized the repression hitherto enforced by parapolice gunmen. Whereupon things such as "thought crime," so-called, provided the pretext for taking activists and intellectuals alike into preventive custody.

José was vulnerable to this new policy of repression because at no point did he cease his activities as either a teacher or as a CNT militant.

The newspaper *Solidaridad Obrera* resumed publication surreptitiously around 1930. Lots of prestigious writers contributed articles and lots of anarchists passed through Barcelona's Modelo Prison at that time.

September 14, 1930 saw a protest rally held at the Palacio de Bellas Artes in Barcelona. It became a rallying point for a wide range of political persuasions. The protest was against the expulsion from Catalonia of Francesc Macià. There was also a demand that political prisoners be set free. The rally was addressed by figures such as Lluís Companys, Antoni Rovira, Ángel Samblancat and, representing the CNT's Regional Committee, José Alberola.

After the rally, on his way home to Minorca, José was intercepted by the police as he came ashore in Ciutadella. He was placed under arrest and told that he had to leave the island at the earliest opportunity, having been banished for his militant activity. And so, barely two years after he was born, Octavio and his family made their way back to Barcelona.

The increasingly eccentric and obtuse Primo de Rivera's last year as dictator was 1930. One example of his eccentricity was his choice of Severiano

Martínez Anido as military and civilian governor of Barcelona and subsequently as minister of the Interior. Martínez Anido brazenly proclaimed his contempt for intellectuals and for the working class. The Galicia-born Martínez Anido had a resumé filled with cruelty and atrocities carried out in Cuba, the Philippines, and Morocco. Primo de Rivera saw him as ideally qualified to contain the anarchists in the capital of Catalonia.

But the dictator's days were numbered and, with CNT support this time, the political parties from a range of ideological positions clamored for the return of a Republic. That very year the CNT called a general strike in December. In retaliation, nearly all of the leadership of the Regional Committee in Barcelona (José for one) were arrested: José served a short term in the Modelo. His recollections from that time were passed on to Octavio; memories of the "university" he had attended in the company of the other anarchists held there.

In the end, afflicted with diabetes and rejected by much of the army, General Primo de Rivera stepped down from power on January 28, 1930. After a softer period of authoritarian rule, the Second Spanish Republic was introduced in April 1931, bringing an amnesty in its wake.

A free man once more, José Alberola spent some time working in a range of the CNT's rationalist schools in Barcelona and Manresa. The Alberolas' travels ended in 1933 in Fraga, a few kilometers from where José had been born. It is at this point that Octavio's memories begin.

The town of Fraga, in the 1930s, had approximately 7,500 inhabitants. Small, rural, dating back to times immemorial, with traces of Iberian, Roman, or Arab influences, Fraga was claimed by both Aragonese and Catalans. Shortly after the Alberolas arrived, the town would undergo one of the most novel social changes the history of the twentieth century had to show. In 1936, for a brief period that lasted less than a year, the entire Bajo Cinca area was under the remit of the Regional Council of Aragon, meaning that the area's inhabitants lived under libertarian communism, with the land collectivized, and private ownership and the use of money eliminated.

The school at which José started teaching was known as La Cultural and was part of the Sociedad Cultural Aurora libertarian *ateneo* set up by the Fraga and district CNT member.

One ex-pupil of José's stated in an interview that attendance at La Cultural was not contingent upon one's being an anarchist or from the proletarian class. However, pupils were primarily drawn from peasant families which were anarchist or proletarian.

As for the *ateneo* we have the testimony of one resident, Agustín Orús, who was a pupil of José's: "The *ateneo* was a real powerhouse; we had an arts group and staged plays, mounting libertarian tours of the villages in the co-marca and we had access to a splendid library that made books available to the members."

Amateur dramatics, literacy classes, health education, and many other subjects were taught there to anyone willing to learn. In next to no time, José and Clara settled in the town, earning the sympathy of Fraga's workers and the enmity, once more, of the well-to-do classes.

Valerio Chiné Bague, another ex-pupil, said of Alberola the teacher: "I barely knew him but he was the only teacher who taught classes at times when it best suited his student ... I arranged with him that I would attend his classes at nine o'clock at night. Even though I was fifteen years old, I could barely read or write since I had been working since I was eleven [...] Imagine my surprise when my boss discovered that the teacher due to deliver lessons to me was Alberola; he told me bluntly that I needed to find myself another job [...] The fact is that Alberola was held in very high regard by ordinary folk and by the workers, though not by the bosses or the monied classes."

Octavio was able to live a "normal" life up until the outbreak of the Civil War changed everything in 1936. He would go to school, play in the street with other children, and from time to time, Clara's family would travel out from Olot to visit them. Virtually nothing from that time has stuck in his memory, but judging by how he speaks of it, it must not have been an unpleasant time.

Sometime in the Future

IN 1936, THE FASCIST wing of the Republic's army mutinied against the Republic. Simultaneously, social revolution erupted in Barcelona, which initially put a stop to the fascist uprising there. The fact that the mobilized populace was able to stop a regular army—as happened in Madrid and Barcelona—can only be explained in terms of the existence of good internal organization on the part of the CNT and its regional committees, as they had spent years making preparations for a potential army revolt. The euphoria felt by Barcelona anarchists at their defeat of General Manuel Goded (who had sided with the would-be coup-maker General Francisco Franco while in the Balearics before flying on to the capital of Catalonia) was cut short by the high cost of their victory: many of their comrades lost their lives on the pavement of the Avenida del Paralelo, fighting the rebels.

The reaction to developments outside of Barcelona varied. In Fraga, José's comrades reacted speedily and brought the situation under control. In Aragon, even though the fascists seized power in Zaragoza, the situation was dominated by the CNT and the republican parties, especially in Huesca. José was put in charge of Education on the Aragon Defense Council.

Within days of crushing the fascist rebellion in Barcelona, the first libertarian columns were setting off from that city, bound for Aragon. The aim was to liberate Zaragoza, opening up access to the Basque Country which was particularly important to the Republic as far as industry was concerned. That entire part of Aragon fell under the control of the Aragon Defense Council and, once established as an entity, the latter set about fostering the process of land collectivization and the abolition of money from exchanges of goods.

Getting a handle on such happenings today, in a world so wedded to corporations and private spaces, is a complicated matter. In some villages near Fraga there were instances of people gathering together in the square to burn money. Anarchists back then were convinced that a revolution was a sort of a "wipe clean and start over," after which a brand-new society could be conjured up from nothing. And so the Aragon Defense Council readied itself to implement libertarian communism as soon as possible. Valuable assets were stockpiled for redistribution to all in accordance with essential needs, rather than their being accumulated. In times of war it is vital—and the anarchists knew this too—that the production of goods continues uninterrupted. Meaning that, above and beyond the process of social change, at no point was there to be any interruption to the production of raw materials or manufactured goods.

Although the vast bulk of the population was poor and illiterate and eked out a living from subsistence farming, the hard thing—really the hardest thing—was doing away with customs and a culture that had been embedded for centuries. Things like money, private ownership, or religion had put down roots over centuries and abolishing them overnight was a complicated challenge.

José cited one peasant woman who, when it came to the distribution of confiscated goods, asked for one of the candelabras seized from the church. The teacher pressed her to explain why she wanted it, as it was utterly useless. Her response was that owning a candelabra had always been a great dream of hers, never having had one.

Into such paradigmatic change stepped Buenaventura Durruti.

The sight of the Durruti Column's militias arriving, with their pointed hats and red-and-black banners must have made an impression on those remote, ancient, blithely unchanging Aragonese villages. A ragtag army of un-uniformed personnel, with weird looking vehicles armored by the whimsical talents of a blacksmith and a collective discipline that defied description. The confederated members of the columns were of every sort: some were true believers, people whose dreams were of "the ideal"; others were simple opportunists in search of material gain; and there were also those who, in the wake of the widespread euphoria that had erupted in Barcelona, wondered what the hell they were doing there, gambling their lives beneath a leaden sun, eating poor rations and unable to take a bath the way city folk normally did.

In the van of the Column came Buenaventura Durruti, a native of León whose charisma there was no denying. He was a direct actionist, an imposing presence with enough oratorical talent to mobilize such a motley crew of humanity.

The Column passed through Fraga in the stifling heat on or around July 26, 1936. Some seven thousand armed individuals traveling through the scorched fields of Aragon, eating whatever they could find, tackling fascists, and spreading the watchword of land collectivization: it was rather chaotic and memorable for the participants as well as for the peasants who saw them coming.

José briefed Durruti on what had happened in the town when the column passed through Fraga. By then, everything had been collectivized already, and José had played a crucial role in that, in Fraga as well as in the surrounding villages. Not that it had been easy, though. José's philosophical anarchist turn of mind prompted him to argue with his own comrades over how their ideas were to be put into practice. Stripping the landowner of his land was normally accompanied by punitive actions and vengeance, as scores were settled arising from many years of exploitation and wretchedness. In many instances, the landowners were shot. José emphatically rejected the use of force and, on more than one occasion, stood up to the more radical elements. We have the testimony of Josefa Calucho Amil who, in an interview, recalled what happened prior to the Durruti Column's outriders reaching Fraga: "Alberola said to those meeting with him: 'And now that you have taken over the homes of the rich, what is it going to take to get you out of them again?' When lists circulated of those slated for death, Alberola hid a number of people in his own home. We all pretended not to know a thing."

"But my father's problems started after the arrival of the Durruti Column," Octavio remarked. "I remember that when the Durruti Column showed up, its advance party took over the town. That unidentified group wanted to shoot those arrested by the local CNT, people like the mayor, the priest and other fascist supporters who were being held in the town hall. My father opposed that and a heated argument erupted: 'The revolution's purpose is not providing opportunities for vengeance, but rather to set an example.' The squaddies left, only to come back to the town hall in the early morning, bringing the prisoners to the cemetery, intent on shooting them. Fortunately, a neighbor woman spotted them and scuttled off to alert my father. He arrived late, by which time some of them had already been shot. He managed to stop them from carrying on, but they threatened to kill him, cursing him and railing at him: 'And which side are you on?'"

"So how did it all end?"

"They left the town but returned a few days later because they had run into some fascist resistance on the front lines, a few kilometers further out, en route to Zaragoza. My father and some of the others from the town got themselves organized and denied them entry to Fraga, stopping them at the bridge across the river. My father hissed at them: 'You are a bunch of cowards. You cannot kill the enemy in the front lines, yet you want to kill defenseless people here in town.'"

"They were a bunch of uncontrollables, right?"

"I do not know what they were, but they had nothing to do with my father's way of thinking. Those were heady, terrifying times and life had very little value. Let's put it this way: those guys were hard to hang a label on but they did a lot of damage to the anarchists.

"Shortly before the so-called May Events in Barcelona," Octavio went on, gliding from one memory to the next, "in 1937, my father had made his way to Lérida for a meting with Felipe Alaiz and José Peirats with an eye to coordinating the magazine *Ideas*. On leaving Lérida and heading back to Fraga, he was stopped by some communist troops from the army of the Republic serving with the military unit at the airport. They brought him into a room. He got wind of what they were planning when he saw armed soldiers threatening him. Luckily, such was the shambolic organization that my father seized his chance and slipped away to safety. José reported to his comrades and complained about the matter to the authorities, who explained it away in terms of lapses in control in the republican ranks. The communist military also apologized and said that the whole thing had been a mistake, that they had mistaken him for a fascist; which was a lie because, from the moment he had been abducted, they had been addressing him by name as José Alberola."

"From what you say, the situation was highly dangerous."

"You have no idea. On another occasion, my father traveled to Manresa to give a talk setting out his opposition to the CNT's collaboration with the government of the Republic. He was against the militarization of the anarchist columns, meaning, their being brought under the supervision of the republican military command. On his way back to Fraga, his car was riddled with bullets by a Control Patrol. Those traveling with my father fired back. The car from which they had been shot at tailed them for quite a while. They escaped by the skin of their teeth. The pattern was the same, but this time it was a case of 'friendly' fire. This time it was personnel from within the CNT who were all for collaboration with the government. Their argument was that the thing was a mistake, that they had mistaken them for fascists. As you can see, it was all very precarious and there had been a huge radicalization in positions."

The land as everybody's property was short-lived. First there were the so-called May 1937 Events or Incidents in Barcelona which largely ended the anarchist workers' power of the CNT. Later, internal differences fostered the rise of the communists who were gaining strength. Later still, after the CNT's influence within the republican government had diminished, the communist General Enrique Líster's troops turned up on the Aragon front and, at gunpoint and in the name of the Republic they dismantled the Aragon Defense Council (and indeed persecuted Council members) and returned ownership of the land to the former landowners.

By then, Alberola had left Fraga for Barcelona. This was in late 1938 and the Republic was suffering Italian fascist and German air raids, deference to Stalin's plans, and the wretched non-intervention policies of France and England.

"Back on the road again, dashing from city to village, teaching in extreme circumstances, evacuating the children due to the air raids, hunger, and short rations ... Can you remember those days, Octavio?"

"Vaguely. The odd detail. I reckon I was around ten years old. We moved to Valencia for a time, staying in Progreso Fernández's home. Then it was on to Viladecans near Barcelona. My father was teaching there, I can remember the air raids."

"What is it like coming under an air raid?"

"Italian planes flew in from Majorca, bound for Barcelona. Some of them bombed the arms plant in Viladecans. Some bombs landed near us. At nights the sirens went off and we went outside as a precautionary measure. The antiaircraft searchlights in Barcelona and on Tibidabo could be seen in the distance. Plus, there was the dull, hollow clump of the bombs. We clambered up a hill for protection and in order to get a better view. One night during an air raid we left home just to be on the safe side. I went with my mother, my father and sister were slightly behind us. We were making our way along the street, heading for a nearby hilltop, when a bomb landed. The shock wave from the blast hurled us against a door. We knew the explosion was very close, even though nothing happened to us, because we could see wounded behind us."

Viladecans suffered as many as three fascist air raids between March and July 1938. The town was a secondary target but, even so, twenty-seven people lost their lives to bombs. July 5 was the day that claimed the highest number of lives. The target of the air raids was the Roca plant, a strategic target since it had been concentrating on the production of artillery shells ever since the outbreak of war.

From the low hills overlooking Viladecans and Gava near the factory, Octavio and his family witnessed the horrors of what was going on in Barcelona. The local topography was high enough to afford them a view of Barcelona under air raid and that, added to the black-out in the villages, left an enduring impression in the memory of an eleven-year-old boy.

"In Viladecans the position was becoming unsustainable and, to be on the safe side, my parents decided to send Helie and me to Olot, to our maternal grandparents. I can remember my grandfather's garden. Every day I used to fetch him a *cistell*, a basket, containing snacks. That short stay in Olot was a fairly quiet time for me, I think. My uncle worked in the local Nestlé factory. They made condensed milk and powdered milk there. You can imagine how delighted I was with such a treasure trove. In war-time no such things are available and there is no describing what a dream it was to have access to such delights."

"Hunger. We haven't mentioned hunger, Octavio."

"Hunger is scary. I remember it from my boyhood, and a child has a tremendous appetite. We were growing up and had nothing to eat. It bequeathed me memories such as the condensed milk. Back then, a militia friend of my father's passed through Viladecans. He brought along a bar of chocolate and I wolfed it down. And felt sick after gorging myself. I also ate radishes that we used to grow in the tiny garden we had at the Viladecans house. We turned up our noses at nothing."

"It is hard to grasp what goes through a boy's head in such circumstances."

"Everything revolved around getting something to eat. Anything you spotted you ate because you never knew if you would get the chance later."

"And your parents?"

"They left Viladecans and passed briefly through Barcelona. Even then the fascists were hot on their heels. From there they set off for Olot from where we made for the border by truck along with my mother and sister. My father made the clandestine crossing of the Pyrenees with some other comrades, the Ocaña brothers, following a different route. They all spoke very good French so it was not too daunting for them to cross into France. My father then made for Paris, to renew his acquaintanceship with Paul Reclus and Renée Lamberet. There was nothing to be done in Spain by then.

A Boy's Eye View of the Retirada

THE WAR WAS DRAWING to an end. With Catalonia gone, there was little hope of dragging out the conflict pending international intervention. The Negrín government's plans were unfeasible. No one came to the aid of the Spanish Republic.

Contemporary film footage shows children in the long line of refugees crossing the border. Children without a hand to cling to, children with wire-thin legs, poorly clad and walking unsteadily through the winter chill of that fateful January 1939. Crossing the border into France and having no notion of where to go.

Along with some other women, children, and elders, Clara, Octavio, and Helie reached Figueres. The truck brought them there from Olot, and in all likelihood it would have turned back to collect more people. From Figueres, the journey continued on foot as far as Le Perthus, on the far side of the border.

"We climbed a small mountain," Octavio recalled, "and slept in an abandoned farmhouse. The route obvious as there was a trail of suitcases and other items people were dumping into the ditch. Because initially, when they had left their homes, people were carrying as much as they could. But as the journey went on and they grew more weary, they dumped their belongings by the side of the road.

"The gendarmes took us to a school from which they had removed the desks and installed some mattresses. That is where we spent our first night in France. It must have been in Le Boulou. The menfolk finished up in the nearby refugee camps in Saint-Cyprien and Argelès. After three days, they placed us on a train that would disperse us across several sites in France where we were taken in. I remember the train having passed through Lyon, which struck me as a ghastly, grey, depressing place."

"And what became of your father? Those must have been very tough times for your mother."

"Of course, as she was left to do everything on her own. As yet, we had had no news from my father. We assumed that he had made it through to Paris. My mother put on a brave face, as did my sister who spoke a little French, thanks to my father. Some days after that we arrived in Tenay in the Ain department."

There is a hasty assumption that has gained traction over time, that France failed to take the republican withdrawal in hand. Officially, as a country, France left quite a lot to be desired and was not equal to the circumstances. This was the natural outworking of the non-intervention policy by which the French government had stood throughout the entire Spanish conflict. Apparently, the socialist Leon Blum's government faced international challenges a lot more important than Spain's internal problems. Even when the fate of Europe was largely being played out in Spain, it stuck by the policy of non-intervention. However, the same could not be said of the French population and displaced persons were met with solidarity efforts. In the region where the little town of Tenay was located, close to the Swiss border, there was a significant show of solidarity.

Thus, a few Spanish refugees—women and children—arrived in Tenay between January 29 and February 8, 1939. The families arriving were placed under strict quarantine, the children were vaccinated, and then the refugees were scattered through various settlements in the Ain department in the Auvergne-Rhône-Alpes region. Tenay in those days was a tiny village. Jean Pélaz, its socialist mayor could scarcely have imagined that these Spaniards would be a foretaste of the Second World War. Because, in the wake of France's defeat in the war, the village and its surrounding area became part of the Nazi system for imprisoning and subsequently deporting Jews, maquisards from the Resistance, and dissenting slave laborers.

Before long the children were being sent to French schools. The village placed great importance on the recent arrivals' returning to normal life.

"What was it like going to school in Tenay at that time, Octavio?"

"Pretty different from my previous school experience. For a start, we could not understand French and there was no war going on. What we did I have no idea and I cannot recall. My sister Helie, then aged fifteen, was the main interpreter between the French people and the refugees in Tenay.

"Tenay's mayor had been on a trip to Mexico sometime previously. He was a rather odd sort. He had one of those wide-brimmed hats like the Mexican *charros* (cowboys) wear and it never left his head. A real odd bird. As it happens, he found out while speaking with my sister that my father was a teacher and that he was in Paris…"

"That's right. We were forgetting your father. What had become of José?"

"My father was in Paris trying to secure passports and some sort of assistance through his French contacts. But neither Paul Reclus nor Renée Lamberet were able to do much at that point."

"And the mayor?"

"Tenay's mayor found out through my sister what was father was doing. And he came up with a brainwave: to bring José to Tenay 'officially' to deliver lessons to the refugee children. He offered to sort out the family's papers."

The CNT, busy trying to resurrect itself as an organization in exile, was not having an easy time of things. The profound falling-out that was beginning to become apparent within the organization was evidenced by the reproaches or accusations traded between its scattered leading lights such as Juan García Oliver in Sweden, Diego Abad de Santillán in Buenos Aires, and Federica Montseny in France. On one side were the libertarians critical of anarchist participation in the government of the Republic. They looked upon that a as a surrender to the state, in which, theoretically speaking, no anarchist believed. They denounced the concessions made from May 1937 onwards, which had allowed Negrín and the communists to grow in influence, thereby delivering the coup de grace to the movement. In the opposite camp was that faction of the CNT that had allowed all that to happen and, worse still, had made the case for having entered into a partnership with something in which they, as anarchists, were disbelievers, i.e.. the State.

This was a very serious business, in complicated circumstances: the CNT, the largest anarchosyndicalist confederation in history, was now in exile in a strange country, and much of its human resources had dwindled.

"In the end, you were reunited with your father."

"My father arrived in Tenay and set up the school for refugees. Not that we lasted for long. Before leaving Paris, his name had been added to the list of teachers bound for Mexico where the Republic had established itself in exile in an attempt to resurrect itself. And so, early that summer, we left Tenay for Bordeaux. There we boarded the *Ipanema*, which the Republic had leased to ship exiles across to Mexico. There was still a degree of pluralism in the Negrín government when it came to passenger selection and so we were able to secure our passage."

The *Ipanema*, the *Winnipeg*, the *Mexique*, and the *Sinaia* ... Clandestine ships carrying a human cargo of the vanquished. Paradoxically, republicans, communists, anarchists, and persons from other parties or political persuasions exiled from Spain found themselves obliged to rub along together, in confines narrower than the defeated Republic, during the twenty-five day voyage to territories unknown.

On June 12, the *Ipanema* set sail for Veracruz, Mexico, with 988 passengers on board. José Alberola was on the SERE (Servicio de Evacuación de Refugiados Españoles/Spanish Refugee Evacuation Agency) passenger list:

"Alberola Navarro, José, aged 41—[...] Political party, none.—Trade Union: National Confederation of Labour—Residence in France [...]—Pre-war posts held: none.—War-time posts: Advisor, agricultural collective."

That was it. Wipe clean and start over. No trade, no children, nothing. Everything was under the name José Alberola and that euphemistic "Advisor, agricultural collective." That was the Republic's slant on the role he had played on behalf of the Aragon Regional Defense Council. Put simply, José had "advised" the peasant.

Most of the exiles taken on board up until 1942 had professional qualifications. Meaning that the Republic itself "struck out" unskilled workers or citizens from exile in Mexico. The selection process served as a screening process, handled by the SERE, the evacuation agency set up by premier Negrín's Republic. Even though no such arrangement had been made between Negrin and the Mexican government.

Mexican president Lázaro Cárdenas, in what was at the time an unprecedented act, welcomed and offered asylum to the republican exiles. Cárdenas put it to the Negrín government, through his ambassador Narciso Bassols that what was needed was: "a careful selection of refugees, entirely disregarding political and social affiliations and ties, with the selection made under this approach breaking down into: 60% farmers; 30% technicians and skilled workers; and 10% intellectuals."[1]

Cárdenas wanted to populate under-populated areas of Mexico with peasants; and inject some fresh Hispanic blood into Mexico as a counter to the United States population growth. However, the ratio of Spanish refugees that Mexico received bore no relation to what the Mexicans had been asking for.

On this score, Octavio maintains that the matter would not have been such a big issue had the personpower involved simply been skilled, that is, had the issue been just about the peasants that Cárdenas was asking for. Mexico was awash with peasants and what it needed was skilled labor, professionals. That way, even though Cárdenas had asked for something different, he would have been bolstering Mexican society with Spanish professionals, artists, and engineers.

"I can remember Bordeaux, grey and smoke-filled and the ship and the trip to Mexico, the passage through the Sargasso Sea where the entire surface is covered in plant life. Oh yes, and the dolphins. I used to spend hours on end just watching the dolphins swimming alongside the *Ipanema*. We met a family of socialists on board. My sister became fast friends with their daughter, Rosita."

"Is that all you can remember of the ship?" I pressed when Octavio fell silent. "I'd have thought a ship was rather impressive in the eyes of a boy. How many ships had you been on up to then?"

"None. But that's all I can remember of the voyage."

"No 'acquired' memories?"

"Yes, yes, yes, of course. I have it stored in here," he points to his forehead. "And it is based on something that happened. But what I mean to say to you is that it is copper-fastened by others. I say this, I say that, an invention ... But not from bad faith or on stylistic grounds. It did happen, of course, but it needs to be handled with care. The spoken memory, in the sense of historical investigation such as we are engaged in, needs to carry weight, but it should also be placed within parentheses unless one can compare it somehow."

"So can I incorporate your invented or almost invented memories in the book, Octavio?"

"Of course. They are only memories, my memories and they are hazy."

EXILE IN MEXICO

There Are No Indians in America

"RIGHT, OCTAVIO, NOW YOU can remember the way you like to, which is to say, relying on your own memories."

"Yes, yes. It's a funny thing, the memory," Octavio replied, warming to his subject. "The moment I start thinking, I can't stop remembering."

"Okay, but don't go wearing yourself out. You were saying that you mull things over in your head. Now your memories are your own. I'm just sorry that, as you were saying the other day, you have no further details to offer regarding the voyage on the *Ipanema*."

I raised the subject of Negrín's SERE, the agency that arranged their passage ... and details that might offer some sort of a lead, but out of the blue, swept along by the dynamics of memory, Octavio remarked:

"The good ship *Ipanema* set sail from the port of Bordeaux on June 12, 1939. Due to technical issues, it was forced off course and put in at the French island of Martinique for a few days. Thanks to a mechanical breakdown, the passage to Veracruz took nearly a month: one of the propeller blades snapped. This forced the captain to stay over in Fort-de-France port in Martinique for a week. The ship had to go into dry dock for repairs. I remember that during that week the chauffeur of the island's governor brought us and Rosita and her sister Pili on a tour of the island. One day, returning via the port and boarding the ship with the Martinican chauffeur to say hello to our parents, the French gendarmes made to bar his way, on the grounds that he was Black. My father lodged a vigorous objection.

"In the end we sailed for Mexico and sighted the port of Veracruz on July 8."

There was great expectancy in Mexico regarding the republican refugees. In the case of the *Ipanema*, they were greeted on their arrival in Veracruz by a municipal band and the city authorities.

"There were no Indians."

"What? I don't follow you."

"Imagine the surprise of an eleven-year-old boy when he is told that he is now in America and, on seeing none of the 'Indians' he had been expecting on that continent from his reading of childish literature and contemporary movies all about 'Indians and cowboys ...'"

"A swizz ..." I suggest, amused.

"Surprise, frustration, and bafflement. Yes, I felt cheated. This was not America, let alone Mexico: and in the streets of that semi-tropical city I could not see any *charros* wearing big black sombreros like I had seen in some Mexican photos and films."

"That's the truth. There are no *charros* and no black sombreros in photos I have seen of the disembarkation in Veracruz."

"Quite the opposite. The *jarochos*, the folks from the port of Veracruz dressed in white shirts, white trousers, and white boots, with a red bandanas around their necks and straw hats to shield them from the sun. I was struck by the curiosity that we aroused, whether on account of how we were dressed or because of our physical appearances, which contrasted with those of the bulk of the *jarocho* population. Although there was also a chance that rumors were rife among them that the Spanish "reds," the communists who had lost the war, were upon them."

That last remark is not something remembered but rather a consideration by the eighty-eight-year-old Octavio. Reds. Defeated communists looked at askance by the conservative classes. Mexico had a well-established Spanish community, which had been living in the country for many years. These were the *gachupines*. In etymological terms, the expression derives from the Nahuatl tongue. Meaning, more or less "the fellow in the spurs" or "he that wears spurs on his shoes"; in short, a foreigner. But over and above whatever meaning it may have had back in colonial times, *gachupín* referred to all the Spanish families long established in the country. Broadly speaking, their leanings were monarchist, they were economically well-to-do with well-established ranches or businesses and, when it came to religious traditions, they were very conservative and prided themselves on their Spanish roots. So they had no hesitation in supporting the fascist revolt and siding with the Francoists in the Spanish war. The *gachupines* were not stingy when it came to sour remarks and rebukes aimed at the republican refugees who could expect no help from that Spanish colony in settling into Mexican society.

Octavio just had to get used to the idea that not all "Indians" are like the movies and that the host country was an unbelievable melting pot of races, cultures, and customs very different from the ones he was familiar with back in Europe.

Scorpions in the Convent

THE NATIONAL CAPITAL, MEXICO City, is an island of cement sprawled across the Mexico valley, in the shadow of the Popocatépetl volcano and built on top of the former Aztec capital, Tenochtitlán. Millions of people packed into one of the largest cities on the planet. One of the things by which the newcomer is taken aback is the gamut of colors and smells and the antiquity of the historical buildings. With their baroque architecture, they resemble their counterparts in Europe but, scrutinized at greater length, the differences come to light and it gives the streets an odd feeling of familiarity about them, the sort of familiarity one might feel in the case of a distant relative. The brickwork is occasionally made of volcanic materials and there is an uncertain verticality that makes the walls appear wooden. Plainly the responsibility for this belongs not just to the architects but to the seismic shifts that have warped everything.

The Mexico of 1940 was in the throes of a strong economic recession that, after ten years, was threatening to become chronic. Well-known local personalities were against the official policy on the refugees; ultimately, this was an influx of communists or "reds." President Cárdenas's political opponents, especially high profile in widely circulating conservative newspapers like *Excelsior* an *El Universal*, tried to gain political capital by standing up against the influx of refugees. And there were other sectors of the population that looked also askance at the newcomers. The trade unions and the peasants had no clear notion of what all these "new Mexicans" were bringing to the country. Despite all this, those exiled by the war in Spain were greeted by an authentic hospitality from the official welcome program and Mexico's intellectual classes.

Once in Mexico, Octavio and his family were brought face to face with the reality of the country, as were so many other refugees from the war. The receptions, complete with municipal bands and fanfares, were over now and they had to earn their keep. To a large extent, the newcomers were reliant

upon the JARE (Junta de Auxilio a los Republicanos Españoles/Aid to Spanish Republicans Council) and upon the previously mentioned SERE, both of
which were set up by the Republic to deliver aid to the refugees. The agencies operated on the basis of funding sent abroad by the Republic before the
government of Spain left for exile. However, with the passage of time, both
agencies underwent an ideological shift and neglected the anarchist-oriented
CNT or FAI exiles.

"Before we turn to the Federal District, Octavio, tell me: what did you get
up to in Veracruz?"

"I seem to recall that we spent several days there, waiting for our turn to
begin the trip to the capital, by train, as I recall it. On arrival in the Federal
District, we were placed in an apartment in a building in the older part of the
city near the Zócalo. In order to get by, my parents had to settle for roaming
the city making door-to-door sales of sausages from a factory that some other
refugees had just opened."

"Turning his back on teaching and getting into business must have been a
big change for a rationalist schoolteacher."

"I remember my mother returning from work, worn out. My sister and
I had just started attending the Luis Vives High School, which had been
opened by some exiled teachers in August 1939. There we bumped into Rosita
again, the friend of my sister who was the same age as her, and Pili, who was
my own age.

The launch of the Luis Vives High School signaled that learning and the
delivery of learning had left Spain along with the Republic. The Republic
in exile had launched a secular, progressive popular school, named after the
sixteenth-century Valencian philosopher and educationist Luis Vives (this
was no random choice: after completing his studies in Paris and having settled in Bruges, Vives had decided not to return to Spain for fear of persecu-
tion at the hands of the Holy Inquisition, and he died abroad). Launching the
school was quite a feat at that time. But the plan was even more ambitious and
the hope was to set up other similar schools around the country, schools that
would eventually adopt the name of the "Cervantes College." They would also
accept Mexican students, which helped the exiled teachers and pupils to settle
in. Likewise, other independent schools were launched by Spaniards, schools
such as the so-called "active schools" that adopted the educational methodology of the French communist Célestin Freinet.

José had not resigned himself to selling sausages. He turned his hand to whatever he could, but at the same time, he was keeping in touch with republican educational circles, as evident from the fact that his children were admitted to the recently founded Luis Vives High School. His return to teaching was only a matter of time: there were about twenty thousand exiles and teachers were sorely needed.

"Octavio, I remember you saying one time that you did not spend much time at the Luis Vives."

"Yes, although I cannot be certain how long. We were left alone with my mother and sister for one or two weeks, because my father had gone to work at an art school in San Miguel de Allende city—the Fine Arts School—as headmaster. He was offered the post by the Peruvian painter and writer (and fellow exile in Mexico) Felipe Cossío del Pomar. My father and he had been introduced by the Chilean poetess Gabriela Mistral, who at that point had yet to be awarded her Nobel Prize for Literature."

"And what of your mother, Clara?" I asked, trying to delve into how she had settled in, in Mexico. "How did she adapt to her new life?"

"Badly. In actual fact, she never really fit in."

"What makes you say that?"

"Well, she was the opposite of my father who was all energy and an extrovert. He would seek contact with the relatives off his pupils, was involved in amateur dramatics, and could carry a conversation with strangers. And simultaneously dash off letters to acquaintances all round the world. He had a life outside of the family. But my mother? No. She was a homebody, with that tragic sense of life that was characteristic of hers."

"I can see that you remember more of your father, beyond his political persona."

"Remembering him is easier. Indeed, there is one thing that annoyed me. He was such an extrovert that on occasion he didn't realize to whom he was speaking. I told him: 'Why talk to them when they do not listen to you?' He used to chat about politics and the arts and anything you like. And did not spare much thought for his listener. He was a very self-assured type. My mother, on the other hand, was shy. She was always able to detect selfishness in people, even among fellow activists, and was critical of some anarchist comrades who would drop by to see us with 'a method in their madness.'"

"Something else that intrigues me about your father is this business of the arts. You say that he had ties to Felipe Cossío del Pomar who was a prominent figure in Peruvian intellectual circles. On political grounds, he left for exile in France and had ties to André Breton, Louis Aragon, the Surrealists ..."

"My father had a real penchant for the arts. In addition to teaching, he was on the look-out for connections with illustrators, painters, musicians, and dancers. And he loved theater. He was always on the lookout for people to give classes at the school. I mentioned to you previously that he had been introduced to Cossío by Gabriela Mistral, but it could just as easily have been by Rodolfo González Pacheco, the Argentinean writer."

"I can't believe that. Your father knew Rodolfo González Pacheco then?" I said, almost cutting him off.

"Yes. From during the war in Aragon, maybe."

Rodolfo González Pacheco is connected to Simón Radowitzky. Pacheco was the son of landowners from Tandil, an Argentinean town smack dab in the middle of the pampas. He left everything behind, intent on changing the wretchedness of the world through the anarchist "ideal." Stirring and impassioned, his plays were out-and-out rallying cries, weapons against state tyranny. His artistic-political activities ensured that he carried the anarchist cause beyond his home ground, first in Buenos Aires and later in a range of Latin American countries. In 1938, he turned up on the Aragon front where, in all likelihood, he met José Alberola. González Pacheco was in charge of the People's Theater Company which, from time to time, used to perform in the collectivized villages along the Aragon front.

"About two weeks after my father left, Cossío fetched us in a car complete with uniformed chauffeur to take is out to San Miguel de Allende to be reunited with my father and settle into quarters at the art school, a former convent. First, we went to a hotel and the chauffeur fetched all our belongings in three trunks. The point about the liveried chauffeur is that Cossío managed to persuade President Lázaro Cárdenas to convert the nunnery for use as a government Fine Arts School. As I found out later, of course."

San Miguel de Allende is a small town in Guanajuato state, located a little less than three hundred kilometers from the Federal District.

These days, the historical town center is painstakingly beautiful and one gets the feeling that specialist staff sweep the town every night. This is because a huge influx of tourists, from the United States above all, has turned the town into a sort of a theme park; colonial architecture, colored houses, heavily ornamented, exquisitely baroque doors. There is nothing out of place, nothing that jars. Work on this has been ongoing ever since the 1940s when tourists began visiting from the wealthy country to the north. The painter Cossío, who naturally had a head for business, promoted the Fine Arts School in the United States. That and another institute in the town, the Allende Institute, offered diplomas validated by the United States government and that attracted a lot of that country's citizens.

"What was the school like, Octavio?"

"My sister and I slept in a room in the nunnery that had a very high ceiling. Our beds sat in the center of the room, under mosquito nets and with our feet sitting in dishes filled with water to protect us against scorpions. That way, they had no way of getting at us. But when we turned in for the night and turned off the lights, we could see in the moonlight that the scorpions were climbing the walls.

We used to play in the convent's central garden, where there was a fountain. Pictures come to mind of the doors to the ground floor rooms where we slept and even of the inside of the chapel where the Mexican artist David Alfaro Siqueiros painted a mural that was left unfinished because he was arrested in 1940 for his role in the attempt to assassinate Trotsky. I still have the images in my head of what is referred today as "the unfinished mural." There was scaffolding and canvases and the odd daub already on the wall. But it is worth remembering because it is indicative of the political climate at the time.

Lev Davidovitch Bronstein (aka Trotsky): at the time that Octavio was living in San Miguel de Allende, Trotsky was already ensconced in his bunker-cum-home in Coyoacán, in the Mexican capital.

His home is a reminder of the end of the story of a man at bay, someone wiped out by forces his own personal resources could not match. In fact, he was murdered while imprisoned by his own security measures, which were useless against Stalin's long reach. First there was the failed assassination bid by Siqueiros and then Ramón Mercader's successful attempt. Mercader murdered him by plunging an ice pick into his brain that very same year, 1940.

Besides being an extraordinary mural painter, David Alfaro Siqueiros was a communist activist of the Stalinist school. Acting on orders received, or out of ideological fanaticism, he orchestrated the assassination attempt on Trotsky. At daybreak on May 24, 1940, he attacked the Trotsky home with an armed commando team. In addition to his secretaries and personal bodyguard,

Trotsky's wife Natalia Sedova and his grandson were on the premises. By some miracle, the raid was a failure but the bursts of machine-gun fire almost struck their target. Before fleeing, the assailants abducted one of the bodyguards, the American Robert Sheldon, who turned up dead in a ditch a few days later. Siqueiros never expressed any remorse for the raid.

"Seems to me that in San Miguel de Allende..." Octavio continued, "that we spent only a few weeks there as my mother soon became fearful for my sister, who was sixteen or seventeen years old at the time. She noticed that students attending the school, nearly all of them from the US, seemed to have come down to Mexico to party rather to study. Which is why she asked my father to give up his post and we all moved back to the Federal District. Her plan was to wait in the capital until my father's papers were sorted out (his naturalization papers) so that he would be in a position to see to the opening of a Cervantes College in Xalapa."

"I can see that your mother held some sway over the household. Your father's project in San Miguel de Allende was a good one."

"Yes, but he could see the reasoning behind my mother's arguments for leaving his job."

"Maybe his heart was not in delivering lessons to dissolute bourgeois."

"Maybe so. What I am not so clear about is whether the proposal to set up a Cervantes College in Xalapa and serve as its director came about before or after we left San Miguel de Allende.

Tragedy in Xalapa

ANOTHER FRESH START. AS if nothing had happened, the Alberolas moved back to the Federal District. While José set off again—for Xalapa this time—the children resumed their education at the Luis Vives High School, and Clara reverted to selling sausages from home.

The Alberola family didn't spend long in the city during that never-ending year of 1940. The prospect of ushering in the New Year once settled in Xalapa held out the promise of stability, something that had eluded them for some time. In late December 1939 or early 1940 the Alberolas arrived.

Bear in mind that financial aid from the CTARE (Comité Técnica de Ayuda a los Republicanos Españoles/Aid to Spanish Republicans; Technical Committee), an offshoot of the SERE, was designed to find work placements for the large numbers of exiled Spanish teachers. Besides, as agreed with the government, they were obliged to offer work to Mexican teachers in any schools they might found.

José was not finding things easy. There were only twenty-six posts for male teachers and nine for female ones. The records of CTARE's activities show that the college was launched in 1940. Of all the centers opened under the aegis of the Cervantes scheme, it was the smallest, with a mere fifty-three pupils. It had great difficulty in getting off the ground, and in 1941 needed additional funding from the CTARE just to survive.

"There seems to be every indication that you completed your primary schooling in Xalapa."

"Yes. We went off and set up home in a refurbished old house where my father opened the Cervantes College with a team of six refugee teachers. In the building, with its central garden and surrounding huge rooms that were used as lecture theaters, the college was launched. We settled into the rear of the garden where the concierge's quarters must have been once upon a time."

"Did you have a hard time settling into Xalapa?"

"Xalapa was a big change compared to the Federal District. It was very provincial, a conservative city where the Church wielded great influence. The *gachupines* in Mexico City were more assimilated but in Xalapa they had a much more telling influence. Suspicions were soon being raised regarding my father's teaching methods."

"And the Church?"

"There was a lot of religious fanaticism. According to the law in Mexico back then priests were not allowed to wear their soutanes on the streets. Processions were not permitted but the law was circumvented because of the strong religious sensibilities. However, in light of the dismal education available in Xalapa, the *gachupines* used to send their children to the Cervantes College, even if the teachers were 'reds.'"

"Tell me a little about Helie, Octavio."

"My sister was enrolled straight away at the city's preparatory-secondary school and I finished my primary schooling at my father's college that same year. A few months later, my sister fell ill after going for a swim in a public swimming pool. Two days later, with her temperature still high, my parents sent for a doctor to get her a sick note to account for her missing class. The doctor signed her off and prescribed her a few injections to bring down her temperature. Shortly after she received the injections, Helie began to go into heavy convulsions. My parents summoned the doctor again and when it turned out that he could not come, they sent for another one. Some time passed, and there was nothing they could do to prevent Helie's death ten days later.

"For my parents," Octavio continued, after a short pause, "it came as a terrible blow. They had gone into exile in Mexico in order to spare my sister and me from having to go through another war, and now here she was, dead, in such nonsensical circumstances ... In the end, the doctors said that it was down to her having contracted typhoid at the pool, and back then penicillin hadn't arrived in Xalapa."

"I have my doubts," I said, casting around for an answer where there was none. "They injected her with something and shortly afterwards she went into convulsions. Sounds like an allergic reaction."

"It was horrific for my mother," added Octavio, changing directions. "She was devastated, and shortly afterwards began to have epileptic seizures, so-called 'incidental epilepsy.' She never got over the tragedy.

"My sister had a civil burial in what was a very Catholic city. The *gach-upines* and conservative class in Xalapa took this as an insult. The ceremony triggered a clash between my father and some teachers. They alleged that a number of students had quit the college on account of the funeral."

"That stance on the part of the *gachupines* was wounding, but the teachers were even more infuriating. If memory serves, they were communists, right?"

"Yes, although they were also possibilists. These were teachers who had struck up friendships among Xalapa's bourgeoisie, most of which were *ga-chupines*. A few of them even consented to have their children baptized or re-baptized so that they could have wealthy *gachupín* godparents. I recall one *gachupín* boy from the school telling my father that, in his home, he had heard one of the teachers, a communist, say that the problem was that my father was an 'artist.' My father corrected the lad by querying whether the word used might not have been 'anarchist' rather than 'artist,' to which the boy replied: 'That's it, that's it, anarchist!'"

The fateful year 1940 ended for the Alberolas in personal tragedy, with the bourgeoisie of Spanish extraction setting its face against them. They were virtually penniless. It was hard assimilating. Once the money ran out, the communist teachers quit and Jose was left alone to front the college with a couple of teachers from Xalapa: one who taught bookkeeping and the other typing and shorthand for adults.

"Your father was, shall we say, on the brink of closing down the college."

"Yes. The rent on the building was too high, so my father switched the college to a different building, complete with rooms, a smaller courtyard and two rooms to accommodate us. I lived there during the five years that my studies lasted, three years of secondary schooling and two of preparatory classes, until, come January 1946, I enrolled at the Faculty of Engineering at the Universidad Nacional Autónoma de México (UNAM/ National Independent University of Mexico) in the Federal District."

"What sort of thing did you get up to outside of the school context?"

"I have various recollections from my five years in Xalapa bearing on my school experiences, given that I was the only Spanish refugee at the school and my friendships, in a context purely Mexican, ensured that I felt just like one of the boys, and then, later, like just another youngster surrounded by other Xalapa youngsters. My interests back then were not that different from those of children and youngsters from Xalapa."

"You mentioned to me once, with regard to Helie, that for a long time after she died you were still on the lookout for her."

"Yes. I couldn't comprehend that my sister was dead, just could not take it in. For a long time I had dreams. I was sure that she had gotten lost and that I had to find her. I had nightmares in which I searched for her or found her and we had to get back home. I also see my sister in other women."

"You were an adolescent by then... You sister must have been a remarkable presence during her short life."

"Yes. I have a snapshot at home that you won't have seen. She was pretty, very athletic, and very happy. It was very easy to befriend her because she, like my father, was an extrovert."

"I would think also that those days were pretty decisive in shaping your present personality. This ability I see that you still have for switching between multiple areas of interest."

"With hindsight I can see that I did some odd things back then. I remember that, at the age of fifteen, I used to hang out with a bunch of youngsters who wanted to be *novilleros*. I went with them on several occasions but I dropped that 'enthusiasm' after I was dragged along by a heifer that showed me no mercy. I was also part of a football team at the time, which is to say, in my pre-university days."

"So much for the run-of-the-mill stuff. But you were interested in other things as well."

"Of course, of course. In terms of culture and politics, during the last year I spent in Xalapa, I attended lectures on philosophy put on by the priests from the city seminary. I had gone to the talks with several of my closest friends from the preparatory class. Later, when we set off for the Federal District to pursue our education, they also helped launch the Libertarian Youth. At the last talk that I attended, I sparked an incident with the priest when he tackled the subject of free love from the Catholic vantage point. I stood up and said that my own parents were in a free union and in addition to their loving me a lot, I felt very happy with them.

"The odd thing about our 'fraught dealings' with the Xalapa clergy was that one of the priests who had spoken most ill of my father at the time of my sister's secular funeral asked him to admit to the college his nephew who was in his twenties and showed no interest in his studies. My father acceded and he was with him up until the college was shut down towards the end of 1946.

The upshot was that the lad graduated in accounts and typing, and the priest turned up to thank my father, saying that he was sorry to learn that he was leaving Xalapa.

"On another occasion, while in prep classes, we were required to wear uniforms. That was, I think, in 1944. I could always come up with some reason for not wearing the uniform tie, shirt, or cap. Furthermore, in order to get out of the two hours of square-bashing at the stadium, I pretended that I could not march in step and ensured that they 'punished' me by leaving me behind in the prep stores. There it was my task to issue and collect back the wooden rifles the others used for their military drills. There was not a lot to do, so I used the time to read science books that I fetched from my father's library. Such reading material was crucial in me generating a huge interest in science and philosophy. I was about sixteen by that point and still did not think of myself as an anarchist. I just had this feeling that I wanted to break away from the grip that the PRI (the monopolistic party that occupied all the political ground) had on Xalapa."

"And in the end you left Xalapa behind to go to Mexico City, to study at the university."

"It is hard to get a handle on what goes through a youngster's head in such surroundings.

"In early 1946, I left my parents behind in Xalapa and took off for the Federal District to enroll at the Faculty of Engineering. I had made that decision a few months earlier in Xalapa along with one of my closest and most like-minded friends, Manuel González Salazar. I had wanted to go to the United States and study but, as a political refugee, that was not happening. My dream at that time and the product of my reading of science books dealing with Einstein's theory of relativity and Planck's quantum mechanics, was to enroll at Princeton University where Einstein was lecturing. Manuel had also wanted a civil engineering career and so off we went together to the Federal District. One year after that, Mario Díaz, another of my Xalapa pals, also enrolled at the Faculty.

"Together with Mario and Manuel, I was part of the most 'politicized' group from the Xalapa prep class at the time. They had both dropped out of the lectures at the seminary, similarly disappointed by the priests' social conformism. In conversation with one another, we were agreed on the need for a fresh revolution in Mexico. Our 'politicization' was the result of a like-minded rebelliousness; but at that point it was not caught up with any hard and fast ideology. Mixed in with it was a degree of admiration for the great Mexican revolutionary leaders and the craving for novelty and autonomy. We held never-ending discussions because, despite any influence of my father's, I was still not an out-and-out champion of libertarian ideas. He used to give us books to read, books by Tolstoy, Kropotkin, Reclus, and so on. But what we cared most about in political matters was Mexico's politico-social situation. Especially the corruption that prevailed among the country's professional politicians. But that was as far as we went. We settled for 'we should...' or 'we ought to set up...' At no point did we make up our minds to sign up with some group or political party. Which was commonplace at the time, since all one ever heard about in Xalapa was the PRI, the Partido Revolucionario Institucional/Institutional Revolutionary Party, which was the only political option available. The talking-point was how to break away from the PRI and get back to the Mexican Revolution of 1910 again. The PRI had been in government in Mexico since 1929 when the various revolutionary factions had decided to amalgamate, and it was founded for the purpose of institutionalizing the Mexican Revolution. A party that clung to power and then, every four to six years, proposed a new president for the Republic. Its excuse was the principle of 'effective suffrage and no re-election' as guarantors of the system's stability and a measure of democracy in that presidents were not eligible for re-election. It was only reasonable therefore that, the PRI being the only party in Xalapa, none of us had any intention of joining it and our political and social concerns were confined to mere gossiping with friends."

Draftsmen on an Hourly Rate

OCTAVIO LEFT XALAPA IN 1946, moving to Mexico City as a student. Even then, the Federal District was a huge blackhole gobbling up more and more Mexicans from every part of the country every year as they arrived in search of opportunity. At the time, the city had a population of nearly three million, a huge figure in the context of the times.

"I read somewhere that back in 1946 the Federal District was an enormous city."

"I was very struck by my arrival in the capital. As you say, it was even then one of the largest of the world's megalopolises. Bear in mind that I was two months short of my eighteenth birthday. A brand-new stage in my life was actually beginning. Remember the Ocañas with whom my father crossed the border into France at the end of the war? They were my hosts when I arrived in the Federal District. One of the Ocañas—Francisco, who went by the name of Floreal—was a great pal of my father's and a rationalist teacher just like he was. Together with his partner, Fraterna, he earned his living in a dye-works."

"But didn't you tell me that José Viadiu had played host to you?"

"Yes, him too. But before arriving in the Viadiu home I spent a few weeks with the Ocañas."

José Viadiu was one of the anarchists of the old guard, from the days of Salvador Seguí and Ángel Pestaña. Like them, Viadiu was rather more moderate in his political stance than, say, the FAI's hard-liners, Durruti or the Ascaso brothers.

"Why the interest in Viadiu?" Octavio asked, rousing me from my ruminations.

"His story is an odd one. I read that, in 1938, anarchists refused to board their children on the vessel that was setting off for Moscow, in the face of air raids and the advance of the fascist army. But the Viadius sent their three children away."

"Yes. It's a very sad story."

"I read that Viadiu was an editor working on *Solidaridad Obrera*. Even though most of the children belonged to communist cadres and families who were by then openly at odds with the CNT, Viadiu booked his children a passage to Moscow. The oldest son, Armando, was very frail and in need of care. Viadiu came under a lot of pressure from the CNT to not send him away, because the idea of shipping the children out had come from the communists and, in a sense, was tantamount to conceding that as far as the war was concerned, defeat was around the corner. However, off the Viadiu children went to Moscow."

"But worse was to come. At the height of the Second World War, Héctor and Armando Viadiu, two of José's sons, joined the Red Army and took part in the battle of Stalingrad. Nothing more was ever heard of them. At the time that I arrived in the Federal District and showed up at their home, José Viadiu and his partner Libertad Ródenas were awaiting the arrival from Russia of their youngest son, Ismael, the only one of the three to have survived. Just imagine how anxious they must have been."

"How was Viadiu earning his living as an exile in Mexico?"

"He was working as a proofreader in the 'La Nación' Print Shop, a cooperative society with a state stakeholding; it produced the *Boletín oficial de la República Mexicana*. I spent no more than two weeks with them. It was a matter of waiting for the grant that we had been awarded to come through."

"A grant I would not have imagined. Looks like the Veracruz government was pretty generous…"

"It was a trifling award, not enough to cover our costs. To make up the difference we put in a few hours each day as draftsmen in architects' offices."

"Why? When you knew nothing about architecture."

"On the bulletin board at the university we spotted an ad for draftsmen to work on blueprints. The pay was lousy but it helped us earn a bit of cash. We were comfortable with the work as it was the sort of thing we used at the faculty.

"And it had just popped into my head that in one of the architect offices I worked in sent me out to carry out a survey of the basement of a church on which construction had been paused for several years. I went out there on two mornings to take measurements and, on my return to the office, set about drafting the blueprints. On the third day the chief architect summoned me to his office and started to give me a dressing down for having 'offended' the priest at the church by having, it was alleged, refused to say hello to him. I told him that on every occasion when I spotted him coming, I had raised my hand in salute. To which the head architect replied that, where a priest was concerned, the etiquette was to kiss his hand. I told him that I was a nonbeliever and therefore had no need to do so. We argued and he said to me, 'Pack up your stuff and get out.' I went to my desk, gathered my things and, before leaving, scrawled in capital letters across all of the blueprints that I had completed: 'There is no God!' Two years later the same phrase caused great disruption in Mexico, after Diego Rivera inserted it into one of his murals in a high-class hotel in the capital. The phrase was borrowed from Ignacio Ramírez, *El Nigromonte* (The Necromancer), a Mexican author to whom we owe it that Mexico is a secular state. He was highly respected in Mexico and since he dated back to before the Revolution, to the late nineteenth century, Rivera had inserted it in order to provoke."

"And you knew Carlos Contreras, the architect, didn't you?"

"True, but not through any architectural connection. The link with Contreras had to do with my father having written to tell me that I should call and give Contreras his regards and see if he might find him a job in the Federal District since my mother was having a hard time coping with my absence."

"And how did José know him? Contreras was a celebrity even then," I said, searching for the papers I had found about the architect.

"He had run into him before we moved away to Xalapa. In all likelihood, he was one of the intellectuals with connections to my father, like the painter Cossío. Contreras held him in high regard. He was very famous and wealthy, and, as far as I can recall, lived in the Polanco quarter, an upperclass residential district. We visited his home several times for dinner. It was a huge mansion with a superb garden."

Besides being an architect, Carlos Conteras was acknowledged as a great town planner. Although, if we are to understand his rise, we have to talk about Miguel Alemán.

Miguel Alemán, the president of Mexico from 1946 until 1952, stands comparison with a lot of leaders in different South American countries at the time. In 1949, with the anticommunist scare at its height, the Americans were caught up in a witchhunt overseen by Joseph McCarthy. Like his neighbors to the north—and his South American counterparts—Alemán spared no effort to rid the country of communists and other left-wingers of the same ilk. He outlawed the Mexican Communist Party and enforced a crackdown on progressive-minded trade unions and peasants through his term of office. Alemán can also be compared with other Latin America presidents of the time because he derived great personal benefits from his term in office; by the end of it, he was one of the richest men in the country. Certain historians even allege that he bears the responsibility for the institutionalization of corruption. Although there is no denying—and this is where the architect Contreras comes in—that under his rule the country experienced a huge upsurge in civil construction. Schools, highways, brand new estates, canals, and hydraulic schemes flagged up Mexico's drive for modernization. In the Federal District, at the time when Octavio was still studying at the university, the University City was on the verge of being unveiled. It entailed a mammoth national effort.

Small wonder that the architect Contreras made his fortune under the Alemán administration. The capital was expanding and, thanks to that, Contreras's signature was on lots of avenues, and he was involved in redrawing the city boundaries, from which he grew wealthy.

But there were other factors in Octavio's extramural life too. One was Helie's absence. From Xalapa, José told him that Clara's epilepsy was getting worse and that she could not bear his being away from home. Looking for some way of easing Clara's depression, José asked Octavio to keep an eye out for an apartment for the whole family to share in the Federal District. He had made up his mind to burn his bridges and shut down the college once and for all by the end of the year.

"But what work was José intending to do in the Federal District?"

"That was why I went to see Contreras, the architect: to see if he could help him out whilst he looked around for work as a teacher. I remember that Contreras was, or had been, president or vice president of the Rotary Club in Mexico. He had his studio in one of the tall buildings across from the Palacio de Bellas Artes, on the corner of the Avenida San Juan de Latrán (which I think he had designed) and the beginning of the Calle Madero. I paid him a visit and he told me that my father could come whenever he liked. He could start out working in his workshop, putting the archives in order and after that he would see what he could do for him."

And so in late 1947, José brought his Xalapa period to an end. He closed down the Cervantes College and once again the Alberolas were back living together in the Federal District. Octavio found a small apartment in the Avenida Baja California for them to move into.

"My father started working with Contreras right away and I continued with my studies and my work as a draftsman."

"It is odd that someone like your father, with such solid ideals, should have had that sort of a friendship, given the highlife that you mentioned Contreras used to lead."

"It was probably a meeting of minds. I remember my father saying over and over, when the talk turned to the chances of the refugees' returning to Spain, what Contreras had said to him about the prospect: 'In the wake of civil wars, exile is useful when it comes to easing the pressure on countries, which is why governments have an interest in stretching it out as long as possible.'"

"What an idiotic thing for Contreras to have said!" I burst out, almost without thinking.

"His remark reflects a geopolitical fact: every state has an interest in preserving the political and social status quo in the world. That way, the right of asylum allows them to seem humane, when their only goal is to cling to power. Which explains why the Spaniards' exile lasted forty years!"

Getting a Handle on Entropy

"WHAT FEW MEMORIES I have of 1946 and 1947 have to do with my mother's health issues and events in the faculty, such as the time we spent several days on a perspective sketch of its monumental doors. This was for the descriptive geometry assignment we had been given by an elderly lecturer of Italian extraction. Apparently, somebody played a prank on him and he reckoned it had been me, and I confessed, rather than naming the real prankster. By way of 'punishment', I had to stand by the blackboard at the start of every class and solve the descriptive problems that he would give us. The upshot was that I was top of the class since the 'punishment' forced me to be thorough in my studies. I finished up on very friendly terms with him and in the end, I told him that I had not been responsible for the prank related to his name, but that I could not identify the real prankster for him. He appreciated that and let it drop. And so, gradually, I learned the rudiments of engineering. Obviously, my fascination with other disciplines such as physics or philosophy endured. Evidence of this was the fact that one physics lecturer, to round off the year, asked his students for a written essay on whatever portion of the course they had found of greatest interest. Since I was still reading science books, I handed in an essay on Louis de Broglie's wave mechanics and classical mechanics. The physics lecturer knew nothing about wave mechanics and apparently only knew about classical physics. He could have rejected my paper but he gave me good marks and urged me to matriculate through the Faculty of Sciences. Which I did at the beginning of 1947."

"Why such an interest in physics, Octavio?"

"I have always had such leanings. Life's mysteries have interested me and they still do."

"Is there any connection between the mystery of life, as you put it, and the disorderliness of human behavior?"

"Sure. When all is said and done, such human disorderliness derives from the universe. We are the universe too. I have long thought that in order to come up with an explanation for human adventure one must go back to the origins. And the origin is matter. If matter has a history, we should delve into that history. On the basis of what we understand we will be able to arrive at conclusions. The fact that we possess the ability to frame questions and that there are questions to be asked about life means something. There must be an explanation that is both biological and material. I think it resides in the proper functioning of matter wherein all manner of subsequent developments within reality are implicit. Hence the importance of trying to understand the universe."

"But doesn't that mean that you are harking back to there being a point at which everything began? Reminds me of Creation."

"No. The notion that everything began at a specific point, that the beginning of matter was conjured up by something, strikes me as somewhat nonsensical. As is zeroing in on it as we do not know much about it. What we can do is try to learn as much as we can, but in a verifiable way."

"And can a notion like injustice be understood or set right on foot of materialist notions such as 'the origin of the universe?'"

"Yes, plainly. Insofar as one claims to be a materialist, the notion of 'blame' or 'injustice' vanishes. In the context of the reality in which you found yourself, there is what you do and what others do. If what the others do is harmful to you, you have a right to react; react as long as your own reaction does no harm to anyone. That, regrettably, is not the way things work. As I see it, one cannot go any further than your own freedom."

"I am still thinking in terms of physics and, say, the universe. Are notions such as 'class struggle' thinkable when it comes to studying the universe?"

"There is no need to go all anthropomorphic with regard to the component parts of the universe. But when it comes, say, to the notion of 'class struggle' we are talking about a social construct. If there is struggle it is because there is one class with more power than another and the latter doesn't like this. Meaning that class struggle is an evolving stage of matter. But it is matter active, matter with consciousness.

"With regard to physics, matter also undergoes changes with regard to other matter. If you hurl something at a stone, the stone moves. The difference being that we speak of 'inert matter,' matter without consciousness. The universe contains different classes of matter and energy. But none is any more important than the rest. It has its place and purpose, or not, but there is a balance. In the case of a human being, we play different roles within society, and some people—and this is the big difference as far as the universe is concerned—think that they matter more than the rest. Even certain social classes ensure that others are done away with."

"But the logic of the universe is disorderliness, entropy," I add, straining to follow Octavio's train of thought. "Like human behavior."

"Yes, a disorderliness that represents another form of order! A disorder as compared with our notion of 'order,' but also a perfect order in terms of what reality, which is to say, the universe is."

"So why the all-too-human struggle against entropy? Why this need to establish an order of one's own?"

"I have never given that much thought. There is no point. The ultimate consequence of entropy is the conversion of energy into heat. There is a variety of theories, and in my student days I wrote an article about this. Apparently, the final disorder of the universe is going to be entirely heat. We cannot identify its purpose. After that there will be a big bang, something cyclical and, from the human point of view, vast. The assumption is that the end of cosmic infinity is going to be heat, order."

"I am finding this hard to understand."

"What actually excites me is matter's capability of acquiring consciousness, to think all these things and, simultaneously, go for a coffee."

We chuckled. Thinking about complex, abstract matters, yet at the same time, feeling hungry.

"Our reality is essentially biological. There are lots of things conditioning us. If your tooth hurts, for instance, your mind cannot focus. Entropy and all that can go to hell!"

"But is there some link between physics and anarchy?"

"Of course, of course. Society is a stage in the evolution of matter. We find ourselves at that stage today. We derive from a material process and insofar as there are relations between us and even though some may think that they are better than others, the option of rejecting authority, rather fundamental to any understanding of anarchy, is basic. Anarchism is a stance that derives from a relationship of equality. Society itself, in matter's current stage, accords a quintessential vale to anarchy, as a repudiation of authority. Once that is no longer the case, issues of anarchy or non-anarchy will vanish.

"Everything is required and nothing exists unless everything else exists. Nature, if we may use the expression to designate matter capable of self-organization, is an order founded upon anarchy and mutual reliance, which are the determining factors in causality in terms of the span of the universe and life. What exists is, one way or another, related and what happens makes a contribution to evolution which is the change and development through space-time, of a 'whole' which, for simplicity's sake, we may carry on describing as 'the universe.' How could one not want to make an active and 'conscious' contribution to said evolution and not think that a more hopeful future is feasible? Listen," Octavio suddenly said, "I need to go and do some cooking. All this talk and it has grown very late."

"Yes, all this is impossible to understand... Especially while cooking. I should be doing some of my own."

"Okay then, let us call a halt to this pondering of the universe's conscious matter, lest our food get burnt."

Willing Theodolites

ONE OF THE MOST dramatic aspects of revolutionary life comes about when committed activism gradually intrudes into everyday living, altering it and shifting it onto a secondary plane.

"When did your whole militant career start, Octavio?"

"I reckon that was back in 1948 and 1949 when I first got involved in student movements and demonstrations; but those are very vague recollections, especially in relation to what the aims were. Manuel González and I had started hanging out with some Mexican anarchist comrades from the Federal District. The Mexican Anarchist Federation (FAM) had been launched a short time earlier. The Mexican anarchists produced the newspaper *Regeneración*. The interesting point is that, although I had had contact, through my father, with republican anarchist refugees, I fell in with Mexican anarchists before I ever fell in with anarchists belonging to the republican exile community. Manuel was Mexican and he was the one who first sought contact. We set up an affinity group. The connection with the Spanish refugees came along later. And so a Mexican-Spanish nexus was established."

"But what did your militancy amount to?"

"In Manuel's case and my own, we tried to engage in practical things connected to what we were studying. For instance, the Mexican anarchists put us in touch with a group of *magonista* peasants. They were near the Federal District, numbering some 150 peasants in a community that had no water supply, even though there was an irrigation canal a few kilometers away. The state had authorized them to dig a canal linking the existing one with their community, if they did the work themselves. They asked for help and off we went."

"I am fascinated by your direct action from that time, such a difference from what goes on these days."

"In the end we got our faculty to lend us a theodolite so that we could go out and mark out the canal. It took us several days to complete the task and we spent those living as part of the community."

"And this was your first contact with what is referred to these days as *indigenismo*?"

"Precisely. We were light-skinned and fair-haired and showed up bringing technical gear from the city. We slept in adobe homes, on the floor. It was a great experience, with people wholly different from those we had known prior to that. In spite of our being so different there was a feeling of brotherhood between us. But even though we were essentially comrades, they were Indigenous and we were whites and there were certain misgivings on their part. I suppose that, as per their experiences with other whites, they felt slighted and were instinctively distrustful."

"Can you remember anyone in particular?"

"There was one, the youngest of them, pretty much our own age who was forever bombarding us with arrogant questions while staring at the theodolite: 'If I was to go to school like you, I'd be able to use that too, right?'"

"That view, this urge to say that, with the right training he too might do the job, was indicative of how he felt slighted."

"The natives clung to the notion 'white men.'"

"The fact is that even today there is a huge gulf between the 'non-native' Mexican and the 'native' Mexican in certain parts of the country. Many times, I heard Mexicans of European extraction saying that 'these other guys' are not Mexicans but Indigenous."

"And is that where you first heard of the Magón brothers?"

"Well, no. I had already read quite a bit about the Magóns. Back in Xalapa, I had read their writings because my father had several of their books, especially Ricardo Flores Magón's books. My father used to dictate from his writings as typing exercises for me at the school, and through them he broached the situation in the country and spoke about the Magóns' influence in the Mexican revolution. They were a big presence in my early efforts. Besides being an anarchist, Magón was a figurehead of the revolution. He must be one of the few anarchists in the world who features in the official revolutionary pantheon of a bourgeois state. You can see him in La Alameda park beside the statue of Juárez. Institutionally, Mexico regards him as a hero."

"When it comes to talk of anarchist figures, people tend to remember the Russian or the French ones rather than Magón. And yet he lived at much the same time as those."

"Yes. Don't forget that he led an uprising in Baja California against

Porfirio Díaz. Like Práxedis Guerrero, he was a big influence on us. Mago-nismo was very important for Zapata who repeatedly invoked it."

"Is there any remnant of it left within today's *Zapatismo*?"

"They invoke it albeit not in a fashion that is to my liking. They politicize it and forget that Magón was not a believer in the state. They skip over his anarchism. The roots of present-day *Zapatismo* are marxist, remember. They place whatever construction upon it that suits them.

"Today's Zapatistas say that they lead through obedience. Which is how they justify their organizing role; they reckon they have overcome the problem of hierarchies. But in my view that remains one of the mechanisms of order. When all is said and done, they still have hierarchy."

"Have you had any dealings with them in recent years?"

"Yes, I had some dealings with them quite a few years later when I was living in France, and we had our differences of opinion. As I see it, as long as they do not brazenly become institutionalized, they have the potential to become an interesting project. But we shall see what the outcome is. My position is that it represents an experiment and has validity as such."

"Harking back to 1948, what other incidents of note were there?"

"There was a lot going on in the Federal District. The University City was under construction and there was a lot of student unrest. President Alemán was none too happy about the ferment that was going on. In the case of the Engineering Faculty, there was little involvement by the students. Whenever there were strikes, only a few of us got involved. Primarily it was campaigns against the PRI, the governing party. There was the demand for university autonomy; it had none. Miguel Alemán was not exactly a left-winger. In fact, from Cárdenas's presidency through to Alemán's, the country was turning more and more towards what is described these days as neoliberalism."

A Stroll Through the Sewers

"I THINK THAT WHAT happened in February 1948 was the start of a lot of other things that came later."

"I don't get you."

"You'll see. On February 9, 1948, we, the 'three Xalapa libertarian musketeers' produced the very first edition of *Alba Roja*, with Manuel González as director, myself as administrator, and Mario Díez Sánchez as publisher. *Alba Roja* purported to be a monthly publication for the 'dissemination of social ideas.' The titles of the front-page articles were very meaningful: 'The Student Question,' 'The Crime of War,' and 'Social Injustice' and there was a poem entitled 'GOD.' I had already started writing articles. I needed to set my thoughts down in writing."

"Meaning that you began writing in a Mexican anarchist review, the same as your father had in *Tierra y Libertad* and *La Revista Blanca* back in the 1920s."

"Yes. And note that in presenting *Alba Roja* our message was: 'Not long ago, we discovered that the name *Alba Roja* has been used on several earlier occasions and has a history of its own. How it was used matters little or not at all to us. As far as we are concerned Alba Roja is a goal, a purpose, an OBJECTIVE: Emancipation of the human race. Death to tyrants and oppressors. Alba Roja (Red Dawn) of the day of FREEDOM in blood and fire. Alba Roja, a brand-new life, light and love in frozen hearts. Red Dawn of the SOCIAL REVOLUTION.'"

"Has a utopian and ambitious ring to it," I teased.

"We took it very seriously," Octavio grinned as he cast his mind back. "*Alba Roja* grew out of the groups of Mexican and Spanish youngsters that we, in the Mexican Libertarian Youth, had been setting up on the basis of what was left in the Federal District of the FIJL, Federación Ibérica de Juventudes Libertarias/ Iberian Libertarian Youth Federation) in exile. I don't recall if it was a singled issue or whether several appeared. But we were greatly enthused by its publication. We decided to seize upon the commemoration of

September 16, 1810 (Mexican Independence Day) and distribute a manifesto addressed to young people and to public opinion generally."

Commemorations of the Mexican revolution brings Emiliano Zapata to mind. Unfortunately, what stuck in most of world's imaginations, where the Mexican revolution was concerned, was the image of Marlon Brando playing the part of Zapata in the movie *Viva Zapata!,* in which he is eventually mown down in a hail of gunfire in a farmhouse. His white charger, like the untameable spirit of freedom, escapes the gunfire and flees into the savage countryside. And that was it. A ghastly metaphor and a gringo with the sombrero of a *charro* plonked on his head pretending to be a Mexican, his skin darkened to invest the character with some Indigenous swarthiness. In cinema terms, however, *Viva Zapata!* is a very fine movie. The director, Elia Kazan, was a *wunderkind* of cinema in the heyday of Hollywood and what can one say about Marlon Brando? Even so, apparently all that stuck was this stereotype of a trigger-happy, macho, angry Mexican *charro*.

But as far as young Mexicans of Octavio's own generation—those with any appreciation of history—were concerned, it really stood out that, in the days after the Paris Commune, the revolution that succeeded and emancipated the peasants was not so much the Russian revolution or any other, but the Mexican revolution.

So, every November 20, on Mexican revolution commemoration day, in a village in Chiapas like San Cristóbal de las Casas, the children, all of them of Mayan stock, parade alongside adults with their painted-on Zapata moustaches and plastic pistols, in honor of the heroes of the twentieth century's very first peasant revolution. Ultimately, they are honoring an authentic peasant uprising by the poor against the Porfirio Díaz dictatorship.

But every revolution has its day after. The winners in the Mexican revolution set up the PRI, a party usually referred to as a "soft dictatorship." Back in the years when Octavio and his comrades were producing *Alba Roja*, a representative of the PRI misdirected the policies of what had once been a revolution towards the most market-driven liberalism in Mexico's entire history.

"Meaning that you decided to do some anarchist campaigning on the very day that Mexicans hold most dear?" I asked, knowing that it was precisely the same for the hypocrites in government.

"Precisely. About twenty of us youngsters had met up at midnight on September 15 for the purposes of the operation. After splitting up into four groups, we set off by car for different parts of the city. Our group had wanted the streets in the city center. After we had posted nearly all of the manifestos we had with us on the walls at the intersection of the Calle Francisco Madero and the Calle Monte de Piedad, a patrol of plainclothed police stumbled upon us and lined the four members of my team up against the wall. After reading the contents of our manifesto, they brought us, under arrest, to the Federal District Police Headquarters. The sun had come up by then and they placed the four of us in a large, filthy cell. Inside, there were about twenty 'ordinary' detainees sitting around on benches against the walls. The police made them move over to make space for us.

The atmosphere in the cell was sinister and menacing and it was like a bandit hideaway, a den of misery. Most of the people there were petty offenders. They had been there for days and weeks, waiting to be heard by a judge. In one of the walls there was a niche with a bucket overflowing with shit. The stench was unbearable.

"Your first brush with the Mexican police. I can imagine how scared four university types not used to seeing criminals at close quarters must have been."

"In our imaginations we must have felt like we were at the entrance to Dante's *Inferno*."

"Plenty of people have described South American prisons like that," I added, thinking of the ones in Brazil or Argentina.

"A taste of what is often the reality of Latin American prisons. We spent six hours there but it seemed like an eternity, though it was nothing compared with how long the other inmates had been kept waiting. Then the four of us were ushered into a cramped cell where we could touch the side walls simply by stretching out our arms; there was a steel door and a toilet at the far end. The only people we saw were the jailers, since we were held incommunicado."

"The Mexican police," I added, knowing what Octavio was talking about, "are a power parallel to the Mexican state: a pseudo-state often seen on television screens these days in the wake of some very murky situations. The main law of physics of the Mexican police is based on how much money one has to offer. Bribery is assuredly the best way of greasing the corps's wheels."

Octavio went on, "You cannot imagine the wonders money can work with the police and prisons. There, whoever has money has access to one, two, or three cells for his personal use. You can furnish them, install conveniences and employ servants and dress in civilian clothing. It is incredible."

"Reminds me of the case of Ramón Mercader. From Moscow, the Stalinists used to send money across so that Mercader, a KGB agent, could lead a more comfortable existence in his enforced 'retirement.'"

"I saw Mercader in prison. Or rather, I did not see him because he wasn't there, but I was in his cells."

"Can you remember the details?"

"Ramón Mercader was housed in Lecumberri prison. With two or three cells for his own personal use. One of them was in the central part of the prison where there was a pigeon-loft, because Mercader was a pigeon-fancier."

"What were you doing there?" I pressed him, intrigued.

"It's a long story and it occurred a year before I was arrested. There was an official representative of the Franco regime on a visit to Mexico. Name of Gallostra. He was killed and two Spanish anarchist refugees were implicated. The perpetrator went by the name of Fleitas and the other one was Benítez. This Benítez had come over from Spain later on, in 1945. Seemingly, Benítez inveigled Fleitas into killing Gallostra. The motive was not very clear and it was unclear whether it was a case of manipulation or some dirty-dealing on Benítez's part. On behalf of some anarchist refugee comrades, I had gone to the prison to help Fleitas. Our view was that he had been persuaded by Benítez, whom we did not know. In order to get to see Fleitas, you had to go to Lecumberri and ask for a gent who had also been a refugee but who was involved in the Mexican underworld. This 'gent' had ripped the tongue out of another person with some pliers ... on account of his being, I suppose, an informer or to ensure that he would not blab. Which is how he came to be known as *El Deslenguador* (The Tongue Remover). This guy had become king of the prison. He was an inmate, but such was his power that he had come to an arrangement with Lecumberri's governor and had a completely free hand when it came to handling internal matters in the prison. To get to see an inmate, you handed cash to *El Deslenguador*, and after that you could talk to whoever you pleased. When I went in, he came to see me in a splendid suit and walked me through to see Fleitas, who was in the central section in Lecumberri. There, in the securest part of the prison, I could see, as if on a tourist visit, Mercader's cells. Not that I saw the man himself, who must have been 'relaxing' elsewhere. It was even said of *El Deslenguador* that he used to holiday in Cuba and, since the deal he had going inside the prison was so good, he always returned. That will give you some idea of the scale of the corruption we have been talking about. The jailers used to stand at attention when he passed by. He was a wealthy man. That is how everything worked."

"Even the best of novelists could not come up with this story of yours," I remarked. "But let's get back to your arrest."

"Some five or six days passed. On the outside, absolutely no one knew anything about us. The earth had swallowed us up.

"Then, one afternoon, they brought us out of the cell with two plain-clothed policemen escorting each of us. They brought us back, in handcuffs, to Police Headquarters. There they brought us into a large office and, after a while, a serviceman entered. He was the chief of police, General Othón León Lobato, who stood in front of the desk beside the portrait of the president of the Republic, Miguel Alemán, which hung on the wall above his head. He started to upbraid us, insisting that Mexico 'welcomed foreigners who were at liberty to go into business and indeed to amass fortunes.' And he underlined the point that three of the four of us were of Spanish extraction."

"I suppose you had been picked up by the political police. In actual fact, right at that moment you were non-existent, having vanished off the face of the Earth. You could have turned up dead in a ditch, a bullet quietly fired into your head."

"That was how we felt, as if we did not exist and as if everything depended on the general standing in front of us. However, I found out later that Alemán himself was aware that we had been arrested. Since he had served as governor of Xalapa and since two of us came from there, he took an interest in the case."

Octavio fell silent. I waited eagerly for him to resume.

"Sorry, lapse of memory. He had just been saying how we behaved thoughtlessly and were carried away by youthful innocence... when I cut the general short by telling him that this was the very thing we were denouncing in the manifesto while the people went hungry. That was as far as I got. He flew into a rage, rang a bell and back in came the policemen, whom he ordered: 'Take them away to the Islas Marías!'"

"I am not familiar with that archipelago."

"Some islands off Baja California. There is another pretty sinister prison there. Back then, being sent there meant never coming back again. We were, to say the least, terrified."

"Yes, of course. But that doesn't change the fact that, from what you say, you were magnificent!"

"And it did not end there. Manuel and I answered back telling him to 'think through the consequences of our detention, that we were students,' etc. I cannot say whether it was our calling upon him to think again or whether his threat had been merely a ploy to intimidate us, but he then summoned an officer. They conferred in whispers and right after that he ordered that Manuel and I be sent back to the police station where we had been detained up to that point."

"But surely there were four of you?"

"Yes. We speculated about why they had separated us from Florico Ocaña and Francisco Rosell. After some time, they were brought back to the cell and we found out why they had been missing. A comrade who had just happened to be passing Police Headquarters had seen us ushered inside by the police when they moved us. Without delay, he went off to alert Florico and Francisco's families. When General Lobato ordered that Manuel and I be taken back to the police station, this was because he had been informed that Florico's uncle and Francisco's father had shown up at Police Headquarters where they had been subjected to identity checks without a word of explanation.

A further two or three days passed without our knowing what they intended to do with us. Eventually, on September 29, we were brought to an old building several stories tall in the Calle Bucareli, near the Secretariat of the Interior. Our custody was strictly unlawful. We remained there in the care of the political police. They questioned us again and then we were handed over to the Secretariat. On October 18, they brought us before the director-general of political and social investigations, Lamberto Ortega. He conveyed to us the government's determination that we would not be extradited and would be released on condition that we signed a document undertaking not to meddle in Mexican politics."

"Rather a velvet touch by the state, when you come right down to it. A month on the missing list and a sort of a pardon," I said as I worked out how long they had spent in legal limbo.

"Yes and no. We found out later that they had come to this decision in the wake of lobbying on our behalf by a range of personalities and various Mexican trade union organizations such as the Confederación de Obreros y Campesinos de México (Mexican Worker and Peasant Confederation) and Enrique Rangel's Federación Proletaria (Proletarian Federation) in the Federal District. Without that outside pressure, there is no way of knowing what might have happened."

Interval

HAVING SPENT A MONTH in the Mexican prison underworld at the age of twenty failed to dampen Octavio's militant enthusiasm. But it did have consequences, such as the virtual disbandment of the Mexican Libertarian Youth. Although what perhaps hurt Octavio the most was the unprecedented critical backlash from the Spanish libertarian exiles, the battling old guard who had been living on Mexican soil for almost ten years. They did not want any complications with their host country. Octavio had broken the silent, unspoken arrangement between them and the former Cárdenas government to the effect that they would play no part in the country's affairs.

The likelihood is that defeat in the civil war was a big consideration, or that their view was that by then they had had enough and invested their ideological commitment into tokenism like the news regarding the CNT diaspora, scattered across different geographical areas, but little else. It was the logical outcome of the war in which they had lost everything. A tragedy that was further aggravated by the world's democracies when they won the Second World War but accepted the option of the Franco dictatorship rather than some other unexpected alternative course in Spain. For instance, in Winston Churchill's voluminous Second World War memoirs, he devotes approximately one page out of the book's almost two thousand pages to the war in Spain. There, he describes the cohesiveness of the army that halted a potential communist dictatorship. What, therefore, was one to expect of those defeated by fascism?

But Octavio was not one of the defeated. He lived through the calvary of the war, exile, and hunger as a boy, but he was spared the moral defeat. Because, among that generation of exiles, a very small number of those who had played an active part in the war as anarchists picked up the torch in the fight against the dictator from their exile. The maquis did, and people such as Quico Sabaté and Josep Lluís Facerías or Cipriano Mera and Juan García Oliver—to name just a few—did. The active struggle against hell and high water was something left for others to prosecute. To a large extent, they came from the next generation. The generation of the children of the defeated.

One can understand the disappointment felt by a twenty-year-old anarchist who felt that he was being belittled and chastised by the very people who stood for what underpinned his ideals. On that account, Octavio began to consider leaving Mexico and freeing himself from the restrictions that prevented him from being active in any Mexican movement. Then again, leaving would have given the Spanish exiles, who were censorious of his direct-action cravings, what they wanted.

Octavio was part of that irrepressible worldwide impulse, perhaps the last of the twentieth century. Like so many young people in the 1960s, the notion of changing the world and rejecting the new economic and moral order, posited by the winning side in the Second World War, proved fascinating to him.

But as the days slipped by, Octavio was coming around to the opportunities presented by his social and economic circumstances. Due to his work as an engineer, he was starting to earn money and this posed a threat to his ideological concerns. The everyday struggle to square what he was thinking with the daily grind was becoming more and more onerous. And so Octavio breached the agreement not to get involved in politics and took over the direction of the Mexican anarchist newspaper *Regeneración*.

"Were you never tempted, Octavio, to jettison everything and get naturalized and fit in and then be able to struggle in the arena of Mexican politics? Or to do something rather more bourgeois, such as renounce the 'ideal' and go after a big Mexican house in Coyoacán?"

"Sure I was tempted," he replied. "My fellow engineering students laughed at me and said 'Oh you'll see, you'll see once you have your car, your house, and get married and have kids.' And those things were on their way."

"You could have been a wealthy man..."

"I came this close. But that was part of what came along later when I was a partner in a company and specializing as a hydraulic engineer."

"Okay. Let's talk about the temptations of capital."

"As I said, we were becoming bourgeois," Octavio continued. "Nearly all the comrades from my university days were slowly blending into a society rooted in money and comforts. As they obtained their degrees and started working, they were compromising. This, among other things, was one of the major factors contributing to the petering out of the fight against Franco."

"Well, it is a fact that material plenty dissipates the struggle for social change," I mused.

"Even some very committed anarchist cadres, who, back in Spain, had been peasants with no possessions beyond their brawn, once they prospered in Mexico, where a lot of them had turned their hands to different trades, became more casual about their ideals because they were so well off. Domingo Rojas, for instance, was a red hot, highly pugnacious anarchist. He had been a member of the *Tierra y Libertad* group. Then he set up a firm that really took off and hired a lot of workers. And then one day they went on strike against him."

"Went on strike against the anarchist because he wasn't paying them well!" I commented with a chuckle

"Yes. Crazy. Some contradiction, eh?"

"Maybe a lot of Spanish anarchism had more to do with the desperate need to leave behind the crushing poverty there was in Spain, and then, on reaching Mexico, where the exiles were white men and enjoyed greater opportunities, they gave it up," I suggested to Octavio.

"There was much more to it than that. While they were in Spain, they were unaware that their rebelliousness derived from their economic wretchedness. On arrival in Mexico, they were shunned, lest they might infect the Mexicans. That shattered their previous dynamism and from then on they started casting around for excuses and pretexts. They invested 90 percent of their activities in earning a living and prospering. And on Sundays, like Mass-goers, they clung to their libertarianism. But it has to be acknowledged that that libertarian commitment was genuine. They remained faithful to the ideology and used that to justify everything else. Domingo Rojas contributed money to *Tierra y Libertad* and on that basis felt himself an anarchist. I found the contradiction very hard to take."

"In what sense?"

"Because," Octavio stated, "holding my tongue amounted to my becoming complicit in such ideological and ethical dereliction. For denouncing such a stance that flew in the face of the anarchist ideal, I ran into a lot of problems with the anarchist old guard."

Octavio was always highly critical of this attitude among the refugees. His craving for direct action against the dictatorship in Spain highlighted the huge contradiction and rabble-rousing in the anarchist exile community. They could not fathom what he was about and cast around for excuses for their do-nothing-ism. The exiled anarchists, whose names, taken together, were the stuff of legend, turned out to be, as far as Octavio was concerned, mere "individuals" full of all the contradictions that that term suggests. And this caused him a lot of heartache.

The CNT had split apart in 1945. Ten years later, the anarchist exiles in the Federal District—quite separate from the remainder of the republican exiles in Mexico—had just two papers, *Solidaridad Obrera* and *Tierra y Libertad*, each representing one of the two factions within the movement. Some looked to the CNT Sub-delegation tied to the remnants of the CNT, which was centered in Toulouse and under the sway of Federica Montseny and Germinal Esgleas. The other camp was the reformist breakaways known as the National Sub-delegation. Octavio and his father lined up with the first group. Naturally, the two factions did not mix, albeit that they still mingled at a personal level in bars like the Tupinamba.

"Can you recall clashes with other anarchist exiles?"

"I don't know if I would call them 'clashes' but there were heated arguments. For instance, I used to argue a lot with Hermoso Plaja and Liberto Callejas, who were quite a bit older than me."

"They say that Liberto Callejas could be very unpleasant," I added, remembering some biography.

"You have no idea. Those two reckoned they were the masterminds, the official spokesmen, but I disagreed. They were forever lecturing about ideology, but in practice there was nothing going on with them.."

"The fact is that, in exile, Liberto Callejas barely survived. He was alone and had financial problems. He never did adapt to Mexico. He had been a journalist and eked out a living writing articles for commercial or lonely-hearts magazines, which left him greatly embittered. Besides, Callejas was obliged to rely financially on the most contradictory comrades such as Rojas."

"Tell me a little about *Tierra y Libertad*."

"Sure. That's where I ran into problems with Callejas. On one occasion they refused to print what I wrote. Because they were very dogmatic and sectarian. I would query a few things, what they took to be established dogmas, and they didn't like it. *Tierra y Libertad* was the anarchist fig-leaf for the day-to-day lives they were leading. I could not fathom how they could reconcile their talk of revolutionary anarchism with bourgeois practices that implied abjuring internationalism and conceding states' right to prevent foreigners from meddling in social struggles. But, aside from them, I did not have much of an organizational connection with the rest of the anarchist exiles. So, for a while, I drifted free of activism."

At the beginning of 1949, Octavio was primarily caught up in his university studies and draftsman's work. He had decided to take time out and let the arrest episode blow over a little. On the one hand as a way of protecting himself against the Mexican state, because now he was on the files of the political police. And, on the other, because he was trying to understand what role he could play in the history of the exile community, of which he oddly felt that he was a part, but which had marked him down for rejection. It was a period when he worked on his writing and satisfied the irrepressible curiosity that has been his lifelong companion. His inquisitive mind steered him through a wide variety of reading, such as the works of Práxedis Guerrero, Magón's poet comrade, who wound up dead during the takeover of a ranch in the dusty little border village of Janos in the state of Chihuahua in 1910.

During those years, Octavio wrote about science, about "truth" as a philosophical topic, sampling the works of Camus, Nietzsche, or Práxedis Guerrero himself. In 1952, he also took part in the very first Mexican Science Congress. As the youngest attender. His paper on "Determinism and Freedom: The Problems of Science" opened the Philosophy of Memories section of the Congress. He went on to win the prize in a philosophy competition on the UNAM radio station. His writings were published across a range of media, and one of them was even published in France.

But of course, for a nomad like himself, the still waters of the inquisitive intellectual were short-lived. Something clicked inside him and he resurrected his activist consciousness, and, following an interval in 1954, Octavio reverted to active militancy.

The Great Doubt

AN ATTEMPT TO UNDERSTAND a movement like the CNT of the late 1950s needs to acknowledge above all else that it had suffered a tragic and terrifying defeat. That defeat was followed by five years when the political panorama, not just in Spain but around the world, was very dark. The Second World War, the Nazis, and the threat of totalitarianism still hung over the West. Among those who had lost the war in Spain, how things turned out had a disheartening impact and fostered skepticism. There was the palpable sensation of a further, worse and worldwide defeat. The Spanish diaspora, with its varying political leanings, clung to the hope that the powers victorious in the Second World War might restore Spain's democracy. But this was not the case. The countries that won the war had little interest in democracy returning to Spain. And remember, after that, the Cold War came along.

Meanwhile, inside Spain there were guerrilla bands, small resistance groups doing whatever they could. But in 1947, the exiles abroad abandoned them to their fate. The Communist Party, or indeed the libertarians themselves, formally washed their hands completely of the armed struggle.

In 1957, Octavio had started working for a firm set up by a team of engineers older than himself but who he had met at school. The country was in the middle of a building boom. Its economic circumstances were improving and, for the first time, he was able to afford a car of his own. The Alberolas moved into a larger apartment on the Avenida Cuauhtémoc, close to a baseball stadium. Octavio has clear memories of those times because there was a huge earthquake (a 7.6 on the Richter Scale) that had an impact on the city and brought down a good number of buildings.

"Octavio, two years after that you renewed your ties to the anarchist exiles in Mexico and became active again. You were more assiduous in attending the homes of the exiled Spanish libertarians. However, your squabble with the members of the *Tierra y Libertad* team and the anarchosyndicalists from the CNT in exile in Mexico rumbled on."

"The problem was that the squabble was not about to come to an end, so there was a sort of a truce. Like most of the libertarian exiles in Mexico, my father and I 'were active' in the a-political faction of the CNT which, since the ending of the Second World War, had overhauled itself and was trying to operate as a local federation of trade unions. But militant activity through that trade union structure was utterly fictitious and ineffectual. At meetings, all that was ever discussed was the CNT's internal issues, in exile or inside of Spain and, at most, the prospects of the downfall of the Francoist return and the chances of going home again."

"But whereas Spain was subject to fascism, there were lots of things going on around the world."

"There is no doubt that the international context was undergoing change. At the height of the Cold War, fresh focal points for emancipation cropped up, such as the revolutions in Latin America. That had a direct impact on me, but not on many other exiles. It left them cold. I espoused a more active stance and bonded with Mexican people."

"In actual fact, you were largely brought up in Mexico, in a Latin American setting."

"Yes. I am the fruits of that. I felt solidarity with what was going on around me," Octavio went on. "It was that which triggered my activism. We felt that this struggle was our business, that it changed us all. Had we stayed in France, I have no idea what might have happened."

"Colette Durruti, Buenaventura Durruti's daughter, who lived in exile in France, never took part in anything, insofar as I can tell."

"Well, I knew Colette, and her sole commitment was to tending to her father's myth. Her activism was tokenistic, but she was never involved in any move made by the Spanish exiles or the French."

One tipping point that left its mark on the activism of Octavio and others of his generation in Mexico, and other South American countries such as Chile, Peru, Argentina, and Uruguay alike, was the United States government's policy towards Latin America. Slowly, the terrific whirlwind that triggered coups d'état and guerrilla campaigns, which shaped the lives of so many people and left all the countries south of the US border strewn with dead bodies, had its effect on Octavio too.

But the contradiction referred to earlier persisted. Sometime around 1955, Octavio had struck up a relationship that, through ups and downs, lasted for several years; this was with a girl by the name of Rosa from the Mexican aristocracy. They even shared a furnished apartment gifted to them by Rosa's parents who wanted to see them married by the Church. When Octavio shied away from any such ceremony, they finally suggested a civil marriage. There was pressure from Rosa's wealthy, conservative aunts who owned a chain of large furniture stores. They even put it to Octavio that he should take over the management of one of the stores, if he were to marry. When Octavio declined even a civil arrangement, they issued him with an ultimatum and sent Rosa away to the United States.

"Having seen your photos from the time I am thinking of the contrast between what you have been saying and what an extremely handsome and elegant fellow you were. You cared a lot about your personal appearance, how people saw you. One has only to look at the way you are dressed in the photos."

"Are you saying that I was conceited?" Octavio shot back, his hands toying with a pencil.

"That was not exactly my meaning, but..."

"Yes, conceited, yes, yes. That applies to me and to others. I was a child of my times. I loved the movies, listening to music, singing, and certain home comforts. I was influenced by that as well as by the prevailing macho attitudes. Even though it may well have been unconsciously, there was no way of avoiding that."

"What was your family life like?"

"I used to help out a lot around the house because my mother was worsening by the day. She was having constant nervous epileptic seizures and was suffering from depression and had taken to her bed. She was so sick that I even had to bathe her. It was a very sad situation for her and very hard on me and my father. Little by little, I was taking over the reins of the family. But at the same time this whole family issue was also the bane of my life. There were other things I wanted to be doing but couldn't. As he aged, my father came to appreciate that he would never recapture his impetuous and creative youth, and this had a tremendous impact on him. He was aware of how uninterested his contemporaries were in social questions in Mexico and so he turned to my friends and my active militancy rather than to the aging exiles. He wrote wherever I wrote, such as for the newspaper *Regeneración*. And he sought out contact with young people and imitated them, to the point where he started smoking. He had never been a smoker... It defied all understanding. He was questing after something but did not know what."

We took a break so that Octavio could rest. I was left on my own in the room gazing at the heaps of books, photos, and various souvenirs by which I was surrounded. It was raining outside. I ran an eye over the texts I had printed up prior to my coming. In one of them Octavio stated, "It was then, I think—in 1955—that my father underwent a prostate operation and, due to a mistake by the doctor, who closed the wound but left some gauze inserted, he spent almost an entire year in the Sanatorio Español."

The operation on José had come at the time when Octavio had just met Aurora Segura. As she was a celebrity, Aurora secured him a meeting with the director of the sanitorium, who recommended to Octavio that they perform another operation on José. The doctors believed that the wound was not healing because it was cancerous, but when they opened him up, they came across the gauze.

Aurora Segura was the daughter of Spanish exiles and enjoyed a fleeting career during the golden age of Mexican cinema, her greatest performance being, perhaps, in ¡A toda maquina! in 1951, starring alongside Pedro Infante. She lived with her mother, who was separated, and they had set some space aside on the terrace of their building, where the laundry rooms normally were, for Simón Radowitzky to move into.

Octavio visited Radowitzky on several occasions towards the end of his life, by which time Simón was very ill. Simón would pass away a short time later, in 1956.

Like many anarchists, Octavio knew the story of the last surviving anarchist avenger from Argentina. At the age of just seventeen, back in 1909, Simón Radowitzky assassinated the Buenos Aires police chief, Ramón Falcón, by throwing a bomb at his horse-drawn carriage. Falcon died the same day. That was only the start of the Radowitzky legend and of the anti-legend as well. Because the better known his resistance inside Ushuaia prison grew—he lived through every conceivable torment there over a period of twenty-one years—the greater the efforts he made to dispel that legend. Radowitzky tried to shun the limelight.

The course of his life then brought him to Uruguay after he had been amnestied and banished from Argentina at the age of forty-one, afflicted with tuberculosis and a harrowing thinness. He later traveled to Catalonia to combat fascism, and saw action in the Spanish Civil War, very close to where José Alberola was building libertarian communism in the bailiwick of the Aragon Defense Council.

Following the loss of the war, Radowitzky ended his days as part of the anarchist exile community in the Federal District of Mexico. He was still in touch with the Spanish refugees, but also had links to the Russian anarchist refugees who had fled Stalinism. He was a native of a hamlet in what is today Ukraine, near Kiev. And thus became a fascinating bridge between Spanish anarchists and Russian anarchists.

Octavio learned from his fellow activists that Radowitzky was unable to find work or to travel. He lived in seclusion in the little room that Aurora and her mother had set aside for him. The remainder of his story belongs to the celebrated solidarity among anarchists and, as part of that, Octavio brought food to Simón several times and kept him company.

"What always impressed me about Simón," Octavio mused, "was the tremendous love he displayed for the birds he kept. Odd that someone who had served so many years behind bars in prison should have kept caged birds."

"You mentioned earlier that you did not know precisely what sort of birds they were. Maybe they were messenger pigeons?"

"Could be, but I can't be sure. I do recall that Simón was quiet and reserved. He was one of the few people who supported my stance on direct action, and disagreed with the Spanish anarchists' 'biding their time.' He supported those of us youngsters who were eager for action. And that mattered a lot to me. That a figure of such renown in anarchist circles would acknowledge us—Florico Ocaña and me and all the others—was very important."

"Why do you think he supported you?"

"Because he refused to accept his fate," Octavio mused. "He was loyal to the 'Ideal,' that everybody talks about and yet no one can quite define. In Simón the 'Ideal' was unmistakable. They tried to use him and spoke on his behalf. He could have taken advantage of his acknowledged status, like other anarchists did, but he clung to his dignity and humility. He did not identify with his myth and sought no advantage from it. He was conscious of the tremendous international solidarity that had helped him survive the calvary of Ushuaia penitentiary.

"To some extent, we can take from that, that he was a great man to the depths of his being. In their meetings and demonstrations, anarchists around the world never forgot him. They were forever clamoring for his release, insisting that he must not die in prison, as he was, in all likelihood, meant to do."

"That is one hell of a burden for the prisoner to carry," Octavio pointed out. "Simón was always conscious of the debt he owed to those on the outside who were campaigning on his behalf."

"I'm going to go all cosmic again, Octavio. I now think that, though dead, Simón still answers us with unpredictable effect. It is thanks to him that we are here and now chatting in Perpignan, you and I."

"Don't be going all cosmic," Octavio laughingly added. "If we start talking about the stars and the universe again, you're going to have to stay the night here. And remember, you train leaves in three hours and we still haven't eaten."

The ˝Beardies˝

OCTAVIO AND I DINED alone. His partner Ariane had already eaten at the day hospital where she was going to therapy to ease the effects of her depression. I had seen no indications of illness in Ariane, even though Octavio had spoken to me of the subtle changes in her personality. We finished off the meal with the obligatory bread and cheese and the chocolate ice cream that Octavio never misses at the end of every meal. Finally, clutching our coffees, we returned to the study to carry on with our chat.

Picking up on the theme of internationalism, in late 1957, Octavio and the Mexican anarchists came into contact with the Cuban 26th of July Movement. This was a natural show of solidarity with incipient Latin American revolutionary movements. Fidel Castro and a small band of Cuban exiles had been in Mexico since 1955 as a result of the abortive attack on the Moncada barracks back in 1953, which had cost Fidel a two-year prison term in Cuba. By the time Octavio came into contact with the Cubans, they were trawling Mexican leftist movements in search of support. At the same time, under the surface, they were stocking gear for an expedition to Cuba on board the yacht *Granma*. Fidel was twenty-nine years old and it was in Mexico that he first met Ernesto "Che" Guevara.

Octavio and his group contacted the 26th of July Movement through a member of the Movement who had arrived in Mexico with Fidel and of whom nothing remains beyond his nom de guerre, Comandante De La Rosa, as they never did find out his real name.

"Do you remember the initial contacts with De La Rosa?"

"There's a hotel in the Federal District by the name of the Hotel Plaza, on the Avenida Reforma, at the junction with Insurgentes. I was there as an engineer to check out the plans for the hydraulic installations of a huge refurbishment that was being carried out. The hotel belonged to a family that owned an important arms dealership. I became acquainted on site with one of the sons, who was running the business."

"But what has this got to do with Comandante De La Rosa or with Fidel?"

"Fidel had been arrested in Mexico along with other leaders of the 26th of July Movement, like his brother and Che and so on. They had already begun training for the guerrilla campaign so that they could later sail for Cuba, and they had established a wide variety of connections likely to garner support for their cause. When the police let them go, they had confiscated their weaponry. Fidel got it all back after a little while because, well, we have already seen that, in Mexico, money talks. The upshot was that the ideal way of pulling this off was through the dealership I mentioned to you. I can only suppose that, with capital resources on the scale required to build a huge hotel like the Hotel Plaza Reforma, the family business was not so much a gun dealership as arms-trafficking. Actually, I have no proof, but I am convinced that they sold more weapons to Fidel's group."

"Were you involve in all this arms business?"

"I think I put the *barbudos* (beardies) in touch with the guys from the dealership, although now, with the passage of the years, I cannot state so emphatically. It all happened very quickly. Our dealings with the Cubans lasted no more than four months. I was involved in the business of the light aircraft: I put Comandante De La Rosa in touch with an ex-pupil from my father's days in Aragon, another refugee who piloted a light aircraft for a crop-dusting company. He told me that he had made several flights to Cuba to drop medicines and equipment for the Cuban revolutionaries up in the Sierra Maestra.

In 1958, we orchestrated a number of public meetings for the Cubans along with Fidel's younger sister, Emma. It was only later, since we certainly never asked who was who, that I saw some photos and started to be able to identify, by name, Raúl Castro, Che, and others whom I had met."

As if talking about a get-together among friends, or neighbors, Octavio named all these figures who left their mark on generations in Latin America. With virtually nothing, these figures had mounted a revolution and, more unbelievably yet, had succeeded in it. They withstood the onslaught from the huge nuclear-armed monster besieging them from the north. Efforts had been made elsewhere in Latin America to emulate the Cuban *barbudos* with greater training, more personnel, and logistical support, but these had failed.

The Cuban revolution was the greatest myth there could have been as far as several generations were concerned. The truest indicator that things could be different and a window opened into a different future. Initially, the Cuban revolution, like the Russian revolution, was not of the communist persuasion but was represented by a spectrum of many progressive tendencies eager for change in a country as poor as Cuba was, a resort for American tourists and a stomping ground of mafia types. Prior to the revolution, Cuba was a satellite of the United States and these *barbudos*, whose portraits gazed down from posters erected on the walls of every progressive household in the 1970s did the undoable: snatched a morsel from the lion's jaws and lived to tell the tale.

Quite apart from any criticisms or historical analyses and any erosion and degeneration in the Cuban revolution at a later date, at the time the achievement of the *barbudos* was something genuinely memorable.

One of the most outstanding rallies in which Octavio took part in solidarity with the Cuban cause was the one held in the auditorium of the Electricians Union. A range of groups of varying left-wing persuasions spoke, indicating support for the 26th of July Movement. Then twenty-nine years old, Octavio spoke on behalf of the Anti-Francoist Youth.

At another meeting held in the Ateneo Español, Octavio spoke alongside Emma Castro, Fidel's sister. She was not that active politically and later married a Mexican engineer. At that meeting, Octavio was again speaking on behalf of the Anti-Francoist Youth.

"I am startled by the variety of political persuasions that backed Fidel. When it comes to the left, it is hard to get the different camps to agree," I remarked.

"Yes, that's the truth. But remember that Fidel and his people back then were not describing themselves as pro-soviet communists. That came afterwards. Dealings with the Mexican communists were not easy. They didn't see eye-to-eye with the 26th of July Movement. On one occasion, they held a meeting that was a homage to Stalin, to mark the fifth anniversary of his death. I went along to distribute posters at the exit in support of the 26th of July Movement and came in for a torrent of abuse. We almost came to blows."

"How did they know you were an anarchist?"

"No, no, it had nothing to do with my being an anarchist. They accused me of being a CIA agent, just like Fidel! They claimed that Castro was an agent working for the United States secret services. Back then, that was the soviet stance vis-à-vis the Cuban *barbudos*. In their view, Fidel and his activities up in the Sierra Maestra were thwarting the chances of elections being held in Cuba which they reckoned they had a chance of winning."

"So where did Fidel stand at that time?"

"At the time," Octavio said, raising his eyebrows, "Fidel was passing himself off as a fighter against Batista. He claimed to be fighting for the Cuban people to recover the country's constitutional freedom, and even argued that he had no aspiration to political power. Draw your own conclusions about the guy ...

"In the end, the Cuban revolution emerged triumphant in 1959. I never set eyes on my main contact, Comandante De La Rosa, again. They took over the institutions and sought links with the Francoist government. Fidel promised us things back then which, as we shall see soon, he never delivered. His metamorphosis had begun."

"And after all these years, how do you feel about Fidel?"

"Aside from the rallies I mentioned, I have seen him a couple of times. At one- or two-hour meetings. I think he was an authoritarian, a hierarch. His organization, even back then, had a military structure with the rank of '*comandante*' and all that nonsense. But he was a very determined person with great organizational ability and a very magnetic speaker. Over time he was turning into a *caudillo* and gaining power. At one of the last meetings in Mexico, another Cuban militant spoke up on behalf of the Revolutionary Student Directory, the members of which had stormed the government palace in Havana. At one point in his address he said that there must be no more *caudillos* and Fidel's group tried to snatch the microphone out of his hands and silence his opinion. I, as the organizer of the meeting, managed to avert that. I was pissed off to see the emergence of caudillo-ism, the blight of leaders forever straining to vest all power in a single person."

"And Guevara?"

"At that time Che was not well known. They didn't even call him Che. That came later, when he was credited with the capture of Santa Clara. His fame grew following Jorge Masetti's interview with him. He was very skinny, still beardless and not much of a talker. During that Mexican phase, he had no fully defined political education. My view of him is that, in his own way, depending on his own circumstances, he was somebody out to break free of his earlier life. Somebody consistent in what he wanted to be and he was, albeit in accordance with an authoritarian mindset..."

"To me, he stopped being a person. And became a myth," I said. "I could never quite see him as a person, given the myths woven around him."

"In the wake of his death in Bolivia, many interests conspired to turn him into a mythical figure," Octavio argued, "as part of a collective craving for generating myths. People were on the lookout for myths and he, what with his struggle and his martyrdom, fit the bill."

"Let us acknowledge that he left his mark on a whole generation, right across Latin America. Guevarism shares some common ground with your own way of thinking. What's is you view of Guevarism?"

"Guevarism meant permanent revolution. Action as the sole guiding thought. If you call a halt to the permanence, the revolution goes stagnant. It does actually overlap with my approach to things, except with regard to how to achieve it. Anarchism and Marxism are both liberation movements. One by means of the destruction of the state; the other by means of the good offices of the state. In Guevarism's case, there was an incontrovertible determination to aim for a liberating revolution. However, I wonder whether, had it succeeded somewhere else, Guevarism might have escaped the process of institutionalization similar to the one in Cuba. Even so, Guevarism was forever on the lookout for revolutionary authenticity through action, a consistency between ends and means and therefore it was and is a valuable experience when it comes to delving more deeply into reflection on the contradiction between authority and liberty."

Planned Coincidences

THE 1950S WERE THE tensest decade of the Cold War. McCarthyist paranoia spread to many countries in the western camp. Anything that deviated from "the American way of life" was labeled communism and stigmatized for it. Which was one of the reasons why Spain became a neat little isolation chamber where, in defiance of every prediction, the fascist experiment was consolidated. The 1950s turned out to be the worst decade of them all as far as anarchism and the CNT were concerned. With its different factions divided and at odds, the 1950s are referred to these days by the organization's members as "the long tunnel."

In addition to solidarity with the Cubans, Octavio and other young anarchists—the children of Spanish anarchists—never stopped thinking about how to crack open the box in which Spain was being held. And he was seduced by the notion of visiting the place incognito. He wanted to see for himself the outcome of seventeen years of isolation and steely fascist control. But how could he get there and back safe and sound? Getting into Spain was not easy. Along the lines of the SS or the KGB, the regime had set up its own political police, the Brigada Político-Social (BPS/Political-Social Squad), which was notorious and highly effective. As in many other cases, it was the sum of small details, "deliberate coincidences" that brought Octavio his chance to travel to Spain. Between 1955 and 1958, Octavio had been writing political articles for the newspapers *Regeneración* and *Solidaridad Obrera*, as well as texts bearing on science. The director of the Paris-based *Solidaridad Obrera*, wrote to Octavio asking him to carry out an interview with Octavio Paz who was working at the Mexican Foreign Relations ministry at the time. Octavio Alberola could see the contradiction between the allure of certain Mexican intellectuals and, simultaneously, the profound repudiation of such muddleheaded intellectualism. Both Paz and Juan Rulfo, or the mural artists Rivera, Siqueiros, and Tamayo populate the overall image that the world was being sold about the twentieth-century Mexican intelligentsia. Paz was a separate case since, unlike the others named, he had publicly repudiated Stalinism, denouncing the gulags, among other things.

Octavio Alberola met up with Paz for interviews on two occasions and in spite of the expectations raised, he admits to having had few opportunities to get through to the human side of the poet who would shortly thereafter be awarded the Nobel Prize for Literature.

And Octavio did have a certain connection with the contemporary Mexican intellectual scene. One of his engineering assignments had opened the doors of Diego Rivera and Frida Kahlo's Casa Azul to him. However, far from sympathizing with communism, Octavio readily identified it as part of the Mexican bourgeois scene. Without casting aside their bourgeois status, Tamayo, Siqueiros, and Rivera had, through their painting or sculptures cashed in on Mexico's poverty or her "colorful" natives.

Another essential point, as far as Octavio was concerned, since it helped him afford the trip to Spain, was his fortuitous participation in a television game show. Competitors had to guess the answers to certain questions that then made up a crossword. And Octavio managed to make it through a couple of stages before being knocked out. This secured him a cash prize that put him in the position where he could now start thinking about that trip to Europe.

But the main trigger was that he met Irene Dominguez who would become his partner for several years. His relationship with her sounds like something out of a novel. Grasping what they went through is a complicated business and entails the acceptance of rationales that are not easily squared with a conventional existence. Between them, they built up something rather different from what is considered to be a "family," with lots of areas of agreement but lots of discordant notes as well. And it was probably here that Octavio tested the coherence between what one wants and what is feasible and one's sense of responsibility. Together with Irene, Octavio acted out the most revolutionary family experiences conceivable. For good and for ill.

"Right, Irene arrives on the scene."

"I met Irene in 1957. She was working as a reporter for *Zócalo* newspaper. As we grew closer, I told her about my plan to travel to Europe, and we decided to go together. She let the managing editor of *Zócalo* in on this and he suggested that he help us out with the funding in return for some reportage and interviews for the paper."

"Okay, but let's take this step by step. You're in your thirties, you meet Irene, you become close, the business of the trip to Europe comes up, adventure, romance, that feeling of freedom one gets from traveling with somebody new on a voyage of discovery. This was your first planned, or, as they use to say, 'emancipated' trip. For reasons as commanding as all those 'obligations' you impose on yourself in political matters."

"Okay," he mused. "Bear I mind that I was about thirty-three years old, what they call the 'critical age.' I was called Octavio because of *El Cristo moderno*, a play they used to stage in my father's school in Alaior, where I was born. It was an anarchist play and so they called me Octavio. So the notion of my being thirty-three years old meant something to me. I was hardly the first, as lots of people go through it. But I pretty sure that I would die at that age. I pressed on and forced myself to keep going when everything around me was telling me to stop. The trip was an adventure but it set a lot of strange monsters loose in my head. One of which was that maybe I was not going to live long."

"But you won't deny that you took off with a beautiful woman to Europe, as lovers."

"It was like a honeymoon. Sure, it was romantic. But I also had a dream that I might get the chance to set eyes on all these people that my father was always talking about, those of his comrades-in-struggle who had stayed put. Irene made it easier for me, among other things, because the option of traveling as a reporter was perfect cover for getting into Spain."

"And up popped Ricardo Vaca Vilchis, right?"

"Ah, Vaca Vilchis! Yes, that was my cover name ... Ricardo Vaca Vilchis was the name of a deceased person," said Octavio. "Through a lawyer, a '*licenciado*' as they say in Mexico, I obtained an official Mexican passport in the name Vaca Vilchis. The whole thing, the passport, the press cards, and even two marriage records. The aim was to bring along the first one, Vaca Vilchis's, so that we could produce it if necessary in Spain. The second was to remain in Mexico so that, in the event of my being arrested in Spain, Irene could demand help from Mexico as my lawful spouse. I remember that I took the photos in the SEMO studio belonging to Senya Fleshin, a friend of Simón Radowitzky's. Senya was a Russian anarchist whose partner was Mollie Steimer. They were both Jews, as was Simón."

"Everything was ready. Now for the start of Vaca Vilchis's adventures in Europe!"

"Yes," Octavio chuckled, and, rubbing his whiskers, added, "not forgetting that the trip was almost called off because when I went to get Irene at her home to go to the airport, her father came out with a pistol, threatening me and telling me to leave his daughter alone. After a heated argument and after Irene announced that she was going with me, her father told her: 'You're no daughter of mine anymore' and 'Never darken this door again.' Irene's father, who had served as General Prosecutor of the Republic for Chihuahua state, took it as an insult that I had talked his daughter into signing two fake marriage deeds."

Reporter Vaca Vilchis's Adventures

OCTAVIO ARRIVED BACK IN Europe in 1957. He brought with him his own memories, those fed by his father's fraught exile, and, in the case of his mother, heart-rending recollections. Returning to Spain had many meanings. Traveling as a couple with Irene while they wrote pieces for the paper that was helping to fund them; rediscovering names he had heard in his adolescent days in Xalapa; names of libertarians who had put down roots in France; and a burning itch to slip, incognito, into the fascist fortress.

"Octavio, tell your initial impressions on arrival in Paris."

"Ah, *oui, oui*, Paris. The first thing I did was to look up my father's friends and get to know them. I was startled to see how small the apartments were in the city. Especially the bathrooms. There were tiny!"

"Big contrast with the Americas where everything is bigger."

"Clearly. In Mexico the bathrooms were generous-sized, huge. In actual fact the way apartment blocks are built in Mexico is in stark contrast to the old quarters of Paris. It really hit me. They were uncomfortable; some comrades were living in apartments where they had to share a bathroom."

"I can hear the hydraulic engineer speaking, as you remember ..."

"I had never thought of it like that. In Mexico I was living according to a certain bourgeois standard of living. Paris was my first run-in with reality. I realized what life was like for a libertarian in exile in Europe. The day-to-day existence, the tight finances, attending meetings on Sundays, the routine, and the symbolism.

I met up with the director of the Paris-based *Solidaridad Obrera*, Joan Ferrer. I saw Gaston Leval, a French anarchist historian who had been in the civil war. Later Irene and I tried for a meeting with Albert Camus, but that proved impossible. And I also saw Colette Durruti, and so on."

"But you also met up with people who weren't acquaintances of your father's, people of your own generation."

"Yes. Such as Salvador Gurrucharri, Joaquín Delgado, etc. This was something novel for me. Remember that, back then, Franco had just been recognized by the UN and 'his' Spain was starting to be accepted and that really frustrated me. This was at the same time that I was frustrated to see all this anarchist old guard dormant and keeping their ideals for Sundays. As I met up with people my own age who reckoned that something could be done about it all and actions taken to denounce the dictatorship, I felt a degree of hope."

"And around the same time there was the maquis resistance and people such as Quico Sabaté and Caraquemada; armed guerrillas mounting incursions into Spain."

"Sure, and other resistance within the country. In Barcelona they had just murdered Carballeira, which just went to show that there was an actual opposition, and that was a hopeful sign.[2] I soon found out that there was the same dichotomy in France as there was in Mexico. There were the same factions inside the anarchist movement. Initially I made contact with both factions."

"You mentioned Delgado."

"Yes. He was in touch with Quico Sabaté, whom I could not meet as he was in jail."

"I am impressed that you mentioned Delgado. Some time later he was subjected to a wretched execution alongside Francisco Granados."

"The impressive thing about Delgado is that they executed him, as the man himself was not 'impressive.' Delgado was quite discreet and very headstrong. I found out from him that Sabaté was keen to get back to the struggle inside Spain."

From Mexico, Octavio and Irene had bought a car, a Dauphin, for the purposes of their trip. But before they got as far as Abi, an accident caused by ice delayed them for a time in that city. They took the opportunity to fulfill one of the aims of the trip and wrote a piece about the Toulouse-Lautrec Museum. Shortly after that, by which time they were in Toulouse, Octavio met with Federica Montseny and Germinal Esgleas, members of the Inter-Continental Secretariat of the CNT-in-exile, as well as with some members of the FIJL. Octavio has happy memories of their first meeting.

Federica Montseny, one of the historic leaders of Iberian anarchism, was possessed of a certain anarchist pedigree as the daughter of Federico Urales, the founder of *La Revista Blanca*. With her great oratorical skills, Montseny was an ambivalent figure during the turmoil of the civil war.

Perhaps the greatest controversy of which she was at the center related to her time as a serving government minister during the civil war. Federica was the first female minister in the history of Spain. At odds with fellow wartime minister García Oliver, together their fingerprints were all over one of the events most widely criticized by the anarchist movement in and outside of Spain. When all was said and done, the anarchist community is opposed to having anything to do with what is referred to as "the State."

Federica Montseny only served as a minister for a few months, but she did manage to draw up the very first abortion legislation and plan the establishment of children's homes and kitchens for penniless, expectant mothers. Unfortunately, none of this ever came to fruition, due to the republican government's precarious circumstances. And, once in exile, Federica showed her other face, the face of a stick-in-the-mud anarchist, resting on her laurels and weaving, hatching a strategy to ensure that "nothing happened" throughout the long tunnel of exile.

Not that her partner, Germinal Esgleas, was any slouch when it came to controversy; he was one of the biggest orthodoxes in the anarchist movement. Esgleas was a genuine colossus of organized inaction. Dubbed by his opponents The Monk, Father Prior, or Brother Gerundio, Esgleas was the founder of the internal school of thought known as "Esgleism," which is to say, the current within anarchism that bided its time and laid preparations for the day-after-tomorrow when the dictator would be dead.

Montseny and Esgleas had no way of knowing that this youngster from the exile community in Mexico, dining at their home in Toulouse that afternoon, was to become the authentic *bête noire* threatening their interests within the anarchist movement.

Octavio crossed the border into Spain via Irún. After a brief stopover in San Sebastián, he began to form his first impressions of the country. By picking up hitchhikers, Octavio got to speak to a priest and, putting discreet questions to him as a curious Mexican—his accent helped in this deception—he was able to learn about the economic and social circumstances of the country. Many people, on learning that the couple were foreigners, revealed their own dissatisfaction with the situation, though this depended on their social status.

However, the risk of betrayal was there, and was very widely practiced in Spain. It was common for people to denounce others to the Civil Guard for political activity, and the regime did all it could to encourage this. Octavio and Irene had to keep their wits about them, foreigners or not. Octavio attended two football matches and watched how people in the pubs reacted, as any anger they displayed was a fair indication of how things stood and how much fear there was among the population. The referee and the players would be called "sonsabitches," and many people found an outlet for their frustration and fear in the rivalry between two football teams. Nevertheless, Octavio still remembers the time that a Civil Guard stepped inside one pub and the football brouhaha evaporated, giving way to closed lips and silence.

In 1957, few tourists entering Spain were treated any differently. They brought money with them and the regime had an interest in that, which proved very useful for Octavio's purposes, as he was carrying messages from anarchist comrades living in exile in France. And this was the reason for his visit to Santillana del Mar.

"Wasn't Santillana del Mar where Franco used to spend his summers?" I asked.

"Certainly was, and we stayed overnight at the National Parador, which, at that time of the year, October, was open to the public. They used to close down a few weeks in advance of Franco's arrival, when he went salmon fishing on holiday. Our cover was that we had been to view the caves at Altamira to do a report for the paper. Our press cards were a great help to us in those matters. They enabled us to earn the trust of the staff at the Parador, and they even allowed us to visit the room in which Franco slept. But our real reason for visiting the Parador was that the Toulouse CNT wanted intelligence about the place as they were interested in laying the groundwork for an assassination attempt. The idea was to plant a bomb near Franco and trigger it by remote control. As I say, I viewed the room but, by my reckoning, the thing was very complicated due to the very tight security measures in place. So that idea was discarded."

Octavio and Irene then left Asturias, bound for Salamanca. They knew that the students at the university there had their own cinema review and that some of them were opposed to the regime. In the canteen at the University of Salamanca they met up with their very first opponents of the dictatorship who were living in Spain. They provided him with the Madrid address of the filmmaker Juan Antonio Bardem.

The couple continued on their way with a few days spent in Lisbon. Octavio wanted to drop in on an old acquaintance of his father's, the veteran Portuguese militant Germinal de Souza, who was living on his own in the Alfama district, in fairly wretched circumstances. Through de Souza, Octavio found out about the activities of the dictator Salazar's police force. They had arrested de Souza not long before and deprived him of sleep for several days on end. His nerves were shattered and he was spooked by everything. For that reason, he refused to take part in any action and curtly remarked that he would be in contact with the Toulouse CNT soon. A dismal fate for a man who was arguably the most prominent Portuguese anarchist. De Souza had held significant positions within the CNT and the FAI during the time of the civil war in Spain. For some reason, he was expelled from anarchist circles and was looked at very much askance in others.

Returning to Spain, Octavio arrived in Cadiz. His plan was to contact the underground CNT there. But the initial approach was very risky and the anarchist comrades asked him to get out of the city as fast as he could. That very day a ship laden with arms and bound for Ifni, where war had broken out between Spain and Morocco, had been set on fire. Octavio left the city whilst the Civil Guard was concentrated on the docks.

On his arrival in Algeciras, Octavio crossed the straits to Tangiers. His recollections of that first trip to Morocco are somewhat muddled. Maybe he was out to gather information about the fighting in Ifni, given that Franco was keeping this war from the public.

Just as Octavio was arriving in Algeciras in mid-October 1957, the conflict was on the brink of erupting. The Moroccans intended to seize Ifni in Spanish Western Sahara. Those were the years during which half of Arab Africa was in the throes of decolonization and there were constant revolts and outbreaks of nationalist guerrilla activity. In the Ifni area, Moroccan guerrillas were out to annex the city of Sidi Ifni and surrounding areas for Morocco.

"We bought a gold watch in Tangiers, which is famous for them."

"A very anarchist thing to do."

"*Oui, oui.* In Mexico some friends had mentioned having sold one of those watches in Spain. A Rolex, I think it was. We could recoup the costs of the trip," Octavio grinned. "A few days after that we returned to Algeciras to travel on to Valencia by road. As we neared Alicante, we stopped off at the Arab-style Santa Barbara castle. My father had a lot of memories from there, from his days as a teacher in the school in Elda. In Valencia, we paid a visit to Progreso Fernández and Concha Estrig, who were very good friends of my father's, and with whom they were still corresponding."

"I read something about Progreso Fernández and was lucky enough to stumble upon the Causa General indictment against your father up in Fraga.[3] They believed that José was the man chiefly responsible for the death of forty people during the war. By which I mean that José was an enemy of some note as far as the regime was concerned. They would definitely have been monitoring Progreso for corresponding with him. Indeed, I find it hard to understand why Progreso Fernández was not rotting in some prison or had not been shot years earlier."

"The mysteries of fascism," mused Octavio. "I suppose he was lucky, very lucky. Because Progreso, a rationalist school teacher like my father, was miraculously spared retribution for his libertarian activism. Maybe the crude Francoist machinery of repression proved unable to 'purge' him because he had resigned from the FAI back in 1934 on the grounds that it was becoming authoritarian. Be that as it may, the Causa General never touched him even though he had been jailed for five months in 1948 charged with being an anarchist."

"It must have been an emotional encounter."

"Sure. But as we were saying before, he was really scared. Scared that they might identify Alberola's son and take steps against him. And, just to add even more fear, I was there on a mission from the comrades in Toulouse. We were to lay the groundwork for Libertarian Youth comrade Liberto Sarrau, who was due for release from prison, to cross over into France."

"And what did Progreso do for a living? He was barred from teaching."

"He had a small workshop making sieves for colanders on the ground floor of the building where he lived. When I showed up with Irene, we introduced ourselves as Mexican reporters, friends of the Alberolas. When I felt more confident, I told him that I was Octavio. His response was to shut the workshop without delay and, after I had passed on the instructions I had been given for him to pass on to Liberto, he asked us to leave. Progreso said that he suspected that he was under surveillance. According to him, José Alberola's son represented a real threat to his safety."

Octavio arrived in Madrid intent upon an interview with moviemaker Juan Antonio Bardem for *Zócalo*. Bardem's standing was higher outside of the country than in Spain itself. In fact, he had already shot two of his major movies, *Muerte de un ciclista* and *Calle Mayor*, which had won awards in Cannes and Venice. Perhaps for that very reason, the regime did not dare take action against him for his known communist party membership, even though the Brigada Político-Social had held him for two nights at the General Security Directorate (Dirección General de Seguridad) in the Puerta del Sol, the much-feared Spanish "Lubyanka." Even though his awards offered some sort of protection, they could not stop Bardem's being censored and shunned in his later years. Their interview took place on a movie set, surrounded by props.

Thanks to Octavio and Irene's Mexican accents, Bardem initially appeared at ease. Octavio attempted to bring up politics by remarking on the situation of the anti-Franco opposition and the underground organizations. However, whether because of his PCE membership or some innate mistrust, Bardem proved evasive.

In the end, before setting out for Barcelona, Octavio and Irene tried to visit the Valle de los Caídos. In 1957, information about what exactly Franco was building there was still quite scarce and it seemed like an ideal opportunity. When they reached the entrance and found no one in the watchman's hut, they decided to head on up the road leading to the basilica.

"I can't get over your deciding to just drive into the Valle de los Caídos. You could have ended up under arrest."

"But we had to try. We were stopped about five hundred meters further in by a couple of Civil Guards. We had arrived as there was a changing of the guard and the replacement pair were en route. We apologized, saying that we had not seen the 'No entry' sign and were just a couple of Mexican tourists on a tour of Spain and Europe and that our eye had been caught by the Great Cross. Feigning innocence, we asked if it was alright for us to take a photograph. They said that if we let them in the car and would take them to the barracks (about a kilometer or so away) they would let us drive on and then do a U-turn and take our snapshot. We enthusiastically agreed. And so we drove around the place and took our photo of the basilica and its Great Cross. That photo later appeared in *Zócalo* and was, no mistake, the very first photo of the Valle de los Caídos carried by the world's press."

"Did you see any workers?"

"No. There was no one there at the time. I know that they were putting the finishing touches on the site because it was inaugurated the next year. But back then we had no idea that they were using slave labor, let alone what was to happen with the transfer of mortal remains there."

"And how did it feel visiting the tomb of a dictator who was having it built during his lifetime, like one of the pharaohs?"

"I knew it was a monument to the 'fallen,' meaning the fallen on his side. But that was all I knew. In Toulouse there was an idea that there was something there but beyond that they didn't know too much. Which is why we were there."

The following day, Octavio and Irene set off for Barcelona via Fraga, the town where the Alberolas had spent the war. On reaching Barcelona, Octavio was reunited with old friends. The couple's plan was to make a quick trip to Alaior, Octavio's birthplace, as he was keen to see Carme again, the family friend who had looked after him as a child.

"What did you do when you got to Alaior?"

"Prior to that we visited Majorca and wrote a story about Chopin and George Sand in Valldemosa. From Majorca we traveled overnight by ship and reached Minorca early in the morning after sailing across some choppy waters. From there we took a taxi to my home-town of Alaior. The taxi driver was taken aback when, as we reached there, I pointed out how I wanted him to go into town. I had recognized the street he was driving down as the street Carme lived in."

"And how did it go? Did she recognize you?"

"I got the same feeling from Carme as I had when I saw Progreso Fernández in Valencia. Her emotion on learning that we brought her news from the Alberolas turned into panic once I told her that I was Octavio."

"That fear again that we talked about earlier."

"Yes, fear was everywhere. Nevertheless, Carme ushered us inside the house and let her children, Laieta and the musician Liberto, know that we had arrived. Carmeta's husband had been shot at the end of the war even though there had been no repression to speak of in Minorca. Minorca was the last place to fall into fascist hands in a war that had scarcely been affected it in any case. Even so, they shot Carme's husband. Most likely because of the connection to my father and for being a member of the CNT. Carme corresponded with my father and we never quite lost touch. Our meeting was very short, a matter of a few hours. We had booked flights by light aircraft back to Barcelona that afternoon. The taxi brought us to the little airport in Mahón, where a Civil Guard dupe checked our papers. I have a vague memory that he jotted some of the details down in a notebook, something that struck terror into my cousin, who had come with us. The sort of fear we are talking about lingered for years, until well after the advent of democracy. Look, in 1981, by which time my Spanish papers had been normalized, I wrote to Carme's son, Liberto; I wanted to pay another visit to the island after all those years. He asked me not to come, saying that he was scared and that it wasn't safe. So I didn't go! Once it gets a grip, fear is very hard to shake off. And in Liberto's case it was because he'd read a piece in the *Menorca* newspaper, later reprinted by *La Vanguardia*, mentioning me as having been the winner of the *El Viejo Topo* award for 1978."

"What lingering memories do you have of Alaior?"

"I couldn't say. There is something that has to do with Helie. I remember how she used to move around the house and yet I spent only my first two years there. Were these remembered images or images passed down by my parents or by Helie herself? I really don't know."

"There is no way that emotive geographical details can be passed on to anyone."

"Maybe. Once back in Mexico, I learned in a letter from Carme that within hours of our departure from Alaior, the Civil Guard had dropped by to see her. They had photos of my father and of me as a child. She told them that we were friends of the Alberolas, over on a visit. I later discovered that in Barcelona too the Civil Guard had visited my cousin's home to ask questions about the Mexicans. Whether they knew who we were we never found out. There was a paranoid, knee-jerk monitoring system.

"After our short stay in Alaior and, once back in Barcelona, we left my female cousin at home and set off on a drive to Olot. My cousin had arranged a meeting with my mother's relatives. The meeting lasted around an hour. My cousin's panic about possible Civil Guard intervention had them on the edge of their seats. We left Olot and after an hour or two crossed the border and headed for Toulouse.

"Once in Toulouse," Octavio continued, "I met up again with the comrades from the CNT Secretariat and from the FIJL, briefing them on my contacts in Spain. When I told them that our plan was to go on to Italy and then to England, the gave me with the contact details of anarchist comrades in both countries. I also saw José Peirats, who corresponded with my father."

"I have several books by Peirats at home. He could be described as the official anarchist historian of the Spanish revolution."

"Did you know he was self-educated?" Octavio asked. "One of the most intriguing cases of self-education and emancipation. A triumph of the anarchist ideal and proof of the importance of education."

As he spoke, Octavio showed me a photo showing him in an immaculate, white, Sherlock Holmes-style raincoat alongside José Peirats, Irene, and Víctor García.

"Peirats, Peiró, and Edo, three examples of the many anarchists of humble origins who, through their own efforts, educated themselves intellectually. In Peirats's case, besides working as a *bobiler* (or brickmaker), he studied, and curiosity molded his fund of knowledge. The same went for Joan Peiró who was a glassblower in a factory. A lot of civil war anarchists, on account of their social status, were denied any chance to study. Peirats already had a reputation for his literary pursuits and, from 1947 onwards, lived in France, after some time as an exile in Ecuador and Venezuela."

"This is an interview Peirats did with Josep Alemany, when he was older," I said to Octavio, holding up a copy that I had brought from Barcelona. Peirats said, "For all the many clashes, frictions, and divisions where the CNT was concerned, it is my belief, taking into account the forty years away from the land of our birth, that, in terms of cultural activities and the like, our emigration was, all in all, a positive experience. There was never any let-up in the publication of newspapers, pamphlets, magazines, and books, some of the latter being highly original. On the other hand, we have left behind our sons and grandsons who will never be Spaniards again but who have made their way into every class and profession in the countries all around the world that took us in. It is still early for those descendants to make their impact felt in so many countries. But it was already apparent in France at the time of the events of May '68. I believe that, aside from the Jewish diaspora, ours is going to be one of the most telling instances in the history of emigration."

"He was talking about its legacy in exile," Octavio replied curtly. "Peirats was opposed to Esgleism but restricted himself to championing anarchist and anarchosyndicalist practice within the framework of bourgeois legality. That boiled down to lawful trade union activity and cultural endeavors: publishing newspapers, pamphlets, lectures, etc. Thus, in his statement he places a high value on exile, regarding it almost as economic migration, on the basis of its publication of lots of newspapers, books, pamphlets, and the delivery of a lot of talks. But such activity was without impact upon the future back home.

"Back then I locked horns with him and with Gaston Leval. They reckoned that the task of the exile community was to 'create well-prepared revolutionary cadres' for whenever we might, with the grace of Divine Providence, I suppose, be in a position to return to Spain. Be that as it may, Peirats had a soft spot for me, on account of his high regard for my father."

Octavio and Irene carried on with their tour, heading for Clermont-Ferrand via Toulouse. There Octavio dropped in on an uncle and a cousin who had moved out of the country prior to the war and who were working in a Michelin plant. Later, in Grenoble, Octavio made the acquaintance of the twenty-two or twenty-three-year-old Joaquín Delgado, by then secretary of the Grenoble Local Federation of the FIJL. They hit it off with each other and Octavio agreed to keep in touch by letter with an eye to the future of the struggle inside Spain. After a few days in Paris, the couple went on to Italy. Octavio learned first hand about the political situation in Italy and struck up connections with various anarchists who would prove very useful in the years thereafter. After visiting Rome, Pisa, and Florence, in Carrara Octavio met with Alfonso Failla who was one of the "leaders" of the Federazione Anarchica Italiana. In Carrara, Failla was an agent for an anarchist cooperative quarrying marble.

Octavio and Irene then passed briefly through Paris before traveling on to London, where they met up with Salvador Gurucharri, known as Salva, and other British anarchist comrades. Salva brought them to the anarchist bookshop of the newspaper *Freedom* where Octavio met Vernon Richards, author of the book *Lessons of the Spanish Revolution.*

"Vernon Richards is a classic," I remarked. "Highly regarded in libertarian circles. What was your impression of him?"

"He struck me as ...," here Octavio paused for thought, choosing his words. "A bit like the refugees over in Mexico. Anarchist discourse galore, but it was never translated into any concrete follow-through. Obviously," he chuckled, "he wasn't going to show up over here planting bombs, but I found him a bit of a windbag. Richards talked more about the past than the present."

"But, Octavio, there is more to militancy than just praxis. Maybe Richards had turned to literary matters and set praxis slightly aside. And is there not, maybe, some validity to that?"

"No. As I see it, one without the other is meaningless," he confidently replied.

"Let me come to that. Throughout your life you have married praxis with theory."

"It is meaningless thinking about an ideal world without trying to build one. There should at least be an attempt to do something, to give it a try. If you are a romantic or an adventurer and you sit at home making sure that nothing happens to you, what use are you?"

"They say that in the Greek *agora* there was a placard that read: 'No participation without a knowledge of geometry.' Meaning that if you wanted to have your say, you had to have dabbled in the discipline of geometry. But the great twentieth century theorists and philosophers broke with that practice. They do their writing from a studio or office with virtually no action, constructing their thought from their reading. Isn't what you are saying dismissive of a Hannah Arendt?"

"No, I am not dismissing her. In my own historical setting certain favorable circumstances for putting what I believe into practice fell into my lap. All I am saying is that one has to give praxis a shot. Had Arendt gone back to Germany in order to act, they'd have killed her and that would have been silly. I cherish the effort required to think and ponder the truth, but I believe in action, in getting involved. You are quite within your rights to pontificate from your armchair, putting forward your propositions, and what you have to say may very well be interesting, but the belief that you have captured the truth, if that is the case, strikes me as a touch ridiculous."

"So, afterwards you headed back to Mexico."

"Yes, but hang on a moment. In my view, and the passage of time subsequently proved this, the most important thing I achieved by going to London was meeting Salvador Gurucharri."

"I read something you wrote in commemoration of him after his death in 2014: '[Salvador Gurucharri] was decisive in my agreeing to take part in the DI, leaving Mexico, and joining that 'secret' agency in March 1962.[4] And I say decisive by virtue of the fact that everyone not only displayed the same enthusiasm, but also the same determination to fight and, in Salva's case, because he was also ready to leave England for France in order to join the clandestine struggle against the Franco regime. As was another young comrade, Floreal Ocaña, Florico, who was living in Mexico at the time.' It must have been hard on you seeing your comrades die," I added.

Octavio clasped his hands together on his knees and settled his shoulders into the armchair in which he was sitting. The room was flooded by the dulcet tones of a French voice from the television set. When Octavio sits in silence, when he gazes into infinity, there is in his blue eyes a perceptible degree of nostalgia which he would probably not acknowledge, deeming it romantic sentimentality.

"Anything else you'd like to add?" I asked, trying to rouse him from his memories of Gurucharri. "Something frivolous about your trip or something about Vaca Vilchis, say?"

"Ah, Vaca Vilchis. The things I got up to after that poor fellow passed away! Taking advantage of our stay in London we wrote a report on the National Gallery. I took a rapid exposure shot of London Bridge and captured a gull in mid-flight. Half a page was given over to that photograph when it was published, and quite a while later we spotted it being used as the backdrop for an advertisement for perfume or such like. The newspaper's director had sold it!"

Irene

UPON RETURNING TO MEXICO, Octavio had difficulty assimilating after the things he had just lived through in Europe. There was a choice to be made between the Octavio who was itching to "do something," to act and get in on the action in accordance with his ideals, and the engineer Octavio, which offered the temptations of a quiet bourgeois existence on good pay, the building of a home with all mod cons, and the longing for well-deserved summer vacations.

"After coming back from Europe, you and Irene started living together."

"Yes, but remember that my parents were there too. On her return to Mexico, Irene agreed to live in the apartment with me because she couldn't go home. We lived with my parents on the Avenida Cuauhtémoc. I can't remember how long we were there, but, as she went back to work and I got on with my engineering career, our finances improved, and sometime between 1958 and 1959 we were able to move into another apartment where we could be alone. Initially I thought that it might be good for my father to have Irene in the family, but this wasn't the case."

"Was Clara that poorly?"

"My mother was ill. From time to time she would suffer nervous epileptic seizures, for which reason I had to be permanently at her side, watching in case she harmed herself. I was looking after her, but it was really hard. Every so often, my father would try to get out of the house to take his mind of it, but she preferred to stay indoors. Little by little, she was getting worse due to her memories of my sister, the absence of her relatives, and her almost total isolation. My father, by contrast, just got on with his life since he thought there was no way out of the situation."

"And how did Irene and your mother get along?"

"Badly. It was very hard for Irene, and one way or another my mother did not want to see me formalize matters. She was terrified of the prospect of our having children. She did not want any children or grandchildren in this ghastly, nasty world."

"And then Irene got pregnant," I added.

"Actually we moved into another apartment when that happened because tensions were running so high. It really pained me see her so much worse, her dignity oozing away each day. I think it was around then that Irene got pregnant with Helie who was born on January 15, 1960. Irene and I had been taking contraceptive measures for some time, but in the end I had given into to her wishes and her reasoning."

"What was in Irene's head?"

"She said that my mother would forget about her late daughter if she had grandchildren and that it would do her spirits and her health good. So when Helie was born we named her after my late sister. During the period when my mother was able to have little Helie by her side, there was no improvement in either her spirits or her health. Besides, she still could not accept Irene's pig-headedness about having a family. On the same grounds, when Irene got pregnant again, later, we decided to name the child Octavio. Irene thought that this symbolic reconstitution of the duo that my sister and I had once been would buck up my mother's spirits. My son Octavio was born on July 4, 1961."

"Strange business."

"Over time, I could also see that Irene had anticipated what I had yet to decide. As far as she was concerned, our returning to Mexico after our European outing implied normalization of our relationship. In spite of what I said and did, in her heart of hearts she clung to the illusion that I would eventually give up on my political commitment and settle into life in Mexican society like the other refugees she knew had done. Hence her insistence on getting pregnant. She wanted—and I thought it only normal—to set up a family and for Alberola the engineer to thrive."

"But your mother never got to know your son Octavio. How did your mother die?"

"She caught a severe chill. We put her in the Sanatorio Español. Ghastly place, as it was run by nuns. My mother was obsessed with nuns and they with her. They wanted her to convert to Christianity. According to my mother, they tried to get her to kiss the wooden crucifixes they wore around their necks and even to place one around hers."

"But was Clara lucid?" I asked, warily.

"She was relatively well. I never did find out if she actually lost her mind. But nuns, she hated them. One day, during her hospital stay, someone left the window of her room open overnight. This was in the winter and her chill soon turned into pneumonia. As her health deteriorated my mother was screaming, 'That's the one! That's her!' pointing at one of the nuns. She passed away the following day."

We were left looking at each other in silence. I had no idea what to say until Octavio finally broke the silence.

"She never got over Helie's death. Always wanted to die because of that tragedy. I can still remember her from before my sister died and she was a different person then."

"And how was your father after Clara's passing?"

"After the initial shock, he was relieved, as I was. Consider this: whenever my mother took an epileptic fit, she sweated a lot, which gave her sores and I used to wash her body down. She had these awful sores under her breasts. That was a very tough experience. The suffering we endured over her condition ended with her death.

"From early youth my thinking was that the family is an institution and this is one of the things that gets in the way of the world becoming more fraternal, more humane. Because the family as an institution feeds selfishness through the family. So I have always striven not to turn the notion of 'family' into a myth by downplaying its importance."

"Meaning that you have made an intellectual effort to deconstruct and redefine the concept of 'family.' But let's get back to the hard facts of the life you were leading. You now had two children and there was Irene as well. Sounds a lot like a family."

"The idea I have just set out also included my kids."

"Of course," I went on. "But I sense that there was a sort of a breakdown in the discourse. Given what you are, Octavio, there must have been."

"Sure, you're right. At the sight of little Helie my discourse went out the window. There was no way I could avert it. Whenever I stepped out for a stroll with the kids, nothing else in the world mattered to me. I took on the role of father. Years later, in Belgium, Helie, who was eight or nine at the time, asked me if I preferred the people around me over her. Specifically, she asked me what I would do if I were on a ship filled with kids that was sinking. Would she be the first one I saved or not?"

"Whoah! And what was your response?"

"I told her that if I had time enough to think it through rationally, which is not the case with a sinking ship, I would save whoever was of most use to society. But I added that, if I were to see her drowning, she would be the first one I saved."

"Which must have left her flummoxed."

"Certainly, because it does not fit with expectations. But that's how it is. You think along certain lines, yet love—in this instance love for one's daughter—can make you act differently. I'll grant that. But that is no obstacle to one's choosing intellectually to have other non-biological 'offspring.' For instance, I have a 'daughter' who is Peruvian. As far as I know, she was the first person ever to receive a kidney transplant in Belgium and she is still alive. Ariane and I met and helped Tania when they operated on her in Paris when she was eight years old. She always comes to see us when she comes to France."

"I reckon that fatherly love must be a comfort to Irene," I said, returning to his story.

"Maybe so, but she knew at the same time that political activity was ongoing and escalating. There was no way that Irene could chastise me for it because I had always made my intentions plain to her. So we lived for the moment, on a day-to-day basis. Irene stoically accepted it and faced up to what was coming. Which explains why, even though she did not share my outlook on life and the drawbacks of the separations that circumstances thrust upon us, there was never any breakdown in our relationship. The essence of that relationship, namely, friendship, has endured to this day. Irene did not share my outlook on life, but she accepted my trying to live it as I saw it, acknowledging that every human being is entitled to live according to his own standards."

"You are very precise when it comes to pinning down where you stood from the point at which you became a father."

"Before we get to grips with the events that I consider most telling about those four years of my life in Mexico, I think I need to do that. Bear in mind the value I place on that existential outlook, that ethic and the need to act consistently at the time."

"You're getting very serious now, Octavio."

"There was a very complex situation in which I found myself obliged to split myself in two and lead a double life in terms both of what I said and what I did."

"I imagine that when you step outside of the law you enter into a frantic spiral from which it is hard to distance yourself and reflect upon what you are doing."

"My head is still spinning. I am thinking about what I did back then. The primary, essential driver in my life was preserving a consistency between what I was saying and what I was doing. I was resisting what was pulling me in the direction of fitting into society; looking for reasons and the strength to help me pursue my commitment to the anti-Franco struggle in a settling of bourgeois prosperity."

"But were you actually conscious of everything you are telling us now? I mean, were you that clear-sighted at the time?"

"Yes, I was very conscious of this double-edged challenge and the difficulties involved. And I was also conscious of my having to face up to the consequences of my actions and that these were ambiguous."

"Give me an example of that duality."

"To give you some idea, one day I was able to go out on a stroll in the park with the kids after leaving my engineer's office. And then, the very next day, going for armed guerrilla training with some comrades on the outskirts of the Federal District."

Between the Official and the Clandestine

AMONG THE CHILDREN OF political refugees, a symbolic reconstruction of the lost homeland is quite commonplace. The tales of exiled parents, of what was lost or of what might have been, is a powerful driver that is a big factor in the molding of those who have grown up far away from the parental homeland and this holds true regardless of the political ideology of the emigrés. Because, strange as it may seem, it is possible to be homesick for a home one has scarcely known at all, or never actually known, as was the case with many of the children of republican exiles born on Mexican or French soil. This is imaginary nostalgia for a lost homeland, and sometimes the imagination carries a lot more potency than actual recollection.

Thus, many of the children of the Spanish refugees in Mexico started banding together regardless of the ideological affiliations of their forebears, with an eye to taking action to unseat fascism. Youngsters of varying political persuasions, driven by the success of the Cuban revolution, made up their minds to join forces in order to combat Francoism. Not without frictions and difficulties, exiled youth launched the Movimiento Español 59 (ME/59 or Spanish Movement 59), just as the Cubans had had their 26th of July Movement (or ME26). The mere sight of the initials invites comparisons. We are speaking here of young people born in Mexico or who had arrived in the country when just a few years old. The main thing they had in common was that they felt uneasy about the inaction of the historic refugees; that, plus the mental picture they had of the land that was crying out to be liberated.

In 1955, Francoist Spain was granted membership in the United Nations. In the specific case of Mexico—which had never recognized the Franco government—there was a degree of ambiguity. Francoism actually did dispatch a representative to Mexico, his task being to establish diplomatic relations and strive to put pressure on the longer-established non-republican émigré community, the *gachupines*. Thus, Manuel Oñós, a diplomat from the Spanish Nationalist Movement, placed an insertion in the Mexican press indicating the Franco regime's intention of marking the anniversary of July 18, 1936 (the date of the "Uprising") with a banquet and to invite lots of diplomats from different countries. There was an immediate spontaneous backlash, as expressed by the painter Xavier de Oteiza: "We went loco ... 'We have to do something!' 'Something has to be done!' We began talking to people and it transpired that everyone was on the same page as us." There was even a plan to kidnap Oñós, although this wasn't done. The republic's embassy in Mexico protested Oñós's move and he was obliged to cancel the plans. Prior to that, some young refugees had spontaneously paint-bombed the home of the fascist official's home. That incident, in 1959, heralded the launch of the ME/59 a few months later. Its members described themselves as nonparty political. The aim was to stir up resistance and opposition to the regime inside and outside of Spain by means of genuinely creative actions. Evidence of this was a funeral held by youngsters from the Federal District as a criticism of Eisenhower's visiting Spain in 1960. The most interesting testimony regarding the short-lived ME/59 is the book that was written by writer Max Aub's daughter, Elena Aub, in which she mentions Octavio as representing the anarchists, a relevant point given that the Aubs were of the Stalinist communist persuasion. Elena described Octavio as a young man "in serious pursuit" of his goals.

"There is a couple of photographs showing you in a ravine training in the use of arms along with some comrades."

"Yes, that was on the outskirts of the Federal District. The heat was frightful. We were having target practice."

"It looks like you were on a picnic."

"The idea was to launch a guerrilla war, Cuban-style. The bunch of us were drawn from a variety of political persuasions and of course we were out to emulate the success of the Cuban revolution. Lots of us were in touch with the *barbudos* and their influence among us was palpable."

"Historical processes are not repeatable."

"I know, I know. But those were very infectious times. Half of Latin America had revolution on its mind. One of the comrades who was there—Alcover—who was, among other things, a republican and a Freemason, was in contact with Bayo over in Cuba."

"Bayo? Colonel Alberto Bayo?"

"The very same. He made his name during the civil war because he tried to capture Majorca for the republican cause. It was a hare-brained operation that even left García Oliver pondering whether to have him shot. Well, the point is that Bayo was providing military and technical support to Castro before the latter set sail for the island on board the *Granma*. In Cuba, Bayo was up to his old tricks again. My friend Alcover was in touch with him and was out to secure help from the Cuban 26th of July Movement through Bayo. Which is why we were training. The idea was to launch a motley republican front with backing from Fidel and Cuba, something that never happened."

"But did ME/59 mount any hard and fast action?"

"Yes. When the Francoists killed Sabaté over in Spain, we organized actions and tried to torch the Francoist 'embassy,' as well as carrying out graffiti, for example. We also clashed with gangs of Francoists at the airport in the Federal District when Franco's latest 'official' representative arrived. I took a lot of punches."

"Meanwhile, you were working away as an engineer, installing pipe-work on vast sites."

"Sure. Everything was booming. My political commitments, as well as my work commitments. In fact, in professional terms, I was in charge of overseeing projects for a building firm set up by some colleagues and friends from the Faculty of Engineering. That meant that I could suit myself when it came to time off, since I had no set working hours. I even had time to get on with the drafting of the book *El ideal de la ciencia*, that I had started writing in the mid-1950s, but which I had never, for various reasons, been able to finish."

"Back then, in the late 50s, if memory serves, it was a time of lots of work and a booming economy, right?"

"*Oui oui*. I had specialized in hydraulic engineering. My job was to carry out projects and oversee the outfitting of the main hotels being built in the Federal District and in Acapulco back then, as well as other schemes like Oaxaca airport. Perhaps the largest project I was involved in was the building of the United States's new embassy on the Paseo de la Reforma. My firm won the contract, on the basis of the specifications set by the US government agency responsible its construction. The work was well advanced when fire accidentally broke out and the press depicted it as a potential attack. Just to be on the safe side, it was decided that I would have nothing more to do with the site.

They were afraid that a link might be drawn between my name and my 'other' activities that my partners knew about."

"Is this when Gloria came on to the scene?"

"Precisely. There was the so-called Hotel Bamer across from the Alameda. It is no longer there as such but at the time it was very important. There were technical problems with the building. You know, drainage, dampness, etc. Since everything in Mexico shifts a little due to the earthquakes, there are always problems. The hotel was owned by the banker Bamer (same name as the hotel) and he had his offices on the first or second floor. It was in those offices that I first met Gloria and we became friends. She was one of the secretaries of the director of the bank."

"You struck up a romance with Gloria. You are forever talking about 'friendship' and you employ the word in various ways. Another facet of your double life in this case."

"Well, I was living a double life in every sense," Octavio added with a barely perceptible smile. "As an engineer I was useful to the firm as I was good at my job, and as long as that was the case, I had no problems. Irene, on the other hand, was very devoted to the kids and did not want to know anything about what I was up to."

"Meaning that Irene did not ask too many questions about your political activities. Her world was the family."

"Spot on. Gloria did have an interest in republican refugees and became part of my political obsession."

"Are you still in touch with her?"

"No, no contact."

"There was something dizzying about your relationship being hidden. An adventure."

"Yes, but there was also something that was kept hidden from Gloria. She knew that I was an engineer, the son of refugee parents, and I was plotting against the dictatorship, along with other refugee progeny. But she never knew about my family situation. When we started going out together she used to come with me on the more clandestine ME/59 activities, in which 'secrecy' as to our real selves was paramount."

"There was a romanticism at work with Gloria," Octavio said, breaking out of the silence into which he had retreated. "We knew that our relationship would be short-lived because, in the fight against Franco, everything lacked stability. Maybe that was the charm: an unadulterated feeling of having no future. She just took it for granted that, some day, I would be leaving Mexico for an unknown fate."

"From what you say it seems that she made excuses for you."

"No," Octavio sank into silence once more, trying to sift through his thoughts after so many years. "More straightforward than that. I believed that there was no need for me to tell her more and drag her into a world outside of my activism. It struck me as more convenient not to go into the existence of other ties that might keep me in Mexico. It was not only the more 'romantic' thing to do but it was more convincing in terms of my plans and commitment to leave the country. I did not want any doubts about my sincerity in that respect or about the authenticity of my behavior."

"Back to Gloria again. But first," I said, looking at the photo of the guerrilla training, "let's talk about violence. When I look at your life and how close you have been to violence, I have a hard time accepting you using it on third parties. I don't see you as a violent sort."

"I have always had issues with the question of violence. I have never been a violent person and at times that has created complications in my life when there was violence all around and it had to be used. I do not like guns. My only contact with them was during those training exercises."

"But the same thing happened too, in respect of the manufacture of explosives in France, years later, when you were striking at Francoist targets."

"Actually, I always strove to keep contact with explosives to a minimum and to ensure that actions were symbolic. With the exception of Franco himself, I never planned to have human targets. We always hit out at agencies, at assets of the regime. I used to have conversations with García Oliver about that. He came from a direct-action tradition and was a man of action. He used to say that killing Franco would open up a whole Pandora's box. I had my doubts even about that. I never viewed the elimination of an individual as definitive, even in the case of an aberration like Franco."

"Getting back to Gloria, I suppose that when the pace of things started to pick up, which is to say, as your engagement with the libertarian resistance against Franco drew nearer, you pondered how you were going to bring your relationship with her to an end?"

"Whether my relationship with Gloria would have gone the same way had I not been mixed up with ME/59 and the progress towards unity within the CNT, I don't know. The fact is that she was okay with our relationship being informal and temporary, given my activist commitment and the secrecy I operated under.

"Gloria came along with me on nearly all of the clandestine actions our group mounted during our time with ME/59. She was known to us all as La Compañera and was present when we planned out the action targeting the premises of the semi-official Francoist embassy in Mexico City in the wake of Quico Sabaté's murder on January 5, 1960."

"Not that you were active in ME/59 for long."

"The reasons why we quit had to do with the ascendancy of the communists in its operations. We were greatly frustrated to find that the communists' policy of national reconciliation vis-à-vis the Franco regime was a brake on any chances of active moves against Francoism. Where the MC/59 was concerned, a different approach stood no chance. The communists would prevaricate and hijack everything. And also there was an inter-continental CNT congress in France, in Vierzon, the outcomes of which raised hopes of reunification, so by that point ME/59 no longer had much meaning as far as libertarians were concerned."

"Meaning that, as the possibility was broached of reunifying all of the Spanish anarchists scattered in exile, it looked more reasonable to you to invest your energies in that direction?"

"Precisely. At the beginning of the 1960s, I was actively supporting the process of reunification of the Spanish Libertarian Movement (Movimiento Libertario Español/MLE), in which the Cuban revolution was a great help. It was at that point that I began to have direct contact with Juan García Oliver. He had made contact with Floreal Rojas, a member of the Libertarian Youth. Every so often, Floreal would travel up to see him in Guadalajara where he was basically living in isolation from official anarchist circles. García Oliver put it to him that he wanted to collaborate with us. He wanted to lend a helping hand to us young libertarians who were agitating for actively taking on the struggle against Franco."

García Oliver

TIME NOW TO TACKLE the role played by Juan García Oliver, Octavio's comrade during his final months in Mexico. García Oliver was one of the key figures in the Spanish civil war, perhaps (no offense to Durruti) the most significant figure on the anarchist side. García Oliver held a curious position and was hard to place, given the ambiguousness he displayed in the events in which he took part. In frames from the historic CNT footage showing him speaking in Montjuich cemetery beside Durruti's grave on the first anniversary of the his death, one can gauge the charisma and oratorical gifts that García Oliver had. He spoke of his fellow fighter from the so-called Los Solidarios group. And eulogized the dead hero in the name the "Nosotros" collective. He also took the position that Durruti was one of the "kings of the workers' guns," answering the onslaught from the bosses' hired guns blow for blow. But years later, in his autobiography *El eco de los pasos*, Oliver was critical of Durruti, upbraiding him for his recklessness and lack of common sense in given historical circumstances. His speech in Montjuich on November 20, 1937 was an emotional one delivered over a lost comrade, and as we listen to García Oliver and see him dressed in that immaculate suit of his, his hair swept back from his forehead and his comrades surrounding him, one cannot but acknowledge his imposing, overpowering personality. As tough as granite and virtually sculptured, García Oliver slowly raise his tone, like a symphony, in a stunning crescendo. It is even more stunning to think that this waiter from Reus turned into one of the most impressive and ambivalent personalities during the tragic war years.

But later there was a different side, as one can tell from his memoirs. Besides his great intelligence and extraordinary gifts of memory (Oliver wrote upwards of six hundred pages entirely from memory, citing dates and fellow travelers from more than fifty years of an activist career), there is an extraordinary ego and arrogance palpable in the text.

García Oliver was accused of being an authoritarian. A harsh term for someone who doesn't believe in attaining power by using power. In his defense, it should be stressed that Spanish anarchism or specifically anarchism in Barcelona, was paradigmatic, having, thanks to historical circumstances, had the option of exercising power. Power, the destruction of which so much effort had been invested, surfaced within anarchism like a time bomb. And anarchism paid a heavy price for its exercise of power, and García Oliver too paid a price, as he had been one of its most significant figures. Some of his detractors alleged that there was a hint of bolshevization about him. In power, García Oliver accepted—reluctantly according to him—the post of Justice minister, a post he filled at a time when the CNT still had some influence within the republican government. His record as a minister, judging by what historians of various persuasions have written about it, displayed laudable organizational talents and a capacity for hard work. He even got along reasonably well with republican politicians who looked upon anarchists as the devil himself. But one thing above all others stood out from his term in office: ultimately, he was the man who gave the go-ahead for the shooting of José Antonio Primo de Rivera, Spanish fascism's major figure. Going by his subsequent exile in Mexico, this was an action that made him somewhat wary of returning to Spain once the dictator had died. In fact, García Oliver ended his days in Guadalajara (Mexico) where he was buried, and he never again set foot on Spanish soil after the civil war.

García Oliver's time in Mexico was marred by the death of his only son, who was killed in a traffic accident. In exile in Mexico, he gave anarchist circles among the exiles a wide berth and eventually severed all ties with his great rivals from the civil war days, such as Federica Montseny and Abad de Santillán.

García Oliver was born into a humble family and received scarcely any primary schooling, which is to say, he only learned to read and write. His true intellectual education—as a man of action forged during the days of "*pistolerismo*" in Barcelona—he owed to the lengthy prison terms he served and to an innate intelligence that was better than the norm. A slow reader, he acknowledged that he liked to "ruminate over" any texts that came into his hands.

The affinity he felt with young people like Octavio, Floreal Rojas, and Floreal Ocaña derived from his identification "with these youngsters who, when faced with greybeards like Proudhon, Bakunin, or Kropotkin, had no hesitation in shaving off the long beards of these anarchist saints, given the need for their teaching to be brought up to date."[5] In all likelihood, he also relished such rebel youth who laughed at the way his former comrades from the days of the civil war wriggled out of outright struggle.

"Tell me how you came to meet García Oliver."

"I don't remember the date, but I think it was in the mid-1960s that Floreal Rojas drove me up to Guadalajara to meet him for the first time. We knew each other because my father and he had served time in jail together—in the Modelo prison in Barcelona, I think it was, during the Primo de Rivera dictatorship. Not that they got on well with each other. Later, during the war, my father opposed the appointment of anarchists to ministries. Once in exile, the word was that García Oliver was out to launch a libertarian party and that he had certain masonic connections. All manner of things were said about García Oliver, but we knew that he had taken a stand against do-nothingism and Floreal Rojas and I made up our minds to get in touch with him."

"But were you an admirer of his?"

"No, not in the least. Even though he was a big name and a prestigious figure and might be of service to us in shaking off do-nothingism."

"By the time you met him, García Oliver was sixty-nine years old and had lost his only son, Juan, who, I think, would have been the same age as you. He was living all alone except for his partner, Pilar. There is a tremendous sadness evident in his memoirs when he speaks of those years."

"Never, not once during all the time I had dealings with him, did he ever speak in the first person or about his family. I was aware of the tragedy, including the accident that he himself had suffered when he was knocked down by a motorcycle and very nearly lost his left leg, but not one word was uttered by him about his private life."

"I always got the impression that he was a bit of an egomaniac."

"He actually was, but at the same time he had a hell of an intellect. He was a very quick thinker and sometimes one had to slow him down a bit. He thought he had come up with something earth shattering and you would tell him 'Hang on there, Juan, you're forgetting this and this and that.' He was always very straightforward in his dealings with me. Showing me consideration and listening to my suggestions."

"He speaks highly of you in his biography."

"He used to refer to me as 'the engineer.' He was a pragmatist. He was tuned in to the anarchists' mindset and saw that the most interesting way to act was what we were putting forward."

"Meaning that, in spite of certain differences, there was this affinity. He always stated that he held the educated bourgeois classes in utter contempt. He stated that the anarchist revolution would only be acknowledged if made by workers and peasants. You were neither and came close to the very thing that he despised."

"Okay, yes. But in my militant career I never made any play of my university education or my 'studies.' Maybe he despised the sort of soap box mounted by a certain sort of intellectual bourgeoisie that blabs on about the left and the revolution. The way one conjures up a 'caste' that talks in terms of what needs to be done."

"It was a sort of a 'class-based' attitude to who was or was not authorized to speak on behalf of anarchy; he was dismissive of student movements, for instance."

"García Oliver had a huge personality and knew that his brain was above average. He knew it and there he was right, even though it pains me to say it."

"García Oliver held Federica Montseny in contempt. But didn't Federica have a mighty 'intellect' also?"

"Well, yes. She did. But Federica was the last word in rabble-rousing." Octavio fell silent for a long time before adding, "And in drawing room anarchist literati."

Octavio sat in silence, hands clasped. Maybe he was remembering how, as far as she was concerned, he was one of the main stumbling blocks inside the movement."

"Give me some more detail, Octavio."

"No, I'm not going to say anything more about her."

"She was not to your taste."

"No. Not at all," he answered curtly. "Deliberately telling lies and unwittingly telling lies are not the same thing. And telling lies in order to profit is just bad."

"And what was she after back then? Why was she telling lies?"

"What 'they were·after'—because there was her partner, Esgleas as well— was to stay on as leaders and make a living out of it. She was a real mediocrity. She wrote semi-anarchistic literature, with educational pretensions, very simplistic. And it sold! It was a pathetic way to make a living and it made a bureaucrat out of her."

"Was there not something of the tear-jerker about *La Novela Ideal*?"

"That there was. That was the worst of it. It was used to moralize, in the Christian sense of the term. In one speech she delivered about Durruti, I remember her talking about 'heroes of the race.' What an ugly word, 'race.' In her view, García Oliver was a 'plague-carrier' and I suffered the same fate after 1961. She and Esgleas treated me like a 'plague-carrier.'"

"It was said of García Oliver that he might have made a Spanish Lenin," I said, changing the subject.

"Yes, A lot of things were said ... It is a slightly tiresome topic," Octavio replied, displaying a degree of irritation. "García Oliver suggested 'going for broke,' as if he was taking about an anarchist dictatorship based on the balance of power in 1936 and he deserved a lot of credit for being so blunt and so unpolitical. My father or Alaiz, on the other hand, believed that the opportunity should be seized to take the transformation of society and work on the revolution as far as they would go. That people would then see that what was being done was worth the effort. No need to impose anything. They were closer to the old educational discourse of classical anarchism. The problem is that one has to act in the historical moment. Back then, ideas had not progressed sufficiently for people to understand that the process of human evolution is a gradual thing and not a sharp break. And realize that a change or an idea comes slowly and, back in the day, Marxists and anarchists alike understood that if there was a disruption such as, say, a revolution, something brand-new could be built from scratch. And that is not feasible. We anarchists destroyed Power so that we might start on the process of change with people. The marxists achieved or gained Power for the purpose of exercising it. And, as we have seen, their exercise of it is the same as all the rest. Sharp breaks are needed in order to generate the conditions for change, but they themselves are not the change."

"I can see that you are drifting into the theoretical now..."

"Let's get back to García Oliver," Octavio replied, turning the tables. "We can pass many an hour on matters theoretical. That much I know."

"So, what happened at your first meeting with García Oliver?"

"García Oliver indicated to us that he was ready and waiting to use his connections to raise the funding that activation of the fight against Francoism required. I saw him as someone clear-sighted, knowledgeable about the dire straits in which anti-Francoism was trapped and, in particular, the Spanish Libertarian Movement. His view was that the MLE needed every one of us. He took a back seat, in a very frank way. He simply wanted to make a contribution."

"And when it came to the practicalities?"

"The SI (Inter-continental Secretariat) at the time was single-minded and in favor of action.[6] An attempt on Franco's life was being hatched. They needed resources and funding. García Oliver had links to the Freemasons. I am not sure quite how. They say that his connection to them started during his short stay in Sweden, but I never discussed this with him. There was talk of his tie to them being an issue. In my eyes, it was not, as long as his intentions were honorable. If García Oliver did have ties to them, it made not the slightest difference to how he behaved.

"A few months later, García Oliver advised me that CNT personnel living in Venezuela as refugees had invited him to come down there. In Caracas, he would see the co-ordinating secretary of the Inter-Continental Secretariat, Juan Pintado. García Oliver made his trip to Venezuela in order to secure funding for the attack that was being planned. Before he set off, he called me to tell me to be on stand-by to meet with them, in the event that my presence might be thought necessary."

"Meaning that the time had come to drop everything else and act upon what Irene had been so afraid of," I remarked, thinking about her and about the little kids.

"I never thought of it in those terms," Octavio replied, pensively. "Ever since I had made up my mind to commit myself, I always felt it was perfectly natural to arrive at that sort of decision. Actually, on the day after he arrived in Venezuela, García Oliver phoned me to say that my meeting them was a matter of urgency. So off I went to Venezuela, and I accompanied García Oliver to all the meetings."

"And what happened in Venezuela? Because you were in Caracas for some time."

"A number of things happened. There were comrades with financial resources down there who were all for backing our objectives. The point now was to complete the planned attack on Franco. We tried to secure funding from the Venezuelan trade unionists because there was a certain connection already in place with the country's union confederation, a fellow by the name of José González Navarro. He had help from Spanish anarchists in the attempt on the life of the Venezuelan dictator Pérez Gimenez. That operation failed and they ended up in jail, but from that point onwards, Navarro tried to help the Spanish anarchists in their fight against Francoism.

"I promised Pintado that Floreal Ocaña and I would take part and it was agreed that we would be kept abreast of any progress in the plan."

"And did you manage to work out anything concrete between yourselves and the Venezuelan trade unionists?"

"Nothing came of it. García Oliver was quite disappointed that he hadn't managed to get any serious commitment from the Caracas comrades and the Venezuelan trade unionists. I don't know whether it occurred to him that he could pull it off because he was a member of the international masonic order, but it all came to nothing."

"Do I remember something about there having been some connection between anarchists and Freemasons in the past? What was García Oliver looking for? For them to cough up money?"

"Strictly speaking there was never any connection between the two movements. Certain anarchists had become Freemasons after the war was lost, and García Oliver thought that he could persuade them to back the fight against Franco financially. The fact is that I was pretty skeptical about this, not that I made any attempt to stop him from trying."

"Have you ever had masonic connections?"

"Yes, and I have had friendships with some of them. It might seem strange, but they never ever tried to recruit me into the order. Maybe because they knew that I hadn't the slightest interest. The masons are a club for making connections and conducting business; like businessmen getting together to play a round of golf and talk about their projects. There were lots of them in Mexico. It was said that one had to be a Freemason in order to get to be president. My co-workers joined the Freemasons for career reasons."

Octavio then returned to the topic: "I think García Oliver joined the Freemasons to protect his personal safety. It seems to have been after his stay in Sweden in 1939 and I'd guess it was more of a strategic move than anything to do with masonic mythology and symbolism."

"And how long did the trip to Venezuela last?"

"More or less a week. García Oliver and I returned to Mexico separately, but we kept in touch from then on. The days went by, and 1961 came along. Finally, at the start of the year some news arrived, but, as feared, the news was confirmation that the planned attack had to be postponed so as not to compromise the CNT's reunification congress due to be held in Limoges in August–October that year.

"Then, given that the reunification of the CNT in Mexico was already an accomplished fact, we joined García Oliver and the most like-minded comrades in advocating for action against Francoism. After I informed them of my intention to go to France on my own initiative to find out if the CNT actually did have any intention of fighting Franco, the decision was made to appoint me as delegate from the reunified CNT in Mexico. And so I was able to travel and attend the reunification congress in Limoges."

"Time to say your goodbyes. Which I can only suppose was not easy."

"Easy? No. But remember: I attended the congress and then returned to Mexico to prepare for my final departure from the country. My trip to the Limoges congress was very tough because, before I left, Gloria informed me, out of the blue, that she was expecting. She said that she was prepared to have an abortion, something very hard to do in Mexico because it was against the law. Through friends, we managed to make contact with a doctor who could carry out the procedure. Since I had to leave urgently for France, I left Gloria what she needed to pay the doctor and she agreed to get in touch with him.

Reconstructing What Remained

OCTAVIO FLEW TO PARIS in 1961. Within days he traveled the four hundred kilometers to Limoges where the congress was meeting. After the rude awakening of defeat in the civil war, the CNT had embarked upon a tremendous, very difficult period of internal reflection, which resulted in its breaking up into many bickering factions. It was twenty-two years before they tried—for the first time since the civil war—to unify and rebuild the union at a congress. This is why the Limoges congress was so important, and one can appreciate the enthusiasm, effort, and dedication that the new breed of anarchists—the children of the exiles—brought to it.

But in Limoges there was a sort of a parallel fight going on: one side spoke up for collective interests and renewal; the other, to a great extent, prioritized personal interests over collective ones. The proceedings and resolutions made up a complicated fabric in which the anarchist ideal was mixed up with personal preoccupations very often dressed up as activities that dated back to civil war times.

Representatives from the various factions arrived from Africa (French Oran), the Americas, France, England, and so on. There was even a clandestine delegation from inside Spain. Each group carried with it the undeniable imprint of its immediate surroundings, which is to say, the context of their home countries, but the biggest difference between them was the huge generation gap. On one side stood the "veterans," the militants who had fought against fascism in the civil war. They were now twenty-two years older, fifty years old and up. Mature, tempered people who proceeded at a comfortable pace. On the other side were the "newcomers," the children of exile, who had left Spain at a very young age or been born elsewhere. With no investment in the myth, they didn't hesitate to make action the priority. They were immersed in the historical reality of the day, like the Cuban revolution or the independence achieved by African nations.

In the articles he wrote after the Limoges congress, Octavio was very clear in his depiction of the young attendees' stance that the veteran Spanish libertarians, the products of their various contradictions, were sitting in their bubble watching the world go by. As they saw it, the older generation didn't see themselves affected by anything beyond "the Spanish question." Octavio was blunt when he ventured to describe these "erstwhile heroes" as weary foot-draggers. Even though he didn't name names, it was clear that he was talking about the likes of Montseny, Esgleas, Herrera, etc:

> Spent men who hover over full stops and commas, men unaware that "militant responsibility" implies their not having any right to bore the audiences at meetings with soporific addresses from emeritus professors of the ideal ... those who live only in the past have no part to play in the present day nor in the future.

This declaration of intent, in the middle of the Limoges congress, irritated more than one quiet attendee at the Sunday meetings. These young people were despised and, as Octavio himself put it, treated like "plague-carriers." As far as Esgleism was concerned, the "promising young man" who had sat down to dinner with Montseny and Esgleas in Toulouse three years before, this youngster with his tried-and-tested anarchist pedigree, son of a rationalist schoolteacher, had turned out to be an out-and-out punk, and at the Limoges congress the young generation blew all expectations out of the water—though it would be fair to say that they had help from some "old hands," like as Cipriano Mera and García Oliver.

What could have been a quiet congress that might not have come up with anything definite, that might have kept the CNT in quiet disarray, as the Esgleists wanted, turned out to be a rejuvenating bombshell where there were declarations and voting in favor of reunification of the historical movement. As well, and for the very first time since the civil war, there was concrete action in the shape of the formal creation of a group to tackle Francoism head-on. And so was born the DI [Defensa Interior], flying in the face of Esgleas, Montseny, and other members of the anarchist royal family. But the latter didn't lie down and accept this. They tried to ensure that the reunification foundered, accusing "Venezuelan" comrades of having turned into company bosses in exile and of lining their pockets, arguing that for that reason the

CNT could hardly associate itself with people of their ilk. But this scheme got them nowhere.

As García Oliver wrote in his memoirs, these young people had "shaved the beards off Bakunin, Kropotkin, and Malatesta." In Octavio's case, he is still on active service to this day. When he describes himself as a maverick (*heterodoxo*) he is simply registering the fact that the means of avoiding turning into an orthodox is very straightforward: one has only to strive to not be one. "Tired and want to rest on past achievements?" he asked one twenty-two-year-old kid who was whining about feeling worn out by certain internal bickering in an Ateneo in the Sants barrio in Barcelona in 2016. "Then rest up for a while and carry on later."

It's worth noting that Octavio hadn't wanted to speak too much about what happened in Limoges. I can only suppose that it was tough, and that it left a deep wound in the brand-new reunified CNT.

Maybe that was why Octavio seemed very loath to cast his mind back and answer the questions I was asking. Reading the articles Octavio wrote back then, another side of his personality comes as a surprise. When he speaks or writes now, Octavio displays a very open attitude to other people's opinions and his antiauthoritarianism is unmistakable, but in those articles, there is a notable vehemence when it came to defining his ideas as against those of the "veterans." He was blunt, incisive, and doesn't hate to repudiate the personality cult and to speak of the urgent need for praxis.

"What can I tell you?" Octavio volunteered, unsolicited. "The atmosphere at the congress was upbeat for those advocating on behalf of reunification and marked by aggressive rancor by those led by Esgleas, who wanted no such thing, because, they argued, the CNT was going to lose 'its essence.' This was a ruse, an ideological 'ploy' used to cling to control of the CNT, hang on to paid positions and waste time while they looked forward to their retirement, like any other Frenchman. Federica and Esgleas were even on record with the French Social Security Agency as employees of that revolutionary venture, the CNT!"

"Quite surreal!"

"As you can see. For them it was almost a case of CNT Limited. They never forgave us for what happened at that congress."

"But did all the old hands think along those lines?"

"No. Each had his own quirks. There was García Oliver, who threw his weight behind us. As did Cipriano Mera. They were 'veterans,' as they were called, but they were still 'youngsters.'"

"At that point the maquis had been cut loose, right?"

"Yes, of course. Facerías and Sabaté ... they had already been 'blackballed' by Esgleas, not that they cared much. They were people who largely ignored the Toulouse CNT."

"The very fact that the congress was attended by anarchists who had come from within Spain meant that the domestic resistance was still alive, from what you say."

"They were crucial. They were the ones most entitled to talk about the CNT. Theirs was a frontal struggle and their lives were on the line day in and day out. And with comrades Ismael and Gorrón from the reunified CNT committee of the Interior, who played a decisive part in getting the DI resolution through, I agreed that I would travel down to Madrid to meet with them. They wanted García Oliver to represent them on the DI once it was established with its base in France. They had a lot of confidence in García Oliver and his charisma."

"Meaning that you would pass through Madrid before heading back to Mexico."

"Ismael and Gorrón had a letter they wanted to give me for García Oliver. Before setting off for Madrid using the Vaca Vilchis alias again, I passed through Toulouse. I attended the FIJL congress at which its engagement with the DI was approved. It was there that my name was put forward as the FIJL representative on the DI."

"The very thing that you wanted. At last, some direct action and direct attacks on the regime."

"That's what struck us as the most consistent course. In Paris, Liberto Sarrau suggested to me that we meet the Cuban ambassador. The idea was to set me up with an entry visa for Cuba so that I might have an audience with Fidel Castro. We wanted to remind him of his promise that he would lend us a hand in our fight against France. We had that meeting with the ambassador and he assured us that he would do whatever was necessary. But the visa never came. I told him that I had to leave for Madrid and his response was that he would forward it to the Cuban embassy there so that I could get the entry visa in person. I was just about to embark on my trip when two comrades turned up at the airport to tell me that Ismael and Gorrón had just been arrested."

"A close call ... Weren't you afraid?"

"There was no time for fear," Octavio replied. "But taking a cold hard look at things, no further arrests had been made and it looked as if I could blithely proceed down to Madrid. So I made the trip because of the Cuban matter and, in passing, paid a visit to the Puente de los Franceses."

"The Puente de los Franceses? Had it anything to do with what later happened to Delgado and Granados?," I asked.

"*Oui, oui.* I took some notes and photos of the bridge with an eye to our assassination attempt on the dictator. But I am jumping ahead... I was pissed off about having to go to the Cuban consulate. I felt like an idiot. They gave me the runaround. I hung around all week for the damned travel visa to Cuba. I realized that we could never expect any help from Castro. Some time went by before I discovered that Federico Álvarez Arregui, a communist from the ME/59 who was in Cuba while I was in Madrid, had been briefed on my plans by the Cubans and had ensured that the PCE made it impossible for me to get to Cuba. I don't know if that was also Fidel's stance, but I know that he had heard about me and had seized upon the PCE's opposition to mess up our meeting. In any case, I had no expectations of Fidel because by then he had direct ties to the soviets, like the PCE. In the end, when no visa was forthcoming from the Cuban embassy, I gave up waiting and decided to head back to Mexico."

"You went back in order to sort matters out, say farewell to Irene and the kids, find out how Gloria was, following the termination of her pregnancy, talk to your father, and close down your career as a hydraulic engineer," I summarized. "Loose ends easily tied up."

"Little things that I had to leave behind in order to begin a fresh life in France," he replied with a barely perceptible smile.

Farewells

OCTAVIO ARRIVED BACK IN Mexico firmly resolved to pack his bags and embark upon a new life as a direct-action activist in France. The time had finally come for him to display the consistency between discourse and praxis that he had been struggling with internally for so long.

"On my return to the Federal District, I got in touch with Gloria. Things had not gone as we had planned. She had not been able to have the abortion, as it proved impossible to get in touch with the doctor. I believed her. Gloria was always open and honest with me, and she was now in the advanced stages of pregnancy. Her mind was made up to keep the child, which turned out to be a girl. Knowing the way my mind worked, she made it clear to me that this was her own choice and that she was taking charge of everything if I was not going to go along with it."

"Didn't you get the feeling that everything all around you was spinning out of control?"

"*Oui, oui,*" Octavio replied, somewhat wearily. "And I took it badly. I had to accept things and realize that there were a lot of things that were beyond my control. I had no option but to take responsibility. At which lively moment Gloria asked me what I wanted to name the baby and asked me to give her my family name. I now believe Gloria was placing a tremendously romantic construction on what was going on."

"Gloria must have been head over heels in love with you."

"In love ... That doesn't begin to explain it ... Scientifically, love ... I don't know ..."

"We are not going to agree here. Love is a scientific fact too. Being in love is a verifiable fact and, if you like, you can investigate and you will surely discover that the endorphins and all associated biological factors have their part to play in it."

"I disagree. Love is a matter of chemistry, not science."

‚w there I cannot agree. Passion is chemical. But love is not and, in my
‚w, it can be tested scientifically."

"I see it as a matter of chemistry too and we could spend a lot of time
mulling it over... Anyway, Gloria looked up to me," Octavio went on. "I was
someone 'out of the ordinary' in her workaday world. And she was the same
in my eyes, given our relationship. We arranged for her to keep me in the loop
and that, once the baby was born, she would be registered as Livia Alberola."

"What about Irene? Did she find out about Gloria at all at that point?"

"No. She found out later. I thought it better not to complicate matters
unduly. I never thought things would get that far, now they were out of control, and I had no option but to suck it up as part of my commitment to the
comrades who were waiting for me over in France."

"How did your father and Irene greet your decisions?"

"Where Irene was concerned, things had been pretty clear ever since our
joint trip to Spain back in 1957–1958. And the same applied to my father. They
were both aware of my commitment to the struggle and when I agreed to
leave, and even though it mortified them, they accepted it. Neither of them
questioned my conscientious motives and my commitment to solidarity with
those who were fighting in Spain," he mused, rubbing his knees automatically.
"Obviously, given the material and political comforts we now enjoy, it is hard
to imagine that sort of solidarity. Whether we acknowledge it or not, today
our priority is preserving such material comforts. Plainly—as far as I am concerned at any rate—there is nothing worth jeopardizing it for.

"But, getting back to my loved ones, my chief concern at the time was
leaving them in the best financial circumstances so that they could cope with
my absence. In principle, once I had done a year in France, I would look into
the chances of going home, even if only temporarily. My departure from
Mexico was a leap in the dark. I had no guarantees. It was only when I was
on the plane that it struck me that there was no holding back now. I imagine
that is the sort of thought that crosses the minds of those on their way into
battle. The anxiety generated by feelings of fear and yet knowing that there
can be no turning back. It's not a matter of being ignorant of the risks, but an
appreciation of a self-imposed duty. The likelihood is that those who sailed
on the *Granma* thought precisely these thoughts. The only difference being,
maybe, that a lot of them set sail with the idea of emerging victorious and
gaining power."

"Yes, bringing one chapter to a close and facing up to a brand-new purpose are quite well known to fliers in pursuit of their destiny."

"Well lo and behold the thing takes years, since I occasionally think the same thoughts, fifty-five years on," said a smiling Octavio. "I can say it out loud now because you have 'forced' me to look back on the past and 'explain' the whys and wherefores of what I did. I reckon anybody in similar circumstances has similar impressions; a heady feeling of being compelled to improvise at the drop of a hat, in unknown territory, with no knowing what lies ahead. Which is why the improvisation is not always logical, coherent, and consistent, and the consequences aren't always fixable."

"Let us get back to the succession of events."

"During the time when I was getting ready to go to France and when the finishing touches were being made to the launch of the DI, I briefed my associates at the architect's firm about my decision. After that, I made it my business to finish off any outstanding projects. Later still (I think this was towards the end of February 1962) I was summoned to take up my place in the DI along with García Oliver and another five comrades. I disclaimed all my rights in the firm and arranged with the director that, in return, he would undertake to pay my salary over to Irene month by month for a full year. I was able to hand Gloria the equivalent of some ten thousand of today's euros, which was a lot of money back then, so that she could pay off her mother's house, where she herself was living."

"I might be wrong here, but didn't you feel any sense of guilt?"

"No, not at all. Although I was perfectly well aware of the implications of my decision for those who were somehow dependent on me, and I did what I could to ease them. It was very hard, but such was the price of consistency. Although that is not to say that I didn't find it hard to do, that it was not a worry to me, and that I was not afraid of the risks, the inconveniences, and the uncertainty of the future that I was voluntarily forging. Naturally, the thing was not to dwell on it but to convince myself that I needed to press on, to forget everything that until now allowed me to enjoy life and, for all the absurd ways in which society operated and its nonsensical purposes, to find reasons for leaving it. Over those months, and during the hours that the flight from Mexico to Paris took, I spent a fair bit of time thinking about the physical and spiritual pleasures that were being cut short once and for all. My life in Mexico was now a thing of the past. What was it that gave me the strength to carry on? Maybe it was my inability to forget about the injustice in the world whilst listening to music and basking in the sun on the Pedregal de San Ángel (San Ángel lava field)."

"You mentioned a convertible to me one time," I said, remembering a remark he had made quite some time ago.

"Ah yes, the convertible! Do you know why I loved convertibles? Because I delighted in taking in the sun. At every opportunity that presented itself, I would be out in the sun and I loved that sort of car because I could take in the sun and drive at the same time."

"Sunshine, beauty, driving ... even after all these years you still haven't given up on these. I can see it in your face," I added, seeing the pleasure the memory brought him.

"Because it is essential to have dreams. Things did and still do fascinate me. I mean the chances of gaining knowledge, using one's senses to drink in the beauty of the physical world, enjoying relaxing times listening to music or sunbathing on some beach, or out in the Pedregal de San Ángel, on one of those lava boulders spat out once upon a time by the Xitle volcano and strewn all around the University City in the Federal District. The time I used to spend getting some fresh air in my lungs and dreaming of a more rational, fairer, more beautiful world, was unique."

"I've never been to the San Ángel lava fields. But I can see that it was your 'spot,' a symbolic place for you."

"I sometimes used to drive out there at night in my convertible, stretch out flat on my back, and gaze up at the stars. Transported into the infinite. Out there I used to mull over matters, biological and philosophical. Matters such as you and I being face to face with each other, yet not knowing exactly what is going through our minds, but being capable of understanding without the need to say a single word."

"You've lost me there. Are you talking about telepathy?"

"No, not exactly. I had in mind the harmony of the universe; we don't know ourselves and we find it hard to guess what the other guy is thinking. Sometimes you cross paths with somebody with whom you might well have a startling affinity and you don't know it. Out in the lava field, I used to dream about being able to 'read' people and pick up on that without needing to say a word."

"Okay, but that all has to do with the randomness of the universe," I said, thinking out loud. "I like it that way."

"Naturally. It is the unknown that makes life that much more interesting. If we knew everything, the mystery would be banished from life, and it's the mystery that prompts you to want to tear away the veil and incites you to act. And out in the lava field, I wanted us all to be transparent. Not to be dependent on speech, but for there to be some sort of logical consequentiality between what other people think and what they can discern in you without the deception of speech. I was intrigued by language and used to ponder on that strange, ambiguous invention, speech."

"I must try to get out and pay a visit to the San Ángel lava field some time. There is much humanity in what you are saying. By which I mean contradiction as well as coherence. The contradiction may well be a generational thing, the sort of thing we all share: the convertible, your stylish shirt and pants, music, and a fondness for sunbathing ... But at the same time there is—and I now you don't like the word because of its religious connotations—a degree of mysticism in the native sense of the term. You wished to be alone beneath a star-studded sky, surrounded by lava from the sacred volcano near the ruins of the city of Cuicuilco, mulling things over as you gazed out at the universe."

"I was yearning to be part of the Pachamama," Octavio said.

"That's a perfect definition. In fact, Xitle, the name of the volcano from which the lava field originated, is the Nahuatl word for 'navel.' It was a holy and a magical place for our first peoples. The hub of the universe."

"I used to enjoy thinking deeply out there and it brought me pleasure. Being a part of the universe is something one feels on certain occasions and, out there between the lava and the stars, with my convertible by my side, that was what was going on."

FRANCE

Arrival in France

THERE WAS A CHANGE of president as the United States entered the 1960s. Secure in its atomic might, the great power that had won the Second World War switched from a victorious braggart, Eisenhower, to new leader, John F. Kennedy. A youthful blond who brought a brand-new cosmetic image to the ongoing policy laid down by the chief powers in the land. As demonstrated by the Vietnam war and meddling in the Southern Cone of the Americas, a readiness to go to war remained part of US policy. Evidence of this was the Playa de Girón (aka Bay of Pigs) invasion, an attempt to end the Cuban revolution; the Cuban Missile Crisis, that came within an inch of sparking all-out nuclear war; or the wretched assassination of Patrice Lumumba, the thirty-five-year-old Congolese leader, an attempt by Belgium to cling to control over her African colony, with CIA assistance. It should be pointed out also that Algeria, the French province consumed by a civil war of independence since 1954, was nearing a successful conclusion. Communism had thereby become the "official" option and alternative to the West, and it split the West's population into those who looked kindly upon the soviet experiment and those who despised it. Every county in Europe, and in much of the remainder of the world, had its own communist faction, which was very good at spreading its propaganda, especially in the realm of culture, to further its own interests. There were lots of instances of intellectuals who freely or out of convenience embraced communist thinking. Some of them adamantly supported the option of the USSR, led at the time by Nikita Khrushchev, Stalin's swaggering successor who banged a shoe on the podium at the United Nations. Those were the years when the Cold War was at its height, with Berlin divided by a wall, and the Stasi, the KGB, and so very many other intelligence and quasi-police agencies mingling with the civilian population. There was audio-visual material galore to indicate what was going on during that time. *Goldfinger* in the James Bond series of movies, or, shortly after it, the spoof TV series *Get Smart*, and the slightly more humorless *Man from U.N.C.L.E.* were products that hinted at the existence of a "free world" at odds with "the other side," where people were "not as free." These fed the collective imagination, so much so that a lot of people still view those years through the prism of those movies and TV shows.

Octavio glided through that decade alongside the intelligence agents and agencies, clandestine and legal organizations, and strategic gatherings held to plan operations or missions. It may sound like some television adventure, but it wasn't. It was dramatic, though that over the years and through the conversations I've had with Octavio, the drama might be seen in a more tragicomic light. But those were years that destroyed lives and lots of Octavio's comrades perished along the way, victims of torture or of the *garrote vil*. Years when the dead and disappeared could be counted in the thousands, as in the case in Latin America.

Octavio arrived in Paris at the beginning of March 1963, having left his loved ones behind in the Federal District, knowing that the victory scored by his ideas at the Limoges congress was a very precarious one. He now had to flesh out what had been agreed, before everything could evaporate. He passed through customs as Vaca Vilchis and was welcomed by Rafael Esteban, a member of the Paris CNT, an acquaintance of José Alberola's. During his first few days in Paris, Octavio lived in the Esteban home, a modest apartment near the Place de Colonel Fabien, where the architect Oscar Niemeyer had erected the headquarters of the French Communist Party some time before.

"Sorry, Octavio. You mentioned Niemeyer to me; I am an admirer of his architectural works, and a question struck me that may be a slight digression from the narrative," I said. "Why do you think the anarchists never won the support of the great architects, writers, and intellectuals acknowledged by the mainstream press, when the communists could?"

"There were lots of reasons, but, aside from Albert Camus or Noam Chomsky, who did speak up in favor of anarchism, the fact is that no outstanding intellectuals ever professed openly to be anarchists."

"But there were communists such as Jean-Paul Sartre, Simone de Beauvoir, Pier Paolo Pasolini, Luchino Visconti, Oscar Niemeyer, Pablo Picasso, Gabriel García Márquez ... the list goes on."

"For sure. The reasons for that are many. Throughout the twentieth century there wasn't much intellectual involvement with anarchism. Remember that, for many of those years, Marxism was the 'official' ideology of the opposition to capitalism. Even a few intellectuals, who these days are highly critical of communism, championed it in their younger day. Not only was communism the prevailing ideology in that regard, but it dominated all the academic media at the time. In many instances if one wanted to be a university lecturer, you weren't going to get the post unless you were a Marxist."

"I just can't understand their attachment to the Soviet Union. For instance, in Italy there were some communists such as Visconti or Pasolini who were gay and the latter a Catholic as well. I'm surprised that they both toed the USSR line when the USSR was killing and jailing people on religious grounds or because of sexual orientation. I don't know if they ever spoke up, but I understand that if you were a communist back then you pretty much agreed with soviet practice."

"In that respect, the communists in each country were very pragmatic. And adapted to necessity. As far as they were concerned, the priority was to get as close as possible to power. And if, in order to accomplish that, they had to embrace different things in each context, including repression in the USSR, they had no difficulty in doing so. The Communist Party had an interest in having influential people who backed it. It was more important that Pasolini was a communist than anything he might be able to accomplish as an individual."

"Maybe the intellectuals thought that the USSR could stand up to capitalism as an option for society?"

"I don't know if they believed that or not. What is surprising is that they failed to recognize that state capitalism, as practiced in the USSR, was the same as capitalism per se. Years later, a lot of these intellectuals who embraced the USSR had to acknowledge that. If you delve into the different trajectories of some of them, you'll find that the Communist Party offered them a lot of opportunities back in the 1960s. They were hailed because the communists we in control of certain kinds of media. For instance, in order to shoot movies in France, unless you had French Communist Party connections you stood little chance, unless you could fund the project out of your own pocket. Jorge Semprún, for instance, had a great career as a screenwriter and was with the Communist Party. For some people, let us say, being a communist was de rigueur, the way being in the Freemasons once was for the sake doing of business.

"Sartre's run-ins with Camus in 1944 centered on the latter's efforts to show greater consistency, greater authenticity. Camus denounced the existence of concentration camps inside the USSR, whereas Sartre in a way argued the need for a certain 'discipline.' Which was, when you get right down to it, an aberration."

"Getting back to your trip, Octavio. Where did the money come from for your airplane fare and that first year's stay in France?"

"The organization covered the airfare. And, as for the first year, I had some savings. Remember that our service with the DI was voluntary and we were unpaid. But inside the organization we did have a travel allowance. And accommodation was always in comrades' homes. Given the actions we aimed to carry out, I thought it would be very hard to find work and earn myself a regular wage. But there was also the fact that I was a foreigner and therefore was legally prohibited from working."

"And did you get around that at the time?"

"Of course. From time to time I did odd jobs in an effort to earn some money. Like helping out a comrade by the name of Moñino who was a shoemaker, sorting out his window display, designing it and doing his books. One day some tax inspectors showed up, along with the immigration police. I was working in the rear of the store. They had come to check if there were any foreign illegals working there. I managed to slip out, miraculously, via the back door.

"I was aware of how hard it would be to activate and set up Defensa Interior," Octavio stated, changing the subject. "I was a realist because, once the DI was up and running, it was going to be hard to get around Esgleas, and Llansola, who supported him implicitly. From behind the scenes, they were egging on militants opposed to unity and supportive of a 'do-nothing' policy to carry on sowing the seeds of discord inside the movement. I was forever asking myself what were the real reasons why Esgleas and Llansola might have wanted to get on board with the DI.

"I think that right after the end of the Limoges congress, the militants from the faction that was against the CNT's reunification stepped up their invective again, through the CNT press proper, which they controlled, targeting those of us who were for it. They explained their hostility away in terms of a fight against reformism, but their only purpose was to unleash a sort of a witch-hunt against what they termed 'reformists.' Why so much venom against us young libertarians who were trying to shake the movement out of the stagnation into which bureaucratism had plunged it?"

"But is that what you thought at the time or is it the benefit of hindsight?"

"There is no way that I can state categorically whether those were my thoughts at the time, or whether my main concern at the time centered upon what my day-to-day existence was going to be like once the DI was up and running and once its operations began. I must have thought about that too, since the actions to be undertaken constituted a real leap in the dark: I was aware of the unpredictable aspect of clandestine struggle against a system that was infinitely superior in terms of material and human resources, against a backdrop like France, which was entirely new and, as far as I was concerned, unexpected. So, over there I was obliged to live life on the run, obliged to adapt and tolerate unappetizing living conditions."

"You found it hard to adapt to France then?"

"Very much so. I didn't speak French, the customs were different, and the places a far cry from what I had been used to in Mexico where I had been living in comfortable modern apartments. In France, most of the people who took me into their houses lived in homes where there was no bathroom, or where there was only a shared bathroom on the landing. The toilets were 'Turkish,' which is to say, hole-in-the-ground affairs. But my real obsession was with getting a shower. In Mexico I was used to showering every day, and in France they thought me a real oddball for wanting to shower every three days, something that struck my comrades as excessive. I sometimes had to go to the public baths because the houses in which I was staying had no shower facility. Or, if they did, we had to heat some water and use it to fill wash-hand basins. Back then the people in the surroundings in which I was operating showered just once a week."

"How things have changed!," I remarked, noting the contrast between past and present.

"Yes, but back then people who were not that well paid lived like that. And I found it really hard to fit in, if I ever did. My acquaintances found this obsession of mine with showering a touch exaggerated. It was a Mexican oddity," Octavio added, with a giggle.

"So you felt like a fish out of water, like an outsider?"

"Yes, but I cast around for solutions or grinned and put up with it because I was eager to get on with what I had brought upon myself. That first year I slept in all sorts of beds, including children's cots, with my feet sticking out at the ends," Octavio stands more than 1.80 meters in height.

"And what were the first few DI meetings like?," I pressed him, changing the subject. "From what you've been saying I get the impression that they were more like democratic, congress-style proceedings, with opposing factions. For instance, two of the people there, Llansola and Esgleas or Ángel Carballeira conducted themselves like out-and-out politicians. Politicians in the professional sense of the term. And given that these were anarchists, that is, in principle, a bit of a paradox."

"Even after all these years, it is hard to fathom," Octavio curtly replied, "but, just to be clear about it, I would need to say something about how I got to Toulouse, where our first meeting was held."

Slogging Through the Mud

SHORTLY AFTER ARRIVING IN Paris, Octavio traveled down to Toulouse to attend the very first meeting of the DI. He was greeted at the station by some comrades from the FIJL and the group immediately headed to a house on the outskirts of the city, where Acracio Ruiz, Juan Jimeno, and Cipriano Mera were waiting for them. After a while, they were joined by Marcelino Boticario, then the general secretary of the FIJL, and Roque Santamaría, the general secretary of the Inter-Continental Secretariat (SI) of the CNT-in-exile. The atmosphere was one of open expectation.

Before I go on, we need to say something about Cipriano Mera. Octavio worked in close association with Mera, who by that time was sixty-five years old. Cipriano Mera took part in the civil war and, at the end of it, was held in the grand concentration camps in Algeria and in Missour in Morocco, under the watchful eyes of the French in both places. In light of the inhumane treatment that the Legion meted out to prisoners, Mera managed to escape to Oran and later reached Casablanca, only to be recaptured there by the French. During the Second World War, the Vichy collaborationists handed him over to the Francoist authorities in Ceuta, who extradited him to Spain. In Madrid, following a cursory council of war, typical of the Francoist military courts, he was sentenced to death. Anxiously he awaited his turn, watching each day as a list was posted in Porlier prison of "the chosen ones," but, through some strange contortion of fascist whimsy, his sentence was commuted to life imprisonment. Since Mera had served with a squad of prisoner bricklayers, after a year he was awarded a twenty-four pass to visit his family, during which time the anarchist organization yanked him out of the country. Mera made it successfully over the border into France and after that made Paris his home for the remainder of his life.

Mera had some unexpected personal idiosyncrasies. A bricklayer by trade, Mera set himself the target of learning to read and write at the age of twenty, and pulled it off thanks to his laudable persistence. Afterwards and over the course of his life, he penned, in his schoolboy hand, one of the most fascinating eye-witness journals about the war in Spain and his prison experiences. In it he placed on record his direct action as an anarchist and his common-sense approach when faced with ignorance about, say, how a war must be fought. By a quirk of fate, Mera rose to the rank of major and later was cast in the nonsensical post—given that he was an anarchist—of lieutenant-colonel. He reluctantly embraced militarization of the CNT column under his command. He had no experience of military strategy, let alone the warrior's trade. And had no qualms about seeking the counsel of professional soldiers from the republican army; his anarchist column (later the 14th Division) was the only one to defeat the Italian fascists at Guadalajara.

Years later, *Cara de palo* as he was affectionately described by his wartime comrades, worked in Paris as a bricklayer and led a very humble existence, along with his partner Teresa and his son, Floreal. Cipriano Mera was one of those anarchists of the old guard, veteran of a thousand battles, who pig-headedly insisted that the regime ought to be harried, the very thing that Octavio wanted to see. Mera and Octavio struck up a very close relationship based on friendship and mutual affection.

"Prior to the DI meeting you had time to talk about pretty much everything," I said to Octavio.

"Boticario and Santamaría laid out the situation inside the movement, explaining the unity issues yet to be resolved and how hard they were finding it to persuade the secretary of the FAI, who was a supporter of 'Esgleism,' to accept my appointment on to the DI. Apparently, the secretary had agreed to my being a representative at the insistence from the FIJL. I briefed them on what I had agreed with García Oliver prior to leaving Mexico and I confirmed his decision to join the DI later.

The following day they picked me up to take me to another house, also on the outskirts of Toulouse, where the DI was due to hold its first meeting with the Defense Commission. Six of the seven of us DI members met there— Germinal Esgleas, Vicente Llansola, Cipriano Mera, Acracio Ruiz, Juan Jimeno, and myself—with only Juan García Oliver absent; also there were four members of the Defense Commission—Roque Santamaría, secretary of the Inter-Continental Secretariat; Ángel Carballeira, SI co-ordinating secretary; Marcelino Boticario, secretary of the FIJL's Liaison Commission; and Florentino Estallo, FAI secretary."

"I remember that in the Monty Python movie *The Life of Brian* there is a very funny bit where the talk turns to the hundreds of factions and posts and sub-posts among the Jewish revolutionaries in Roman times. And to some extent, all those initials, the positions, the entire structure that we today find hard to fathom in every respect, tickled me. So why were you such a supporter of setting up quasi-ministerial structures?"

"Know something?," Octavio replied with a giggle. "My view back at the time was the same as yours. Not as clear cut as now, but it struck me as a bit nonsensical. All these initials and sub-initials were a product of the times. Other parties such as the Communist Party or the socialists were awash with secretariats and under-secretariats and agencies."

"Yes, but why something so bureaucratic in a movement like the anarchist movement?"

"Because it mattered that we have a structure in place so as to add solemnity to what was being done. It was a bit of a nonsense and so was the jargon.

"'Defensa Interior,' 'Defense Commission,' 'Inter-Continental Secretariat' ... If you take them literally, it is unfathomable. There was a sort of a hollow structure.

"And in the anarchist ranks, its internal structures turned the organization into a myth. The reckoning was that, even if they were not real, the creation of structure meant that the organization was. And as long as the organization was around, there was a movement. It was a bit surreal. Later it was the case that some people represented no one but themselves. In my case, I was more of a believer in spontaneity, and the whole thing got on my nerves, but I had to embrace it if I was to take part."

"And that is discounting the amount you had to waste your powers of memory in remembering all those posts and sub-posts," I said, to laughter.

"That's what the organization was all about. Acknowledging that there was no substance behind it all is saddening. There were some people who paid their dues and nothing more. There was no authentic trade union activity being carried out. I was at the end of my tether because it was unadulterated nonsense. I was never an advocate for the arrangement and, even back in Mexico, that was how I thought about it."

"Meaning what?"

"That I am not a believer in posts, accredited titles, and stuff like that. Remember that, even though my career was now at an end, I never used the title 'engineer.' I never wanted any sort of title at all. My interest was in learning, rather than any diplomas or parchments of accreditation."

"These days there is a craze for titles and sub-qualifications, pretty much like the secretariats we have just been poking fun at."

"Yes, it's nonsense. And lots of people laden with qualifications aren't even capable of thinking."

"But back to that meeting of the DI down in Toulouse..."

"Santamaría opened the meeting," Octavio explained, "and he labored the point that this was the necessary continuation of the resolutions passed by all three libertarian wings, the CNT, the FAI, and the FIJL. That is, that the DI needed to be funded after the seven comrades who were to serve on it had been chosen. But, unfortunately, the 'pro-España' drive to raise the roughly ten million francs allotted to the DI as its budget under those resolutions had brought in only a third of that sum, up to that point. Santamaría reminded us that the DI's activities had to be funded exclusively out of contributions coming from the Movement and its members. He then briefed us that García Oliver had appointed me to act as his representative and that I would be reading out the letter in which he spelled out his view of the situation of Francoist Spain and the world at large. He suggested, further, a strategy for the DI's conspiratorial activity consistent with the libertarian goals set out by the CNT's Limoges congress."

"Let's go over what was said at Limoges, because it implies talking about the state of affairs in place in Spain at the time. What was in the García Oliver letter that you read out?"

"García Oliver's letter explicitly stated what he and I both reckoned the DI had to be: 'First:, through its token operations, a reminder to any who had forgotten it, that the Franco dictatorship was still cracking down brutally on any signs of popular protest, and that the consistent thing to do was to mobilize active solidarity with those who were fighting and suffering that crackdown. Second: simultaneously, an attempt to bring about the end of the dictator's life, this being the only way of ending the status quo embodying the 'Spanish question' and of blowing the lid off the 'Pandora's box' inside which the Spanish people's future was trapped...' Once I'd read the letter, the floor was thrown open for comment, and everybody expressed agreement with what had been said. We thought it was fundamentally necessary that action be taken to try to fell the dictator by means of an attentat. And that is where we left the first meeting. We agreed that we, the six members of the DI who were there would go on to meet with the coordinating secretary to work on the practicalities of our getting ourselves organized and allocate the portfolio that each member would be responsible for.

At the second meeting, the very next day, the atmosphere was cooler and more tense; I thought there was a slight hostility directed at me. Esgleas, Llansola, and Carballeira did not display any great cordiality. In reality, it was the same feeling I had had at the Limoges congress. It was discernible that their hand had been forced by circumstances. Nevertheless, there was agreement on abiding by the strategic policy determined the previous day and neither Esgleas nor Llansola opposed this or passed any comment. We, the four other DI members, interpreted their attitude as an indication of assent. However, when it came down to the practicalities of how to carry our mission forward, we were surprised at Esgleas's eagerness to have the propaganda portfolio and Llansola's to assume charge of the attentat against Franco, leaving the other five of us—Mera, Jimeno, Ruiz, García Oliver, and myself—to get groups and gear ready to launch symbolic operations.

Next thing we knew, Esgleas asked for a hundred thousand francs and Llansola for a million. It was agreed that, to cover the task that Mera and I were to accomplish with backing from Jimeno, Ruiz, and García Oliver, we would have an allocation of five hundred thousand of the francs at that time to start and after that, more money would be forthcoming as the need and opportunity arose. These sums were intended solely to cover the outlay involved in the preparation and mounting of the agreed activities; no DI member was to receive payment for his voluntary contribution. The final point at the meeting related to how we were to coordinate with one another. I agreed to act as organizer, since I was the only one who could travel at a moment's notice. Esgleas and Llansola then left with Carballeira and the rest of us stayed on to thrash out how we were going to keep ourselves in the loop.

"Sure and that was vital, because, if memory serves, Jimeno was living in Morocco and Ruiz in London."

"Correct. Apart from the Esgleists, Mera and I were the only ones actually living in France. Naturally, we were not able to pass comment afterwards on the outcome of the meeting and the behavior of the stick-in-the-mud trio. Behavior that struck us as fairly responsible; because, setting aside their haste to secure the portfolios awarded to them, which was pretty suspicious in itself, they had voiced no objections. Of the four of us, I was the only one who thought it might be possible to work hand-in-glove with them inside the DI. Both Mera and Ruiz and, to a lesser extent, Jimeno had their doubts as to the others carrying out their allotted missions in good faith."

"A thought occurs to me here that I want to share with you. Were the 'Esgleists' a lot more afraid of the return of what they termed the 'great bête noire' of the stick-in-the-muds?"

"You are referring to García Oliver, right?" Octavio responded. "Sure they were scared of him. There were only a few militants of his stature from the old days still around. Mera was one of them, but he had neither the clout nor the charisma of Federica Montseny or García Oliver. They were the last big names surviving from the days of the war."

"Together with Abad de Santillán."

"Abad could not command the membership support that the other two could. He had never been a militant beloved by the CNT membership, though he was respected. But at the time he was hors de combat in Buenos Aires.

"García Oliver was an inspirational thinker. Look, he even suggested that a historical figure of international stature should fly into Madrid to hold a clandestine press conference attacking the regime, and then seek refuge inside the Venezuelan embassy. It was a matter of digging in there, relying on the prior acquiescence of the government of Venezuela, and then launching an international campaign to denounce Francoist rule. To cap it all, I hinted that Federica was the person best qualified to spearhead this operation. She, of course, indignantly declined."

"It was a good plan, but I'd guess it too would have declined."

"Months later I saw Federica and we had a 'run-in,'" Octavio giggled. "She accused me of wanting to kill her! Even though I had suggested that my father take her place. My father was all for it, but he lacked Federica's prestige."

"Was anybody taken aback by the outcome of the meeting and how the 'Esgleists' had conducted themselves?"

"Yes. Mera was. What surprised him the most was Llansola's having sought the task of coordinating 'Operation Cabeza,' which was the code name we have given to the attempt on Franco's life, and Esgleas's having endorsed it. Despite such misgivings, we agreed to press on and await the outcome of my meetings to coordinate with them.

"The history of a maverick movement such as the anarchist movement is tremendously complicated for anybody who might like to compare it with a political party. Maybe that is where its weakness lies, in terms of how society's ideological palette is organized; because the anarchist movement does not have a direct hand in the means used to reach power, like elections or legislative chambers.

"The drama that the exiled anarchists went through was that, even though anarchism was not a political party, some of those within its ranks, including the most militant of them, conducted themselves as if it was. The addressing of this first challenge, the setting up of the DI, signaled the beginning of an outright struggle by some in order to bring influence to bear for the benefit of their personal interests.

"We can see such sort of activities at present, say, within the so-called 'trade union bureaucracy.' But in the case of the CNT, the FAI, the FIJL and other anarchist organizations, bureaucratization was a slow, creeping process that revealed that some people, like Montseny or Esgleas, were genuine titans of do-nothingism. When all is said and done, they never came up with any other way of earning money in France and there is no record of their having worked for a wage nor plied any trade beyond paid anarchist membership. Federica was a writer, but never turned her hand to writing for official outlets like a commercial publishing form."

"When was it that you started to spot the characteristic inertia displayed by the 'Esgleists?'"

"After that DI meeting. Esgleas's purpose in his and Llansola's taking up the two most telling portfolios in the task that the DI had set for itself was different. Through their inaction, they were delaying the project as they were not about to lift a finger and they prevented us from getting to grips with it and trying to push it forward."

"How?"

"Two or three weeks after that meeting, I realized that I had been mistaken in my assessment of that stick-in-the-mud trio's stance. Not just because it was the first and last DI meeting at which they would be present, as they didn't show up for any more, but because of their attitude to me. Indeed, capitalizing on a trip to the south of France to check out and activate a number of safehouses and arms dumps, I passed through Toulouse and seized my chance to call in on Esgleas. I wanted to talk about how propaganda efforts were to be coordinated with the actions that Mera and I had under preparation. He said that he couldn't see me. Even so, I made up my mind to call on him the following day."

"The sort of attitude one might encounter from any official within a state ministry."

"Indeed. Throughout that time Esgleas behaved just like a civil servant. His conduct was decisive in whittling the action down to a purely bureaucratic modus operandi. Ever since the war, some comrades had grown used to the few leading in the name of all. And in 1960s France, it became standard practice. There was an established bureaucracy. Although, of course, it promoted and managed cultural and solidarity activities. Almost like a business venture."

"And were they in paid positions?"

"Within the SI there were five salaried posts paying dues into the French Social Security system. In addition, Federica was paid a wage as director of the newspaper *CNT*. And Esgleas received a wage as secretary of the IWA, if not of the CNT, plus director of the newspaper *Solidaridad Obrera*, published in Paris, as that too was a paid position."

"And in what way was that different from, say, the Communist Party?"

"None. It was amazing. The abnormal modus operandi of an organization that purported to be 'trade unionist' and 'anarchist.' A few militants living off the backs of the membership. Hence the battle to cling to internal office."

"Why did this all come about, do you think?"

"I think this degeneration had to do initially with the political collaboration with the republican government at the time of the Spanish Civil War. And later, five years of ghastly exile that resulted in dispersal and the retreat from activism of lots of comrades who had carved themselves out a niche in French civil society. This spawned a centralized organization based in Toulouse, the purpose of which was to liaise with the membership scattered around France, Europe, and other continents. The centralization conjured up a standing panel of individuals. This was useful for people like Esgleas who had no trade of their own, and those who found it very hard to survive in France without the CNT."

"And how did your dealings with Esgleas at the time end up?" I asked, trying to discover if they carried on seeing each other or collaborating.

"I turned up unannounced at his office and, after his surprise subsided, his reaction was to wriggle out of discussing the subject. In light of that, I told him that he should tell me bluntly whether or not he would collaborate with me. His response was that there would be no further communication between us. I tried for a meeting with Llansola later, through Carballeira, and the upshot was the same, evasive answers and he would let us know. It was obvious that they were stalling…

"In light of their attitude and before setting off for Paris, I briefed Santamaría and Boticario about what was going on. They advised me to alert the other members of the DI so that the other five of us could take charge of all that had been decided at the first meeting. Gurucharri and the other FIJL comrades were in agreement with this."

"And was that decision endorsed by all the other militants?"

"Once back in Paris, I had a word with Mera and the other three DI comrades as well as with the other comrades working with us. They all expressed agreement with our taking over all of the tasks assigned to the DI."

"After which you started organizing everything."

"Yes. April was a very busy month for me, in terms of trips and meetings in France, Italy, and Switzerland with groups and comrades prepared to serve as part of the DI infrastructure and play a part in its activities. Actually, I was the only DI member dedicated full-time to these training and coordinating tasks. Mera was still working as a bricklayer and was only able to go along with me on trips and to meetings from time to time. His presence was especially important, especially when it came to mobilizing the CNT's and FAI's 'defense groups.' These were groups mostly made up of comrades Mera's own age who had been through the civil war and they respected him. Unfortunately, there was a mismatch between what Mera thought and reality. It was put to them that there was a chance of resurrecting the struggle inside Spain, refloating contact and support networks there. But they proved evasive. They all backed out. And—this was a real pain for us—some of them scolded Mera for still being alive."

"I don't follow," I said, in disbelief.

"Remember that he had been condemned to death in prison shortly after the war ended? Whenever the chances of going back to Spain were brought up, there was a guy in Bordeaux, a guy Mera held in high esteem, who would say that he had his doubts about how he had managed to avoid the death sentence."

"What an asshole. Mera was the very embodiment of moral dignity."

"Cipriano was very much affected by that experience. I talked him into cutting off all these guys on the grounds that they were not about to contribute anything to the cause. Their militancy was unadulterated nostalgia. Mera was very important to us, what with his name and his past record, but in some cases that was not enough."

"I was very impressed watching the video of Mera's funeral, years later. There were hundreds at it."

"He was much loved by all. In the flesh he was soft-hearted and without artifice. I saw him many times in Paris along with his partner, Teresa. They cherished me like a son. Mera appreciated me and regarded his own son as apolitical. Because that son, Floreal, was never involved with nor did he have anything to with the anarchists."

"Did you see him that way? Did you see yourself as his son?"

"Of course. I felt like I was a part of the family. I agreed with them and chatted about all sorts of things. They were my family in France as well."

"Were you aware of how your loved ones were getting on? Did you speak with Mexico?"

"I was in correspondence with them. I had a number of letter-drops where I received letters. That is how I found out that Gloria had given birth to my daughter, Livia. And that Irene and my father were keeping well. Bear in mind that I knew hardly anyone in France. Though I saw a lot of comrades, male and female, emotionally speaking, I felt very much alone."

On "Delegated Mission"

1962 WAS A VERY fraught year for the Francoist regime. After all the years of dictatorship, some segments of Spanish society were starting to display a rebellious streak and putting up opposition of sorts.

In light of this, Octavio and other comrades labored the need to keep tabs on "the course of developments" because other political factions such as the socialists and communists—and indeed, forward-thinking quarters in the Church—were exploiting the malaise. In the Communist Party's case, its penetration of the unions and the universities in Spain had been under way for quite some time.

In April 1962, Octavio began to organize the infrastructure that would be required later if attacks and demands were to be made in the anarchists' name. Among other things, Octavio had to make countless trips to re-established broken connections and seek out fresh ones.

At the beginning of May, Octavio left on a "delegated mission"—in the jargon of the day—which meant he was acting as a representative of the Spanish libertarian movement. His aim was to visit Portugal and Morocco for meetings with people who might be useful in the upcoming actions.

Octavio arrived in the city of Oporto, where he was due to meet with General Humberto da Silva Delgado's underground representatives in Portugal. The meeting was arranged by libertarians who had connections to that segment of the opposition to Antonio de Oliveira Salazar, the Portuguese dictator. It looked as if they too were itching to get in on the action.

Ever since 1932, Portugal had been saddled with Salazar's Estado Novo (New State), an authoritarian government influenced by Benito Mussolini's fascism. Once in power, Salazar boosted the Portuguese secret police (PIDE), which was gradually eliminating the opposition.

At the time of the Spanish civil war, Salazar collaborated comprehensively with Franco's fascists and even supplied a battalion, the so-called Viriatos, to fight for the cause.

After the Second World War, in which he flirted with the Germans and Italians without quite abandoning the alliance he had with Great Britain, Salazar ensconced himself comfortably in power, infiltrating his secret police into every sphere of Portuguese society. However, with the passage of time, the opposition, including former allies such as Air Force general Humberto Delgado, began to stir. In 1965, by which time he was deemed a threat to Salazar, a PIDE commando made an incursion into Spain, were Delgado was in hiding, and murdered him.

In 1962, there was also the active, direct actionist opposition movement, the DRIL[7] (Directorio Revolucionario Ibérico de Liberación/Iberian Revolutionary Liberation Directory), which, just the year before, had been behind the spectacular hijacking of the *Santa Maria* liner plying the Caracas-to-Lisbon route, with some six hundred people on board at the time. That operation had drawn the attention of the world to the Portuguese and Spanish dictatorships. General Delgado had links to the DRIL and the latter to the anarchists.

Octavio stayed over in Oporto and, along with a Portuguese contact, visited an empty building where he met several people who had taken part in General Delgado's campaign for the presidency. They were middle-class folk, academics. The meeting was cordial enough but their message was that, for the time being, they were in no position to go into action. Octavio agreed that if the DI were to strike in the future, its operations would also be claimed in the name of an Iberian Liberation Council (Consejo Ibérico de Liberación/CIL).

Without further delay, Octavio then moved on to Morocco where he was to have an audience, on behalf of the MLE, with one of King Hassan II's chief advisors. That meeting was facilitated by a Spanish republican lawyer in exile, who was on very good terms with the advisor to the Alawite ruler, and it took place in Rabat in the offices of King Hassan II's advisor in the government palace.

Morocco had just crowned its king, who inherited the crown of the Alawites who owned much of the land in the country. The kingdom, which was still trapped in a sort of Middle Ages, had an aristocracy (the *majzen*), connected to the Alawites who still lived in the most offensive opulence. Hassan II, in keeping with what was then going on elsewhere as well, introduce a sham parliamentary arrangement.

Casablanca was home to DI activist Jimeno, Octavio's main contact. But what possible interest could anarchists have had in a regime that eliminated any political alternative that didn't see eye-to-eye with the monarchy? The answer to that was possibilism, as both Hassan II's government and the anarchists might make political capital out of potential collaboration.

A lawyer well disposed towards the libertarians mentioned to the anarchists exiled in Casablanca that the Alawite ruler was prepared to turn a blind eye to operations mounted from within Morocco "by Spanish republicans," as long as the latter backed Morocco's claims to Ceuta and Melilla. The purpose of Octavio's trip was to try to persuade Hassan II to allow the creation of an underground radio station in Tangiers. In theory, there was still a chance of retrieving a radio transmitter from Venezuela, which had never been put to use. The anarchists had not overlooked the tremendous influence exercised by Radio España Independiente, better known as "La Pirenaica," the PCE radio station broadcasting from Bucharest.

The audience with the Moroccan advisor was a brief one. The bureaucrat explained to Octavio and the comrades living there that Morocco would let the lawyer act as go-between whatever decision the Alawite government might come to.

Octavio then made his way back to Casablanca where he was a house guest of Jimeno. He didn't spend a lot of time there, as Jimeno arranged a meeting for him in Agadir, a city in the south of the country, with some CNT comrades who were working in the port and had volunteered to smuggle arms and personnel into Spain via Algeciras. These were the same men who had helped General Delgado enter Spain a few months before he made his way to Beja in Portugal, where he was to have headed a military revolt against Salazar.

"Have you any other memories of Casablanca?"

"Sure. There is one particularly telling one," Octavio shot back. "Before heading off by bus to Agadir, I had an accident that very nearly ended my trip to Morocco, not to mention my life. I was staying in Jimeno's home and he and his wife had gone out early. When I woke up, I popped into the bathroom for a shower. I closed the door, and while I was showering, I began to feel dizzy. I sat down on the floor since I couldn't catch my breath and was drowning. I dragged myself to the door and stepped outside. I was semiconscious. After a while, Jimeno turned up and, once he was over his shock, he explained to me that when I closed the bathroom door I should have left the window open to let in some fresh air to replace the oxygen being burned up when the water-heater was switched on. That was a lesson that has stayed with my whole life!"

"Good job ... or we might have been finishing this book right here," I joked.

"Well, that was the preamble to my trip to Agadir, which had been half-leveled by the earthquake that had hit the area two months earlier. I only spent one day there, but it was like something out of Dante. The earthquake struck on February 29, and left the city basically a wasteland. All around me was ruination and destruction. In fact, it was evacuated shortly after I was there, and rebuilding resumed nearby because parts of the city was damaged beyond repair. "

"So you made the trip to Agadir for just one day?"

"Exactly. Just think; in my lifetime, I have traveled much of the world, yet seen virtually nothing. I was only in Agadir to carry out a 'delegated mission.'"

In the port of Agadir, I met up with comrades who were working on fishing boats. We would be in touch in the near future whenever we needed to smuggle gear or personnel into Spain. I only spent the one day there, after the whole chore of the return trip down from Casablanca. The next day I returned to France and finished off my 'delegated mission.'"

Clandestine and in Action
Twenty-Four Hours a Day

OCTAVIO'S UNDER-THE-RADAR EXISTENCE IN France during the first year of his stay there had to do with what was going on in that country. France was immersed in the war in Algeria, one of its last important colonies with provincial status. In October 1961, shortly before Octavio's arrival, Paris was the scene of a huge demonstration by French citizens of Algerian extraction. Under the direction of Maurice Papon, a Second World War collaborationist and the man responsible for the deportation of thousands of French Jews to death camps in Germany, the French police used unprecedented means to break up the demonstration. The incident became known as the "Paris massacre." French police murdered hundreds of the demonstrators and dumped their bodies into the Seine. Later, the police shipped dozens of detainees to the Pierre de Coubertain stadium where they were tortured with complete immunity. The death toll was reckoned at upwards of two hundred.

Those were also the years that saw the launch of the Organisation de l'Armée Secrète (Secret Army Organization/OAS) a far-right, ultra-nationalist terrorist group set up by General Raoul Salan. The OAS sowed terror with its attacks on the Algerian insurgents, that being its main raison d'être.

"I imagine that having Papon as prefect in Paris was no help at all to a clandestine."

"No. Those were difficult times. The CNT was in touch with people who were working with the Algerians and fighting against the OAS. Besides, when we started organizing everything related to the DI, we took especial care of our movements; not for our own sake but because the French police were on the look-out for other groups and we might be swept up in the raids they were forever mounting. Plus, the OAS was hand in glove with the Franco government and had ties to the Brigada Político-Social. Every so often, Charles De

Gaulle's government would trade favors with Francoism. If the Francoists took a tougher line with the OAS or briefed the French government on the Algerian rebels, the French government would clamp down harder on us or pass on information about us.

"Meaning that there was effectively collaboration between the French government and Franco's?"

"Naturally. And why not? We were aware of that problematic situation, even though it occasionally worked in our favor. For instance, one French intellectual suggested to us that we contact Ahmed Ben Bella, the Algerian leader of the Front de Libération Nationale (FLN/National Liberation Front). We were following the Algerian rebellion with enthusiasm, even though we had virtually nothing in common with the Algerian FLN, in terms of our ideologies."

"Meaning that you did have a measure of contact with the FLN?"

"Essentially with French people who were working with it and with us, people such as Alain Pecunia and Bernard Ferry. They had communist backgrounds and had worked alongside the Algerians."

"But back to the 'Spanish question.' What was going on in Spain that made launching an action a matter of such urgency?"

"In Spain, from that April onwards, there was a flurry of strikes and demonstrations with the resultant political crackdown. The strikes, begun in the mining basins of Asturias, spread to other provinces and breathed fresh life into the anti-Franco opposition, in exile and at home, as it tried to seize upon every spontaneous backlash from the miners as justification for its 'peaceful opposition' policy.

"The Asturian miners, who lived in wretched conditions due to their working conditions and pay rates, were demanding improvements at work, in terms of working hours and job security. Given the inflexible response from the bosses (in cahoots with the Francoist state), they started organizing a systematic trade union opposition. However, it should be pointed out that working conditions were not the sole trigger for the strike. Several miners had relatives living abroad in Belgium or France and, when they came home on their summer holidays, they explained what life was like in countries where democracy was in place. This also helped trigger events. In the wake of the demands came the usual response from the Francoist employers: seven miners were sacked at the San Nicolás (Nicolasa) pit in Mieres (Asturias). Looking at testimony from the time, one cannot but be impressed by the part played by the miners' wives who charged the strikebreakers and scatted corn at them, as they regarded them as 'chickens', or handing out leaflets crudely run off on home-made mimeographs known as *vietnamitas*.

"Claudio Ramos, the notorious BPS torturer in Asturias, oversaw the crackdown. This was the very first popular backlash against the regime. Thousands were arrested and a lot of the organizers ended up being tortured and jailed in Larrinaga in Vizcaya, a place with a longstanding sinister history. A lot of strikers were forcibly banished from Spanish soil, thereby 'dispersing' the power of the strike. It's interesting to note that the violence was a consequence of the regime's anxiety. Franco was afraid that a massive protest wave—as had been seen in other provinces—would sweep the entire country."

Octavio and his comrades' hurry to activate the DI was understandable. Nearly every political party, in exile or underground, had backed the strikes. Especially the PCE, which had Dolores Ibarruri—Vizcaya-born—broadcasting over La Pirenaica and urging the strikers to hold out at all times. That radio station undoubtedly had a huge impact in Francoist Spain. An influence that was communist, of course.

Octavio insisted that the communists had it easier because of the enormous resources that the USSR supplied to the PCE for mounting all sorts of activities. Unlike them, the anarchists had no one but themselves to rely on, and that, added to their internal differences, made it very easy for them to be overtaken by history. In record time, and on the basis of what few resources it could command, the DI was ready to go into operation. There had to be a demonstration of the MLE's determination to play an active part in the fight against the Franco regime. That way, they could also expose the involvement of worker-based Catholic organizations like the HOAC or JOC in the strikes. These later organizations were out to underline the notion that the Church was committed to social protest, which was false, because the official Church was still a fundamental pillar of Franco's rule.

Moreover, outside the country, that April, Paris hosted the First Conference of Youth Organizations of the Democratic Opposition, orchestrated by the still extant Movimiento Español 59, which had been under complete communist control since its launch in Mexico. Later, Rome hosted the International Conference for the Freedom of the Spanish People, with intellectuals and personalities from many countries taking part. Most of them were "fellow-travelers" with the PCE. The aim of both congresses was to bolster the notion of the PCE as leading the opposition to Franco.

"There was no denying it. We either got involved or we would fade away as a movement. Besides, the situation cried out for active solidarity.

"Even today, I am stunned by the tremendous benefits the communists and socialists of the day derived from proclaiming themselves the real opposition to the regime," he went on. "They proclaimed themselves the only ones authorized to talk for the anti-Franco resistance. Though they were singing from the same hymn sheet as the Franco regime, which dubbed every opponent a 'communist.'

"The communists profited from the circumstance because they had the wherewithal to do so. And, if they could, they benefited from the way the Franco regime misrepresented us. At best, we were antifascists, and they stripped us of our anarchist outlook. There were also dirty tricks such as when I was arrested in Belgium some years later. The media alleged that we were being funded by Peking.

"The communists' approach was to deny us; we did not exist. The communists could not acknowledge anarchists or Trotskyists because there was only one way of understanding communism, and that was: State communism along the lines of the soviet model.

"The last two weeks of 1962 were earth shattering," Octavio continued. "We were putting the finishing touches on preparations for token actions that would signal the launch of the DI. I spent a week traveling through southeast France with Mera. We called on a radio engineer who was getting some transmitters ready for us to use in the attempt on Franco's life. We also made contact with the Basque comrades from the CNT in Hendaya: Ángel Aránsaez, his partner Julia Hermosilla, and another guy whose name escapes me. They were to supply us with intelligence in the mounting of the San Sebastián attack.

"Towards the end of the month, García Oliver arrived from Mexico to join the DI. We gave him the run-down on what we had achieved over our two months of activity, especially in relation to Operation Cabeza. Everything was in place for us to launch our actions by early June, and the San Sebastián attack was scheduled for August 1962."

"Some organizational feat on your part. Just over four months had passed since that initial meeting."

"Well, getting the infrastructure up and running in such a short time was down to support from the FIJL in France, where it had been in more or less clandestine fashion for some time past. Almost immediately we were able to call upon contacts and bases in Paris and other French cities and had access to the arms dumps the libertarians had built up and guarded following their involvement in the maquis and in the liberation of France at the end of the Second World War. Furthermore, Mera and I were in touch with about twenty comrades who were deeply committed to us, albeit that they were working and leading 'normal' lives. This was great at the logistical level; I was able to stay in their homes in nearly every city they lived in. Which facilitated an operational and, at the same time, a fuller clandestine existence."

"What did García Oliver get up to when he came over?"

"We 'set García Oliver up' in Paris in a service room left to us by a French comrade on the seventh floor (there was no elevator) of a building near the Sant-Fargeau metro station. Due to his leg injury (following his road accident in Guadalajara) this left him very ill at ease. Two days later, he was off to Toulouse by train for a meeting with Santamaría, Boticario, Mera, and me. There was a meeting between the Defense Commission and the DI; but the only ones who showed up were Santamaría, Boticario, and we three; the stick-in-the-muds Esgleas, Llansola, Carballeira, and Estallo were by then blatantly in opposition to the very existence of the DI. So, from then on, our dealings with the Defense Commission would be funneled through Santamaría alone."

"And the French, how did you get along with the French? So far the only comrades you have mentioned have been Spanish."

"That first year, there were not many French. The bulk of the population was part of the backdrop surrounding me. Like the French language, which I spoke very little at the time. Though having said that, I did, from time to time, have dealings with the French comrades who were assisting us."

"As a general rule, clandestine living is a lot more daunting that ordinary life. You probably age more quickly," I jested.

"Yes, I haven't the slightest doubt about that. But do you know something that pissed me off about all those years?"

"Tell me."

"That, for security reasons, I did not retain a single snapshot showing me and Cipriano Mera together. I would love to have had one to look at and commit to memory."

The DI's Short Span

OCTAVIO HAD WAITED SO long for the launch of the DI actions, and he had sacrificed much of his "regular" life in Mexico for them. Circumstances outside of the anarchist organization, specifically in Spain, were ideal. Similarly, the moment was well chosen, from a geopolitical viewpoint, because there was a considerable number of left-wing movements emerging, especially among university students whose expectations and appetite for change were running high.

Octavio spent quite a bit of time regaling me with his recollections of the facts set out below. Despite the intervening years, he still found hurtful recalling the experience and it had cost him a lot of effort writing about what occurred, even in cursory form. His text was brief and dense. Ever the optimist, Octavio has set out his memories in writing as if this were a task that he found pleasant and, betimes, liberating. However, in the case of the DI, what transpires is his indignation, his frustration with opportunities lost, and a need to speak out and explain those times.

Those were tragic times for Octavio and his aspirations as an anarchist. Tragic in that three of his comrades were sent to the gallows and others found their dreams shredded by lengthy terms in Spanish and French prisons; but tragic also because the setbacks came from within and were headed by figures such as Federica Montseny and Germinal Esgleas, from within the CNT and FAI, organizations in which many people, such as Octavio, Mera, Gimeno, García Oliver, and a huge number of now anonymous volunteers, had placed all of their hopes, efforts, and expectations of direct action as a means of ending fascism in Spain.

"Well, the tragedy inflicted upon the anarchists in exile, in France above all, where the CNT's and FAI's heartland was, was on a scale that was immeasurable and perhaps terminal."

"I've read what you have written, Octavio. The six pages you first forwarded, plus the supplement that arrived two days after that."

"And what did you think of them?"

"For the first time I detect a certain bitterness in what you wrote. Very intense. I think it cost you a real effort writing them."

"Bitterness? No, no," he shot back. "There's no bitterness there. Intensity, yes, but no bitterness. Just outrage.

"DI operations against Francoism began on June 5, 1962 and, with varying degrees of intensity, continued until mid-1963. But just when their continuation would have been most needed, we had to call an end to them due to a series of external and internal considerations," said Octavio, choosing his words carefully. "I say 'considerations,' although it would be fairer to say 'an odd and shameful coincidence of interests.'"

"Explain, please, Octavio."

"For there to have been an overlap of interests between Francisco Franco's fascist Spain and General Charles De Gaulle's democratic France was logical enough, in terms of raison d'état, but both championed capitalism above all else. But the weird thing, the really odd thing, was how Esgleas and the other do-nothings from within the anarchist ranks, chose to serve as the tools of outside interests that were out to end the DI and the anarchists per se.

"How should we account for such an abject coincidence? Fear? The unadulterated economic concern with preserving their paid bureaucratic posts? Or in terms of something more despicable, ignominious, and self-serving? To this day we still do not know what really underlay such a coincidence. Or at any rate, we have no objective explanation for it. All we can do is suggest a few hypotheses, but without forgetting that this behavior was a decisive contribution to the sinking of the DI."

"I'm trying to get my head around it, but it is not easy," I admitted. "How far did this whole suspicion go?"

"It is hard to understand, I know. The anarchists were a shambles in 1963. There was very little actual participation, very few people prepared to 'act.' Such a situation was greatly suited to the thriving of bureaucratic machinery and to the spread of do-nothing-ism, as indeed was the case."

"Okay. But not everyone was in on it. What about the maquis? Ramón Vila Capdevila aka Caraquemada was killed in an ambush in Rajadell in 1963, when he was on his own."

"Caraquemada? Caraquemada's true story remains to be written," Octavio added curtly. "When the DI was launched, Mera and the rest of the veteran comrades thought about reactivating the maquis. We even visited Marcelino Massana in Paris, by which time he was quite old and disillusioned with the CNT. He could see that the real prospects of reactivating the maquis, a style of fighting that was obsolete by the 1960s, were zero. Massana even told us that the bases he had had inside Spain, along with the peasants and such, had been lost completely. On his advice, the DI ruled out maquis activity as a strategy.

"Nevertheless, despite their desertion and the DI's being in a sort of a limbo, Llansola and Esgleas, without consulting with the rest of its members, had plans to justify their own involvement by dispatching Caraquemada into Spain."

"But why were they going to do that?"

"Because they were even then campaigning in the lead-up to the approaching Toulouse congress. Their aim was to gain the upper hand within the congress and be re-elected to the important posts they had lost at the Limoges congress. Since they could not be sure that they could command a majority, they had an ace up their sleeves: that they were the ones who had reactivated the maquis. It was a sort of a medal that they would award themselves if need be. The problem was that Caraquemada was gunned down shortly after crossing the Pyrenees. He was getting on in years by then and shouldn't have re-entered the struggle using methods dating back to the 1940s."

"But Esgleas and Montseny always shunned the maquis movement," I remarked, recalling an interview with Federica Montseny that I had read a short while before.[8]

"Sure, but it didn't matter. Anything went when it came to their justifying themselves. Along with Mera and the other comrades, we could not credit the level of these people's cynicism. They literally sent them to slaughter."

"Octavio, could you provide us with a definition of the 'do-nothing-ism' (*inmovilismo*) of the day?"

"The term was in use among the militants of the time and it indicated an all-encompassing policy: hold on to power, any way you can. Do-nothing-ism amounted to restricting the anarchist movement to organizational activity alone, meaning, confining one's militancy to internal squabbling; its point was to wash one's hands completely of anything practical, whether in the country of exile or the country from which one had been exiled. For this to happen, there had to be ongoing internal frictions. If there were none, they were conjured up and never-ending meetings held to 'set things straight.' The do-nothing strategy at these was to manufacture some evil that represented a deviation from anarchist purity, and as part of that dynamic, the stick-in-the-muds portrayed themselves as the authentic readjusters, alarm bells, and saviors of the ideal."

"Which is to say unadulterated political practice in the professional sense of the term."

"Precisely. Furthermore, you only mattered inside the movement if you agreed to play this game and play by the rules. A bit like what goes on in the so-called 'democracies' or the western countries. There are set rules and, ipso facto, nobody queries them. Nobody wanting to take part in democracy asks himself whether these rules are an undiluted curtailment of free participation. In the anarchist case, the killer was, supposedly, none of that existed, since we do not play by the rules of western democracy."

"And was *inmovilismo* the death knell for Spanish anarchists?"

"Yes, of course. And proof of this came at the Montpellier congress in 1965. The opponents of do-nothing-ism, which had a strangle-hold on all the posts within the organization, were expelled from the MLE. It was the end of the anarchists as an organization. Even the Paris Local Federation, with its four hundred members, was expelled."

"An out-and-out coup d'état."

"Exactly. It was the end of the organization. Methods did not matter. Not even collaboration with the French state, intimidating or disowning comrades. Anything went."

"In light of the sort of tumor you're describing, let's talk about the chief culprit, Germinal Esgleas."

Octavio sat in silence for a moment before responding:

"They used to refer to Esgleas as *El Fraile* (The Monk) on account of his great talent for intrigue, like a monk in a monastery. He was in charge of everything and he used it all to his benefit. But he was not on his own; he was part of a 'clan,' an anarchist royal family that included his partner Federica Montseny, who was herself the daughter of fellow-anarchist, Federico Urales.[9] They were all based in the Toulouse area. There, there was someone key to understanding the relationship between *inmovilismo* and the French authorities. I refer to Tatarou or Tataró, a superintendent from the French political police, the Renseignements Généraux, the man in charge of keeping tabs on the libertarian movement and keeping the French government briefed on what the exiles were up to—especially CNT members. He was the official go-between with Esgleas and Santamaría, passing on the demands of the French authorities, and it was the mutual respect between them that allowed the anarchist organization to operate within the law in France. Those demands included their not meddling in France's internal affairs and not trespassing against its foreign policy. But in 1963, under pressure from the Francoist government, France insisted that the DI be brought to a halt and, for that reason, among others, Esgleas saw to it that the DI couldn't carry on."

"This is shocking. I'd never have imagined that things went that far."

"There are two explanations for it. My own focuses on the need for a salaried post. The great blight on the movement was that it had paid positions."

"You are very elegant when it comes to describing what happened, Octavio. But I imagine that the alternative explanation of the facts is less refined."

"The other explanation is García Oliver's," Octavio pressed on. "He was a lot harsher in the charges he leveled at them. But he was never able to prove anything because there was no documentary record. García Oliver said that when the Germans occupied France in the Second World War, the Gestapo handed certain persons over to the Franco regime, people like say, President Lluís Companys or Joan Peiró, both of whom were shot in Spain. Whereas they, and especially Federica, were not handed over, even though their whereabouts and identity were known. García Oliver had a theory that Esgleas and Federica collaborated with the French authorities and later with the Gestapo. Come the end of the war, the Gestapo archives fell into soviet hands. Being communists, the latter passed the information on to the PCE, which then manipulated it and used extortion on both of them in order to destroy the libertarian movement."

"That's a bombshell of an explanation," I replied, stunned by what I had just heard.

"García Oliver's theory was much debated, including with Mera. At the time, we were unable to bring anything to light because there was no evidence. If there was any real evidence, it must have been among the papers and documents of the NKVD in Moscow. If we had had access to them all, our position would have been very different.

"García Oliver detested Federica Montseny and her father, dating back to the days of the war. They dismembered the CNT, and as a result the PCE was able to claim a monopoly on spearheading the anti-Francoist cause."

"And what is your own view of García Oliver's theory?"

"I was never into the conspiracy theory. And today I have no wish to find out because there is no point any more. But I do know this: through their obsession with clinging to salaried posts, Esgleas and Federica destroyed the movement. She, as director of the CNT's newspaper throughout virtually the entire period of exile, and Esgleas by switching backwards and forwards between general secretary and IWA secretary. These were all fixed positions in a movement that permitted none. Though that was not the only factor that demolished the movement. Loss of heart and widespread disillusionment of the militants created the soil in which that could prosper. Not forgetting the tremendous repression to which we were subjected by the Spanish and French police."

"And what became of García Oliver?"

"García Oliver was in a precarious situation and took the failure of the DI as a very bitter blow. His resolve crumbled when he found that he was unable to handle clandestinity the way he once had. He was sixty-two years old and his health was not as it had been. Life in Mexico had brought a change of lifestyle. Besides, he had nothing to contribute at a personal level. He had high hopes of raising funding on the basis of his personal prestige, but that didn't work. After returning to Mexico, he still tried to help out through contacts in Venezuela, but that too failed. He was greatly embittered as a result and that was how he finished in the anarchist movement."

"Were you never afraid of the *inmovilistas* turning you over to the French police or even of the latter's deporting you to Spain?"

"The thought crossed my mind from time to time but I was very much on guard. I was never an habitué of 'official' anarchist circles such as the premises on the Rue de Sainte Marthe in Paris or the Rue Belfort, the CNT's Toulouse headquarters. I was at all times mixing with very trustworthy comrades. I weighed up the risks and proceeded accordingly."

"Octavio, I know you may not have much appetite for this, but could you clarify what happened with the attempt on Franco's life in San Sebastián as part of Operation Cabeza? It has been much talked about and I understand that a lot of nonsense has been spoken about it."

"Ah, *oui, oui* ...such as Jordi Conill's involvement in things. Such nonsense! A concoction by the BPS. He had no hand in anything they say."

"How did the operation go?"

"Without question, the attack on Franco in San Sebastián was one of the most daring actions we came up with. August 1962, it was. We knew that the dictator spent every summer in San Sebastián at the Ariete Palace. Blessed with the sort of luck that dictators enjoy, Franco arrived at the palace a day after we had detonated the bomb. Operation Cabeza failed in its purpose of ending Franco's life, but it did affect his nerves for quite a long time. In it, we proved our operational capability and the DI's determination to move beyond token actions. Similarly, even though we had not achieved our objective, we demonstrated that the Caudillo's life was crucial to the continued existence of the regime."

"Can you tell us exactly what happened?"

"We had help from Julen Madariaga from ETA, even though he knew absolutely nothing of the operational detail at the time. I cannot say whether or not he thought the radio equipment he passed to us was intended for use on a clandestine radio station. That was his only contribution. We planned and implemented all the rest. By ship from the French coast we smuggled in the plastic explosive for detonation by remote control, and two comrades planted and armed the device."

"And who were the comrades who risked their lives like that?"

"They were French. I have never named their names nor am I about to, even though I have no idea if they are still alive. A number of reporters tried to get the information out of me but I had promised them I would never tell."

"You also had another remarkable operation in Italy, I believe it was?"

"Yes, along with a group of young Italian anarchists, we kidnapped the Spanish honorary vice-consul Isu Elías in Milan on September 29, 1962. This was in solidarity with a young Catalan student anarchist, Jordi Conill, who had a death sentence hanging over him. Cardinal Montini, the future Pope Paul VI, asked the regime to show clemency, which provoked Franco's wrath. In the end, Franco was forced to back down, commuting the sentence to a thirty-year prison term. World public opinion picked up on that operation and it aroused sympathy, especially among the younger generation of the time. And we also mounted an action at the Valle de los Caídos. But let us leave it at that. I see no need to catalogue all of the actions mounted at that time because they can already be found in a number of books and because the boycott targeting our operation was what most marked our activity. The DI's history has yet to be written. I reckon that, on the basis of what we have been talking about, we can offer a few answers to the questions just raised."

Octavio's refusal to expound further upon events was a tribute to those who had put their lives on the line and, in the absence of material resources, who had shown that they possessed inventiveness and solidarity in holding the regime to account.

The DI based its strategy on two approaches: denouncing fascism and targeting the life of the dictator. On the one hand, it was a matter of focusing international attention on the dictatorship in Spain and exposing its fascistic, anti-democratic character lest it reinsert itself in the comity of nations, and on the other hand, there was this yearning to do away with the dictator. Even though the latter purpose was never achieved, the failed attempts unexpectedly did generate fear. Franco feared that his life and the lives of his hierarchs might be cut short by some unpredictable attack. The DI's real strength lay, not in its actual capacity to act, which was limited, given the resources available, but the fact that it could create the sensation that an attack might be imminent. And it worked, because the dictator was afraid for his life. He was tormented by his own demons and the alleged conspiracy embodied by the Jews, Freemasons, communists, and anarchists. Unfortunately, Francoist paranoia also led to the deaths of innocents, persons who, simply because they were suspect, wound up being executed or ended up in the awful dungeons of the Brigada Político-Social.

The DI lashed out at Francoist interests abroad by, in some operations, say, planting low explosive devices in the offices of Iberia airlines—one of its favorite targets—in Rome or on planes in the airports in London, Frankfurt, or Geneva. No person was injured, since the aim was to point the finger at the regime. These campaigns targeted tourism, the regime's chief industry. And operations were mounted against Spanish interests in Mexico, Copenhagen, and London, among other places. But in addition, there were operations mounted inside Spain itself by domestic commandos in Barcelona, Sabadell, Madrid, Valencia, et cetera.

The actions triggered an enormous crackdown inside Spain where huge numbers were arrested, because the BPS did not hold back when it came to repression. Anyone was likely to be an anarchist. To get some sort of idea of this, let us look at the two most dramatic cases. The first is that of Jordi Conill, a Catalan student. Conill was arrested by the BPS along with other comrades in Barcelona. It was the old, old story. For twenty-three days he was tortured by Antonio Creix's henchmen and ended up admitting his part in the bomb attacks in San Sebastián and the Valle de los Caídos, a confession in which there was not a word of truth. And, given the high-velocity fascist court system, he was sentenced to die by *garrote vil*. When his death sentence was commuted, Conill passed through a range of Spanish prisons, during which his ideological leanings swerved toward communism. He was released in 1972, after serving ten years.

The other case, the consequences of which were graver yet, was that of Delgado and Granados. They were both arrested in Madrid on August 1, 1963 and charged with complicity in two attacks—again, untrue—one against the General Security Directorate (DGS) and the other against the headquarters of the Falangist Syndicates. This time, the regime really stepped up the speed of its summary procedures. That reduced the chances of the DI's retaliating against Spanish interests abroad.

Under torture, the detainees confessed to taking part and were condemned to death in seventeen days, a record unequaled in the world's courts. Sentence was carried out to the letter: death by *garrote vil* on August 17, 1963 in the face of a worldwide campaign that even triggered demonstrations like, say, the one held in Paris. As he had earlier stated apropos of his first stay in France, Octavio was especially well acquainted with Delgado.[10]

Granados, Delgado, Conill ... upwards of a hundred people were processed by summary trials and courts martial between January and April 1963. They were virtually all anarchists and, if not, were accused of being such by "the imperium of the Law" as the regime put it. We won't go into those who served lengthy terms in prison, but we mustn't forget them either.

To finish, let us shed a little light on the case of the young Scottish anarchist, Stuart Christie. The idea behind the operation proposed by Carballo and in which Christie would be implicated was quite a risky one. Carballo would plant the explosives—which would be smuggled to him by an innocent British tourist by the name of Christie—in the parking lot at the Bernabeu Stadium, where Franco's car would be parked prior to his attendance at the final of the Copa del Generalísimo match. Just as he did every year, Franco would be in attendance to present the trophy. Both men were arrested and found themselves in the clutches of the BPS on August 11, 1964. There is every indication that Stuart Christie was on file with the British police and that the latter had tipped off the Spanish BPS.

Because he was Spanish, they could mistreat Carballo and sentenced him to a thirty-year prison term. He became the longest-serving of the regime's prisoners and was amnestied in 1977, after the advent of democracy and once the dictator was dead.

On the other hand, Christie, as a foreigner was treated better by the regime. Nevertheless, he was sentenced to a twenty-year prison term, although he was released in 1967 and expelled from the country.

These events triggered and accelerated joint crackdowns by the Spanish fascist state and Europe's democracies—especially France—out of their fear of possible revolutionary replication that DI operations might inspire in the youth of Europe. These states pulled out all the stops to end the operation of the DI and they mounted raids on French libertarian youth in mid-1963.

"I don't think there is any way of justifying the moral duplicity," Octavio suddenly declared as part of some inner soliloquy, "and consciencelessness of Esgleas and company. So for the answer to the DI and its end we need to look elsewhere than in militant ethics."

After a tense silence, during which his breathing was audible from the other side of the television, Octavio dryly added: "In order to grasp the extent of the treacherousness of the stick-in-the-muds, we need only remember how they acted following the murders of our comrades Francisco Granados and Joaquín Delgado in Madrid. Shortly after that, and while we were still reeling from the blow, the French authorities carried out a round-up of the young libertarian supporters of the DI. A lot of people were arrested and there was a lot of uncertainty. Capitalizing upon the moment, the French authorities authorized the holding of the CNT congress in Toulouse, so that Esgleas and Llansola might capture control of the SI, which is to say, control of power within the CNT and cripple the DI once and for all.

"Faced with that sort of thing, how can one not have questions? How was one to carry on with one's commitment to activism? Yet, in 1964, the libertarian youth from the FIJL and some old CNT hands did, just as we still do."

"And how can you do that? Given the circumstances, a split was feasible, or withdrawal from the movement. From what you have been saying, they wanted everything to deteriorate."

"In order to answer your questions, let me start with a reminder of what García Oliver wrote about the DI in his memoirs, *El eco de los pasos*. Let me read it to you."

The DI, which brought together some very old militants of proved revolutionary credentials, with other young, intelligent members of the youth,
mounted an operation that lasted for six months. [...] To all appearances, a
mere six months of concerted action on the part of the DI, the Organization's armed wing. It would have required another year at least to complete
the task embarked upon, which was nothing short of somehow ending the
dictatorship in Spain. Unfortunately, it was a fight that required financial
resources galore. Ever rich in terms of fighting men but ever poor in terms
of funding, they had to call off the attempt to liberate Spain. However,
that was the only time that the Organization had taken on the Dictatorship; and also the only time that any Spanish organization, prior to ETA,
embarked upon a collective struggle against organized Francoism [...]
Unity was brought about, the DI was set up, a start was made on the struggle, and just when a stronger surge suited to the logical move beyond an
initial trial phase should have been mounted, it all stopped dead. Even the
unity. Because, yet again, dissensions, differences, and incompatibilities
resurfaced.

"I am not sure if there could be a more accurate summing up of what the
DI was, what it did, and why that libertarian 'collective struggle' ended the
way it did, but, for all of García Oliver's elliptical language it is not hard to figure out the names of the people he does not name as bearing the responsibility.

"The problem is that today we have little or no information about those
times. And, even if we did have it, it's hard to comprehend how the very comrades who drafted the resolution on the DI should have gone on to sabotage it
and to have collaborated, knowingly or unconsciously, with the Madrid-Paris
police 'axis' in order to destroy it. As García Oliver said, the DI represented
the only time that the Organization tried to deal with the Dictatorship."

"So why didn't you go back to Mexico, Octavio? I am having a hard time
understanding what you did. Your father was over there, as were Irene, Gloria,
the kids, and even, forgive my frivolity, home comforts."

"Because Europe too held worthwhile, enthusiastic, fellow-feeling people
who thought the same way I did and who wanted to carry on with the struggle. Get it?"

"No!" I replied, emphatically. "Because only you knew the true worth of
those male and female comrades and, I imagine, many another factors that

ensured that you didn't walk away from it all. I see a young man, cornered, persecuted as a clandestine by the machinery of the French state, shunned by his own comrades, frittering away your many talents by that point."

"You are talking about me," Octavio replied after a moment of thoughtful silence, "but I am talking about a collective circumstance. We are not talking about the same thing."

"But we are talking about you, Octavio."

"Yes, and at that point I was somewhat collective. Understand?"

"You're going to have to convince me of this symbiosis between the 'collective' and the 'self.' Because I understand you being part of a collective, if it would have you, but, and I am sorry to say it, one part of the collective wanted nothing to do with you."

Yet Octavio prioritized the collective. The few who thought along similar lines back during those tumultuous times in 1963 did not have things easy. The onslaught of repression in Spain and France and the (by then) brazen lack of support coming from the CNT, were big complications in Octavio's everyday existence. And to make matters even worse, in October 1963, the young libertarian Francisco Abarca, who had dodged the crackdown on the FIJL in France, was arrested in Belgium. Which ended the solidarity coming from Belgium, given that that comrade's importance was as a go-between.

Short of resources, what was left of the DI focused its efforts on campaigns in solidarity with those behind bars in France and Belgium and on trying to alter the situation inside the CNT. They demanded a meeting at which they could confront Esgleas face to face. The youngsters from the FIJL still believed in the chances of sparking an internal backlash by the membership against "Esgleism."

Octavio wasn't optimistic about the chances of that. He didn't trust Esgleas and Llansola, and even Santamaría, whom he had once felt a degree of affinity. The previous year, before García Oliver headed back to Mexico, Santamaría had shown just how fragile his commitment to the "collective struggle" was when he refused to help García Oliver in his attempt to wring financial assistance out of the World Federation of Free Trade Union Organizations for laying the groundwork for attacks on Franco. Later, Santamaría lied to Mera and Octavio and, at the CNT's 1963 congress in Toulouse, failed to brief those present on Esgleas and Llansola's resignations from the DI. And finally, in 1964, Santamaría accepted Esgleas's refusal of a "face to face meeting" with Mera and Octavio, on the grounds that dealing with the issue would have to wait until the next CNT congress.

"Where did you stand during the interregnum of the DI between 1963 and 1964?"

"I supported efforts by all the comrades who were trying to spark a backlash by the membership against the dangers of the libertarian movement's disappearing. I couldn't walk away from the fight after the sacrifices made by all the comrades who had gambled with their freedom or their very lives. On that score, ego doesn't matter. Because, in spite of everything, there was a lingering effort to press on with the struggle; some of us wanted to thwart the Franco regime's efforts to "tie up the loose ends" of its institutional continuity. We also wanted to reinsert anarchism into the social and political struggle inside Spain. Can you see why I made up my mind to stay in France?"

"Okay, I get it," I said, "but given your circumstances, how were you able to fight off the disenchantment and hopelessness?"

"There is much talk of the 'will' as a concept. But the will is a product of circumstances. It is not so much courage, your urge to fight back, it is more the external conditions supporting you or forcing you to carry on. I carried on because, to a large extent, circumstances forced me to do so, rather than my having any will to do so. I am aware that I was no hero to be imitated, but that it was circumstances that enabled me to carry on."

"Did it ever occur to you to get active elsewhere?"

"To me, that was unthinkable. I couldn't be a hypocrite as long as there were comrades behind bars in Spain. I never felt hopelessness. Our sacrifices had not been in vain. In the face of authority's excesses, surrender is the worst option."

"Did you have further contacts with the component parts of the organization?"

"Yes, sure, with Boticario. Remember that Boticario, as the co-ordinating secretary of the International Secretariat and with Santamaría's assent, handed me five thousand francs so that I could return to Mexico."

"Meaning that they wanted to see the back of you."

"Not quite. As we mentioned earlier, my safety was in peril. But I refused to leave because, in February 1964, after Pascual and all the young libertarians were released, we met up again in Paris. We agree on the need to press on with the fight inside the CNT. All this while waiting to find out what the CNT might determine in its upcoming vote.

"It was at a further meeting in Paris, with Mera and the FIJL comrades, that Pascual announced that several comrades reckoned there was a need to raise funds to bring Irene and my kids, Helie and Octavio, over to France. And the Esteban brothers would provide me with work off the books for as long as I needed. At that point, the future of the collective struggle was pretty uncertain and the prospect of my staying in France was, in the eyes of those comrades, the best solution to my rather precarious situation as a clandestine."

"Over the time you had been living in France, Octavio, I have observed two very different facets of your most recent time in Mexico. The first is obvious, that you were older than you had been in Mexico and that has an impact on people, you had broader experience and thought differently. But the second aspect that caught my attention is the loss of a certain 'lyricism' and of the hedonistic personality you had had when in Mexico. Life with just a bit, a tiny bit of rest and frivolity. You had no San Ángel lava field to fall back on in France."

"There was no chance of lava fields," Octavio retorted with a laugh. "But hang on, the 'Lava Field' was to come. In 1964 I was very wrapped up in activity. I didn't have time to think or to listen to music, one of my greatest delights. I was wrapped up in an atmosphere where the organization was everything and the individual was superfluous in the face of it. Over in Mexico, individuality ruled the roost. Over there I could take cover in my individuality. During those first few years in France there was no time for individuality, nor for looking for it, let alone finding it."

"But that must have been tremendously stressful."

"Stress? I hadn't the time for such matters. My life was one unrelenting continuum."

"Okay, but that grinds one down, right?"

"*Oui, oui*, I agree. Yes, but I had no option but to get on with things. I had to press on."

"Tell me about Irene and the kids."

"I reluctantly agreed to their coming over. Given the precariousness of my situation, I wasn't very sure that they were doing the right thing by joining me. Besides, have you any idea what it means to pluck two young kids and their mother out of a country as different as Mexico and drop them into a clandestine lifestyle in Paris, with its cold, wet winters? And it all depended on what might happen at the forthcoming Montpellier congress."

Having resigned from her job and leaving José Alberola alone in the apartment where they lived in the Federal District, Irene, Helie, and Octavio junior made the trip to Paris in early 1965. Octavio and his family lived an on-off clandestine life in the service rooms in comrades' homes. Meanwhile, Octavio was working as a painter for the Esteban brothers and, from time to time, with comrade Pedro Moñino, keeping the books for his workshop and making his shoe store display.

But this precarious arrangement was dragging out infinitely and was made all the more complicated when Irene fell unexpectedly pregnant. Since there was no possibility of her having an abortion or giving birth legally in France, it occurred to Irene and Octavio that the solution was for her and the kids to move back to Mexico, which they did in September 1965.

"Honestly, Octavio, I cannot get my head around what was going on with you. Just can't."

"It was the same with me. So much so that I came very close to giving it all up and heading back to Mexico with Irene and the kids."

"You must have been pissed off with this failed family episode."

"Just think. But as I was saying before circumstances were driving me on. I carried on working clandestinely in Paris, meeting up with comrades from the FIJL and like-minded CNT people until along came the disastrous Montpellier congress in August 1965. There, the FIJL and any of us who complained of the Stalinist, do-nothing performance of 'Esgleism' were expelled. These were comrades who had been trying to encourage continuation of the collective struggle that the CNT and the FAI had abandoned. That was the beginning of the end."

"Do you want to talk about the Montpellier congress?"

"Not worth the bother. It was tedious and bureaucratic. Personally, I took no part in it, for reasons of safety, and only attended the 'reserved sitting.'[11]

"Both at the 1963 Toulouse congress as well as at the later one in Montpellier, anarchist unity was undone and the FIJL severed its connections with the CNT and the FAI. So the libertarian youth and a few of anarchism's older hands decided to go it alone and carry on with the fight against Francoism, outside of the parameters of 'official' anarchism.

"All manner of things occurred at both congresses and they were humiliating. At the one in Montpellier, the stick-in-the-muds accused Mera of having pocketed the money set aside to cover my fare back to Mexico. There were even a few people who tried to punch him. But it should be pointed out that a prominent member like José Peirats backed us. Peirats did not approve of the actions of the DI, but he faced down the 'Esgleists.'"

"Is there any suggestion of forgive and forget vis-à-vis the stick-in-the-muds? Are you over it after all these years?"

"Not in the Christian sense of the word. I'm a determinist. I strive to with-stand unfavorable circumstances and try to swap them for other, favorable ones. There is no point in my wishing somebody ill or forgiving him. Finding their behavior out of order prompts me not to condemn but to oppose such behavior. I cannot forgive because I have never condemned. That, I think, is the most logical stance."

"But my understanding is that, for many, maybe because of the Christian education imposed on us in the West, condemnation is part and parcel of ban-ishing resentment from the body. A form of justice, so to speak."

"I never felt resentful. I felt anger and I made a stand against that sort of behavior. When dialogue was out of the question, I made my stand, as I still do to this day, and faced the consequences."

"It hurts to see the most repugnant mechanisms of hireling politics also cropping up in movements such as the anarchist movement."

"Hurtful and yet human. We anarchists point the finger at institutions rather than at individuals. It is the mechanisms that lead us to act and force us to decide in their name."

"Meaning that nothing is achievable under the aegis of institutions."

"Precisely. Because those institutions spawn unnatural behaviors and warp people. Governance does not allow the doing of god. Governance implies im-position upon some for the benefit of others. When you govern, you are on one side or the other. With those sorts of mechanisms, the game is up. One's supposed ethics are done for. And if you stay in the fray, you are somehow out to gain ground in order to overrun your rival's ground and you become part of the game. Which is to say, you embrace it."

"So what are we to do?"

"The best course is not to get caught up in that dynamic and to avoid it. But I only got to appreciate that later because, in 1964, I wanted to change the system from within. With the passing of the years, I realized the pointlessness of fighting on when the organization, the system, is corrupt. I am not a be-liever in political associations. Sooner or later, everything ends up corrupted."

"How did this canker of power within the MLE begin?"

"In the case of Germinal Esgleas and Federica Montseny, the trajectories and strategies they followed from the Limoges congress of 1961, when Esgleas volunteered to draft the structures of the DI, up until the 1965 Montpellier congress, at which he laid it to rest once and for all, are such as to suggest that they acted with forethought.

"First, by putting his name forward out of demagogic opportunism, as drafter of the DI resolution and by agreeing to serve as an active member of it and indeed, being issued with funding for that purpose. Second, in performing a U-turn and stepping down from the DI, which had previously been endorsed at the 1962 CNT plenum. Third, when he and Llansola accepted and took up posts on the SI at the 1963 Toulouse congress, where the stewardship of the DI was approved, despite the raids that the French authorities had unleashed against the FIJL in order to decapitate it. Fourth, when Esgleas declined to meet with the members of the DI in order to sort out the problem created by his resignation and Llansola's, even as they accepted the posts of general secretary and coordinating secretary on the SI, respectively, which was incongruent as the congress had specifically given its approval to the continuance of the DI. And, the finishing touch, because they let time go by without sorting out the matter. They waited until 1965 before convening and holding the congress, where, after repealing the decisions of the DI, they could offer the good news—pleasing to the French and Spanish authorities—that there would be no further 'collective struggle' against the regime coming from the CNT.

"In the face of such a coherent performance, how can we deny that Esgleas was directly responsible for the end of the movement? And let us not get into the methods employed, the expulsions of individuals and groups, in order to satisfy his desires: triggering a further split in the libertarian membership in order to leave behind a CNT that was sheer tokenism. He knew what he was doing, which is why, not being able to discern why he did it, all I have left, right now, is the financial motive, namely, his and Federica's need to survive at the organization's expense.

"But the responsibility for the ending of that 'collective struggle' must be shared by everyone, by those who aided and abetted them, 'apoliticals' and 'politicals' alike, and by those who, so as not to get drawn in, let them behave that way over so many years."

"These things are very much alive in your memory," I said, witnessing the clarity and wonderful restraint displayed by Octavio in his narrative, there being no sign of anger of fury.

"That's the truth. Experience teaches us to keep the complexity of the human being and personal relations ever in mind. Above all, in the case of the exile, which was more than merely geographical, and was also internal and time-limited... That may perhaps be the only way we can account for the behavior of the few who wound up speaking for all."

"It may well also be one of the circumstances that your will weathered it all. We might describe the position of not yielding in the face of the actions of individuals like Esgleas 'rebel tenaciousness.'"

"Probably. I can recall," Octavio went on after a lengthy pause, "the still-lingering indignation and the determination to press on; because the clash with *inmovilismo* was no 'generational conflict' but was a 'clash of values,' two contrasting views of libertarian ethics and revolutionary militancy.

García Oliver, Mera, Jimeno, Acracio, Pascual, and others were older militants, yet they thought the same as the young ones. As well as being on our side, they treated us as equals. They made no claim to any sort of 'generational transmission.' They were wholly aware of the importance of the moral backing they were bringing and the deferred to us when it came to the initiative for action. Because they were militants in tune with their ethic and libertarian action."

A Brand New Day-To-Day

AFTER THE PERIOD THAT had just ended, with the disappointments of the DI as food for thought, it was a case of back to beginning. This is where the "will" that Octavio talks about came into play. His "will" prevented Octavio from walking away from it all and returning with his nearest and dearest to a country that, in all likelihood, understood him better than the hostile France to which he had yet to adapt.

The anarchists' fragile unity had just been smashed at the 1965 Montpellier congress. The schism was so bitter that it quite possibly signaled the end of an era, a shared history of many years of struggle, war, and exile in different locations around the world. But, beyond the foundering of unity and the formal consolidation of the "Esgleist" stick-in-the-mud policy, in Octavio the break-down acted as the launch of a militancy less fettered by bureaucratic restrictions bound up with initials from the past.

The Montpellier congress receded into the past and Octavio embarked upon a further phase of clandestine life that was rather different from the preceding one, hopes riding higher because he was up for anything. The demise of the DI released him once and for all from committed activism within the CNT. In spite of everything, Octavio clung to his affinity and activism alongside the FIJL. But what did the Libertarian Youth stand for back then? Essentially, they were young and not so young people—as Octavio usually says with a giggle—that supported the DI and who, in the wake of the 1965 Montpellier congress, stuck together. Few of them were active. But they enjoyed the backing of some local federations of the CNT, which had continued functioning as such in spite of their having been expelled. In addition to the militants within France, there were also FIJL personnel in Venezuela (like Víctor García [real name Germinal Gracia]), in Britain (like Acracio Ruiz), or others in Belgium and elsewhere. In contrast to the previous stage, the split brought a resurgence in internationalism and with that came a rush of heterodoxy and shared experiences in different countries with different issues. Somehow, these youngsters had reverted to the essential anarchist building block, that is, the affinity group. And they liaised with others from nationalities other than Spanish, people such as the youth in Milan, Sicilia Libertaria, the Provos in Holland, and so on.[12]

"Of course, the exchanges with, say, the Dutch Provos, were interesting. One thing that strikes me as setting apart you people from the FIJL was that you were very much shaped by the frontal struggle against a dictatorship, Franco's dictatorship. That had made you pragmatists. By contrast, the Dutch Provos were, so to speak, more lyrical. They posited that art or humor could be agents of change."

"Of course. They had no dictatorship to unseat. Beyond our short-term aims, we were out to weave international connections, and, in the case of the Provos, who mounted hilarious actions, *happenings*, or squats, contact with them was based on revolutionary solidarity. I traveled to Amsterdam with Salvador Gurucharri and met up in their *squats* and we agreed to work together on actions, albeit retaining our autonomy at all times. It was the same with the Gioventù Libertaria (Libertarian Youth) in Italy, with whom we had a great affinity. These new connections brought me a renewed confidence. Now the only problems and dangers came exclusively from the outside and from a dearth of resources, free of sabotage carried out by the anarchists proper.

Besides, restricting myself exclusively to acting as the organizer of actions was now at an end. Now I was free to be a participant as well. That allowed me to act with greater consistency with the libertarian decide-and-do ethic."

"And in your personal life, how were your spirits?"

"In personal matters, there I was, back on my own again, the way I had been during my first three years in France. I was therefore more autonomous. What had changed was the belief that the temporariness of my separation from Irene and the kids was dependent on the circumstances surrounding me. The prospect of a return to Mexico was looking increasingly unlikely. It was no longer a case like it had previously been of my voluntarily spending a year in the service of the organization. In 1965, things were different because my personal circumstances were no longer what they had been, in terms either of my social integration or of my militancy."

"Meaning that you were completely at the mercy of the circumstances."

"At the time, yes. I stood by my duty of solidarity vis-à-vis the comrades fighting inside Spain and with those who were still behind bars, even though there were no ties to them. By that point, the two things driving me on were the duty of solidarity and the circumstances created by the pursuit of that obligation."

"And the chief consequence," I interjected, filling in the context, "was, I suppose, the FIJL's decision to carry on down the road marked out by the DI."

"No. The DI had been laid to rest at Montpellier. The most serious thing that occurred there, albeit informally, was a split in the anarchist ranks. We were two irreconcilable camps as far as our notions of how to practice libertarian ethics were concerned. Do you know what the 'circumstance' was that made us rush back into action?"

"Nothing comes to mind."

"Something very, very perverse," Octavio added, taking some time to reflect. "Ever since 1964, the Francoist regime had been hatching yet another machiavellian ploy. The plan was sponsored by representatives of the Falange, in cahoots with a bunch of veteran CNT militants from Madrid."

"I suppose you're talking about what had come to be known as *cinco-puntismo*, on account of the five-point program posited by what we might term the 'heretics'?"[13]

"Everything they were saying about its being a potential counter to communist infiltration of the Vertical Syndicates was mind-boggling. In order to bring this off, negotiations had already been opened in Madrid between some alleged National Committee of the CNT of the Interior and members of the Vertical Syndicates. Apparently, with the blessing of Franco and of the Opus Dei members of the government."

"So the FIJL was compelled to pick up the gauntlet and thwart the success of any such aberration."

"We had no choice in the matter. It was obvious to us that those 'negotiations,' which brought the anarchists into disrepute, not only offered Francoism some breathing space, but were made possible by the do-nothing course being followed by Esgleas within the CNT. We opened by denouncing the entire business in a review and went on to mount specific actions to place the plight of the prisoners and whoever was suffering the repression in Spain on record.

"The review in question was called *Presencia libertaria*, the first edition of which came out in March 1966. It carried an article entitled 'Options of the Spanish Left vis-à-vis Francoist Strategy and Reality.' I had returned to my writing and, from late 1963, onward had been publishing articles in libertarian publications, mainly in *Ruta*, published in Caracas. In one of those articles I locked horns with the French anarchosyndicalist comrade Gaston Leval. The matter in dispute revolved around the use of violence against Francoism. Leval took the line that the priority at that point in history was 'to train trade union cadres for when Franco dies.'"

"And when did the FIJL's operations start?"

"The decision to resume operations was made at a meeting with the FIJL Liaison Commission in late 1965. At that gathering, Luis Andrés Edo volunteered to denounce the *cincopuntistas*' 'negotiations' at a clandestine press conference in Madrid."

"Tell us a little about who Luis Andrés Edo was."

"I met Edo in 1962. At all times he supported the DI and was active in the CNT's Parisian Local Federation. Edo's background was in a different kind of past. He was no historic exile, since he came from Spain, meaning that he arrived in Paris after the *Retirada*. He had a very strong personality and we saw eye-to-eye regarding the action policy to follow. With the passage of the years, especially after the advent of democracy in Spain, we went our separate ways, which kept us apart for a fair time, but towards the end of his life we were reunited. At the time we are talking about here, we were acting in concert with each other and were on very good terms up until Franco died. On a number of occasions from 1966 onwards, Edo entered Spain, which earned him several years in prison more than once. Edo was intelligent and my dealings with him were always very candid."

"Going further back somewhat, what was your role in the first operation planned in conjunction with the FIJL?"

"I was put in charge of preparing and mounting an operation that would reverberate internationally in support of this denunciation of the *cincopuntistas*. It was, as ever, a matter of reminding the world of the duty of solidarity it owed to the Spanish people, who were obliged to put up with the Francoist dictatorship."

An Artist Up for a Fight

THIS FRESH BURST OF activism led to Octavio's becoming acquainted with other people and to his slowly integrating into the country. It was during these years that Ariane, Octavio's current partner, appeared on the scene.

In the home in which they live today in Perpignan, one wall is covered with lots of black and white photos. One shows Ariane, sitting, shoes off, smoking and grinning, and surrounded by painting gear. Behind her there is a half-finished painting. This photograph was most likely taken some time around 1970. Ariane is slim, not too tall, with wavy brown hair and piercing eyes. She is unpredictable and quite capable of switching in a second from a frank smile to a harpoon-whaler's gaze and running you through, ensuring that you are forever losing your train of thought. Ariane has an unsettling personality, and her presence demands a reaction. She speaks very good Spanish, the fruit of the years she has shared with Octavio and her dealings with exiled Spanish anarchists. But what affords us a rough guide to Ariane's personality is her painting. Figurative, with firm brush-strokes and, here and there, radiant colors, it can glide gently from the impressionistic to the Fauvist. For instance, there are smooth blue patches clashing violently with an angry red. Or not. Or else they simply blend delicately into a transfigured green passing itself off as yellow. So, with color as her signature feature, Ariane paints portraits of close friends that border on the abstract. Among these is one of Agustín García Calvo, their comrade in the FIJL. There are glimpses of Ariane's own lightning flash gaze in her paintings. Fiery sparks spraying from the viscous oils. But also, having most likely wearied of the internal torment, other paintings switch subject and nature dominates everything. With her landscapes and impossibly colored skies, Ariane conveys her innermost feelings very well in her paintings.

When Octavio met Ariane, she was studying fine art in Paris and would have been twenty-three years old. Ariane was, then, a member of the French Anarchist Federation (FAF) in Paris. Octavio met her through Milhaud, an

Algerian whom he was hanging out with at the time and who had a certain connection with French anarchist university students.

"How did you take up with Ariane, Octavio?"

"It was on a trip that four of us comrades made to a port in Normandy. She acted as our guide as we went shopping for a small fishing boat that we wanted to use in an operation I had in mind for Spain. But the price was too high and the boats weren't in ideal condition. So we decided to drop the plans to buy one and we all headed back to Paris. In addition to Ariane, comrades Pedro Moñino and Vicente Cañizares, who had helped us out with funding in our DI days and who were now ready to fund the purchase of a boat, were along on the trip to Normandy. Also along was Milhaud, a young man from Kabylia; he was supposed to have served as our sailor, because, as you might imagine, we had no idea when it came to crewing a boat."

"Meaning that, to all intents and purposes, you were introduced to Ariane by circumstance."

"Yes, to begin with it was something entirely unimportant. In fact, that first contact with Ariane would definitely have been my last had fortune not intervened a short time later. A few days before setting off for Rome to lay the groundwork for the operation due to announce Luis Andrés Edo's press conference in Madrid, there was a knock on the door of what might be called my apartment (a bedsit plus kitchen where I was staying in Paris at the time). I opened up and it was a girl carrying out a survey for Social Security. My answer to her was that I was just passing through France and I quickly shut the door again. After a few minutes there was further knocking. It was the same girl again and she asked: 'Don't you recognize me?' The girl conducting the survey was Ariane who was on a temporary contract. She was dressed completely differently and that had made her unrecognizable."

"Unbelievable coincidence."

"Ariane stepped into the apartment and we chatted for a while about our trip to Normandy. She told me that she was a painter, and I asked if she might like to come with me on a longer trip, bringing along her painting gear, easel, luggage, etc., in which to conceal a couple of handguns and a submachine gun that I had to smuggle over the border to Rome."

"That's some way to meet girls," I laughed. "Quite the seducer..."

"Seduction didn't come into it at all," Octavio retorted, also laughing. "Besides, it was only after a fair while that I formed an attachment to her. But

I'll acknowledge that sounds odd. She was already familiar with this sort of conversation from her membership in a French Anarchist Federation group. Talking to her about weapons or operations was not as odd as it now sounds and she knew that we Spanish anarchists were fighting Franco. So she was not unduly bothered. Anyway, her father, since deceased, had been a member of the antifascist resistance during the Second World War."

"Yes, but, as far as I can make out, dating back to that meeting in Normandy, Ariane became a 'permanent' feature of your life. There may have been no affection yet but there was affinity. What happened after that?"

"Ariane carried on with her work and we arranged to meet up in two or three days' time. She would let me know her answer to my suggestion that she come to Rome then—and her answer was yes.

"One week later, we set off for Italy. We were driven there by a Spanish emigrant comrade who was living in Germany and whose name escapes me. There was another young French libertarian along, Gilbert Rera, who was supposed to help us with preparations in Rome. The arrangement was that, if we ran into problems at the border, Ariane and Gilbert would claim to be a couple of hitchhikers that I had picked up on the motorway. That way they could remain free and report the trouble, in the event of my being arrested."

Contact in Rome

"WE CROSSED THE BORDER without any problem," Octavio continued, "and arrived in Rome, where each of us sorted out his or her own lodgings. We only met up at certain times in different pre-agreed locations; we were all on the lookout for logistical information for the operation. Ariane as a painter and Gilbert as a student of architecture. The comrade who had driven us down headed back to Germany. And so it was that, after a week of assessing the difficulties of an attempt to kidnap the Spanish ambassador, I decided to wait no longer and to focus on the ecclesiastical attaché to Spain's embassy to the Vatican. Edo had delivered the clandestine press conference in Madrid at which he denounced the *cincopuntistas'* negotiations and had gone underground so that he could claim our operation from there. At which point I summoned to Rome comrade Juan Andrés aka 'El Viejo' who was active in the Libertarian Youth in Tours. When he arrived, we met up with Milhaud who had been in Rome over a month and had rented two apartments on one of the summer beaches closest to the city. Now we were to act all together for the first time."

"And who were those who would be going into action?"

"Milhaud, El Viejo, and myself. The day after El Viejo arrived, we abducted the ecclesiastical advisor, Monsignor Marcos Ussia. To be on the safe side, Ariane and Gilbert left for France immediately."

The abduction of Monsignor Ussia took place on April 29, 1966. The cleric was held for twelve days, with the Italian police able to establish precisely nothing. The operation was an unprecedented success and was covered by all the world's media. Not only was it a success in terms of its reverberations in Spain, but also because it drew international attention to the situation inside Francoist Spain. In addition, the operation showed that the anarchists conducted themselves very differently from the fascist rulers of that country; indeed, some time later, Monsignor Ussia was forced to acknowledge that he had been treated impeccably. The operation allowed anarchists "outside of the

CNT" to explain to all and sundry why they had been driven to act like that and resort to violence. Unlike the Franco regime, which was cracking down brutally on workers and students, they strove to keep the violence to a minimum. Even the press was forced to stress this point.

The operation was claimed on behalf of the First of May Sacco and Vanzetti Group, due to the proximity of the symbolic date. Octavio concedes that the choice of name was random and it then became the official designation of the FIJL's armed wing. After the Rome operation, operations mounted thereafter were claimed in the name of the First of May Group.

The Ussia kidnapping earned the anarchists a lot of sympathy from every segment of anti-Francoist public opinion. It exposed the connivance with the dictator's rule on the part of the Church and all the states that claimed to be democratic. In France, the TV stations picked up on this and interviewed Mera about it. In Italy, the government demanded the resignation of intelligence chief General Giovanni Allavena, who had failed to prevent the abduction, and that the perpetrators be arrested.

Octavio didn't go into detail about the operation, as he felt no need to do so, so we shall look to the account by Antonio Téllez who, as a great pal of Octavio's, heard the story from his lips on more than one occasion.

Even though Octavio may have claimed that it was all down to improvisation, the abduction can be looked upon as a work of art. In terms of how long it lasted, the absence of leaks, the absence of violence in it, and the impact it made across the word. Ussia was unable to offer any clue as to his kidnappers. Milhaud and Octavio, to shake off suspicion, hadn't spoken around him, so had not made themselves identifiable on the basis of their accents. The kidnap victim had not been able to provide any clues as to his surroundings when captive, as the room was windowless and a medium wave radio had been left on continuously, playing Italian light music. What Octavio designated as "improvisation" had missed nothing.

"As for myself," Octavio added, "after dropping off Monsignor Ussia near the Vatican radio station premises, I brought my two comrades to the empty second apartment that we had previously and deliberately refrained from visiting. They would stay there until the heat had died down.

"Then I was off to Venice, changing buses several times, and from there it was on to Switzerland from where I finally made my way back to Paris. Through some FIJL comrades, I secured a French passport in the name of

Juan Andrés, El Viejo, who had remained behind in Rome with Milhaud, as his own passport was Spanish and might arouse suspicions. To hand over the new passport, French comrade Jean-Pierre Duteuil, from the Anarchist Students' Liaison made the trip down to Rome (he would later play a significant role in May '68 alongside Daniel Cohn-Bendit). They made the return trip to Paris together, because Juan Andrés didn't speak French. During the trip, he pretended he couldn't speak. Milhaud stayed on in Italy, as was his personal choice."

"How did Esgleas, The Monk, react to these happenings?"

"Some sort of backlash was only to be expected. The Toulouse CNT, through a press release, of which the Francoists later made much, described our operation as 'thoroughly negative.' The jesuitical hand of 'Friar' Esgleas is discernible in that release:"

> We know nothing of this matter. It was a maverick action, assuredly mounted by members of our organization, but without any connection with leadership bodies. Given where the political struggle currently stands, we reject such a thoroughly negative initiative. At a point where within Spain there is a coming-together of anti-Francoist personnel, this is not the time for launching initiatives that may act counter to efforts for unity coming from significant sections of Spanish opinion.

In order to avoid actions counter to "significant sections of Spanish opinion," the CNT "leadership" opted to condemn—yet again—an operation that exposed the sham of Francoist liberalization and the *cincopuntistas*' flirtation with the Falangists. In Esgleas's view, it was merely the handiwork of libertarian militants "without any connection with the leadership bodies." So much for the role of "Esgleist" apolitical "purism" in that setting. Esgleas even floated the rumor inside the movement that the FIJL was backing the *cincopuntistas*.

"So, by the time you got back to Paris, you knew who Ariane was."

"*Oui, oui*, by then she was a part of the 'group.' We saw each other again and she offered me her apartment to sleep in from time to time. On occasion, I even did some work for her mother 'off the books.' Shortly after getting back from Rome, it must have been about five months later, 'I became intimate' with her. But there was never any intention of our becoming a couple, of course."

"What was Gilbert up to?"

"He helped out with other operations as well. He was a shy type, a chemistry student who came from Alsace, where he may well still be living. He lent us a hand in specific operations from time to time."

"I imagine that in the wake of the Rome operation there was a climate of success and euphoria?"

"Naturally. Everybody wanted to get in on some operation. The Rome job was a huge morale-booster. Later I met up with Edo who by then had returned from Spain, and with other FIJL members, in order to weigh up the outcome of the operation and to discuss operations to be mounted in the future. But even before then, we had to weather the occasional attack by the do-nothings. Edo was especially targeted.

"In France, quite apart from the sympathies aroused by the operation and its outcome, the CNT 'leaders'—while avoiding any risk to themselves—set about trying to raise doubts about the First of May Group and Luis Andrés Edo. The newspaper *Le Combat syndicaliste*, which was under the control of the *inmovilistas*, found itself required to publish—albeit for the first and very last time—in its 'Open Forum' column, a response from a French anarchosyndicalist to one such slanderous attack:"

The upshot of the abduction? Interviews with anarchists on the radio, on TV, and in the press. The operation revived memories in Spain, showing that the anarchists have not given up. The kidnappers can only be congratulated. Making propaganda on anarchy's behalf, holding the Rome police up to ridicule, how, in the wake of it all, could there be any belief that they were in cahoots with the Church? Did they not force the Pope into making a stand against Franco? They achieved something important. They at least are living in the present rather in the past like some older militants who once had credibility, or in the future, like others who make anarchy the way they would construct scale models once their working hours are over or when they have time on their hands [...] Our reckoning is that the French CNT can only express its solidarity with these comrades and afford moral and effective support, if need be, to similar projects so that anarchy may live.

G. DEBRAS

And the Fight Goes On

FRANCO WAS AGING, AND from the point of view of the dictator and his co-horts, the plan was to slowly tweak fascist rule in order to guarantee its insti-tutional survival. In theory, that would involve "democratizing" Spain, while preserving the underlying values of the *Movimiento* and its component parts in that democracy. Contrary to what many political parties such as the PSOE and the PCE argued, the regime was not crumbling, but was merely sloughing off its skin, like a snake.

In order to pull this off, what was needed above all else was a clean-up, a surface-cleansing of what was going on in Spain as far as the international scene could detect. A statement of good intentions translated into actions striving to show off Francoism's good practice to the world.

In early June, the Francoist authorities had released Bernard Ferry and Guy Batoux, two of the three young French people arrested in October 1962; they had been sentenced to thirty- and fifteen-year prison terms, respectively. Ferry for his part in an unsuccessful DI operation against Iberia airline tar-gets in Valencia, and Batoux for an attempted attack on NATO interests in Madrid.

"I suppose your chief aim in 1966 was to expose the fact that this Fran-coist *glasnost* was a complete sham?"

"Our sole focus was a boycott of it. Because, in order to let some fresh air into the house, the regime proceeded to introduce reforms along institutional lines. For instance, it eliminated prior censorship of the press and transferred political prosecutions to the civilian courts. Remember that before that they had fallen under the remit of courts martial. It was a sham, but, as it still fell short when it came to containment of the political instability at home, the re-gime stepped up its propaganda surrounding the patriotic claim on Gibraltar. This was further playing to the crowd in an attempt to steer public opinion. Because the big strategy was the forthcoming December 1966 referendum on the State Organic Law. The shambles of the elections culminated in 95 percent of the poll endorsing Franco's remaining in place."

"What plan of action did you come up with?"

"We had to cash in on the impact of our Rome operation, and not let the tide of international opinion in our favor go to waste. At a FIJL meeting we decided to strike in Madrid: we wanted to expose the sham opening-up of the regime and Franco's ridiculous jingoism regarding the claim on Gibraltar. Bear in mind that Franco was simultaneously gifting areas of the nation's territory to the Americans for their military base installations. And so we started making preparations for a further operation. In late August, when we heard from comrade Alicia Mur that she had gone ahead and rented an apartment in Madrid, Ariane traveled down to meet her. They were to monitor the frequency with which servicemen and United States embassy staff visited certain bars in Madrid. We intended to abduct a ranking United States serviceman, Rear-Admiral Norman G. Gillette, the United States chief of staff in Spain.

"Ariane went to meet Alicia Mur at the Prado Museum and waited for an hour. When Alicia failed to show up, she went back the following day, again without success. By contrast, she did meet up unexpectedly with comrade Antonio Ros who was in Madrid on a different and domestic FIJL mission. Ariane expressed her surprise to Ros at Alicia's failure to show and Ros persuaded her to return to France: the staff at a stall in the flea market, where his contact was, had told Ros that morning that his contact was 'under arrest.' To Ros, the only explanation for Alicia's failure to show for the rendezvous was that she too had been arrested. Ariane headed back to Paris and, within days, Alicia contacted her to express surprise that she had not sought her out at the Prado. The rendezvous had failed due to a misunderstanding over the time, and the business about Ros's contact having been "under arrest" was a semantic misunderstanding. Ros had confused the expression '*en arresto*,' which in the slang of the flea market stallholders back then, meant 'taking time out due to illness' with 'under arrest.'

"A lot of time had been wasted, and speed in the operation was of the essence. In the interval, three of the comrades due to play a part in the abduction were already in the apartment in Madrid. But all was not well between them. One, Inocencio Martínez, decided to head back to France, having quarreled with one of those involved. As a matter of urgency, one of us had to go to Madrid to sort the matter out and replace him. We held an urgent meeting and, after the matter had been talked through, Luis Andrés Edo volunteered to fill the gap. He insisted that he had been the one who had put forward the name of the comrade who was creating the issue. And so Edo made his way to Madrid, and Ariane and I stayed in Paris, awaiting further progress in the operation.

"But things did not go well for this second, risky operation. On October 28, a few days after Edo had left Paris, the regime's radio and newspaper outlets reported that Edo had been arrested, as had Alicia Mur, along with Antonio Cañete, Jesús Rodríguez Piney, and Alberto Herrero Dativo. The Francoist press carried this report:"

> An armed gang [...] with plans to kidnap an important foreign VIP in Madrid [...] The gang was led by Luis Andrés Edo who was general secretary of the Local Libertarian Youth Federation in Paris, and a member of the anarchist gang that kidnapped the Spanish Embassy to the Holy See's ecclesiastical advisor, Monsignor Ussia [...] In the apartment where they had set up their "headquarters" and where, it has been stated, they intended to hold the victim, police officers discovered a Sten submachine gun, a Parabellum pistol, with pertinent clips and ammunition, phony passports used in their entry into Spain, as well as documents reflecting the instructions sent down from Paris, with full details as to successful completion of this "second Ussia operation."

There was also some mention in the media of Octavio Alberola as the brains behind the operation. This was the first time that the Francoist intelligence agencies had let on that they were perfectly well aware of who Octavio was and the clout he had in operations. This could have meant a number of things: a stepping-up of the pressure on the French intelligence services to track down and arrest Octavio, as well as an attempt to represent the FIJL resistance to Francoism as the handiwork of just a few individuals—the sort of thing they had done back in the days of Facerías, Sabaté, et cetera.

You Never Desert a Comrade in Danger

LUIS ANDRÉS EDO WAS one of those self-made anarchists, all commitment and determination. A man of great character, he didn't always see eye-to-eye with Octavio. They were "active together" throughout their lives but, on more than one occasion, these two personalities, with their capacity for "seeing things clearly," clashed. Edo was active within anarchism, forever questioning even fellow militants. He had a fascination with some of the stick-in-the-muds' (*inmovilistas'*) outcasts, like Laureano Cerrada, another "blackened" figure, albeit one that was highly controversial and flatly rejected by those who were not.

From Edo's passage through the prison system, in which he displayed his relentless determination, he has left us his historical testimony on conditions in Spanish prisons during those dark times. In his writings, he also lifted the lid on the sectarianism of the inmates and the brutality of the prison system.

Up until 1978, Octavio and Edo were on very good terms with each other, their being fellow militants and friends being factors in this. But one day, disagreements between these anarchist activists regarding the part they should be playing in the recently installed Spanish democracy created a distance between them. A lot of years passed before Octavio and Edo would find common ground again.

While Octavio and (what would turn out to be) the First of May Group had a stand-by plan against the eventuality of arrest, the capture of Edo and Alicia Mur's group in Madrid was a hard knock to accept. Edo and Octavio had anticipated that, in the event of arrest, the regime's policy on Gibraltar would be denounced. But that called for swift action, the devising of a brand-new strategic plan and securing a decent defense for Edo. The France-Presse agency announced that the celebrated Madrid lawyers, Jaime Cortezo—a leading light in the Christian Democrats—and Alfonso Sevilla would handle the defense of the five arrested anarchists.

"Initially, Edo and the other detainees were to be hauled in front to the Public Order Court, which the Francoists had just about finished setting up."[14]

"Don't you believe it. Although the choice of lawyers was good news, on November 5, Jaime Cortezo told the press that the Public Order Court had declined the file and that it was being passed to the courts martial. So the five were at risk of being tried before a Summary Council of War, which, as you know, might go so far as to impose the death penalty."

"You mentioned legal means of defending the detainees. But what moves had you planned on the FIJL's part?"

"Pretty simple but ingenious ones. Anticipating the possibility of arrest, Edo had on him a document signed by the First of May Group denouncing the Francoists' jingoism in laying claim to Gibraltar while ceding Spanish territory for American military bases. As well as denouncing human rights breaches. The idea was to use that document to get the police to forward it to the Francoist minister of Foreign Affairs, Fernando María Castiella."

"And why him?"

"Because he was the minister handling the issue of sovereignty over Gibraltar and he represented the reform-minded wing of Francoism. Edo later confirmed to us that the gambit had worked. On reading it, the police quickly altered their violent attitude towards the five. A few days later, in prison, they had an offer from two lawyers willing to assume their defense.

"Despite the seriousness of the situation, there was a degree of optimism. In the final phase of the dictatorship it was obvious that its heirs were confused about how the succession to Franco would go. There was a hard-line faction close to the Falange and another what we might call a reformist faction. Thanks to that, the lawyers had certain room to maneuver, as there was a real tug-of-war between the two factions inside the regime and Edo's fate and that of the five detainees depended on the outcome.

"But given the unexpected turn taken by events on November 5 when the case was passed to the court martial, lawyer Jaime Cortezo decided to hold a secret meeting with Octavio in Paris. He wanted to brief him on two possible strategies and run them past the organization. Octavio told the lawyer to let minister Castiella know that the FIJL, through the First of May Group, would carry on with its international harrying efforts. With an eye to the United Nations General Assembly in New York, which was due to deal with the Spanish claim to Gibraltar, they would release a document denouncing the detainees' predicament. The intention was thereby to make maximum capital out of the situation and use world opinion to bring pressure on the regime and to protect the arrested comrades. Simultaneously, in several European cities, protest demonstrations in solidarity with the prisoners had begun on October 30. Seizing on the circumstances, the First of May Group set about laying the groundwork for a support operation that would resonate around the globe and to release to the public the document that Edo had been carrying with him."

"And what did this operation that you were hatching consist of?"

"We drafted a document entitled 'Patriotic claims on Gibraltar and mortgaging of the territory of the nation. American bases in Spain.' It was distributed to all the delegations scheduled to attend the United Nations General Assembly in December. Towards the end of November, Ariane traveled to New York to prepare a clandestine press conference on hotel premises. We were in cahoots with a correspondent from the Agence France-Presse who recommended to us another reporter from the same agency in New York, a great friend of Edo's. A week later, I joined Ariane in New York, and on December 9, the Agence France-Presse reported the clandestine press conference regarding the case of the five anarchists arrested in Madrid and the Spanish government's claim to Gibraltar. By then the United Nations General Assembly was in session. The Agence France-Presse release went out six hours after the conference and was broadcast widely around the globe. In the Latin American newspapers, the text of the conference was published virtually in its entirety."

"We were not professional subversives, nor did we claim to be. The issue was, and still is, either resort to improvisation or stay home...," Octavio said once. Despite the enormous pressure to reach the right decision in limited time, thanks to the powers of imagination of some First of May Group people, improvisation turned into a means of claiming responsibility that required virtually no infrastructure or other resources, other than the solidarity flowing from within and outside of Spain.

It is important to see the essence of what was stated at the First of May Group's press conference in New York in December 1966. This is part of it:

The commando team of anarchists arrested on October 24, 1966 in the Spanish capital would, the very next day, have abducted, not the United States ambassador to Madrid, Angier Biddle Duke, but rather Rear-Admiral Norman G. Gillette, had the Spanish police not uncovered its hideout in time and thus frustrated Operation Durruti. This was spelled out on Thursday, December 8 in New York to several journalists called to a Manhattan hotel by Octavio Alberola, in charge of coordination between the Peninsular Committee and the Foreign Delegation of the Iberian Libertarian Youth Federation, who declared that he had made the journey from Spain especially for that press conference, the first his organization has held in the United States. Alberola revealed the conditions in which the abduction was to have taken place, by way of a traffic accident that they intended to fake between the Torrejón base and Madrid: later, the rear-admiral would have been relocated to an apartment in the capital, from which, in the presence of a group of foreign correspondents, he would, as a "living symbol of the American occupation in Spain," have been present for a reading of a document from the FIJL.

That document hadn't been made public because of the uncovering of the plot, so Alberola disclosed it to the New York reporters shortly after dispatching a copy to U Thant, the United Nations secretary-general, as well as to the delegations from every country belonging to the UNO. In it, the FIJL denounces "the patriotic rabble-rousing of Franco's government in asserting its claims over Gibraltar and its complicity in the aggressive plans of the America armed forces," which, Alberola declared, "draw from their bases in Spain logistical support of basic importance for the imposition or escalating warfare in Vietnam, through the thermo-nuclear menace posed by the bomber planes of the SAC." Alberola then underlined the following points:

I. According to him, the amnesty declared by General Franco is nothing but a sham and there are still many of political prisoners in Spain.

II. There is no truth in the claim that the Spanish totalitarian regime is moving in the direction of democratization and that the December 14, 1966 referendum should represent a fundamental step in that process.

III. In the reckoning of the FIJL, Operation Durruti, though thwarted, has produced a positive outcome in terms of the repercussions it has had, and the intention is to proceed actively with the struggle until its short-term objective has been accomplished: the release of all political prisoners and an end to repression in Spain, through the restoration of freedom of assembly, association, and expression.

Following the press conference, Octavio and Ariane had to return to France as a matter of urgency, although this was not that straightforward given their clandestine status. This was their opportunity to leave the country, Ariane for France and Octavio... for Mexico.

"Octavio, before we get down to your arrival in Mexico, I'd like you to explain what your impressions were of New York back then. Because that was a time when there was a lot going on over there. In the United States, there were, for example, the Black Panthers."

"Ah, yes, of course. I am sorry to tell you, though, that I had no dealings with them, other than being familiar with their struggle. I only had contacts with some of their exiled members who had fled to England. Remember that I was only in the city for ten days."

"What did you do in New York?"

"Prior to the conference, we made contact with a young comrade from the Industrial Workers of the World (IWW[15]) and with Siles Forti, brother of Liber Forti who had let us have his address during his visit to Paris, a few days before Ariane was to set off for New York.

"The young guy from the IWW brought us to the home of an old anarchist of Russian descent, Sam Dolgoff, near Chinatown. Dolgoff was an old anarchist from the days of Emma Goldman and Alexander Berkman. He knew Senya Fleshin, the Jewish photographer with whom I had had dealings in Mexico. He was an old IWW trade unionist from the 1920s."

"That is the first mention you have made of Liber Forti."

"Yes, he was one of the most interesting people I met over many years. In 1966, Liber Forti was cultural consultant with the Bolivian Workers' Centre (COB). He was just back from Cuba, having gone there with a union delegation for a meeting with Fidel. Meanwhile, Che was already over in Bolivia setting up the Ñancahuazú guerrilla campaign, despite opposition coming from the Bolivian Communist Party.

"But, getting back to Sam Dolgoff, I have to say that he was a tremendous host. After the press conference, the young IWW guy drove us to La Guardia airport so that we would not miss our flight."

And so, for the first time, Octavio returned to Mexico in complete secrecy. Almost five years had passed since he was last there.

"Your being back in Mexico was a good opportunity to be reunited with your family and friends."

"I stayed under the radar, except for Irene, the kids, and my father. After surprising them, I spent a few days alone with them until I heard from Ariane and the FIJL comrades. After that first week, I met up with Floreal Ocaña and Pepe Alcober, among others.

"Whether I would go back to France or extend my stay in Mexico hinged on the news I was waiting for. In the end, I received news about the trial of Edo and the other four prisoners. I had to get back to France as soon as possible."

"And you met up with Aldo, your third child with Irene."

"Of course, of course," Octavio answered, not making much of the fact. "But I cannot recall being unduly emotional. Such was the hassle I was caught up in, and so enormous was the pressure over the prisoners in Spain that I have no family memories of note. Besides, there was the security factor. I was living constantly on the alert and it was stressful since I had to be wary of everything. Not because the Americans from the CIA might come for me, since I had no great fear of them. But I was trying to prevent news of my presence in Mexico from reaching Spanish intelligence. I was sure that there were no recent photos of me from that time, and their inability to track me down was a weapon in our armory."

"Were you able to see Gloria?"

"I didn't get to see her. Her or the girl, Livia."

"Why not?"

"It was an accident. It wasn't that I didn't want to see her, more that I could not. When I got back to France we carried on corresponding as usual."

"What else happened while you were in Mexico?"

"Something that, as you will see, was also a factor in my missing Gloria. It had to do with the 'problem' that Edo had created for us after the Public Order Court deferred to the court martial. It was suggested to him that he should take part in a planned escape by a bunch of ordinary inmates and he decided to throw in his lot with them. All that Edo asked was that we send a team down to retrieve him once the escape had succeeded. We decided to support him and a connection was made through a go-between. Contact established with the ordinary prisoners in Madrid who were orchestrating the escape and who had nothing to do with us. One of our comrades went down to Madrid but was forced to return to France shortly after he got there. The breakout had been postponed and it was left that they would let us now just as soon as the conditions were in place for another attempt."

"What happened?"

"That is hard to say. While Ariane and I were in New York, we sent a letter to the Francoist minister Castiella in which, while making no mention of the escape business, we held him accountable for anything that might befall Edo. Because we didn't know what may have been behind the escape plan, meaning, whether it might not have been a trap set by the regime itself. And in January 1967, the FIJL comrades informed me that the sending-in of a second team had also not worked out. And now the 'contact' was insisting that I go to Madrid in person.

"Towards the end of January, I was informed that a third team was ready and waiting on the border. When I was not among them, the 'contact' with the ordinary prisoners involved in the escape made himself scarce and our comrades made their way back to Paris. Two or three days after that, with several 'persons unknown,' the 'contact' went to the homes of two of the comrades who had gone down with our teams as well as to the home of a French comrade who received Edo's mail. Overbearingly, they demanded to know how I could be located."

Realizing the danger that he was a priority target for the BPS, Octavio decided to go into action once again. He had to influence the outcome of Edo's trial, as the military had unexpectedly refused to try the case and sent it back to the Public Order Court. And so Octavio made his way back to France. He organized a direct attack on Spanish interests, in England this time. In a letter, the First of May Group warned minister Castiella that they were poised to strike, depending on what the TOP might do with the case.

In mid-March, Ariane traveled to London. Octavio arrived later, and within days so did the other three comrades from the group: Gilbert, Silvio, and a young Italian by the name of Ivo Della Savia. Straightaway, they started monitoring the movements of Spanish Embassy staff in London and it didn't take them long to find the homes of the ambassador's secretary and of the legal attaché—potential targets.

In April, the group had news from the defense counsels. They had fears that the TOP might postpone the trial of Edo and his group indefinitely. In response, the First of May Group acted by detaining the ambassador's secretary for some hours in the garage of her home. Her instructions were that she was not to inform the police but should report the situation to the Spanish ambassador immediately and deliver to him a letter meant for Minister

Castiella. They cautioned the regime to proceed with the trial of Luis A. Edo's group immediately, warning that if there was immoderation in the sentencing, there would be detention of diplomatic personnel, regardless of gender, and that the detention would be indefinite. They also issued a reminder of the case of Stuart Christie, who was still imprisoned in Carabanchel.

The operation did not reach the press until mid-1968 when *ABC* newspaper, reporting the arrest of a bunch of libertarians in Valencia, alluded to "First of May Group intimidation operation." In the end, the TOP announced in mid-May that Edo's trial would be heard on July 4.

Meanwhile, in line with the improvisation, the members of the group remained in London, except for Della Savia, who returned to France for security reasons.

The trial proceeded on the appointed date. The Court didn't take that long to reach its decision and the sentencing was: three years and three months in prison for Jesús Rodríguez Piney and Antonio Cañete; three years, six months for Alicia Mur; and nine years, three months for Edo. Alfredo Herrera was released, having been sentenced to a mere three months, already served. It was the first time a Francoist court had passed lower than usual sentences, given that there had been weapons involved. In Stuart Christie's case, there were no hopeful indications, and he remained in limbo in prison.

Over in France, Octavio and the FIJL decided that, despite the success of their pressure campaign, operations had to continue: the regime had to be hounded and things invested with more internationalist flavor, given the context in Spain and around the world at the time.

"Octavio, you've mentioned the May '68 events before, but…"

"*Oui*, yes, I know. I was getting ahead of myself. I was keeping it for the end of this chapter," Octavio replied. "On the first of May, a week ahead of Edo's trial, a gang of four persons unknown entered my father's home in Mexico City and murdered him."

Remembering José

OCTAVIO HAD VERY LITTLE to say about what happened to his father. José Alberola's murder was, at the time, a murky affair, but the passage of time has allowed us to reach certain conclusions.

According to the Mexico City evening paper *Últimas Noticias* of May 3, 1967, what happened was this: "Thus far, there have been no leads in locating, let alone identifying, the four young men indicated to have been the alleged perpetrators of the murder of literature teacher José Alberola Navarro, who was found hanged and gagged in the apartment in which he lived[....] The above was reported this morning by the detectives charged with the investigation and they have added that, in clearing up the incident, they have only some very confused information from the building's female concierge to go on."

José's killers were four in number and, according to the police and to Irene, who found José's body, they had tied him up and strangled him after he had been interrogated to no avail, judging by the visible bruises.

Nothing was taken from the apartment, where he lived with Irene and the kids—who were, luckily, absent at the time—but, going by the quantity of papers scattered about the floor, they must have been looking for information. All the documents and written papers found had clearly been scrutinized by the killers.

The murder occurred on the first of May, quite a symbolic date, given the name of the anarchist group in which Octavio was active.

By that time, the international deployment of the BPS against Octavio had been underway for a couple of months, and now agents were dispatched into France to harass some of his anarchist comrades in an effort to discover his whereabouts. Had they found him, they would likely have killed him. But Mexico was not like France and it was easier to smuggle in a commando team or hire some local killers. The former was more likely responsible for José's murder, as a bunch of Mexican thugs would not have taken time out to rifle through papers and search for information. Apparently, the murderers thought that in the home of the seventy-two-year-old veteran rationalist schoolteacher they might find information that would give them the jump on the movements of his son. Or maybe they'd found out that Octavio was in Mexico and were after him. They were late in arriving, but they left a dead body behind as a calling card.

One week later, under the byline of Alfredo Semprún (a known and reviled Francoist "plant" in the journalists' union), *ABC* carried an article complaining about Octavio Alberola giving talks in which he accused the Spanish police of having murdered José. Octavio never publicly spoke on the subject. Semprun was ahead of developments, his words "adding a signature" to the murder. He knew very well what had gone on in Mexico, judging by the details he reported.

José's murder and the talk around it goes to show the huge importance that the regime credited to Octavio, to the extent that, a number of local media outlets put in print that he was Spain's Public Enemy Number One.

Months afterwards, the police classified the reason behind Jose's murder as "robbery," but the story of José Alberola's murder is much darker and more complex. Unfortunately, due to the dearth of first-hand evidence, potential explanations never went beyond mere conjecture. But the speculation was boosted by Otto Skorzeny, a Nazi implicated in Operation Odessa, who lived in Spain for a decade. The likelihood is that Skorzeny was a consultant with the BPS's international teams, which there is everything to suggest had been behind José's murder.

Was a commando trained by Skorzeny involved in José Alberola's death? Perhaps time will tell. The theory that the Austrian Nazi was implicated derives from investigations carried out at the time by Stuart Christie and is spelled out in some of his books.[16]

The State of Affairs

ONE OF THE EVENTS that made the deepest impact on young people during the 1960s was opposition to the endless Vietnam War, which started back in 1955. In many countries, the universities were up in arms about it. There was a backlash from a very wide variety of sectors, but there is no doubt that popular opinion on Vietnam was unanimous, regardless of varying ideological leanings. Even youth sectors with no particular political affiliations demonstrated their solidarity, protesting the atrocities being carried out in Vietnam.

Consequently, after a long time, the demand that the war be ended was one of the reasons—though it was not the only one—that Spanish students began to copy the example of the student struggles in Berkeley in 1964 or in Berlin between 1965 and 1966—no matter how severely the regime cracked down on them.

The young anarchists from the FIJL, swimming against the prevailing trend within the CNT, actively involved themselves in protests against what was going on in Vietnam and especially in support of Spanish students. The First of May Group claimed a number of actions against the interests of Spain—which was intent on remaining on the Americans' good side. One such action involved gunshots fired at Spanish Embassy vehicles in London on August 20, 1967, leaving an unsigned message on the windscreen of one of the vehicles. This was one way of denouncing the plight of imprisoned comrades, especially Stuart Christie.

A further action on the same day consisted of the US Embassy in London being raked with machine-gunfire; this was claimed in the name of the International Revolutionary Solidarity Movement. It was a means of denouncing the aggressive policy of American—or, as it was called at the time, "yankee"—imperialism in Vietnam and its brazen support for dictatorships around the globe. This created a great stir in the press, given the importance of the country where the attack was mounted.

These token actions created uncertainty. In none of these cases, as Octavio stresses, was there any question of anyone's life being threatened. These days they might seem like naïve actions when set beside the actions of other direct-action movements of their day, like the RAF in Germany or the Red Brigades in Italy, which did claim lives; this was the originality of the First of May Group. It was one of the few—not to say the only—movements in Europe that utterly refused, right from its inception, to consider the use of physical violence as a method of struggle.

"To get a handle on our attitude," Octavio said, "it's important that one understands the historical context. In many countries across different continents there were protests and guerrilla wars. In my view, the 1960s and part of the 1970s witnessed the last twentieth-century efforts on the part of the left (regardless of which of the many factions in existence was involved) to alter the order established in the West after the Second World War. The old revolutionary thinking was being called into question. In the Marxist and anarchist camps alike, the course ahead required a re-think. During those years, some of us tried to pursue our critique of capitalism through to its ultimate consequences and reformulate revolution, in order to have a coming together onto common ground and to seek out other overlapping areas."

"At the time, Richard Nixon was on the brink of being elected president of the United States and with him would come Henry Kissinger, the chief architect of the massive destruction of incipient revolutionary movements in South America. Did the First of May Group have contacts with South American guerrilla movements?"

"Yes, through Liber Forti, for instance, who had connections to the Bolivian guerrillas through the Bolivian miners' union. And also with Uruguayan anarchists, the comrades from the Uruguayan Anarchist Federation (Federación Anarquista Uruguaya/FAU). We had links to Gerardo Gatti."

"Gatti was an anarchist," I stated, quite loudly, trying to get my bearing, "from a faction that, by that time, was quite small in Montevideo and Buenos Aires both. The guerrilla factions, and the non-guerrilla factions, were of a communist, Trotskyist, or Maoist hue. Not to mention experimental groups like the Montoneros in Argentina, who were left-wing Peronists."

"Yes, but bear in mind what I said earlier: Gatti was kidnapped, tortured, and killed for being an anarchist. And recorded as disappeared. Just the same as communists, Trotskyists, Maoists, or Montoneros were. They perished in disagreement with one another, in the face of capitalism's overwhelming aggression. Because, in that setting, capitalism did not and does not hesitate. And it draws no distinctions. They were all the same enemy that had to be beaten. As I was saying earlier, our weakness lay in our not appreciating that we all had to work together."

"You mentioned Liber Forti. Did Liber or you have any ties to the Ñanchuazú guerrillas?"[17]

"Yes, though not in any active way. Liber never had any links with Che Guevara himself, but he did with Régis Debray."

"Who later linked up with Che."

"Exactly."

"Do you think that what they say about Régis Debray and Che is true?"

"That Debray somehow had something to do with his death? No, not for a minute. That is nonsense," Octavio replied emphatically. "Che was not betrayed by Debray, nor was he betrayed by the Argentinean painter Ciro Bustos. The Bolivian military had been on the trail of the Ñancahuazú guerrillas for quite a while. They and the CIA were perfectly well aware that Che was no longer in Cuba and might be in Bolivia with the guerrillas."

"Tell me about Che's death."

"Keep in mind that the picture you have of Che in your head and what we know about him today are the image and figure that popped up after his death."

"Let's get back to the transfiguration of people into myths," I said, knowing how Octavio disliked myths.

"Outside of the most militant circles, Che didn't enjoy the stature he possesses these days. Meaning that he was not an 'all-rounder.'

"In regards to Che's death and the First of May Group there is one thing I would like to mention. Some weeks prior to his death, through our Italian comrade Eliane Vincileoni, we received a request from Giangiacomo Feltrinelli.[18] He asked that we organize the kidnapping of a Bolivian ambassador in order to protect Che's life. We failed to do so in time, and Che was murdered on October 9, 1967. In any event, I have no way of knowing whether, had we managed to pull off the abduction, we might have saved his life. I get the impression that the CIA was not alone in having passed 'sentence' on Che."

So it was that, a month after Che Guevara's death in the mountains of Bolivia, various left-wing action groups mounted several simultaneous operations involving bombs—though there were no victims—at the United States embassies and interests in Greece, Spain, Holland, England, and so on. Those actions, which triggered plenty of comment in the world press, left the First of May Group obliged to issue a subsequent press statement denying the supposedly pro-Castroist character credited to those happenings and reaffirming the Group's determination to carry on with actions in solidarity with those fighting dictatorships around the globe.

Though back in the 1960s Octavio had been a direct-action activist, that was not the only way of opposing the establishment. There were other currents that didn't see change as requiring armed struggle and that didn't embrace Marxian dialectics. A lot of people applied the notion of "revolution" to other facets of human behaviors, such as sexuality or art.

During the 1930s, the anarchists had championed notions such as "free love," "nudism," "feminism," etc. But as the years crept by, stagnation crept into the evolution of these especially avant-garde notions championed by anarchists. In contrast, there was a resurgence in the 1960s because the emphasis that the hippie movement (the California long-hairs who smoked marijuana in rural communes and practiced free, uninhibited sex) placed on free love.

While none of this had gone unnoticed in Octavio's circles, what with living under the radar and mounting purposeful actions, he had no time for country picnics and ruminating on the meaning of life. Besides, his relationship with Ariane was hugely important because it linked Spanish refugees with the groups of humanities students who would later be involved in the rebellions of May '68 and who were interested in digging deeper into matters other than direct action.

"What sort of relationship did you anarchists have with artistic movements? We were saying earlier how a lot of people were ready to grapple with revolution from different angles."

"The arts were very different back then," Octavio replied.

"Okay. These days the main connection of the arts is the market, on which it is utterly dependent. No revolution there, absolutely none. But in the 60s or the 70s, the arts were loaded with social criticism. Take the protest song, for instance."

"We had dealings in Paris with the Situationists, with Guy Debord and others from the movement. In some of their texts they mention us as an example of the challenging of revolutionary institutions. We also mingled with painters, because the arts were up for debate and the subject mattered to us."

"The Provos used to say that the left needed structures, which is what led to bureaucratization and that turned those structures into a system. They called for change via the imagination and sense of humor."

"Yes, fine, but here art is just like science; it depends on the work of each artist or each researcher. Such work is not connected with an over-arching idea but with the mode of interpretation. Everybody has his own way of life and way of interpreting. We used to identify with artists who were sympathetic with our ideas. But if the artists stuck to mere theoretical speculation or pointless aestheticism, the affinity was reduced and was of no interest to us."

"How do you feel about the arts and anarchism, by which I mean, the relationship between them?"

"Given that I regard anarchism as an approach to life, a *modus vivendi* and not some sort of a sect, ideology, or faction. Of all of the modes of expression open to a human being, and art is one of those, I connect with a type of existence that is free, rather than dogmatic or sectarian."

"For myself, at present and with the odd very valid exception, art these days has lost this approach you describe. These days there is a huge aesthetic preoccupation, but, in my opinion, few artists stand up to power. Besides, any criticism of the system that emanates from art is, if it is harsh, ignored by the media."

"But back then it was. Although there was a lot more social conflict, as a result of which artists 'became contaminated' by the social friction. Their oeuvre thereby became that much more radical. Today, in more changeable times, art is changeable too. Art is the expression of what life is like in every age. Art that moves us is not possible where everybody's thoughts are filled with the consumption of goods. It is meaningless, since human existence has been reduced to a commodity. Resulting in the banalization of art. The present being banal, so is art. To the extent that battles against conformity crop up, art will turn more non-conformist."

"Yes, but nowadays we have social developments fully mirrored through art. For example, the living drama of Syrian refugees crossing the Mediterranean is, to some extent, rendered banal by audio-visual media or social networks. There is so much 'art' spewed out over the Internet that in the end saturation point is reached and it is drained of its impact or message of denunciation."

"I think that the fact that there is less sensitivity to that drama is due more to people's being completely overshadowed by consumerism. Which the media abets. No sooner has something come to pass that it is turned into a commodity. Like that image of Che Guevara printed on T-shirts. The essence is boiled down to nothing. Even death. Now it no longer has any meaning, nor does it trigger outrage. This is a perverse mechanism of the media."

"I have just thought of a graffiti by Banksy. Right after it was painted, the whole thing was taken down and turned into a commodity. And I know that because I saw it in the media. I think that once everybody finds out what happened through the media, that stretch of wall is worth millions."

"*Oui, oui*. Because they are enchanted by it. In fact, that is what they live for. It's how they are. How we go about subverting the situation and get back to the essence is something I do not know."

"Maybe there is no solution," I added, rather skeptically.

"That doesn't work for me," Octavio replied, emphatically. "There is a solution. My nature will not countenance pessimism and there's always a way out."

"Do you think a solution to such banalization of everything is collapse, maybe?" I asked, rather disbelievingly.

"Of course. The system is not infallible and therein lies the basis for my optimism. The system is shambolic, and sooner or later it will collapse. History is littered with examples of this. Collapse may prompt us to cast around for and try out escape routes. What matters, therefore, is turning the evidence into issues in order to generate worries, confrontations, and resistance."

"Getting back to historical matters, Octavio, what happened when you got back to Paris following the actions in London?"

"Not long after arriving in Paris, we drew up a manifesto in which the First of May Group issued an appeal 'to all the world's revolutionary organizations and movements.' In it, the basis for practical solidarity was spelled out. There, in more or less condensed form, we placed the emphasis on unity of action in the face of the common enemy of all the world's revolutionary movements. We posited the need to set aside our petty differences. As all of the guerrilla nuclei in Latin America used to assert, 'the revolution is not the birthright of any party but of revolutionaries who make up their minds to fight for it, weapons in hand.'"

"In Spain, though, Francoism's plans held firm, even though there was a semblance of a loosening of the binds of repression."

"Those actions had an impact on the modus operandi of the so-called western 'democracies,' remember. On September 23, 1967, a month after our most recent action, Franco pardoned Stuart Christie, who had served only three of the twenty years to which he had been sentenced back in 1964. In so doing, Francoism was hoping to seduce the international opposition and especially the European opposition; to diminish the impact of our actions and the growing labor and student agitation at a time when Francoist Spain was looking to gain formal entry into the European Economic Community (EEC)."

However, for Octavio, it wasn't all laying the groundwork for actions and membership of the First of May Group. Then he was also taking part in meetings of the group that published the review *Presencia*. There was much to think about, from the meaning of revolution and what was happening in the world through to manifestos from the FIJL and the First of May Group, and Octavio set out in writing what his thoughts were on many matters: trade union reforms and the student movement in Spain, the fragmentation of anarchist syndicalism... Nothing likely to be of any significance was overlooked in his articles.

Meanwhile, inside Spain, the incipient institutional opposition was searching for its place, somewhere where it might act in the event of the transition. Some of them were hoping to carve themselves out a place in the coming democracy. Others, like the anarchists, were churning out rhetorical opposition messages but were fragmented and had no definite course plotted. On the part of the regime, the last pawn moved on the domestic political scene was Admiral Carrero Blanco in his appointment as formal deputy prime minister. That appointment starkly reflected the real nature of the Franco regime's political evolution. Naturally, by 1967, the dictatorship was no longer a bloc of compact interests and ideologies. The internal contradictions within the Francoist power system, Spanish neo-capitalism's hopes for the future, the political ambitions of generations that had not been through the civil war—inside or outside of the *Movimiento*—pressure groups lobbying on behalf of international interests, those in office because of their merits during the "crusade," and the up-an-coming ones eager to take their place, created a situation without precedent over the previous thirty years. In fact, in 1967 there was open and almost public skirmishing between all these factions over what would come after Franco.

With all that in mind, Octavio and the FIJL started to focus on the domestic opposition to the regime: because from within the Spanish student movement, a faction had emerged—the independents—and it was not long before they were being described as "the *ácratas*." Their approach allowed the rank and file students to step outside of the trade union structures that sought to absorb them. The organization of the Madrid Democratic University Students' Trade Union (Sindicato Democrático de Estudiantes Universitarios de Madrid/SDEUM), which had no leaders and was all for free association, was profoundly attractive to the anarchists of the FIJL who volunteered whatever collaboration it required.

"Octavio, what do you think it was that triggered this blast of fresh air in Spanish universities?"

"I think that what was going on abroad was the biggest driver behind the optimism inside Spain. A confluence of the guerrilla campaigns in Latin America, national liberation movements in the Third World, the Black Panthers' revolt in the United States, and a series of student uprisings on university campuses in America, Europe, and Asia had radicalized the revolutionary approaches of those who rejected society's authoritarian structures. Hence the stepping up of contacts and collaboration on common actions between young libertarians, the Dutch Provos, and antiauthoritarian young people elsewhere. The young libertarians inside Spain were in need of such contacts."

"And when did the student protests take off?"

"There was a resurgence in student unrest in mid-January 1968 in Madrid when the university authorities shut down the Faculty of Political and Economic Sciences until March, resulting in all of the students being denied the chance to matriculate. The student backlash came quickly thereafter and a bus was set on fire the very same day. Everybody was caught off guard, even the student leaders themselves. Various actions followed for a number of days. I remember a statue of Christ being defenestrated from the Faculty of Philosophy and Letters in Madrid, and pamphlets were handed out on World Vietnam Day, attacking the lecturing staff, etc."

"That business of defenestrating a Christ figure strikes me as very 'provo,' in the context of Francoism, meaning very Dutch. Rather creative."

"It was a great thing," Octavio laughed. "Right away, the regime organized a Mass to make amends for the defenestrated Christ figure! It was grotesque. The Mass was attended by Manuel Lora-Tamayo, Fernando María Castiella, Alonso Vega, the archbishop of Sión, and Blas Piñar, a member of the National Council of the *Movimiento*, among other regime bigwigs."

"But there was a price to be paid for it, right?"

"Sure. Minister Fernández de Miranda declared, 'Passion and subversion are out to destroy our university,' while the press began to name a lot of intellectuals who needed persecuting. By contrast, on March 8, the *ácratas* themselves provoked an incident that was the final, spectacular act of the 1967–68 year; it was the high point of the Madrid student movement. Their action in repudiating Jean-Jacques Servan-Schreiber's declarations created ripples around the world."[19]

"What happened with Servan-Schreiber?"

"In Madrid that French journalist had addressed a packed Aula Magna. He already had under his belt a 'triumph' in Barcelona where he delivered another university address to two thousand people. In Madrid, though, he faced cat-calls from the students and the car in which he sped away from the campus came under a hail of stones. The car struck a number of students, triggering complete chaos. It was a great sensation in the world's press.

"Shortly after that, the most high-profile *ácrata* students were arrested and charged with being ringleaders, even though they had always made a point of averting any clearcut dividing line between militants and sympathizers. This sort of practice of *ácrata* ideas, that is, the rejection of authority figures or leaders, became, from then on, a feature of future antiauthoritarian student revolts, because they placed the emphasis on concerned action rather than on leaders."

"And faced with that, what external solidarity efforts were you planning?"

"As regards Ariane and myself, the news that the libertarian students had been arrested reached us just as we were both in custody in Belgium."

"How did you come to be arrested in Belgium?"

"We were on our way to trade our car for a larger model with an eye to carrying out a plan."

"What had you in mind?"

"We intended to kidnap Alberto Ullastres, Spain's first representative to the European Community under Francoist rule. We already had somewhere picked out where we could hide him, and the two comrades with whom we were to have carried out the operation had just arrived. Martínez and another comrade whose name escapes me. The Belgian police arrested us, Ariane and me, at the car dealership. After trading in the car, we were supposed to pick up Martinez and the other guy. When they realize that we weren't coming, they made themselves scarce. We discovered many years later that we had been betrayed."

"Would you like to say something now about 'plants'?"

"No, no. We shall come to grips with that when the time comes, because back in 1968 it never occurred to us that our arrest was down to a 'plant.'"

"Weren't you afraid of extradition to Spain?"

"No. Not of that. The Belgian government was socialist and would never have given the go-ahead.

"The odd thing is that our arrest didn't make it into the newspaper until March 8, and that was through the French paper *Le Monde*, which carried a report from the Reuters agency in Brussels to the effect that the Belgian police had confirmed they had been holding us for nearly a month. In fact, Ariane and I had been in custody since February 9, albeit held in some sort of unfathomable legal limbo."

Detained

OCTAVIO'S DETENTION IN BELGIUM was his second time in jail, after his arrest in Mexico back when he was twenty years old. Not bad for somebody who had spent so many years living under the radar. In fact, his "precautions," as Octavio refers to the safety measures that were a feature of his life, had been quite effective. For him to have fallen into the clutches of the police, there had to have been a leak from inside the First of May Group. But the interesting point at the time was the frantic efforts of the press to criminalize that handful of anarchists who were trying to spike the wheels of the Francoist dictatorship. The first to report his arrest was *The Times* in London. It linked Octavio with operations against American agencies in London, Turin, The Hague, and to the attacks mounted against Spanish, Greek, and Portuguese embassies in The Hague two days earlier, on March 3, 1968, attacks claimed by the First of May Group.

Speaking of these actions, *The Times* stated:

> ...an underground Spanish anarchist group allegedly based in Belgium and credited with the responsibility for the wave of bomb attacks carried out in London and The Hague. Its leader, known as Juan el Largo (Mister Big) is in custody in Belgium and it is thought that his group in all likelihood means to demonstrate that this set-back has done nothing to curtail its combativeness.

Within a few days of that—on March 19—the Paris-based French paper *L'Aurore* carried a lengthy piece, almost a full page, on the actions of March 3. They quashed the idea of an international conspiracy in which all the revolutionary extremes had supposedly joined forces.

Beneath the headline: "Police, fearing another anti-American 'blue night,' stand guard day and night over US establishments in the capital. Funding comes from Peking. The leaders are Spanish '*anars*,'" the article read:

"We shall start over! This is going to be a hot summer! The western world will be blown to smithereens!"

So said, in a series of inflammatory leaflets, the First of May Group, following the wave of attacks launched on March 3 in The Hague, London, and Turin, targeting Greek and Spanish embassies, consulates and American cultural centers. The guerrillas have not wasted much time. Now they have reentered the fray in the very heart of Paris [...] with 250 ARMED COMMANDOS.

The First of May Group, which has made a specialty of dynamiting American embassies and interests, is assembled on the basis of a very motley recruitment. At its base, a core of Trotskyists and Spanish anarchists dating back to the Civil War. They have retained their appetite for the struggle. Organized into small, wholly autonomous five- or ten-man commando units, they satisfied themselves a long time with irritating the Francoist authorities, slipping surreptitiously into Spain, planting bombs on Iberia airplanes, kidnapping monsignor Marcos Ussia, the Spanish Embassy's ecclesiastical counselor in Rome on May 1, 1966 to press their demand for an amnesty for anti-Francoists. Then, when revolutionary guerrilla war spread through Latin America, the actions of the First of May Group took on a wider reach. They switched from being straightforwardly anti-Francoists into being determinedly anti-Americans, accusing the United States of supporting the bourgeois governments of Latin America and of sending Green Berets to train the police forces cracking down on the guerrillas. This new trend inside the First of May Group was boosted by pro-Chinese personnel who infiltrated the organization. The funds for the printing of leaflets and pamphlets, for the purchase of plastic explosives, and the organization of attacks now comes from Peking, arriving via either Rotterdam or Switzerland. The Netherlands, which has a very large Chinese colony, became one of the chief platforms of the group, which can call upon 250 armed commandos there. The remnants of the Provo movement defected to the organization. [...] In recent months, the First of May Group has been bolstered, especially in West Germany and in Berlin, by revolutionary students wishing to protest against the Vietnam War by means of a series of sensational attacks and demonstrations [...] ITS BOSS KEEPS TO THE SHADOWS. The group has also specialized in the desertion of American soldiers by organizing escape lines that lead to East

Germany. In spite of everything, the leadership of the group remains in the hands of the tiny core of Spanish anarchists that founded it. Its main boss, forty-year-old Octavio Alberola, known as Juan el Largo, a professional revolutionary of Mexican origin, has his headquarters in Paris. From there his reach extends to every capital in Western Europe, organizing and overseeing its commandos. In February, he was arrested for possession of illegal weapons, in Brussels. Concerned with the protection of new United States and NATO installations, the Belgian police had caught him by surprise, in the belief that, being thus decapitated, the movement would perhaps be stalled. The response came a few days later, on March 2, with the series of attacks in several countries. In France too, the First of May Group has shown that it had no intention of becoming inactive. Its leader, Juan el Largo, has taught them to proceed without him.

From Spain, Alfredo Semprún reentered the fray [as indeed he would continue to do for any years in his private crusade against Octavio].

Once in Brussels, Alberola made contact with several "comrades" from the organization, though they are not members of the group, and together with them, and after renting a house, he set up a surveillance and tracking agency with which he managed to identify reasonably accurately the routines of the Spanish ambassador, his habits and practices, as well as the usual timetable of arrival and departure at Embassy premises. It was also discovered that "Juan el Largo" who was accompanied by an extremely beautiful young Frenchwoman, rented, in the latter's name, a house in the vicinity of Brussels where he was intending to hide Señor Ullastres and, later, a red, "driverless," small engine capacity vehicle.

ABC, September 4, 1968

"Octavio, this all reads like something from the funny papers. You were 'the Bad Guys.' And you yourself something akin to a Goldfinger."

"Did you see the nickname they invented for me? Nobody within the FIJL referred to me that way. It was sheer invention by the press."

"What was the First of May Group's internal organization line at the time you were picked up in Brussels? It is hard to get a handle on what operational structure you had."

"Well, think of the First of May Group as the active expression of the FIJL. It was a collective name. In operational terms, which is to say, mounting actions, there were very few of us, about a dozen, including Ariane and myself. But that was no obstacle to like-minded comrades in other countries deciding to mount joint operations with us. Though we were not, as happens in an organization, articulated, meaning that we were not dependent upon one another. In terms of operational personnel, if we add in those sorts of collaborators, there were no more than fifty of us.

"In my own case, I was living on a day-to-day basis in the homes of comrades and working whenever I could, meaning during my few periods of inactivity. I never had a fixed residence. Actions were funded on the basis of voluntary donations to the FIJL from comrades, young and old."

"Meaning from those 250 pro-Chinese operational groups reported in the press and supported by the Dutch..."

"That was sheer fantasy too and, besides the ravings of journalists, we found out from our lawyer, Roger Lallemand, that the Belgian socialist government was in difficulty about putting us on trial when we hadn't mounted any actions in Belgium; we hadn't done anything really criminal. And there we agreed with them. We had no interest in making our arrest known internationally either. We knew from Salvador Gurucharri that other comrades from the group had carried on hatching a series of actions in March. But there was a hiatus and, until February, it proved impossible to retrieve the only submachine gun that the police had not discovered. It was in the Brussels apartment rented by Ariane under a phony name. Thanks to the assistance of Ariane's mother, we did get it."

"Meaning that the retrieval of the guns was a 'family affair.'"

"Pretty much," Octavio laughed. "All of the foregoing prompted us not to draw attention to our arrest over those weeks. And the time was also not right for us to claim credit for what we had intended to do, namely, kidnap Alberto Ullastres, the Francoists' first official envoy to the EEC."

But, very much against the will of the Belgian government and the detainees themselves, the press kept probing the wound. In the French magazine *L'Express*, in its edition of March 11–17, there was another lengthy piece from its special correspondent in the Netherlands. Repeated there were the same fantasies that the reporter from *L'Aurore* had been peddling about the First of May Group having had significant help coming from Holland.

The interesting point about the piece was that, after describing the group's actions since the abduction of Ussia in Rome—and blaming them on anarchist activism in Europe—it identified the sponsorship as coming from 'the resurgence of anarchism, founded in 1872 by Bakunin' and it declared and gave advance notice of the preparation—by anarchists—of a long, hot summer for the year 1968. The title of the article could scarcely have been more explicit and insightful: "'Anars' getting ready for a *hot* summer."

"Where was all this discourse in the newspapers leading to?"

"Well, like everything in the papers, we were slowly falling out of fashion. Beyond the journalists' fantasies, the fact is that when our arrest became public knowledge we were able to be more explicit as to the goal we had been out to achieve and to ensure that we faced trial in late April so that could make that public.

The upshot was depicted in the Belgian newspaper *Le Peuple* of April 30, 1966:

> Chamber 22 of the Brussels Correctional Court, chaired by M. Fischer, has taken fully into account the unlawful circumstances of Octavio Alberola, anti-Francoist activist, detained on February 8 for being in Belgium unlawfully.
>
> Alberola was faced with four charges of using a false name, having a false passport, entering the country unlawfully, and possession of weapons. He has been acquitted on the first two and, for the other two, received a minimum sentence: one month in conditional detention and one month's imprisonment, covered by time served in preventive custody.
>
> [...] Alberola had come to Brussels to see S. Ullastres, head of the Spanish delegation to the Common Market, to secure from the minister the release of political prisoners. In the event that this proved unachievable, his mind was made up to expose the horrors of political repression in Spain to the press and to the EEC organizations [...] Alberola's intended purpose has been achieved [...] Alberola has issued a very timely reminder that in Spain, "the land of millions of tourists," there are men still locked away for life. One of the many typical cases is that of Miguel García. Gravely ill, he is denied his freedom, even though he was due for release many months ago.

"There was an announcement in the Brussels newspaper *La Dernière Heure* that 'his girlfriend, Ariane Gransac, from Paris, who was arrested with him but later released, has been acquitted.' Indeed, two or three weeks before, Ariane had been freed and expelled to France. Within days of the trial, Miguel García was released and, several months after that, was able to come to Belgium to see me.

"In any event, the most salient point is that within a few days of the hearing of the trial, on May 10, the first night of the barricades erupted in Paris. This was the eruption of May '68, partly confirming the premonitions of the *L'Express* special correspondent."

BELGIUM

May '68 Seen Through a Hole

THE BUILDING IS SHADOWY, made of granite, and has crenelated towers. Dark and dirty, the mock castle, erected in the late-nineteenth century, replicating a Shakespearean fortress, is a prison in use to this day. It goes by the name of the Saint-Gilles prison and, since the 1960s, it has also been in use as a holding center for terrorists and subversives. These days it houses jihadist inmates accused in connection with the outrages in Brussels.

This was where Octavio wound up after his first European arrest. Imprisoned in Belgium, a country in transition under a socialist government. Following treachery on the part of operatives inside the First of May Group, Octavio served about a month in preventive custody, while the Belgian authorities tried to decide what was to be done with the thorny issue of the arrested anarchists. There was no clear consensus from the Brussels Courts of Justice, which was torn between granting Octavio asylum in the country and moving him somewhere else, beyond Belgium's borders. It might also have been reasonable had the Belgian courts set him free while his asylum was (or was not) being processed, however, given that France's refusal to grant asylum and the way social developments were shaping up in Paris, the Belgians decided to hold Octavio in a sort of a legal limbo, trying to play for time.

"That was the first time you had been arrested in Europe. I don't think the Saint-Gilles prison was any worse than Mexican prisons."

"It was a prison that looked so old and so sinister that I thought it must have been built centuries ago. There wasn't even a washstand in the cell. For personal hygiene, they left us a pitcher of water and a basin and, for calls of nature, a bucket that we traded every morning through the hatch in the cell door. By way of a cell neighbor, I had a Flemish youngster with a radio. Thanks to the radio we were able to listen to the Belgian and French news reports

on what was happening in Paris and right across France. Communication between cells was forbidden, but there was a heating pipe through the wall that
separated ours, and we were able to chat through the gaps. From time to time,
the young guy would put his radio there and we could pick up the news from
France. One of the stations was repeatedly playing the Jacques Dutronc song
'Il et cinq heures. Paris s'éveille'(It's five o'clock and Paris is waking up), a song
that was emblematic of May '68 in France. There is a strange vigor to the lyrics;
it describes Paris, Bob Dylan-style, but the sensation is that everything is on
the brink of exploding. It pretty much reflected the prevailing sentiment. The
song was like a hymn to events.

"My young cellmate, who must have been in his twenties was not politicized, but he was a rebel. He was awaiting sentencing because he had bitten
the ear off a foreman in a fight at work. As he was Flemish, his spoken French
was nearly as bad as my own, and there was a natural affinity between us. We
spontaneously shared all the news that left the authorities in a darker mood.
By the time I went on hunger strike, he had already been moved to a prison in
the Flanders region. I never heard from him again."

"And what made you decide to go on a hunger strike?"

"I wanted the Belgian government to decide what they were doing with
me. Even so, on daily exercise in the yard, other inmates who had found out
about my circumstances would give me food. But I am not about to relive
those times or my daily routine in the prison, let alone the stifled emotion as
I listened to the names of Daniel Cohn-Bendit or other libertarian students
from the Anarchist Students' Liaison (Liaison des Étudiants Anarchistes/
LEA) or from the 22 March Group mentioned on the radio or to read about
them in the papers. I will state that, though I was a prisoner, I felt like I was
part of the rebellion, vicariously, through them. May '68 was a time when absolutely everything was being put in the dock; it was for a good reason the
saying was 'Be realistic: Demand the impossible.'"

This time, however, the rebelliousness was not coming from the heart of
the proletariat. Unlike the Russian revolution in 1917 or the French revolution
of 1789, where the despairing masses burst in upon a system from which they
had been excluded—they having nothing to lose but their lives—in Paris in
May '68, the backlash came, not from their having nothing to lose—because
the rebels "did have something to lose"—but from their having everything to
gain. May '68 was an intellectual revolution querying the way that society was

living. Everything was up for redefinition: childhood, gender, sexuality, and of course, the way society was organized.

The facts are well known and require no explanation; a simple ban at Nanterre University and at the student residences in Antony (male students were banned from the female student residential halls) triggered the initial protests, which were crushed in the worst possible way by the police. That sparked a serial backlash from the students. Throughout France, protests started to grow exponentially. Put simply, the students did not feel that they had a stake in the prevailing status quo. Later, the labor movement joined the protests.

Anarchist participation in the events of May '68 in France was inevitable; a lot of the students' demands overlapped with those of the anarchist ideal. In fact, those seen these days as the "leaders" or leading personalities back at that time—people such as Daniel Cohn-Bendit, known as "Dany the Red"—had anarchist affiliations in 1968.

In Spain, as in many other locations around the world, these happenings didn't go unnoticed. On May 18, 1968, for instance, the singer Raimon performed at the Faculty of Political, Economic, and Commercial Sciences of the Autonomous University of Madrid in an auditorium packed to overflowing. Outside, of course, "*los grises*" (the greys) were waiting for the crowd with horses and truncheons at the ready. As Raimon said in his song "18 de maig a 'La Villa,'" "*Per unes quantes hores, Ens vàrem sentir lliures*" (for a few hours, we felt free).

"It must have been quite unforgettable being in Paris at the time. Even today the spontaneity of it was is striking."

"It was a lot of things coming together and not just the business in Nanterre, remember. It's not like it came out of the blue; it had been building up to a spontaneous chain reaction of earlier rebellions."

"After the event, a lot of people tried to make capital out of May '68. Virtually the entirety of today's progressives were in on it," I added, with a hint of sarcasm.

"Except the communists. Remember that you won't find a single pro-Soviet communist or former communist staking any claim to it!"

"Why is that?"

"Because the communists didn't want any spontaneous rebellion. They were out to channel the rebellion and master it. And, when the strikes started, which is to say when labor started to link up with the students, they were shocked because the labor element, which they looked upon as their property, slipped out of their control. In fact, the communists threw their weight behind the authorities. They arranged what later came to be known as the 'Grennelle meeting,' Grennelle being the street address of the Ministry of Labor. There, the communists got the government to grant a 30 percent wage increase as a way of cutting short the factory occupations."

"But among the photos of the '68 events, there's Sartre and there's Simone de Beauvoir among the participants. Weren't they communists?"

"By that point they were Maoists. They had severed their links with French communism, which was then in the throes of Eurocommunism. We had also had the Prague Spring and there was lingering Soviet repression there and that led to a great backlash against Moscow-aligned communists."

"What connections did the FIJL people have with the French student anarchists?"

"The FIJL-LEA connection had been in place prior to and outside of the university setting. At Nanterre University, for instance, there were connections with the anarchists from the LEA, who were also students, and with the Maoists and Trotskyists or the 22 March Movement in which Daniel Cohn-Bendit was active.

There were FIJL comrades, such as Tomás Ibáñez, who had also been members of the LEA ever since its creation in 1964. Tomás had written a lot about this matter. He is younger than me and he was there. When he was active in the Parisian young libertarians group back, in 1964, he suggested that the anarchist symbol should be updated. That led to the devising of the circled A as a symbol representing all the various anarchist groupings. That symbol became notorious through the events of 1968.

"Through Tomás we came into contact with Jean-Pierre Duteuil who was in Rome when we abducted Monsignor Ussia. He was a very close friend of Dany's."

"Dany the Red, you mean?"

"Yes, they were very great chums. We had met up on several occasions in his apartment prior to my being arrested in Belgium. I saw Dany at a meeting when he was active in Nanterre University, but I never knew him particularly well. He wasn't as well known then as he became after '68. Dany was a daring, fearless, very blunt student. He was attacked for being Jewish and that meant that lots of people came out in sympathy with him.

"When I was arrested in Brussels, I had with me in my overcoat an address book that the police confiscated. His name and phone number were in it. The information was in code, but the Belgians passed the information on to the French police. Also listed there were Peirats and Alicia Mur, among others. In May, the French drew up an expulsion order targeting them for not being French. But they weren't able to expel them because of their refugee status. Dany was informed that he was slated for expulsion while on a trip to Frankfurt, as he was a German passport holder, so he couldn't reenter France.

"I could say more about Gaby Cohn-Bendit, his brother. In my view Gaby was the great influence overshadowed by Dany. We were great friends."

"Tell me something about other influences on what was going on back then. Woodstock, Marcuse, Wilhelm Reich, the Situationists..."

"*Oui, oui*, these were all big influences. As were South America and Vietnam, remember. And since the USSR was ambivalent with regard to Vietnam, certain influential intellectuals broke away in favor of other schools of communism.

"There was widespread questioning of everything. And that included of the left, since it was out-and-out bureaucracy. Everything was being queried, including those pushing for change, because they were part of the set-up.

"We had contacts with the Situationists who were a cultural subversion movement. And for safety reasons I was unable to attend meetings with them, but Tomás Ibáñez could. They gave us moral support in our actions and in our question of the do-nothing-ism (*inmovilismo*) within organized anarchism."

"I find them a bit of a contradiction. A little while ago I read *All the King's Horses*, the emblematic novel by Michèle Bernstein, who was Guy Debord's girlfriend at that time.[20] As you might imagine, it's a compendium on how to live and the Situationist approach based on creating situations of a social nature that break down the vicious circle of our education and smash through the routine etched deep within us."

"And what did you make of the novel?"

"Sheer, unadulterated frivolity. Manipulation rather than situation. We human beings have been doing that, manipulating, for centuries. I believe that the novel is essentially exasperating in its lack of interest."

"Yes, yes," Octavio chortled. "I can see that the novel has put you in a bad mood. Don't forget that, even though they presented themselves a subversives with regard to the arts and other matters, theirs was a subversion that gave the figure of the artist pride of place. That's elitism. In which regard the Situationists were the last word in frivolity. They felt themselves to be different, which is why they subverted not a damned thing. Critiquing ideologies, social structures and making that one's project is by itself a lapse into superficiality. One cannot change reality with a few simple symbolic details. I think the Situationists were a product of Parisian society, a product of the Parisian milieu. They were unable to be much different from what was back then, which is to say, pointless theory, meaningless aestheticism, etc. That's what being a Parisian intellectual was all about.

"These days I view them through a sort of a deterministic prism because I think we are the products of an evolution and not of what we might like to be. You may strive to match actions to thoughts, but where you came from, your background is also a telling factor. I have never argued that Situationism was one of the driving forces behind May '68. But it suits some people for that to be believed because, that way, what happened remains trapped with an elitist superficiality and it underrates the authentic spontaneity of what the real rebellion was.

"For us anarchists, May '68 was a backlash from anarchist rebelliousness, which had little to do with Situationists. These days it is all well and good talking about them and crediting them with a decisive influence."

"You're a bit hard on them, and on the Parisian intellectuals."

"Hard? I'm not so sure," Octavio said. "We need to be realists. I am talking about the majority but of course there were exceptions. There are actions which, due to the circumstances, transcend the present and look to the future. For good or for ill. Sometimes they reach no further than the individual, as I believe may be the case here, when we assess alongside their biographies. This is not so much a criticism as an expression of regret. Society evolves through the idea coming into contact with reality. In the Situationists' case, the rhetoric went no further."

"And Ariane? What was her experience of May '68? She was there."

"I'd say her view is a lot more critical and measured. Ariane had her doubts about the May '68 leaders boosted by the media, as subsequent developments proved right. These days, some of them are very comfortably ensconced."

When speaking of May 1968 there is no way of avoiding mentioning the cultural developments that occurred in the West during the 1960s. In his book *Antipsychiatry*, for instance, David Cooper argued that madness was, as an illness, socially generated, and that the mad—the ones that displayed signs of disturbance—were not. Thus his writings talked about releasing the mentally ill, about their directing their own treatment, since a sick society was not equipped to do so. The ideas in the books of the German physician Wilhelm Reich—who tried to build a machine for measuring orgasms—also ran deep. Reich measured orgasms in "orgone." According to him, an orgasm was an energy source.

But it wasn't all literature back then. The influence of LSD, the engine and liberator of minds—as it was described—was evident in music, which also assumed a political message with Bob Dylan or in records like Jimi Hendrix's *Band of Gypsys*, or, more specifically, in Hendrix's song "Machine Gun," in which he made his Fender Stratocaster guitar scream, aping the noise of machine guns in the jungles of Vietnam.

Vietnam was ever present. Eternal Vietnam, because more tons of bombs were dropped there than in the whole of the Second World War. The Vietnam of the burning child racing naked and hopeless towards the camera that was filming her.

And within all this ferment in creative and social matters, everything was up for question: sex, the State, art, history, gender, etc. It was the heyday of the campus events of May '68 in France which, over the years, lingered like a whimsical tantrum by French youth, blurred media images, but which was, let us not forget, part of a global eruption.

The youth in the 1960s were in revolt in what would probably be the final backlash against the winning powers of the Second World War, against the rules they imposed on what the individual ought to be like and how society should be organized. And the backlash was spontaneous, violent, and, to some extent, innocent. A creative collective backlash that was not looking to be organized, much less looking for anybody to tell it how it should.

"Octavio, how would you define May '68?"

"I see those events as a watershed moment in the struggle for social change and human emancipation. Both because it was a youth rebellion determined to rattle the political, social, and cultural stagnation of French society, as well as questioning the purpose and the very meaning of the bourgeois politics of democracy. That aim was, and still is, confined to the winning of power and the straightforward running of the so-called 'welfare society' from the State. A goal that is shared by reform-minded democrats and purported revolutionaries alike. The aggravating circumstance being that in both cases the ideology driving the 'management' was the capitalist ideology of never-ending progress in productivity and consumption by means of a growth economy. 'Development' and 'growth,' this modern world religion that has shown itself to be so effective in ensuring submissiveness in the people."

"How did you keep abreast of what was going on while you were in prison?"

"Besides the radio-set I mentioned before, it was through Ariane. After she was released and expelled from Belgium, she arrived in Paris just a few days ahead of the closure of the Sorbonne and the very first demonstrations in the Latin Quarter."

"And when were you yourself released, Octavio?"

"Not until July 8. My hunger strike, begun on June 19, triggered a solidarity campaign by most of the left-wing organizations in Belgium. As I have said before, during my strike, a number of inmates slipped me some food during daily exercise in the prison courtyard. Food that I ate, of course. I must have been a week into the strike when, during one of those strolls, the guards pulled me out of the line to frisk me. And when they discovered a hunk of bread and a banana in my pocket, I was hauled up in front of the prison governor who threatened to put me on punishment. As he saw it, it was dishonest going on hunger strike and surreptitiously eating. My answer to that was that I wasn't on hunger strike because I was a masochist but in order to secure my release; it was a political act. I added that if he was to punish me, my lawyers would make the news public and that would furnish them with further grounds upon which to demand my release. I was not put on punishment, but after that incident, I had to take my exercise walks alone, up until my release came through."

Educator in the Abbey

BEHIND THE WALLS OF the Saint-Gilles prison, the days slipped by and the head-spinning caused by events in France diminished. Eventually, as the result of pressures by his Belgian lawyers and the solidarity groups, Octavio was released; he had been granted political asylum in Belgium. But events brought him face to face with a brand-new reality. Octavio was involuntarily "retired" to Solières, a tiny little Belgian town in Liège province, surrounded by fields, trees, and the stone houses that studded the landscape here and there; stranded in the heart of the place where, in a number of battles, the victors in two world wars had settled. Rather a complicated set-up for a direct action anarchist. Alone, under surveillance, obliged to turn to a new profession in order to make ends meet, Octavio set out on an unexpected new phase in which he stared out through the window at the world.

The lawyer handling Octavio's case, Roger Lallemand, had come to an arrangement with the Belgian socialist government that his client would be kept under house arrest. Prior to his time in Solières, Octavio had been invited to spend the entire month of August at a Belgian Socialist Party (PSB) holiday center in a small coastal town near Ostend. His lawyer had agreed to this as part of the conditions of Octavio's release. Every day, Octavio had to sign in at the police station in the nearby town. Ariane paid him a visit that same month, slipping surreptitiously across the border once or twice; so did some FIJL comrades from Paris.

In Solières, Octavio found work through the good offices of some Belgian socialists as a tutor at a medical-psychiatric-educational institute. The institute was ensconced in Solières Château, an eighteenth-century abbey. He lived there over the years that followed, in a little house right in the middle of the parklands surrounding the abbey.

"What were your initial impressions of that 'forced' retirement?"

"Once I had settled in, I wrote to Irene and Gloria to bring them up to date with what had been happening and fill them in about the new circumstances I now found myself in. I was at a strange time in my life as I was in no position to make any forecasts or personal plans. The Paris comrades were aware of my situation and I knew something of them through Ariane. During the five months I spent in prison, my main concern was to secure my freedom as soon as possible and to re-establish contact. I was eager to learn of the consequences for several of our LEA comrades after May '68 in France and about the various activities they were wanting to carry on with.

"But once 'free,' my most pressing need was how to actually survive. Which is why I took the tutoring job at the abbey. Comrade Francisco Abarca worked at the institute as administrative director, as did Joseph Orval who was director of education. Orval was an educationist who used the experiences of the Russian Anton Makarenko in order to keep discipline and educate the almost two hundred children attending the institute. Most of them had behavioral issues and a few also had psycho-mobility problems; they were all in the care of the Belgian Justice Ministry's social services.

"I worked there from October 1968 until early 1974. It was a crucial time or me: I was getting back to normality, to a 'law-abiding' life, albeit within the very confined urban setting of a village. And I had begun assessing the consequences of May '68 because, in the wake of what had occurred, I had to set a new course for my life as a revolutionary activist."

"But you were doing a job you had never done before."

"That was the point. The institute was managed by the Belgian Socialist Party and was little different from Belgian government institutes of the same sort. For the first two years, as a tutor, I was in charge of the senior classes, youngsters aged between fifteen and sixteen, and for the last three years I was chief tutor and coordinator of the teaching staff. The working hours were as you might expect of a penal institution much as capitalist society: up at seven, breakfast, lining up in ranks and off to class. Then, accompanying them to lunch and then back into class for the afternoon. After five o'clock there were various educational activities up until seven. After dinner, they had to be walked to the dorms where they had to be put to bed by nine o'clock. I used to work straight through for two weeks and then had three full days' rest.

"The kids were a handful in the sense that they came from socially excluded families with alcohol and other problems of that sort. There was also a group of kids with physical disabilities. The kids were regarded as victims of society and the idea was to turn them around."

"I can't picture you there. What I mean is, I don't believe you were in agreement with the center's rules."

"*Oui, oui*, obviously there was no common ground. But, given my circumstances, I had no option but to accept it. I didn't teach but I was involved in cultural activities. I was working with highly rebellious seventeen-year-olds. We used to go to the theater, to the cinema, etc. We built forts, meaning paper-and-plasticine castles. The theory being that while they were doing this you could talk to them about what life was like in the Middle Ages."

"And how did you get along with the students?"

"Well, my French still wasn't that good," Octavio laughed, "but I tried to be their friend. We hit it off and our relationship wasn't bad, except for the occasional isolated crisis. What I could not deal with was the Makarenko method. The students carried a report card with them and any time they completed a cultural task we had done with them they were awarded fictitious cash that could be spent at the commissary. They had to run things themselves as if in some sort of little republic with its courts and all. It was a parody of society, since we were the ones who were obliging them to do it."

"So, by chance, you ended up doing something akin to your father's line of work?"

"Well, it wasn't the same thing. But what I had been through with my father helped me out in the real setting of the institute. This approach to education was no different from the prevailing model, whereas my father's practice had been. It was a significant difference and a great experience as well.

"One night there was a fight. One boy, who had come to blows with everybody, just refused to be calmed down. He made me see red too. I ended up getting into a fight with him and, I being bigger than him, I immobilized him on the floor. For a few seconds, I lost it, but when I regained my composure and even as I was pinning him down, I started laughing and said to him: 'Can't you see that there is no sense in our fighting like fools?' He began to laugh and, in the end, he calmed down."

"Very much an educator's response. Faced with a behavioral issue, you finish up having a behavioral issue of your own."

"I wasn't in control of the situation until the very end," he laughed. "But it was spontaneous. I told him: 'I can go crazy just as easily as you.'"

"But in the end the story you tell is the tale of a contradiction, of an antiauthoritarian acting like an authoritarian."

"Sure, sure. Many a time authority comes into play because you want to sort out some problem as quickly as possible. As you rightly say, there's something very contradictory about that. I was constantly asking myself: what am I doing here?"

"Is it not comparable, but on a quite different scale, with what happened in the Spanish civil war, where the anarchists wound up as government ministers?"

"Man, of course," he laughed. "But school shouldn't be a place where power is deployed, the way it is in a ministry. In spite of everything, a school is an attempt to make a contribution to the child's ability to protect himself in society. Even in the taming of them, a contribution is made. However, the mere fact that you are forced to operate along authoritarian lines cuts deeply into whatever the child gets out of the education and tames him but little else; even during my time in Solières, albeit in the attempt to spare him bigger problems in later life.

"The Solières years were not a good time for me. Loneliness, separation from my comrades, the fact that I could not see eye-to-eye with what was going on in the school I was not quite depressed, but I had a hard time carrying on. In that respect, Joseph Orval, the headmaster, was always understanding. He was au fait with my circumstances and my obligations as an anti-Francoist activist. Orval was a left-winger and a Freemason, but above all he was a humanist. It was no wonder that we struck up a great friendship that endured up until his death about ten years ago. He put up with my take on application of the Makarenko method during the time I was chief tutor. Because I got rid of the obligation to form up in ranks and make the pledge to the flag at morning assemblies; meaning that I altered the way discipline was enforced.

"Orval understood that in the conditions in which the school and Belgian society were operating, implementation of the Makarenko approach to education was a fraud and, essentially, did not set out to make the kids self-managers but, as in the democracy of their elders, it forced them to cope with the system's rules by going through the motions, because the hard fact was that we tutors oversaw operations. So much so that, after 1975, Orval stepped down as head of the institute and went back to giving lessons as a music teacher. I saw him often in Paris. He even played a part in a fictional movie we made in the

1980s with Geneviève Dreyfus-Arman, her kids, a few neighbors, and a bunch of friends from Paris."

Out of his relationship with Joseph Orval, who realized what a hard time Octavio was having living in isolation, came the arrival in Solières towards the end of 1969 of Irene and Octavio's kids. Orval had arranged for Irene to be hired to work in the institute's commissary. Her reappearance was the result of several months spent mulling over the situation that had arisen inside the FIJL and Octavio's legal standing in Belgium, which did not look like it was going to change in the near future as the Belgian government had decide to hold him under house arrest indefinitely.

"I still find Irene's return wonderful. There had been some big changes in your life, Octavio. And there was Ariane... Irene agreed to move to Belgium when she already had, I imagine, a settled family life in Mexico."

"Well, it occurred to her that she and I might go back to living as a couple."

"What about Ariane? You were already in a relationship with her," I said, gazing at a photo of them both, taken around that time on some beach in, I think it was, Normandy.

"My relationship with Ariane at the time was based on action. Within the movement and as part of revolutionary activity. We never based our life as a couple on anything stable, the way a normal couple would. Proof of that is the fact that Irene arrived and moved in with the kids, and Ariane kept on seeing me. Irene knew what I wanted and what my intentions were because I never made a secret of any of it from her."

"Yes, but I can see your photos with Ariane from back then and I can see that you were happy. You looked like a couple."

"My relationship with Ariane was no barrier to my feelings for my kids and Irene. I made no distinction between friendship and love. It's a way of acting out my relationship with other people on a basis of freedom and solidarity, one that I have practiced all my life. As I see it, relationship conjures up no particular obligation in my head and my affection and solidarity are not restricted to one or more people, but extend to everyone else," Octavio replied, emphatically. "Such restrictions are imposed by society and that includes today's society, which says that before something can be there has to be something else, even should the two be antithetical. Love, unless it is free, is not love at all. Proof of that is the fact that one cannot be forced to love. People are being hypocritical when they say 'I love you, I love you' and forget to add 'obedient,' unless they add on 'free' and act in a manner congruent with that ambition. I never thought of living as a couple as the tomb of one or the other person's freedom, nor of the family as 'family,' as an institution like the state, a hierarchical set-up in which one's private life, in the form of the family, assumes a public profile. Just to be clearer about that: I have never regarded the family as anything other than a private, circumstantial form of the public relationship between human beings. Hence, in my eyes, the family is sugges-tive of a freely entered into relationship and it would never occur to me to live the sort of 'family life' in which relationships are, as in the state, hierarchical and un-free."

"I don't think there's any rule governing all this, Octavio. Some couples are lifelong matches."

"Of course there isn't any rule. Although a lot of people have an interest in imposing one. What I am saying goes for me, for my life. I am not setting out to weave a theory; I am merely defending my right to think the way I do and to strive to be consistent with that."

Changes

THE GREAT TSUNAMI OF May '68 was receding, and slowly the power of the state was re-embedding itself and returning to the everyday "normality" of French society.

Several months after the Sorbonne had been evacuated by the French police, those parties close to General De Gaulle secured an overwhelming majority in the elections. Not only did this electoral success allow them to carry on in government, but they were now free to demolish many of the social gains made by May '68. The aim was to get back to the previous normality as soon as practicable, while trying to digest all the libertarian concerns and demands that the youthful challengers had articulated during the months of ongoing agitation in the country. The result was an unprecedented crackdown against French and European youth activism.

What had occurred had a big impact on so-called leftist movements. In the case of the anarchists—and in particular of the exiles from the FIJL— this led to a considerable crisis. As a result of the arrests of young libertarians in France over the preceding years, or the arrest and retention of Octavio in Belgium, the consistent militancy of the most active members of the FIJL was affected. The FIJL Liaison Commission therefore had to split itself into three entirely autonomous commissions residing in locations that were quite far apart in geographical terms. But the engagement of the more active youth militants in Paris with the May '68 upheaval had brought fresh air and fresh ideas into the movement. Thus, on the pretext of defending the autonomy and spontaneism fomented by May '68, criticisms were emerging of the FIJL's centralistic modus operandi and its policy line. And the serious point was that these criticisms were coming from some of the people who had until now been its most ardent supporters.

"What was going on in the FIJL?"

"It is complicated to explain. In mid-1969 I was faced with a crossroads similar to the end of the DI. At the time, abandoning the struggle was unthinkable, and it still is, although the conditions were not the same."

"I also think that you were growing up."

"Sure. We were casting around for some other way of explaining it, but with the passage of time it has become very obvious that age was one factor. Work, personal life, and the family were beginning to be the priorities... Another was personal expectations, as is only normal as we grow up.

"Differences of opinion had begun to surface at the FIJL plenum in December 1968, though it was really in April 1969 that a rift began to emerge between the members. There was no split, because the agreement was that militants had a free hand to stand by the policy line and prioritize organizational efforts within Spain. Conditions were not ideal for carrying on with the struggle collectively, the way we had done up until then..."

"Let me draw a very far-fetched comparison. As a rule, there is to group endeavors a starry-eyed process that very often coincides with a certain stage in one's life. As the members of the group grow older, other needs crop up and different curiosities arise. For instance, in rock bands, one's useful life is very clear. With a few exceptions, the members of those groups all fall within a certain age range and the groups break up because the members no longer feel the need for collective creation."

"The phenomenon is the same. For a while you see eye-to-eye because your needs overlap. Look, there's the curious case of one comrade who gave the movement a lot of backing and who was one of those most deeply involved in May '68. Later he was one of the most critical voices within the FIJL. He then fell in love with his current partner who was the ex-partner of another comrade. She had to return to Barcelona on an important job and he, who was living in France, left everything behind to join her in Barcelona, regardless of all the risks that that entailed with Franco still alive. His personal need, what you call 'love,' could not be denied. In Barcelona, he had to go through a period of complete militant inactivity. Like those rock groups you were talking about."

"Could that rule be applicable to countries? I sometimes think that some of them lose their raison d'être."

"Much more so in the case of entire countries! Besides, how were they formed? Once upon a time, there were no countries and people moved backwards and forwards. Countries are such artificial things and make so little sense..."

"Getting back to the FIJL, I guess there was also a degree of ideological disillusionment."

"Without a doubt. Triggered by the protracted and pointless internal battle with the conservatism of the older libertarian membership and also by frustration about the evaporation of the high hopes of May '68. As had happened on other occasions since the end of the civil war, it ended up leading to the 'disappearance' of a lot of militants who had helped to breathe life back into the FIJL and Spanish anarchism over the previous ten years.

"Initially, the criticisms and demands for decentralization were justified and they appeared to reflect an authentic 'spontaneist' intent. But subsequent developments showed that the criticism was just a pretext: the people who were supporting it stopped cooperating in the FIJL and focused on their personal lives."

"Which is to say, the choice between carrying on with the struggle or not carrying on with it."

"That's it. The choice of whether or not to quit the struggle cropped up in my life again. I can't remember if I hesitated about it. And I made up my mind again to carry on with revolutionary activity. I saw it as a duty, on grounds of ideological cogency and because I regarded it as an objective requirement, given the social backsliding we were faced with. Political reformists used this slippage to get the better of the May '68 revolutionary impulse, drain it of its potential for subversion and harness it for their own purposes.

"The priority was to keep up the subversion, when faced with those out to harness it, and press ahead with May '68 without breaking with the existing legal arrangements. It struck me as crucial that we rebut those who claim to have forgotten that a wakening up to authoritarian alienation was possible in the shape of attempts to smash the laws and hierarchical structures of established society."

"But that spontaneous rebellion was as short lived as the foam on the waves."

"True, the subversion was not on the same scale as it had been during the high tide of May '68. But even though it may now have been coming from small groups, it was still active, interesting, and relevant. Besides, it was still multifaceted and multi-voiced."

"What do you mean?"

"That in nearly every country there was an extra-parliamentary left made up of three revolutionary strands that had previously despised one another: the Trotskyist, the Maoist, and the anarchist; not to mention the small, non-aligned activist youth groups that had been brought to the surface by the swell of May '68—in France as well as elsewhere in Europe.

"Plus, the facts compelled me to keep up my ties with subversion elsewhere. Some of those involved kept in touch with me because they valued what the First of May Group had done up to that point."

"How could the one possibly have been linked to the other? I am thinking of the Maoists: China was in the throes of the Cultural Revolution. They supported it and it has been established that the Chinese Cultural Revolution was human and cultural carnage alike. Its consequences are still under examination."

"Fine, but at the time this was not known, and both the Maoists and the Trotskyists were striking 'spontaneist' poses. There was common ground in certain areas and this paved the way for contacts and association."

"And how were you able to link up with all this from Solières?"

"At the school we had access to an offset printer for educational use. From the moment I arrived in Solières, Abarca and I had Orval's blessing in night time printing of propaganda for the FIJL. In 1969 we printed two pamphlets, 'Ways that the student revolt has been defused' and 'A Brief History of Anarchy, so-called'; these were the results of a meeting I had in Paris with Agustin García Calvo and some of the young *ácratas* from Madrid who had recently left Spain behind for exile."

"Hang on a moment. *You* were in Paris?"

"Of course. At no time did I abide by the monitored release to which I was subject. If I could, I would to slip away for a time. That year I paid two or three visits to Paris. I capitalized upon my three-day rest periods at the institute to make the trip with help from friends who use to come and get me in Solières and drive me as far as the French border. There, there were some comrades who smuggled me across into Valenciennes, and from there I used to catch the train to Paris."

So, despite spending the years in silence in Solières, Octavio contrived to create around himself a sort of a scope for activism. In November 1969, Miguel García, released from prison in Spain after serving twenty of the thirty years to which he had been sentenced back in 1949, following the commutation of his death sentence, paid a visit to Solières. His time in prison had been so traumatic that he was literally incapable of uttering a word for several months. Octavio recounted that they brought García to see a specialist and he stayed there for two or three weeks, before leaving for England to meet up with Stuart Christie.

Towards the end of the year, a seminar on May '68 was held at Solières château. Organized by the most progressive wing of the Belgian Socialist Party, it was attended by Trotskyists and Maoists who had made their names in the events in Paris. The organizers included Roger Ramaekers, who ran the Belgian cooperative movement and who had defended Octavio while in custody in Saint-Gilles. By the end of the seminar, Orval and Ramaekers invited Octavio to speak. Another of those involved, having traveled up from France, was André Glucksman, a philosopher of Jewish extraction—and, at that point, a Maoist—who had already published his first book *The Discourse of War*; he stood up to Sartre and the post-structuralism to which the latter subscribed.

"Octavio... small printing press, meetings with leftists and philosophers. Was the Solières institute some sort of a den of conspiracy?"

"Oh, *oui, oui*," Octavio guffawed. "And we debated everything. Those were great times. We traded views with Trotskyists and Maoists. Though they were short, those seminars were very productive."

Europe in Flames

THE DEMOCRATIC EUROPE OF the 1970s was not impervious to what was going on elsewhere in the world. In political terms, the great European democracies were striving to keep up the onslaught mounted by capital and the state; one way or another, they were out to banish May '68 from the collective memory. In the United States, the policy line laid down by the CIA and Henry Kissinger at the height of the Cold War was not that different. Strident anti-communist paranoia, fear that the "accident" that had occurred in Cuba might spread to the rest of Latin America, spawned plans for unprecedented international paramilitary action. Although it may have been a stable geographical area, Europe was not overlooked by these policies. Let us not forget that half of Europe was in thrall to the Soviet Union and, since the end of the Second World War, places like Italy still had their Communist Party and a powerful extra-parliamentary left. The priority for the authorities was halting the trend with Western Europe that was out to consolidate a stable extra-parliamentary current operating outside of the controlled code of rules of democratic congresses. The gamut of motley extra-parliamentary ideological factions had to grapple with the state and the most conservative elements in society and, in the Italian case, even with fascist groups.

Italy was a typical example of this confrontation. On December 12, 1969 a bomb went off in Milan's Piazza Fontana, claiming seventeen lives. The affair was very murky and the state pointed the finger at Italian anarchists, comrades of Octavio's, accusing them of having carried out the bombing.

"The Piazza Fontana business signaled to some extent that the 1970s had arrived."

"Of course. Europe was radicalized by the start of the 1970s. By then there was more to it than idealistic principles. And there was a significant fascist backlash."

"To what extent were you affected by that?"

"Well, Abarca started to be fearful of the fallout from the 'fascist plot in Italy.' He was afraid that in the wake of the bombs in Milan we might find ourselves targeted for an attack in Solières. He stated that he had seen some oddballs in a car with no license plates, hanging around the vicinity of the chateau. And he even issued me a hunting-rifle so that I might defend myself, because our little house was very isolated in the middle of parklands. I never did find out whether or not there was any truth to it all. But the fact is that the fascist plot sparked an out-and-out anarchist hunt in Italy and there was a danger that it might spread elsewhere."

"What was the bombing of the National Agricultural Bank in the Piazza Fontana in Milan all about?"

"It was patently a fascist provocation. In the initial round-up after the outrage, our comrades Giovanni Corradini and Eliane Vincileoni were arrested. At the time, they were the driving forces behind a revolutionary current that was pretty influential in leftist circles in Milan. In the second round-up, which also encompassed anarchist circles in Rome, comrade Giuseppe Pinelli was arrested. His death on December 15, after he was thrown from a window while under interrogation, was reported by the police as suicide.

"The Pinelli case dragged on until quite recently. In fact, in the Piazza Fontana there is a plaque commemorating his murder. And so far no one has been held accountable for his death.

"And I am afraid that no one ever will. Any more than for the prison suicides of the main leaders of the German Red Army Faction, the RAF. Indeed, Dario Fo wrote *Accidental Death of an Anarchist*, based on the Pinelli affair. Pinelli's death and the jailing of the dancer and novelist Pietro Valpreda were all part of the crackdown. Pinelli was a very highly regarded comrade. The last time I saw Giovanni and Eliane was when they came to Paris in 1967, in connection with the proposal made to us by Giangiacomo Feltrinelli that we hatch an operation to rescue Che Guevara, who had been captured in Bolivia. I saw Pinelli just the one time in 1965 or 1966, in relation to a trip to Italy, because I slept at his home. I think I had seen Valpreda back in late 1967, with Ivo Della Savia, who was also arrested in Belgium in connection with the outrage in Milan, even though he had nothing to do with it."

"Feltrinelli also perished in strange circumstances."

"There are doubts surrounding the Feltrinelli case. He was from a wealthy family from Lombardy. He was a communist and owned a very reputable publishing house. I think his firm was the first to publish Lampedusa's *The Leopard*. But, as the 1970s wore on, he became increasingly radicalized in favor of armed communism. When the Piazza Fontana outrage occurred, he went underground, fearing that fascist groups might kill him. The circumstances in which he died strike me as nonsensical and highly unbelievable. I cannot picture him handling plastic explosives at the base of some electricity pylon. Apparently, the plastic charge went off prematurely. He wouldn't have carried out that sort of operation in person because he was on the fringes of direct action.

"Actually, it had never occurred to the far right that the anarchists might have stepped away from armed struggle in the 1970s. It was groups with marxist backgrounds that were espousing it.

"And you can see this in, say, Italy or Germany. We didn't see eye-to-eye with this. From our point of view, there was no point mounting violence on the same scale as the state. Getting drawn into extremely violent operations— like Andreas Baader from the German Red Army Faction was—and tackling the state head-on, causing many deaths, made no sense to us."

What Octavio had just mentioned was part of a flurry of murders that have gone down in history as "accidents" or "suicides." The most startling of these was the suicide of the German RAF leaders. On arrest, they had been held in complete isolation in a purpose-built prison, Stammheim. Baader, Ensslin, Meinhof, and Raspe turned up dead on October 18, 1977. To all appearances they had committed suicide, some by shooting themselves, others by hanging. Irmgard Moller, the only one to survive these "suicides" said that her comrades had had no plans to end their lives, and a lot of evidence subsequently surfaced, which supported that. In the Spanish context, one need only mull over the case of Enrique Ruano, a member of the People's Liberation Front (Frente de Liberación Popular/FLP). Arrested by the BPS in 1969, Ruano died after he was thrown from a seventh-story window. His death was depicted as a suicide by the Francoist press, but over time, it was proven that Ruano had sustained a bullet wound, after which he had been thrown from the window.

Clearly, in Europe, there was a determination to eradicate any nongovernmental attempt to change society. In 1990, the Italian president, Giulio Andreotti confirmed that, in the 1970s, there were paramilitary commandos set up by NATO. Even today we know very little definitively about these, due to the seal on court records at the request of that organization and the intelligence agencies of the countries concerned. Andreotti at the time was referring to what is called Operation Gladio. In the case of Italy, for instance, those far-right paramilitaries went so far as to carry out outrages, up to and including coup attempts, like so-called Operation Plan Solo. But what was the point of Gladio? Presumably to throw a wrench into the works of any sort of movement inimical to the interests of the capitalists and the CIA, by acting as though that the outrages were coming from far-left groups, as in the case of the Piazza Fontana example. The object was to discredit the left generally and communism in particular.

There is a similarity between Operation Gladio and the Operation Condor, which was being carried out in South America at the time. And behind it all was the long reach of the CIA and US minister Henry Kissinger. However, although the mechanics were similar, the countries in which they were operating were very different. The European democracies were a lot sturdier than the South American ones. In fact, no European country was stripped of its democracy, as they were in South America.

Operation Gladio, so-called, in its Plan Solo avatar, started in 1969 and set out to create escalating tension and panic among the Italian populace. After the Milan outrage, there was another in Rome and so on, a total of four massacres in all, in various parts of the country.

In 1998 General Vincenzo Vinciguerra confirmed the existence of a NATO-sponsored organization with the connivance of the Italian secret services. Apparently, Plan Solo is to be credited with the bombing of a Bologna railway station, which claimed eighty lives. Plan Solo was also somehow implicated in the murder of Aldo Moro in 1976, credited to the Red Brigades. Moro faced a revolutionary trial before a "people's tribunal," and was sentenced to death before finally being executed on June 24, 1969.

Maybe Aldo Moro paid with his life for his refusal to agree with the United States administration, which was insisting that the Communist Party had to be completely excluded from the Italian parliament. There was definite CIA pressure being put on the Italian government and, thanks to that, there was an obvious ratcheting up of the escalating violence in the country and a resultant militaristic course by the Red Brigades. This is not an attempt to absolve the revolutionary armed group from blame, but to register the fact that state violence had a polarizing impact on revolutionary movements.

These days, it's obvious that the states of Europe have shown little willingness to try to shed light on what happened. From the 1990s on, there were

only a few timid efforts made in Italy, Belgium, and Switzerland at a parliamentary level—not that they came to anything conclusive. Operation Gladio
remains shrouded in mystery, with a lot of its cohorts still on active service in
other areas of influence.

"Earlier you referred to a certain paranoia, given the rumor that there
were far right groups at work. What was the extent of that concern?"

"I never did find out if the prowlers that Abarca spotted were real, but
from that point onward his behavior changed. He became distant and cool in
his dealings with me. He put obstacles in the way of our use of the offset press
and, as a result of this change of attitude, I stopped asking him to drive me to
the border when I was making an illegal crossing into France. From then on, I
had to rely on some Belgian friends.

"Fortunately, Orval's approach to me was the same as it had been ever
since I arrived in Solières.

"With the exception of the Angry Brigade in Britain and a few other
small groups in Holland or Italy, the revolutionary groups between 1968 and
1970 were not of anarchist extraction but, in most cases, drawn from a range
of Marxist tendencies that were open to armed action.

"The fact is that we, the FIJL or the First of May Group, were a very different sort of group. Our fight was against a dictatorship, and the groups I was
talking about just now were, with the odd exception, operating in democratic
states. In the Angry Brigade's case, for instance, the target was the state and
the policies of the prime minister. They were the only ones with whom I saw
eye-to-eye since their operations did not involve armed violence against actual
people. They were actions against interests that had some material or symbolic
value."

"Were ex-members of the FIJL or the First of May Group involved in any
actions with the Angry Brigade?"

"No. We knew a number of English libertarians or Spanish ones living
in England, people such as Salvador Gurucharri, but he was never involved.
In fact, right then, what we needed was discretion. I was in touch with Stuart
Christie; but, both of us having been prisoners, we had to make a show of our
steering clear of militant action."

During the 1970s, in Europe, like their counterparts on other continents,
a lot of revolutionary groups chose the armed struggle route. One has only to
recall organizations like the Red Army Faction (Germany), Lotta Continua,

Potere Operaio or the Red Brigades (Italy) in the early 1970s or, in the Latin America context, the Tupamaros (Uruguay), the MIR (Chile), or the ERP (Argentina). There were even actions in Canada, with the Quebec Liberation Front. Not forgetting the performance of the Palestinian resistance organizations Fatah or the Popular Front for the Liberation of Palestine (PFLP) in the near East. There followed a flurry of revolutionary trials, kidnappings, and extortion raids, resulting in lives lost in many cases. However, the anarchist movements of the time rejected physical violence as a method of struggle. Even so, as far as the state authorities were concerned, communists or anarchists, it was pretty much the same thing.

In Octavio's case, given that he was under surveillance and always under suspicion, he had to be that much more discreet and cut back on his clandestine sorties as much as he could. Evidence of this is the fact that his only trip to Paris at this time was in January 1970. He was aware of how things stood and so he strove to get on with his educational work and to live a normal family life in Solières.

The 1970 Paris trip was so that he could attend a get-together of several of the *ácratas* from the circle around Agustín García Calvo, who met up with friends at a coffee bar in the Latin Quarter of Paris for a chat. Agustín García Calvo and his circle's aim was to respond to the fresh Francoist crackdown on the strikers in Asturias and Andalusia. In addition, the Franco regime was preparing a show trial in Borgos against sixteen ETA members arrested in 1969. The regime was pushing for death sentences and 752 years' incarceration for the accused. The group set about planning the abduction of the Spanish ambassador to UNESCO, Emilio Garrigues, cashing in on the fact that one of the young *ácratas* in García Calvo's circle was the son of the ambassador's cousin and was au fait with the official's movement. But weapons for the operation still had to be obtained. Octavio lobbied the FIJL to supply them. But on March 5, Octavio discovered through the French paper *Le Monde* that the operation had fallen through. *ABC* carried the following report:

> Spain's permanent delegate to UNESCO, Emilio Garrigues y Díaz-Cañabate, has been the target of a kidnap attempt in Paris, the perpetrators of which have been arrested [...] These are the Spaniards Juan García Macareno (24), José Cabal Riera (21), and Jorge Cañizares Varella (31) who have refused to identify the organization to which they belong. "Our

action had an exclusively political aim," they declared during the hearings.
"We were out to apply pressure to the Spanish government to secure the
release of our comrades, detained in Spain." The trio, whose leanings are
anarchist, had been living in France since last summer.

Through his column in *ABC*, Alfredo Semprún fingered Octavio as the in-
stigator. The Francoist BPS aimed to pressure the Belgian government, which
had arrested Ivo Della Savia a few days before in Brussels. Della Savia was accused in Italy of having connections to Pietro Valpreda and other indicted anarchists. The press depicted Ivo as a member of the First of May Group.

"Octavio, you were a long way away when the attempted abduction of
Garrigues took place."

"That's right, in Solières. But the kidnap attempt was blamed on me.
Within a few days of the arrests in Paris, Belgian police showed up to question
me. When I declined to tell them what I did on my days off work and just
mentioned that I spent them in the countryside, the minister of Justice reim-
posed the requirement on me that I report in person to the police station in
Huy, some fifteen kilometers from Solières, on a weekly basis, reminding me
that the house arrest order was still in force.

"The situation was becoming complicated and it was several months before I could venture beyond Solières. I couldn't even go to Huy railway station
to collect the films we had been shooting at the children's institute. Even so,
over the course of the year, a range of groups in several European countries
remained in action and they were claiming their operations in the name of the
First of May Group: operations that were also getting press attention.

Given all that was going on and being unable to do anything else, Octavio threw himself more into his work at the institute, into family life, and
into the friendships he had struck up in Belgium—people such as Belgian radio and television reporters Claudine Bodineaux and Marie-Paule Eskénazi.
Along with a bunch of like-minded friends, the female reporters decided to
rent a cottage near Solières. The plan was to meet up with Octavio and Irene
on weekends and days off. Octavio recalled these get-togethers as if they were
family gatherings, at which they would dine, sing, and discuss this and that.
And since the gang included couples with children, Irene and her kids were
able to mix with them and break out of their isolation.

"I see the group that took shape in Solières as a sort of a commune."

"Something like that. The reporters belonged to a current of contestation heavily influenced by May '68. In the house there were arguments about couples and the family, the relationships between men and women, feminism... Claudine and Marie at that time assembled, in a very special and unforgettable way, a bunch of disaffected Belgian intellectuals. That link enabled us to get acquainted with one another and to form friendships that have survived to this day. Every so often, we would meet up with them and whoever was around. There were no rules about couples or families. It was an ongoing experiment on the basis of the personal experiences of each of us. Ideologically close, the keynote was tolerance and it was all very open and free. At these encounters in which we ran things for ourselves, there were upwards of twenty of us, plus, every now and then, invited Belgian intellectuals from a range of camps that had dabbled in communal experimentation in Belgium during May '68. I remember that one time the debate lasted a whole weekend, because a young reporter who worked for *La Cause du Peuple* (which was at one point run by Jean-Paul Sartre) had come along. The argument revolved around Maoism and the search for a reconciliation with Marxist-Leninism, something I reckoned was impossible. Or around things such as spontaneism or antihierarchy within libertarianism. At the time, most European Maoists backed a less authoritarian revolutionary praxis, consonant with the spirit of May '68."

"Let's get back to the armed struggle in the 1970s. It was a particularly tough time in many places around the world."

"As early as 1971, student movements started to turn more radical in various places around the world and with that came a temptation to switch to armed action. But, to the extent that that temptation took the shape of dabbling in clandestine violent activity, its isolation and error also became more entrenched and telling, following skirmishes with the forces of order as they were drawn into indiscriminate violence that knew no ethical boundaries. Especially within groups that drew their inspiration from authoritarian ideologies."

"Earlier you mentioned that one of the groups that was spared that authoritarian ideology (with pro-Stalinist or pro-Maoist leanings), was the Angry Brigade in England."

"Indeed. The Angry Brigade stuck to the anarchist policy of symbolic violence, something along the lines of the First of May Group. There is a huge contrast between symbolic violence and physical violence. There is a long and complicated debate to be had here, I know. Symbolic violence was what always set us apart from armed struggle groups and movements with their roots in authoritarian ideologies and hierarchical internal structures. The only thing we posited as a major necessity was the elimination of Franco.

"I can remember countless occasions when it proved necessary to explain this and debate it with the majority of the comrades and groups who approached us about playing their part in the struggle. It wasn't easy getting them to understand the need to be consistent with the ethical and educational purposes behind the revolutionary solidarity that was the driver behind our actions. We tried to explain to them how we were taking on the system for the purpose of defending the freedom and rights being snatched away by the power of the state and capitalist interests. Because competing with the authorities with an eye to replacing them is not the point. The enemy is authoritarian institutions and not the individuals representing or serving them. Violence is down to the authorities leaving you no other option. Revolutionary struggle is a matter for the people and not for some vanguard making decisions in the name of an idea. Hence the educative nature of our actions; the refusal of submissiveness, the setting of an example and incitement to follow it. Being aware that revolution, in the sense of change, had to be brought about by individuals, by the citizenry rather than by some gang. The road is long and onerous. One has to be clear about the importance power held for the system, its determination that it was not going to let its grip be loosened and, if need be, to resort to the most extreme violence, if necessary, to hold on to it. Authoritarian regimes would have no hesitation in cracking down brutally on any form of opposition to the notions of 'power' and 'the exercise of power.' They would be even more ruthless with those aiming to subvert the notion, because they represent a threat to the interests of the system and its very existence. Something that the authorities are always going to defend against all comers is the grammar of power, the established rules of the game. You have the case of the Angry Brigade trial in England."

Octavio's reference was to the British anarchists arrested in London on charges of having been behind the spectacular operations mounted by the Angry Brigade in England, between May 1970 and the moment when they were arrested by the Special Branch and Scotland Yard's CID on August 20, 1971. Even though the involvement of most of them in these actions was never proven—and they caused merely material damage—the court handed down five ten-year sentences for conspiracy, with four acquitted for lack of evidence, ignoring the important campaigns mounted by intellectuals insisting that they be released. Stuart Christie, Octavio's friend and former collaborator within the DI, was one of the accused in the so-called "Stoke Newington 8 Trial." In his case, there was an acquittal. The accused were blamed for taking part in upwards of twenty-five bomb attacks and two machine gun attacks on embassies, in which no one had been hurt. Nevertheless, nothing could be proved and the sentencing was intended "to set an example." The prosecution started: "The eight accused who claim to be revolutionaries and anarchists, have attempted under a variety of names to disorganize and attack this country's democratic society."

But opinion in the British press failed to back the court. The trial, which created a great stir in the media, was the longest in the whole of British criminal history—it lasted until December 1972—and highlighted the contrast between the authorities and the solidarity among the accused. It afforded British public opinion an insight into the deeply ethical motives behind the international revolutionary solidarity displayed by the Angry Brigade members. Even a conservative newspaper like the *Daily Telegraph* felt compelled to carry this remarkably clear-sighted editorial:

> Painful though it may be in certain particular instances, recourse to bombs or other weapons against tyrants and dictators of every sort who cannot be toppled lawfully and peaceably through the ballot-box is understandable. Where there is imperfect democracy [...] violence may seem like the only way of broadening electoral rights. The actions of Prescott and the Angry Brigade constitute a welcome outcry that shows that perfect democracy [...] do not put paid to all the stirrings of violent opposition. We have a tendency to believe that the will of the majority is the general will and that minorities quietly await their turn, confident that one day they will be majorities. But it does not always happen that way. There are those who reckon that our democracy, perfect though it may be, is a corrupted sham—to the point of thwarting all hopes—in terms of the allegedly radically tainted economic and social parameters within which it operates. To them, such mechanisms are purely arbitrary.

However, most of the British press sought to imply that the thinking underlying the Angry Brigade was supported only by London groups and the *underground* press. For instance, they were critical of the fact that its members lived "in communes." Nor was *Freedom*—the mouthpiece of the British Anarchist Federation—sparing in its criticisms. Among other things, it stated:

> In the wake of the devastating results of the repression there is no way out other than to mount an inglorious retreat into conventional political activity, or, if not, to sink further into the shifting sands of terrorism, with all its attendant dangers—a dilemma that has always eventually prevailed in previous campaigns and which is hard to wriggle out of.

Those dark prognostications were borne out neither in the case of the First of May Group nor in the case of the Angry Brigade, since these never went beyond symbolic violence.

On the other hand, *Freedom* was right where Germany and its Red Army Faction (RAF) was concerned. Setting aside the idiosyncracies of each country, one of the many factors in this physical violence was the Nixon-Mao pact that came out of the American president's visit to Peking in February 1972, as well as Nixon's summit with Brezhnev in Moscow the same year. Such rapprochements between the "big three" was orchestrated by Henry Kissinger in order to launch peaceful coexistence even in the midst of the Vietnam war, even under the threat of an atomic apocalypse. Behind the scenes, the Cold War raged on.

"And how did you in Solières perceive what was happening with the Angry Brigade?"

"I have an anecdote predating the trials in London and it deserves to be placed on record. In anticipation of the trial of the Angry Brigade comrades, Stuart Christie mentioned to me that a well-known BBC producer was shooting a documentary on the Angry Brigade and wanted an interview with me. Christie told me that it was very important that I take part so as to demonstrate the links between those arrested and the First of May Group's libertarians fight against Francoism. I agreed and Ariane set up a meeting, which took place clandestinely in Paris in the autumn of 1972."

"I saw the documentary *The Angry Brigade*. Lots of drama and some pretty stirring music. In it, the connection is drawn between the Spanish exiles and the Angry Brigade."

"Yes, there was a sensationalist tone about the documentary. Remember that it was made by the BBC."

"Meaning that, as shown in the documentary, which was shot in Paris, your situation was clandestine. Meaning that once the documentary went out, the Belgian courts would see that you had slipped over to Paris."

"Actually, there was no need. On the way back to Belgium, fed up with slipping through the little border village near Valenciennes, I made up my mind to travel on by train. Shorty after crossing the border, the French police who boarded the train in Maubeuge in France to carry out passport checks, seized mine, a Nansen passport, made out in my name and took it into a different carriage.[21] After a while they came back, saying that I was to accompany them. They held on to me until the train pulled into Charleroi station in Belgium. There we got off the train and brought me into a room in the station. Some time later, the French gendarmes told me that I was to travel back with them to Maubeuge where they would issue me with an expulsion order. I refused to go with them, saying that they would have to bring me there by force, which they did after handcuffing me, and the Belgian gendarmes did nothing, no matter how much I shouted and protested that I was working legally in Belgium.

In Maubeuge station, more gendarmes were waiting for me with a van and they brought me to the gendarmerie post there. There I was placed in a cell and the gendarmerie commander sought me out to tell me that, as it was a Sunday, the Interior Ministry in Paris would forward an expulsion order on the Monday or Tuesday for me to sign. I had to remain there, which was odd, as it was not their usual practice to arrest people in order to tell them they were to be expelled. When expelling you, they would allow you some time, a few hours or even days, to leave the country under your own steam.

Faced with this situation, I asked the gendarmerie commander to let me put a call through to the director of the institute in which I was working in Belgium, so that he could drive down and collect me. I suggested that I would leave him my address so that, once the expulsion order came through, he could inform me so that I could return to Maubeuge and sign it. I cannot say if the francs I gave them to allow me to make the call had anything to do with it, but the fact is that I was allowed to call Orval. Within hours, he showed up to fetch me and I was allowed to go.

"Two or three days after that, the head of the Maubeuge gendarmerie called to tell me that the expulsion order had reached him and that I needed to sign it. By that time, I had taken advice from my layer, Roger Lallemand, who recommended that I do not go as they would arrest me. When another call came through from Maubeuge, I told the gendarmerie commander that I could not come because I was under house arrest. He flew into a rage and abruptly hung up the receiver."

In Belgium the word was out about Octavio's clandestine border-crossing and this infuriated the minister of Justice. Weeks after that, Octavio was informed by his lawyer that the deputy prime minister, André Cools, was intending to meet him and had invited him to his home in the town of Flémalle, near Liège, for dinner. Given that Octavio was banned from leaving Solières, the deputy prime minister who was also the mayor of Flémalle, arrived by car to collect him. Cools was a rather odd socialist—years later he would be murdered by the Italian Mafia—and, addressing Octavio as *camarade*, expressed his own sympathy for the Spanish *anars*. However, he did ask that Octavio cause no further border incidents because it would be very hard for him to stop a fellow socialist (albeit a *right-wing* socialist) Justice minister acceding to the German authorities' demands to have Octavio extradited to Germany.

Through the strange avenues of the intelligence services, the German authorities were linking First of May Group actions with Germany and, above all, had suspicions about (non-existent) relations with the German RAF. Specifically, they were accusing Octavio of involvement in the trafficking of machine guns.

"So, you were marooned in Solières and the history of the 1970s went marching on. You were watching it all from a window a long way away, Octavio."

"I had no option but to sit the situation out until something might come along and change matters. I was wasting away in Solières and there were important things going on in the outside world, things such as the Pinochet coup against Salvador Allende in Chile. And the inevitable occurred shortly after that."

"What are you referring to?"

"Salvador Puig Antich was arrested in Barcelona on September 22, 1974. That fact was crucial in my life in Solieres."

"How did you learn of the Puig Antich matter?"

"Through the newspapers and some comrades in France. When Salvador was arrested, a part of the Iberian Liberation Movement (MIL/Movimiento

Ibérico de Liberación) to which he belonged took shelter in Toulouse. One of them was Jean-Marc Rouillan who founded the Action Directe group in 1979. In Toulouse they made contact with French libertarians who then looked to Marcelino Boticario for help, and he briefed me on what was going on. They wanted or help in trying to thwart Puig Antich's execution."

"But you were getting news from Spain, specifically from the MIL group?"

"Some. I was aware of the setting up of the MIL and other autonomous anarchist youth groups in Catalonia since 1972. They intrigued me because they repudiated all connections with classical anarchism. Nor did they have any links with the FIJL, which by then had all but disappeared, so I had no direct links with them.

"When Boticario contacted me, ETA had not yet killed Admiral Carrero Blanco (which they did on December 20, 1973). Even so, we were afraid that they might pass a death sentence on Puig Antich. My response to Boticario was that I would help them out and we set up a meeting in France."

"And you slipped over the border yet again."

"I went to Brive-la-Gaillarde. There I met up with Boticario and the French comrade Bernard Reglat from the Imprenta 34 group in Toulouse. That group was crucial in my decision. Once back in Belgium, I applied for a three-month sabbatical from the Solières institute."

French Farce

ACCORDING TO OCTAVIO, THE MIL was a quasi-libertarian and quasi-Marxist group: it was autonomous and independent of any other organization. The MIL questioned the authorities, but at the same, seemed to be enthralled by them. Octavio admitted that he was ignorant of a lot of its activities, although he sympathized with it because of his commitment to the fight against the dictator.

In Octavio's eyes, the MIL, or Puig Antich, was less significant than the tremendous impression it has had on lots of Catalans, generation after generation, even up until the present day. In Barcelona the significance of Puig Antich was perceived clearly and, in a certain stratum of society, including divergent political factions, nationalist or otherwise, Salvador Puig Antich is remembered as Francoism's last great victim, which is odd because Juan Paredes aka Txiki, from ETA, was shot in Barcelona in 1975, at the age of just twenty-one and yet he is barely remembered in Catalonia.

On the international scene, politicians from democratic parties, such as Willy Brandt in Germany and, indeed, the Vatican lobbied for the sentences passed on Puig Antich and an unknown German, Heinz Chez, to be commuted. All to no avail, however. In the dictator's twilight years, the Francoist dictatorship was especially insistent upon deploying the *garrote vil*, that medieval instrument of torture, as an exemplary punishment. Puig Antich had been arrested on the grounds that he had killed sub-inspector Francisco Anguas Barragán. During the trial, Carrero Blanco, the rear-admiral intended heir of Franco, had died when the vehicle in which he had been traveling was blown up by ETA. That led to an acceleration in the trials of Puig Antich and Heinz Chez. Both offenders were the last to be executed using the vile garrotte vil machine, following a fast-track trial overladen with lies and misrepresentations.

However, few remember the MIL, the Iberian Liberation Movement. The MIL was a tiny group of students—some sources say that it had no more than fifteen active members—plainly influenced by the events of May '68 in Paris. The MIL linked up with the exile community in the south of France and its membership even included some French people, such as Jean-Marc Rouillan. Essentially, its activities consisted of robbing banks and spending the proceeds on labor propaganda publications.

"So you realized, with the attempt to act linked to the Puig Antich case, that the Solières phase in your life was drawing to a close?"

"In a way, yes. It took a lot for me to apply for leave of absence. Not that I was worried about holding down my job in Belgium or for fear of the risks of further clandestine living. The reason was a bit more complex. I can still feel the worry, the pangs I felt when, upon returning from one clandestine trip to Paris and as I was nearing the Belgian border, my eyes were met by the horizon darkened by those endless slag heaps that littered the region after decades of intensive mining activity. Those mining districts were famous for their inhuman exploitation of the workforce over the years. I remember that every time I passed that way to get back to the institute and thought about my future in Belgium, I used to ask myself: how long is going to go on for? Furthermore, the contradictions of my job at the institute where I had the feeling that I was domesticating the youngsters and turning them into sheep so that they could then be absorbed back into society, were becoming less and less feasible for me with every day that passed. Applying for a three-month period of leave was necessary because things were about to kick off. The idea was to spend that time in action and then go back to Solières. But things did not work out that way."

"Meaning that things didn't go as planned. What happened with Irene and the kids?"

"Well, with the passage of time and while I was in custody, and since she wasn't happy in Solières either (in that she felt cut off and without any definite prospect), we decided that the best thing was for her to go back to Mexico with the kids. That was during my fourth month in prison."

"With hindsight, that must have been a dizzying, irrepressible moment, right?"

"Yes. And different from anything I had been through before. The core of the problem was it would be hard for me to achieve my aim of living under the radar again. Because the Puig Antich affair was a matter of extreme urgency. We already knew how quickly the courts martial worked under Franco. Plus, the conditions for action within France were not the same as before. Now my picture and my particulars were circulating around police circles in Europe. So I was readily identifiable and a menace to the others who were also under the radar with me. However, the problem as I saw it was the argument that Boticario and Reglat from Toulouse had used to persuade me that I could usefully contribute to the—granted—somewhat desperate attempt to save Salvador Puig Antich's life. They both thought that my being known to the services was a fact outweighed by the international reputation of the anti-Franco struggle that I would be bringing to any action. Even if we failed or were arrested."

"Which is to say that it was important that you should denounce the Puig Antich affair and get the press on side."

"That's how it was. Bernard Reglat was very emphatic when he set out the reasons why they had sought me out. They were greenhorns when it came to direct action and figured that they, and what was left of the MIL, would not be bringing to the action the record of libertarian anti-Franco struggle that I could contribute by claiming it."

"What do you mean they were greenhorns? When it came to kidnapping, you mean?"

"Yes. There had already been two failed kidnap attempts and they couldn't work out how to operate effectively alongside the Toulouse MIL 'youth.' In one of the attempts, on the night of January 16–17, 1974, four team members—Jean-Claude Torres, Miguel Moreno Patiño, Michel Camilleri, and Pierre Roger (from a Toulouse group close to the MIL)—were arrested at a police checkpoint near Paris. That set-back, and the fact that those members of the group who had escaped arrest insisted on carrying out sabotage attacks in late February, persuaded Reglat to do without their help and get us—as people close to the Imprenta 34 group membership—to handle the orchestration and carrying out of a further kidnap attempt. But then the regime executed Salvador, murdering him on March 2, before we could mount the operation. Even so, we stuck to our plans."

"Why was that?"

"Because, even after Salvador's death, his comrades Josep Lluis Pons Llobet and Oriol Solé Sugranyes were still facing prison time. Because a kidnapping would not only highlight the barbarity displayed towards Puig Antich but would bring attention and pressure that would help them. The operation went ahead, raising fresh funds. But on April 17, just as we had everything

pretty much ready to go, I was arrested by the political police at the Rambuteau metro station in Paris, the Renseignments Généraux."

"In what looked a bit like a replay of your arrest in Belgium. Somebody
had been loose-lipped."

"Clearly, but we still hadn't made the connection at that point. What happened was that I was returning from monitoring the Iberia offices at midday
and had just parked the car with its Belgian license plates. Off I went to keep
the rendezvous with Ariane and, to check that I was not being tailed, I stepped
into the metro station and then straight out again, a run-of-the-mill security
measure. By doing so one could see who was keeping close and if they were
tailing you. In the corridor a dozen plain-clothed Renseignements Généraux
officers swooped on me.

"Judging by the initial questioning at the police station, I thought I had
been recognized at the Iberia offices and followed from there. I assumed that
the Belgian police had tipped the French police off about my having gone
missing from Solières and that the secret services were dogging my footsteps
in Paris.

"I would later learn that the Spanish police, through Inocencio Martínez,
had tipped them off that I was at the Rambuteau station, as had previously occurred in Belgium, but the fact is that the police were over the moon that they
had tracked me down and arrested me. One of them said that they had been
on my trail for years. After searching the car, they brought me to the Interior
ministry for questioning. They wanted to know where I was going at that time
and who my contacts were. My response was that I had just arrived from Belgium and had slept in the car. The toiletries and change of clothes in the back
were evidence of that. They must have been expecting to find weapons, as they
jumped for joy when they came upon a filthy, grimy bag in the trunk. But their
faces dropped when they searched inside and found nothing but a car jack."

The business of Octavio's arrest and the days thereafter were like something out of a *Fantomas* movie featuring Louis de Funes. The police officers'
clumsiness and their inability to think things through were evidence of that. It
was like a sort of a French farce.

The police moved Octavio to the Interior ministry and, following a series
of interrogations, an order was issued expelling him from France—the one they
had sitting ready since 1968—as a result of his having been arrested in Belgium.
Octavio spent the night in the "mousetrap" at the Palace of Justice. Apparently,

the French authorities were intending to charge him with unlawful entry into France, but they couldn't because Octavio was the bearer of a Nansen passport. The next day, at two o'clock in the afternoon, thanks to Ariane's having tipped off lawyer Yves Dechecelles—who had worked with Spanish anarchists previously when Luis Andrés Edo was arrested—a *habeas corpus* application was made and, when his arrest was confirmed, Dechecelles quickly tipped off *Le Monde* which made Octavio's circumstances known the following day. Had the circumstances been different, the news would not have had much of an impact, but a few weeks before, the president of the French Republic, Georges Pompidou had died and France was in the throes of an election. Interior minister Jacques Chirac—who must have been afraid that in that context Octavio's arrest might be exploited by the opposition led by François Mitterrand—decided to deport him to Belgium without further ado. Legally speaking, it was a reasonable thing to do, as Octavio had still not done anything.

"So the farce was partly due to the elections?"

"Clearly. There are a lot of strange goings-on during elections," added the laughing Octavio. "But what Chirac had failed to consider was that the Belgian authorities refused to have me back. As far as they were concerned, I had already given up my right to asylum by breaching my house arrest and leaving Belgium illegally. They owed me nothing, and certainly had no interest in welcoming me back again.

"Chirac pressed the point and wanted rid of me as quickly as possible. Some hours went by, and before midnight four RG officers showed up, took me from the cells, and bundled me into a car. A further four officers climbed into a second car. I guessed that we were bound for the French-Belgian border. There, in a village the name of which eludes me, they handed me over to the head of the district border police. That would have been at just after two o'clock in the morning. And so, I spent the remainder of the night there, pending the outcome of Chirac's negotiations with the Belgian government.

"On the following morning, impressed by the manpower deployed on getting me there and by Chirac's role in the matter, the head of the border police, who must have taken me to be someone of significance, invited me to breakfast with him at a local restaurant. We ate and waited in vain for Chirac's negotiations. At midnight the order arrived that they were to drop me at a nearby Belgian border post. Chirac's henchmen managed to get the commander at the Belgian border post to turn a blind eye to my crossing into Belgium, without any legal records being made of it. Seemingly, the man in control of the border crossing was in cahoots with the French authorities in respect to other matters of which I knew nothing.

"We crossed the border at daybreak and the French gendarmes dropped me at a border checkpoint where there were two Belgian gendarmes waiting under orders from their superior to let me through. Since no one was quite sure what to do and I had maybe six or seven francs in my pockets, I mentioned to the gendarmes that I had a girlfriend, Marie-Paule Eskénazi in the city of Mons, twenty or thirty kilometers away: she was a television news presenter working at the RTB studios. They were impressed by this and their faces changed as they volunteered to escort me to those 'magical' TV studios. They called their superior who, eager to be rid of me, authorized them to bring me to Mons by jeep. We arrived at the RTB studios and I sought out Marie-Paule while they looked around (there were just some nondescript administrative offices). But Marie-Paul was not at work that day. So, I used the francs I had to call through to my lawyer, Roger Lallemand, who told me to hang on. An hour after that, Belgium not being all that big, he showed up and suggested that I get out of there, pronto. He knew that the Belgian police were under orders to place me under arrest and would charge me with entering the country illegally. Lallemand gave me some cash so that I could find somewhere to lie low. I had ruled out a return to Solières and, rather than going underground in Belgium, had decided to head back to France via the crossing I had always used near Valenciennes."

"You've left me breathless, Octavio. Besides, going back to France strikes me as a masterstroke."

"And it worked out well because neither the French police nor the police in Belgium had been expecting it. Once back in France, I re-established the contacts that had been interrupted by my arrest on April 17. Everything was in position and, though we had changed target, the abduction went ahead. Two weeks after that, in Paris on May 3, we kidnapped the Bank of Bilbao director, Baltasar Suárez."

The abduction of the banker Baltasar Suárez was claimed by the GARI, that is, but the Internationalist Revolutionary Action Groups. They were made up of the remnants of the MIL, from the First of May Group, and from French autonomous anarchist groups like Imprenta 34. One way or another, adopting whichever name they felt like, it was an extension of the spirit of active solidarity that was the river behind the former DI. The international press was thus forced to talk about the executions, repression, and thousands of inmates in Spanish jails. Basically, the GARI abided by the watchword of symbolic violence, because there was no threat to the banker who was held for three weeks. The actions subsequently mounted by the GARI targeted material assets or were surrealistic acts of violence, like the time they guillotined the head of the king of Spain in a museum near Paris. In 2013, Josep Lluis Pons Llobet (his name in the underground was Queso) one of the imprisoned MIL comrades recalled what their thinking was in prison at the time about these operations to help them:

> [The kidnap operation was a source of strength to us] in keeping up our morale and appetite for the fight and made a remarkable contribution to bringing into international disrepute the Spanish government and its institutions that had, two months earlier, executed our comrade Salvador Puig Antich.

The banker was released in the early morning of May 22 in the Jardin de Vincennes in the Ville Lumière, and within a few hours of that, Ariane, the Scotswoman Jean Weir, and Octavio were arrested in the city of Avignon. The arrests continued, with a further six comrades picked up in Toulouse and Paris. They were accused of complicity in the kidnap but, as the actual perpetrators eluded arrest and the place where the banker had been held was not identified, the anarchists were let go on conditional release in dribs and drabs, for lack of evidence. Once again, the arrests were the handiwork of an informer, but they had no proof of any of those arrested having been involved in the operation.

By October, Jean Weir, Ariane, and Octavio were the only ones still in custody: on November 12, Jean was freed and Ariane followed on November 29. Octavio was freed three months later, on February 13, 1975, on conditional release and, yet again, under a house arrest order. Except this time the order applied in Paris and the house was the home of Ariane's mother.

"Impressive, Octavio. You had escaped from your stay in Solières at last. You were now in the same boat as before but in Paris where your comrades and Ariane were."

"In legal terms, my situation was no better but I was in France now, which suited me better. During those first few months I found myself obliged to report on a daily basis to the Police Judiciaire headquarters in the famous Quai des Orfèvres, to sign on. It was there that I bumped into Robert Broussard, the notorious head of the 'anti-gang squad' which arrested us in Avignon, and he frowned every time he set eyes on me.

"And so ended my two stints of clandestine living and I reverted to being a citizen ... pretty much like all the rest. That was in 1975."

A Done Deal

LIKE SNAKES DO, THE fascists ensconced in Spain finished shedding their skin. The final step for this to succeed was inevitable and a matter of biology. One day, the individual who was the symbolic representative of all those fascists departed the scene. It was the death of one of Europe's longest serving dictators; for some obscure reason known only to the victors in the Second World War, he had been left in power for many years, making and unmaking the fate of Spain according to his heartless whim.

"And so that was the end of Franco."

"Indeed. He died in his bed. I found it hard to take. I knew that, after the failure to bring the dictatorship to an end, his biological extinction allowed the dictatorship's official policy and machinery to carry on along the same lines in a democracy, in Franco's absence. It amounted to a natural ideological survival of economic interests and the absence of justice.

"We were looking for a different sort of change. I could see that there was absolutely no way for me to amend what was dubbed 'the Transition' because the opposition, the so-called 'communists' and 'socialists,' were committed to this change-over, which was a done deal. What I felt in the wake of the dictator's death was impotence, albeit mixed with a need to carry on down the road, as Machado would say.

"Months after I was freed on conditional liberty, Franco was still signing execution orders and, in spite of international campaigns, a number of FRAP and ETA militants were executed. There is a photo showing me at the demonstration in Hendaye, where I had traveled by car with a BBC film crew, the very same one as had interviewed me in connection with the Angry Brigade, because I was still officially under house arrest in Paris. I was conscious of the ineffectualness of peaceful protests in averting the crime, but I also appreciated that they needed to be held.

"This was followed by turbulent times with the Caudillo's protracted and tortuous death, which started on October 15. It took him over a month to die. And the final outcome, which not only encouraged celebrations of Franco's death, brought those wearisome days of uncertainty and the macabre spectacle of an old man sliding towards death.

"Which is why I did not see these things as cause for celebration. But at the same time, I found them disheartening and they bolstered my belief that one period of history was drawing to a close and another one beginning. For Spain and for the world, as well as for me. Even so, circumstances played into Franco's hands. The democratic powers were a great help in this, everything went swimmingly and his luck was in. Valery Giscard d'Estaing brazenly backed the transition towards capitalism in Spain."

"And what about the CNT?"

"As you know, there were a lot of comrades keen to resurrect it inside Spain... In my view any such 'reconstruction' was now meaningless. Bear in mind that they wanted to reform it around figures such as Federica Montseny and Peirats," Octavio stated, a certain inflexion creeping into his voice for the first time.

"What did your FIJL comrades do?"

"Some of them—such as Edo and Gurucharri—got caught up in this harebrained effort. It was a disappointment. I realized that going down the structural route would lead to a repetition of the bickering over 'committee' power, as the exiles had experienced."

"So, after the whole odyssey you had started out on with your parents, you, the last of the Alberolas in exile, decided against a return to Spain?"

"I was aware of my situation. If I left for Spain, then, given that I was under a house arrest order, France would declare me a fugitive. Belgium had already declared me illegal and there was no refuge for me there. Nor in Germany. I was not ready to go underground in Europe. Besides, confining myself in Spain was not worth the bother. What would the point be? So that I could struggle with comrades in order to rebuild a CNT that was more dysfunctional than ever? As I said to Edo: 'Do you think you are going to get anywhere with Federica at the head of the CNT?'"

"I still have some doubts, Octavio. You offer a very political reading of Franco's death. I'd like to hear more about your own situation."

"Sure. But what I am telling me cannot be separated from myself. As my father used to say: 'Politics and reality cannot be separated from the individual.' Where there is no politics, there are no individuals. That's right, isn't it?"

"Sure, I am not disputing it. But you were a prisoner, Irene went back to Mexico. And what did Gloria know about you at the time?"

"To appreciate how I felt back then and why I did not raise a toast to the death of the dictator, you have to remember the circumstances in which I found myself in the wake of our arrest on May 22, 1974.

"Franco's death crept up on me while I was out on conditional release after February 1975. When I saw that puppet Arias Navarro and the communiqué reporting that Franco had died, I knew that there were great 'changes' on the way, but that such decisions would not alter the balance of power in Spain. There I was in Paris, my movements very restricted due to my being under house arrest, and I was completely at the mercy of circumstances. I was not working on anything but I was clear about one thing: I was determined to prepare a legal defense against the French state."

"Meaning that you wanted to become legal in France, set causes to one side and get back to being an upright citizen."

"Of course. Franco's demise was not, at that time, any guarantee for the future where we were concerned. It didn't matter that the offense of which we stood accused had been committed in furtherance of the fight against a dictator. And preparations for the trial was a chance to remind public opinion what Francoism was. It was one way of carrying on with the fight."

"Tell me about what happened over the months before, when you were in custody in Paris."

"During the first few months, my basic concern was with turning my arrest into a trial in order to extend the media interest aroused by the kidnapping of the banker. In addition, I tried to exonerate the arrested comrades of any responsibility for the operation. Something in which we were successful and which ensured that they were released pretty quickly.

"But things didn't work out as anticipated, and Irene moved back to Mexico. I also wrote to Gloria, briefing her on my detention in France and how everything was entirely uncertain in terms of what lay ahead. She wrote back offering me the assistance of some relatives of hers who were lawyers, that they might open negotiations with the Mexican authorities with an eye to their granting me a fresh right of asylum once I was a free man again. My reaction to that was that it was out of the question and that she should be focusing more on herself and her own life and not go on sacrificing herself for some impossible dream."

"Which must have been very hard on her. You were telling her that she should forget about you."

"That was the last letter I sent her," Octavio replied after a thoughtful silence. "And no answer came. I never had another letter from her over the months that I was still locked up. Returning to Mexico was not going to happen. It was not what I wanted. But throughout almost all of the time that I was inside, I was torn between optimism and pessimism regarding the prospects of release and the final outcome of the trial to which the French courts would subject us one day or another."

"You were afraid of getting a lengthy prison term, right?"

"Yes, even our own lawyers were pretty pessimistic about the outcome. They knew that in such cases the prosecution asked for twenty year sentences. And even though I didn't think I would get that long, even several years meant losing a big chunk of my life... But at no time did I resign myself to defeat, nor did I stop doing whatever I could in defending our actions. Especially after the examining magistrate told our lawyer that he had read all our letters: mine and Ariane's alike."

"Meaning that you had written to Ariane when she was still in custody or after she was freed and those letters had been intercepted ..."

"Exactly. Which worked in our favor; because from that point on whenever we traded letters jail-to-jail, as well as in the case of any I sent out to outsiders, knowing that the examining magistrate would be reading those letters, I was forever exposing the democrats for their guilt in colluding with the fascist dictatorship in Spain."

"Was Ariane your only contact on the outside?"

"No, during my time in custody I was writing nonstop. I sent letters off to newspaper chief editors with comments on news their media had reported about Spain. This enabled me to strike up a relationship with the editor-in-chief of *Le Monde*, André Fontaine. During my last few months in prison I also corresponded with Claude Bourdet, a very well known and admired journalist and author. He had served in the Resistance against the Nazis and been in concentration camps in Germany."

Octavio's letters from prison were, according to his lawyer Yves Dechezelles, crucial in getting the examining magistrate finally to smile upon his application for provisional release, tabled at the beginning of February 1975. In contrast with Italy or Germany, where the courts took a really hard line on revolutionary movements (one has only to think of the Meinhof trial, or those charged in connection with Potere Operaio or Pinelli's death in police head-quarters in Italy), in France the law was more benevolent or, at the very least, the judge to whom Octavio had been assigned was. Ariane and Octavio were, to some extent, indulged, allowed typewriters and books and documents so that they could carry on inside prison with the writing of the book they were preparing for the Ruedo Ibérico publishing house.

Octavio recalled those days as a time of the utmost tension and stress. Whatever evidence the police and the intelligence services might have pro-duced against them would have justified a maximum sentence from the courts. However, nothing of the sort happened.

Once freed, Octavio was staring at indefinite house arrest and confine-ment in Paris. His most urgent need was for some way of earning a living. Ahead of him, in the near future, he would have to rethink his activism via à vis the nascent democracy in Spain and vis-à-vis the social situation in France. And, in keeping with his inclinations at the time, Octavio carried on with his literary activity, writing for papers such as *Presencia* in France or *Ruta*, the anarchist mouthpiece in Venezuela. In his brand new status as an almost-free citizen, he was in a position to calmly mull over the direction in which society was moving.

"Can you offer us a summary of how you were thinking around 1976?"

"Basically, I was thinking about the irrationality and nonsensicality of capitalist 'comforts' and about the notion that everything had to be left to, say, 'technological progress.'"

"You were a few years ahead of the trend. These days the pitch is that with the right motivation you can do anything, other than fall in love with it," I said.

"*Oui, oui.* The business about technology is nothing new. As a result, in my articles I pondered the need for an overhaul of the critique of capitalism and ideological propositions about emancipation; from the theoretical as well as the practical points of view. My thoughts were that this was a task not merely for those of like mind, but also for 'all those in the Marxist and the an-archist camps alike, who had not resigned themselves to being mere onlookers in history.'"

"And what were you left with after all those years as a clandestine?"

"Well, there weren't all that many years, just the six, I think," Octavio laughed. "And about the same length of time under house arrest, which is not exactly convenient or easy. I don't know what I was left with after it all. Having done what I had, I suppose."

Octavio then fell silent for a time. He had been talking for upwards of two hours, non-stop, about his days in Solières and the whole tough time as a clandestine in Belgium.

NORMAL LIFE

Paris is an Island

OCTAVIO EVENTUALLY SETTLED IN Paris where he remained for the ensuing years without too many geographical relocations, given his status as someone sentenced to house arrest.

We had come in our conversations to the mid-1970s, particularly sensitive years in terms of social unrest, state violence, and the reshuffling of the spheres of influence of the various empires that had emerged victorious from the Second World War. Viewed with the benefit of hindsight, the 1970s produced an enormous number of revolutionary movements—a wide variety of Marxist ones and, to a lesser extent, some anarchist ones—to which, especially in the West, young people looked for a counter to the economic and social plans of the United States and its allies. The upshot of that phenomenon was that capitalism took the countering of dissent very seriously. The aim was not only the physical elimination of rebellion, but also, to eradicate it the way a surgeon cuts out a tumor. To cite just a few examples, there were the thousands who were "disappeared" in Argentina, Uruguay, or Brazil. Or who crushed the Stroessner dictatorship in Paraguay or Banzer's in Bolivia in the early 1970s. The list goes on and on: to many the names mean nothing, just lives lost in time and remembered by only a few. Idealistic young people violently killed, their associates eliminated and above all, with the passing of the years, lives tragically lost as a result of the state's terrorism against dissent.

Looking back, the decision by 1970s' youth to espouse violence as an agent of change seems surprising. Dying for a cause when there is a relatively stable welfare state assured is unthinkable in developed, western twenty-first century countries.

One interesting observation is that for barbarism to proceed in the developed western countries of Europe and the United States there was not the same impunity one saw in the so-called Third World countries. In places like Germany—with violence used against the Easter Berlin Tupamaros or the RAF—or in the United States—with violence against the Black Panthers, for instance, the dirty war mounted in order to round up these dissident radical youths had yet to be clarified. Everything was covered up by the very state that eradicated the problem through deployment of its means of repression.

During those awful years of armed struggle and radicalism and ferocious state backlash, Octavio revamped his life, effected a turnaround in the activism that had been a feature of his life for as long as he could remember and, shrewd as he was, he was a sensitive eyewitness to what was going on the world. His first challenge, during the early months under house arrest, was how to achieve a brand new social status. While he was a clandestine, things were very clear: the enemy was the state. But how can one come to terms with the opponent when you are part of him?

"To an extent, the democratic system allows a degree of radicalism, but, beyond that point, it cracks down angrily on it and makes you an outlaw. I am not talking about actions. It is just that if you become too much of a nuisance they create problems for you. In your case, you had to proceed with caution."

"I knew the risks entailed in the clandestine struggle. By contrast, in that brand new situation, I had to give up coherence and trying to oppose the system to the extent that I was able to. I felt trapped by the system. And as time went by I realized that I was accommodating myself to my surroundings. Which was an odd feeling for me, although hardly new, as I had been though it before in Mexico. It also had its advantages: I could bring legal solidarity to those in need, like the South American exiles."

"And as for Spain, what was the change in your personal circumstances and your previous struggle as part of the FIJL?"

"In 1975 I was wholly convinced that I was watching a turn around in the historical cycle of battles for human emancipation. As the last two remaining fascist dictatorships in Europe to have outlived the defeat of Nazism fell, so the political anachronism that covered up the true nature of the social conflict in class societies also disappeared. As had begun to become evident in Portugal with the end of the Revolution of the Carnations and the consolidation of a bourgeois democracy.

"But it would be a nonsense to deny the emotions aroused by the Revolution of the Carnations and the death of Franco; because, even though in both instances it was obvious what they would leave in their wake, how could one not be moved by actions that, one way or another, ended many decades of dictatorship?"

"The Spanish case and the Portuguese were different."

"Yes. Clearly the fact that Franco could be laid out dead in his dress uniform ended any illusions regarding a Portuguese-style change. How could one delude oneself knowing that the 'transition to democracy' was going to spawn a bourgeois democracy even worse than the Portuguese one?"

"But back to your situation. What did you do next?"

"I had no option but to take it for granted that I was a reasonably normal citizen. Albeit a citizen of the normality the prevailed everywhere, the normality of a capitalist status quo. Besides, my new 'normality' was restrictive: I had to report to the Interior ministry on a weekly basis for the first year and once a month over the ensuing years to secure a 'provisional residence permit.'"

"Yet you were back close to a lot of comrades who were still living there and who had not gone back to Spain."

"Yes. That was a positive but, now that you say it, I remember that 1975 was the year Cipriano Mera died. Which may well have been another reason why I had not gone overboard in celebrating Franco's death. Cipriano passed away a month before the dictator did. I remember what the word was among us at the time. We regretted that Mera had not had a chance to take that satisfaction with him to the grave. I remember a lot of things about his funeral, which drew a large crowd of some five hundred people. We were all very moved by Cipriano's death, having great respect for him.

"In his later years, Cipriano was with Frente Libertario, one of the factions thrown up by the split within the CNT. The last time I saw him was on the premises where they used to meet in the Place Monge. I recall having seen Teresa, his partner. There was a great tenderness between us as if we were all family. But by then Cipriano had dropped out of practically everything due to his poor health. I attended the funeral along with Agustín García Calvo and other members of the *ácrata* 'mob' that used to get together at the La Boule d'Or bar in Paris's Latin Quarter."

"What were those get-togethers at the Boule d'Or like?"

"It all began with a crackdown on the *ácrata* group at Madrid University, years before. Agustín García Calvo was living in exile in Paris and lecturing at Lille University. He encouraged get-togethers at that Latin Quarter bar in the Place Saint-Michel. We used to gather there in the afternoons, once or twice a week, and took part in some very enriching discussions. A lot of people dropped by; Fernando Savater for one, before he turned into what he is today, plus Carames, Víctor Gómez Pin, etc. I had a particularly close connection with Agustín. Our friendship dated back to my days in Belgium. And our friendship extended to Ariane as well. Agustín turned up in my life at an opportune time and, even though he was older than me by two years, circumstances ensured that our paths crossed just when I needed that most, when I was casting around for other ways of rebelling against the system.

"There is an amusing story about Agustín back then. In 1975, I think it was, Brezhnev visited Paris. Just to be on the safe side, the police banished Agustín to Corsica for the duration of the Russian president's visit. It seems that the British police associated him with the Angry Brigade. So Agustín wound up in Corsica, along with other alleged 'terrorists' ... from the far right."

"Those get-togethers at the Boule d'Or must have been mind-boggling!"

"Some time later, when he returned to Madrid, Agustín carried on organizing get-togethers, at the Ateneo. Those too were very famous. Agustín was a big personality. He was a very high-level intellectual, on a par with Chomsky, as a linguist. And he also wrote plays and poetry."

Octavio's living within the law enabled him to get on with his life without dwelling on worries about being arrested, informed on, or kept under surveillance. 1977 saw the passing of the Amnesty Law in Spain, under which the refugees were amnestied. And so, for the very first time, Octavio secured a Spanish passport in his own name. Having a passport was a symbolic thing since there was no way for him to leave France legally. Not until 1981 was Octavio able to make use of the document.

The French state was very clear as to what Octavio and former FIJL militants had been up to in earlier years. So, in 1976, on the eve of King Juan Carlos's first official visit to France, they were placed under "house arrest."

"Now, with hindsight, I think that being under house arrest was a very strange feeling of freedom; a sort of disability, of ongoing mental tension. Not just on account of its being temporary and uncertain in terms of the hearing and its outcome, but in terms also of all the material and family and whatever other issues were posed by the waiting. Decisive circumstances in personal as well as activist terms."

"Even so, I bet the big change in your life was the ending of your 'official' activism on behalf of Spanish anarchism."

"Yes, insofar as I was no longer tied in to direct commitment to a specific struggle. I started taking a more personal, more autonomous, more selective approach to my libertarian activism. Not that it was easy while I had an 'imminent hearing' hanging over my head. Besides, they frequently called me in for questioning on a variety of pretexts or subjected me to house searches and other monitoring methods and that carried on until 1981. All of the factors helped consolidate my cosmopolitan vision of the world and my position in it by means of local activism that added to my interest in what was happening in France at the time."

"By which you mean outside of the Spanish exile context."

"Although I am no nationalist, up until 1974 I felt myself obliged to commit myself wholly to the fight against Francoism. But this was a 'nationalism' imposed by the circumstances and had nothing to do with ideology or conviction. So, once the Spanish people thought that they had won back their 'democratic freedoms; which most of them appeared to have been wanting, I thought it was legitimate to redirect my activism and solidarity along more internationalist lines."

"That's a curious notion, talking about 'nationalism' like that. How is that such an outmoded creation like the nation persists when it's the transnationals that are running everything?"

"Don't forget that nationalism is alive and well in the media, propaganda, and sports. They have even come up with national competitions with anthems being sung. Capitalism still has a use for Nationalism."

"It remains a mighty weapon for which the right lays claim from time to time."

"And not just the right. The so-called 'left' who once upon a time described themselves as 'internationalists' also make a great show their nationalism. I remember visiting Peru one time. The Peruvian Marxist trade unionists sided with Fujimori over some silly squabble that Peru had with Ecuador over a plot of land. And they argued his case! Defense of the homeland and all that nonsense."

"As for internationalism, I imagine you had in mind the fact that, on the other side of the world, half of the Americas were suffering under civil wars and state terrorism."

"Fresh dictatorships as bloodthirsty as (or more than) their European pre-decessors popped up. This was one of the reasons prompting me not to get directly involved in the process of rebuilding the libertarian movement within Spain during the early years of the Transition, even though I had been moni-toring its progress. Helping our comrades, who were fighting the dictatorships in their homelands, was my priority as an activist."

Looking for a Life

"ONE THING WE HAVEN'T touched upon is the everyday routine of your new life within the law. It can't have been that easy finding work after so many years devoted exclusively to activism, right?," I asked.

"Initially, given that neither Ariane nor I found it easy to find steady work, it was hand-to-mouth. We found temporary employment through the good offices of friends and comrades, but those were clandestine jobs because the French authorities refused me the refugee status that would have allowed me to secure a work permit and find legitimate employment. Some of the clandestine work that proved a big help to us was secured through Robert Ariño at the Galeries de France and working for the firm of the haute couture designer Paco Rabanne. We used to mount and issue the invitations for launches and exhibitions."

"I just can't picture you in Paco Rabanne's surroundings."

"Hang on, hang on," Octavio chuckled. "It didn't last that long. The connection was through Robert Ariño. He was the partner of Olga Rabanne, Paco Rabanne's sister. Ariño was a painter and knew Ariane through his ties to a bunch of anarchist painters. Ariño used to feed us invitations from Rabanne just to have us make up the numbers. But the person who really supported us at the time was Ariane's mother, who let us have the apartment where she was living near the Place de la République.

"On another occasion, shortly before he returned to Spain, Agustín García Calvo 'hired' me to redecorate his apartment in the Rue de Bièvre.

"We also redecorated Ariane's mother's new apartment and others belonging to friends and workmates from L'Oréal. In so doing I had help from Silvio and other Italian comrades living in France as refugees. We turned our hands to pretty much everything in order to make ends meet.

"Although, in hindsight, I reckon the stability in our personal lives and affections was also a big help to our fitting in."

"Such as?"

"One peculiarity of the times was how eclectic we were in terms of human relationships. For instance, the ties we formed with some young people of Ariane's acquaintance and whom she had helped during the five months she served in Foris Morangis prison. They sought her out looking for some warmth because, having been in prison, they felt shunned. We formed an affectionate relationship with them and every so often would organize meals or weekend outings to a farmhouse made available to us by a girlfriend of Ariane's mother."

"You were both behind bars at the same time. In fact, it was from prison that you co-wrote *Spanish Anarchism and Revolutionary Action*."

"That's the very period I am talking about. There, Ariane also made the acquaintance of an Irish nun who was a visitor, rather than a guard, and who was very sensitive to the female prisoners' issues. Ariane became friends with several ordinary prisoners jailed for things like theft, fraud, minor offenses, etc.

"There was greater dependency, of an almost family kind, in the relationship with one of these young women, by the name of Catherine, who had given birth to a daughter while in prison. Because following the birth of Virginie, known as Nini, we had to look after her and sort out the problems her mother was making for her. Over the years, our relationship meant that we turned into her 'mentors' and the same applies today. A while later, Ariane wrote a book about her prison experiences. It was at that point that we came into contact with Félix Guattari who was very much caught up in that topic at the time. We also ran occasionally into Michel Foucault who was looking into the prison issue."

"What do you make of the whole theory Foucault came up with regarding power, and his notion of a 'physics of power'?"

"Well, I can tell you that I am pretty much in agreement, though there are a few things in it that strike me as a bit contradictory. Especially where he tried to define power as a relationship. Because power is a relationship and it is everywhere. Power as an institution, the state or the family, is part and parcel of this modus operandi, this relationship."

"Getting back to the family and as you found your feet in your everyday lives, contact with Irene and your kids became more regular."

"In that regard, in late 1978 Irene sent over our son, Octavio, who was having problems with her. Once in Paris, I enrolled him at the Liceo Español and he lived with some friends of ours in the Rue Léon Jouhaux. Shortly after that, my daughter Helie came over as well but she went back to Mexico after a few months, whereas Octavio carried on with his education in Paris.

"Life in Paris went on like that until 1977 when the French Bureau for Refugees and Stateless Persons granted me refugee status, a status I had had ever since I landed in Mexico back in 1939. Thanks to the granting of it and a contract I had for work in a printing shop I was able to secure a French work permit. I was finally able to work legally as a maquette-maker/offset printer for newspapers. I started off with the Impressions J. Debarge firm and finished up with *Le Quotidien du Médecin*, working there up until retirement in late 1996.

"The printing firm lifted us out of financial straits, and as I was working irregular hours I was able to have more time to spare for my solidarity activities with regard to Latin American comrades and activists from French and Spanish groups."

Anarchist Particles

1978 SIMPLY CONFIRMED THE way the world was heading. The dictatorships in the Southern Cone of the Americas embedded themselves, and countries such as Chile, Argentina, Uruguay, and Brazil were plunged into dark years of repression and totalitarianism. The price to be paid for labor and youth activism over the previous years was enormous. To take just one example, the term "disappeared" began to earn acceptance as a worldwide definition of what was by then a mechanical methodology: in the South American case, it was a means of repression and of eliminating views that did not fit with the strategy laid down by the American CIA and the big transnational economic interests. In fact, it's no wonder that experiences such as that of Argentina are categorized by the experts as "genocide."

In Europe things were different. Outside of specific instances of physical elimination of the individual, in the Old World there was no need to reframe states and enforce the policies we have depicted as in place in South America.

Inside the so-called "European left," and, in particular, in the case of Spanish anarchists, finding a niche or scope for activism within the parameters of Spanish democracy was a very complicated challenge. Octavio responded to this process by keeping his distance, trying to ensure a consistency between his thinking and his deeds. In this way, Octavio worked on a review at the time, *El Topo Avizor*—a magazine collating anarchist thinking in a variety of formats (articles, jokes, illustrations, etc.).

El Topo Avizor started back in 1977. The publishers' intention was to participate in the debates stirred up by the contradictions and derelictions of the Spanish "Transition" inside the various strands of revolutionaries, Marxist and anarchist alike, which were questioning that process, either in order to buttress a more "clean break" approach or in order to try to act in a manner consistent with the aspirations for liberation of the end of the Civil War and the forty years of dictatorship that had buried them.

"What was *El Topo Avizor* like?"

"Well, it stated off in a very humble way, with meetings in Paris out of which the earlier issues of the magazine emerged. Later, in its second phase, when it was published in Barcelona, it also set itself more ambitious targets.

"The editorial meetings in Paris were very open and horizontal. No directors, no secretaries. The point was to retain the spontaneity as much as we could. There was a bunch of us in Paris and later contributors from various places, like Stuart Christie in England. From Paris, Campillo was one of the driving forces, together with me and some younger comrades. I was pretty deeply involved in the thing; I found the atmosphere among us and the putting together of the magazine attractive. That's where I first met Fernando Aguirre, with whom I was very friendly."

"What was the affinity factor at *El Topo Avizor*?"

"Well, first and foremost we were a short-lived group as we only managed to bring out five or six issues in Paris and a further two or three in newspaper format in Barcelona. Most of those involved were young, except for Antonio Campillo and me. We were all of one mind in looking upon the 'Transition' as a fraud, a trap. As we saw it, more than a shift from dictatorship to democracy, the real purpose of the 'Transition' was to strip the Spanish working class of any revolutionary notions and set Spain on the road to the 'democratic' capitalism that prevailed in every other country in western Europe. A Europe that was supposedly 'democratic' but which persisted in turning a blind eye to the outrages of the military dictatorships in Chile and Argentina; a Europe indifferent to the communist totalitarians' crackdown on dissent and blind to the persistence of *apartheid* in South Africa or the Israel-Palestine conflict, et cetera."

"Meaning that you were not focused solely on matters Spanish."

"Of course not. Because our view was that the world was still awash with capitalism's grave and unsolvable contradictions, be that capitalism private or state capitalism, and with ruthless power struggles. At the same time, being libertarians, the essential point in those circumstances was to keep clear of the internal strife within the CNT and the MLE, which were just then trying to rebuild in Spain. Later, in 1979, the *El Topo Avizor* team fell apart; some people disappeared, others even got drawn into the 'committee-centered' process of rebuilding the CNT. Camillo himself finished up years later as a pretty well-known 'talking head' on Spanish television."

"The anarchists' role in Spain at that point in history must have been a big influence on all you outsiders."

"It's hard to define. The demise of the *El Topo Avizor* team as well as of the Autonomous Workers' Groups (Grupos Obreros Autónomos/GOA), Solidaridad, the Libertarian Workers' Organization (Organización Libertaria de los Trabajadores/OLT), the Libertarian Communist Movement (Movimiento Comunsita Libertaria/MCL), and many others that had cropped up over Spain bore out my belief that there was an ideological and practical mismatch between the young and the libertarian movement's various historical factions. As a result, building an organization that could accommodate every sort of libertarian sensibility was a very complicated business. There was no way to build a cohesive ideological proposition any more than personal relationships could be accommodated. The convergence between the historical groups looking to the CNT was very fragile."

"Meaning that they could not see eye-to-eye. Why was that?"

"I think that they were, one and all, swimming and marooned in nostalgia; the veterans in nostalgia for July 1936 and the youngsters in a nostalgia for May '68 and its antiauthoritarian bent. As we know, nostalgia binds us to the past and turns us into a historical anachronism. Which was how the hopes raised in many by the mass rallies in San Miguel de los Reyes, in Madrid, or the Montjuich rally and the Jornadas Libertarias Internacionales (International Libertarian Festival) in Barcelona were deflated. The ongoing tension between groups who were looking for a model of the CNT reflective of their own wishes, later sparked an ideological and organizational struggle that made it impossible for different discourses and practices to exist alongside one another, bringing the collective effort and the message being sent out to outsiders to a standstill. The most serious thing, as I see it, was that debate between libertarians became an impossibility."

"Did you in any way point an accusing finger at what you were seeing?"

"There is telling evidence of precisely that in the text I wrote at the time entitled 'Ethics and Revolution (The Dialectical Clash of Our Times),' for *El Topo Avizor*, published in Barcelona by a group of Marxist and anarchist intellectuals. That piece earned me the *El Viejo Topo* Prize that year.

"Further evidence would be a letter written to the editors of *Bicicleta* review and published in its December 1979 edition, in which there was a reference to the 'rumpus in Barcelona' and the wrangling over committee posts and control of the Catalan CNT's newspaper. After expressing my doubts about resolving the crisis by means of a 'straightforward collective *mea culpa*,' I ended by restating my stance 'via vis the expulsions and sackings' when the man in charge had been Luis Andrés Edo: this was proof that 'one can be as sectarian on behalf of pragmatism as one can on purism's behalf. And that one sort of sectarianism is the same as any other and that between the lot of us we are killing it (the CNT).'"

"You just mentioned Luis Andrés Edo. You had been active together and grappled with a range of prickly situations in actions on behalf of the FIJL's First of May Group. As I understand it, there had been a cooling of relations between you over the years, due to differences over the anarchists' role during the 'Transition.'"

"Edo decided to stay in Spain though he spent some time in Perpignan where I ran into him on several occasions, as I also did with Martín Artajo. Inside the CNT, there was a battle for ownership of the Federation. Edo was up to his neck in those struggles. For instance, Edo and Artajo were involved in the approach made to the International Institute for Social History in Amsterdam when a number of CNT personnel went there and reasserted ownership over the historical CNT archives deposited there. I wasn't in agreement with that, given that it was few deciding for the many. The CNT archives are nobody's property. So how can you trot along and demand them in such a bullying, authoritarian manner? It created a wide gulf between us."

"But not wide enough for you to turn into his enemy?"

"Right. Edo was involved in the reconstruction of the CNT right from the outset. That's when the alliances and the squabbling and the power struggles set in. On one side there were the heirs of 'Esgleism,' because Esgleas was dead by then; and on the other, you had the Frente Libertario Faction. They all espoused a very sectarian line. Edo ended up turning into a sectarian himself, something he had fought against for so many years. For instance, he was especially exasperated by the review *Bicicleta* in which some of us were denouncing these frictions. They even orchestrated the burning of copies of the magazine due to their opposition to its contents."

"The way the fascists would once have done."

"Yes. And, sad to say, Edo was involved in some of those actions. There were even instances where they came to blows with other comrades. Very sad. Years later, at the anarchist encounter held in Venice 1984, Edo was still stuck in that position and he was involved in another authoritarian incident. His ideological faction tried to deny a Dutch comrade the right to speak, attempting to deny him the mic when his turn came."

"But you speak of him as someone to be admired. In fact, on reading Edo's autobiography, I was struck by his exposition and clear-sighted opinions.[22] How could he end up with fist fights at meetings or refusing somebody the right to speak at a congress?"

"Well, it didn't end up with fist fights because some of us took a stand against that and separated them," Octavio stated, curtly. "Edo was never involved in physical violence, though he also never made any effort to avert them. For a few years this created a distance between us. But Edo's sectarianism blew up in his face because, years later, he was a victim of his own sectarianism and was expelled from the CNT and ended up in the de-federated CNT which still exists in Barcelona. From that point on, Edo reverted to what he had previously been and resumed his contact with me."

"These sound like schoolboy squabbles."

"Well, yes, that's right," said Octavio, after a pensive silence. "We anarchos have all sorts in our ranks. Every anarcho carried an authoritarian world within him and we are not immune to the human passions everyone shares. Remember that we are born into and live in this world of authority and unsolidarity, features of humanity that are very hard to get under control. I've tried to struggle against it all my life. It strikes me as a nonsense to fight just because you do not agree with somebody."

"As you were explaining earlier, not seeing eye-to-eye implies forcing the other person to think the way you think."

"Not seeing eye-to-eye means not seeing things the same way," Octavio asserted. "It's nonsense to be part of the same struggle and claim that we all have the same overarching preferences. Of course, we are going to think along different lines. But that's it. Besides, in the case of the CNT, the legality of this faction or that ... what is the meaning of all this validity or legality business? Do you know what the most nonsensical thing was? The most telling of those sectarian approaches was that it became impossible to articulate rational options when faced with the sectarianism in the libertarian press and official CNT media. Those of us who were in disagreement could only find an outlet in reviews like *Bicicleta* and *El Viejo Topo*, which were not quite part of the anarchist movement."

Student

ONE POINT OF INTEREST worth highlighting with regard to Octavio's adaptation was his return to education and his need to add to his store of knowledge. Not that Octavio ever lost his innate curiosity but, as he repeats at every opportunity, his curiosity or yearning to study played second fiddle to circumstances.

It wasn't long before opportunity came along. And so, by then almost into his fifties and due to the shutting down of the newspaper on which he was working, Octavio found himself temporarily jobless. He had been working full-time for over a year and, if you found yourself out of work in those circumstances, you had the option of taking a university course. The French state use to pay you a full wage and then, for a full year, 90 percent of that wage if you were to go on to higher education. And so Octavio enrolled at the School for Further Studies in Social Sciences (EHESS) in Paris.

The EHESS was one of the most prestigious colleges in French academia and was meant for people who already held doctorates or had to their credit academic-type work that might justify their pursuing their studies there.

There was a panel to evaluate past achievements and determine whether or not the applicant should be admitted. This was Octavio's case: it was thanks to this latter procedure that he enrolled in the Cinema and History course in 1978, under the supervision of the historian Marc Ferro. Ferro took him on as a student on the basis of reading his book *Spanish Anarchism and Revolutionary Action*, published in Spanish by Ruedo Ibérico publishers and in French by Christian Bourgois publications. Octavio attended seminars given by the thesis supervisors and took part in the "Russian Revolution and Cinema" course delivered by Ferro himself.

"Did you enjoy your time studying?"

"It was really splendid. I used to listen to the seminars, do a bit of research into the topic, and then we would discuss it together. That is how it went for two years, at the end of which I had to submit my final thesis. That made you a graduate of the school and this enabled you to carry on with follow-up studies as a DEA, which is to say, dig deeper into the information you had acquired. I had some very good history teachers there, such as Pierre Nora, Robert Paris, Madeleine Rebérioux, Jacques Julliard, etc."

"What were the circumstances of the Latin American students?"

"A few of them were exiles and, as I remember them, very inflexible in their Marxist-Leninist views. This was displayed in the courses that the historian Robert Paris used to give on fascism. I soon discovered a real affinity with Paris and, over time, we became great friends. I even came to contribute to the *Dictionary of Latin American Revolutionary Militants*, which Paris was overseeing but which, regrettably, he was unable to complete.

"But, before I forget, I had another reason for enrolling at the EHESS: I needed an excuse to ask the French authorities for permission to leave French soil and travel abroad, on the pretext that it was required if I was to progress my thesis. I wanted to consult the CNT archives on deposit at the International Institute for Social History in Amsterdam, since the title of my thesis was *A Comparative Approach to Spanish Trade Unionism through its Revolutionary (CNT) and Reformist (CGT) Currents*. Bear in mind that the CNT's historical archivers were held in Amsterdam."

"I can see that there was a method behind your application but I don't get the underlying motive. Why did you want to leave the country if there was no need for you to do so?"

"Because that pretext, which was nothing of the sort as far as my studies were concerned, was a way of forcing the French authorities into amending my administrative status. It didn't work, but it allowed me to rally support when the French courts made up their minds to put us on trial for GARI activities back in 1974.

"My first attempt to secure leave to travel outside the country was made at the start of spring 1979. They turned me down and so a 'support committee' was set up, circulating through France and Spain a statement signed by French intellectuals, including a number of the lecturers from the EHESS. On that occasion *El Viejo Topo* carried an article of mine with an introduction from its own editorial staff expressing their solidarity: 'Today we are publishing an article from one of the winners of the El Viejo Topo Award last year. Given the 'odd' situation in which our contributor has been for the past several years...'

In that article, entitled 'Anarchism and New Anti-Authoritarian Currents,' I complained of the intolerance that prevailed in ideological debates within the Spanish libertarian movement and came down decidedly in favor of an open, non-authoritarian anarchism that repudiated exclusivism, sectarianism, and dogma. The very fact that it had to be published in *El Viejo Topo* was itself indicative of the extent of the intolerance prevailing in Spanish libertarian media at the time."

"Meaning that you had the feeling that you were wasting your time on pointless debates?"

"Which is why I was focusing more on what I could do in France where I was having this very enriching intellectual experience at the EHESS. It was as if I had a ringside seat in the devising of a scientific thought struggling to break free of academic and ideological restraints."

"Reading your piece in *El Viejo Topo*, I see an exercise in honesty and a proliferation of ideas, plus a ferocious critique of the left. Actually, you find the same sorts of fault in Marxism and anarchism alike. I don't know if there are any other anarchists so starkly self-critical with regard to the bureaucratization, loss of purpose, and drift in the historical western left."

> Anarchism bears an equal part of the responsibility: because while it has not, thus far, managed to spearhead any successful revolution, it is guilty by omission: by having vanished from the social context within which these struggles have taken place.
>
> [...] For a start, because—anarchism not being a political movement, a competitor in the pursuit of Power—not only can it not make political capital out of the revolutionary bankruptcy of the Marxist-Leninist or social democratic parties, and offer itself as a solution-in-waiting, but because socialism's demobilization of the masses accentuates the marginalization of microscopic anarchist coteries and their preaching in the wilderness.

"You took a bit of a risk by closing your article by suggesting alternatives or potential routes to the present as it stood at the time:"

> For that reason, revolution today may well consist of taking full cognizance of the extreme difficulty of changing the world and at the same time

existing, of trying out an autonomous praxis in the bosom of the masses in order to get the latter to overhaul the traditional religious and monkish notions of allegedly revolutionary parties and organizations [...] Let us start by demolishing those parties and every authoritarian organization that look to the revolution or, at the very least let us deny them our contribution.

"Obviously, the critique didn't go down well with a lot of people. But I was pointing out what was happening: those contradictions and the whole lie within anarchism. Or should I have stuck to the notion that just because you describe yourself as an anarchist that that means you are an unblemished soul? What nonsense. Even in my own case, for instance, take the number of things I had done against my will in Belgium. One cannot cling to the lie and feel clean just by describing yourself as an anarchist."

"Your article still holds water today. Elsewhere in the text you mention this blind faith that human beings and the capitalist system share in progress as the instrument that is going to release us from everything. A sort of a religion of progress."

"It wasn't like I had come up with anything new. There had been a lot of talk about that in 1975. How can one put such trust in technology when we have progressed with such effort from cave-dwelling to writing? How could anyone think that we are now in a position to determine what the future will bring? Such nonsense! Because what we don't know is vast and infinite and we lack a lot of clues as to where humanity is heading.

"Remember when I used to go out to the San Ángel lava fields in Mexico, partly for recreation, pondering the universe, gazing at the stars? It is ridiculous to think that you are the center of the universe. What we may be thinking right now is provisional and will be turned upside down later."

"What you're saying brings me back to Alberola the 'engineer.' There must have been great satisfaction in being able to return to that part of your personality, which had been hibernating for so many years. I have in mind the field of abstract thought."

"Sure, but I wasn't working as an engineer any more..." Octavio retorted with a laugh. "And don't forget those were almost normal times. I was affected by the precarious circumstances in which I was living, the threat of a kidnap trial hanging over me, and many years in prison should it go against me. I wasn't sure whether I was going to stay in France, go back to a clandestine existence, etc. When I was denied leave to go to Amsterdam, I took it badly. Besides, the unemployment pay didn't last for long. I was lucky in that a female comrade found me work at *Le Quotidien du médecin*."

"And did that get in the way of your studies?"

"No. The interesting thing was that my work at the print shop had no set hours and left me quite a bit of time to move ahead with my studies and the seminars at the EHESS or to keep up with my efforts to help out Latin American comrades who, by that point, were having to grapple with the state terrorism of Operation Condor in Chile, Argentina, Bolivia, Paraguay, Brazil, and Uruguay.

"In 1980 I graduated with my diploma in History and Cinema from the EHESS. One had to have it in order to progress to further study and also because the lecturers and my fellow students were insistent upon it. Among my colleagues I especially remember Nicole Canto who was working on a thesis on the 'Mujeres Libres' (Free Women) organization during the Spanish Civil War, and Geneviève Dreyfus who was working on another one on the Spanish exile press.

"I often bumped into them both in the course of my historical research in libraries and archives and so on. I hung out with Nicole in Parisian feminist circles and dropped in on some communal living arrangements in the years after May '68.

South America in Flames

DURING THE 1970S, ESPECIALLY toward the end of the decade, Octavio was very enmeshed with those driven out of their homelands by the Latin America dictatorships.

Anarchist solidarity where South America was concerned is very little known. The usual assumption is that, since the South American opposition movements were of the Marxist persuasion, solidarity was forthcoming only from other Marxist groups. But let's not forget that in many Latin American countries the labor movement began at the start of the twentieth century and was marked by anarchist trade unions. The FORA in Argentina, for instance.[23] That changed, and over the years Marxism gained the upper hand. But there were still anarchist remnants in those countries. Like in Bolivia where the powerful miners' union was, at first glance, Marxist, but had retained a lot of the distinguishing features of anarchism. Out of which the bridges to Europe grew.

"Could you say something about the efforts to try to get Gatti, the Uruguayan anarchist, out of Argentina?"

"Still fresh in my memory are the many overtures that Ariane and I made between 1976 and 1978 to boost, here in France the worldwide campaign launched by the family and comrades of Gerardo Gatti Antuña. Unfortunately, these days he is just one of the many 'disappeared.'"

"I remember, right at the start of our activity, one of those involved was Liber Forti who had been forced out of Bolivia following the Banzer coup and had fled to Chile and then later to Argentina. There, his situation turned even more dangerous with the election of María Estela Martínez de Perón, aka Isabelita, and the entry onto the repressive scene of the formidable para-police apparatus the Argentinean Anti-Communist Alliance (Alianza Anticomunista Argentina), or Triple A. Towards the end of 1975, Liber had a chance encounter with Geni Fuentes, a Chilean-Spanish comrade who was on a trip to

France from Argentina, and was able to get a message to me. Liber wanted to
reach Régis Debray, through his partner Elisabeth Burgos. Liber wanted public acknowledgment from Régis Debray in order to help libertarians, wanted
in the Southern Cone, to seek asylum in France.

"Shortly after that I got to see Elisabeth. This must have been five or six
months after Videla's coup in Argentina. Unfortunately, a month or two later,
I met up with Elisabeth again to let her know that Gerardo Gatti was now
among the missing."

"Were there other solidarity efforts?"

"From that point on, Ariane and I were in frequent contact with Elisabeth who put us in touch with Simone Signoret to raise support for the international campaign, being mounted by Gatti's family and comrades to lobby
for some clarity as to his fate. The link with Simone Signoret lasted for many
months and I seem to recall that, in late 1977 or early 1978, I went to her home
with Mauricio, Gerardo Gatti's brother, and family members of other disappeared persons."

"Simone Signoret was one of the media figures most involved with what
was happening in South America. What was your impression of her?"

"Well, at the time I met her, she had split from Yves Montand. She was
living on her own in an apartment in the Latin Quarter, across from the Palace
of Justice. Unfortunately, she was an alcoholic and, every time we visited her
home, she was clutching her bottle of whiskey. It was a very difficult time in
her life and she was on a downward spiral. She was no longer who she had
once been and was just back from a trip to Russia, which I think was a disappointment to her. She was a straightforward woman, full of solidarity and
very respectful of us. As well, I think our former struggles against Franco
commanded quite a bit of respect from her. She was caring and unassuming,
but she lacked the physical and mental capabilities that she had definitely
possessed in previous years. Simone signed support documents and put us in
touch with people she knew."

"Did Régis Debray help you out?"

"Régis Debray had been freed two or three years earlier, having been arrested in Bolivia for his connection with Che Guevara and the guerrillas. Liber
and Régis had met each other in Cochabamba. When I broached Liber's situation with Régis, he said he could get his hands on an official document that
would get Liber out of Argentina legally. He got hold of an invitation to the

International Theatre Festival in Nancy, thanks to Jack Lang, its then director. That invitation allowed Liber to travel to France with his partner, Ana. The cost of the trip was covered by Ariane and me, and by Régis, who had just won the Femina Prize 1977 for his novel *The Burning Snow*."

At Octavio's mention of Liber Forti, I couldn't help but remember how the man first appeared in my life. I never met him in person, but when I was working on my graphic novel about Simón Radowitzky, Octavio happened to mention in a letter that Liber had known Radowitzky in Mexico City. He gave me his address and I wrote to him. Three or four days later, Liber replied.

All I have to say to you today, given the time commitments I currently have, as both Octavio and Ariane will have also told you, and as I am a couple of months short of my ninety-fifth year and, given the life that it has fallen to me to live, there are lots of such commitments [so] I have a few jobs in front of me that need completion, given the heaps of documents, correspondence, archives, etc., that I have, requiring classification with all of the existing paperwork around. Would you be able to hang on for a few days? That way, as I can spare some bits of time for remembering, I can set out for you whatever data memory allows me to convey to you, the things I lived through with comrade Simón.

Ninety-five years old, Liber was putting into order the papers he had amassed over his life as an activist and, in an extraordinary feat of memory, forwarded me a text containing what he could recall of Radowitzky back in 1956.

In what few dealings I had with him by mail, Liber displayed the personality of a live wire, committed to his life's two great passions: one of these universal, which is to say, humanity and justice; the other personal, which was theater as a medium for spreading education and justice.

"You're always talking about Liber Forti. I understand you were quite good friends."

"When it came to solidarity Liber was a pragmatist. I first met him in Mexico but have no great memory of him there. Our relationship started when we met up again in France. Liber was a born internationalist. We met, although I cannot be certain about this, through Eduardo Colombo or Jorge Periés, two anarchist Argentinean doctors living in France. He was someone I trusted implicitly up until he died a year ago. Ariane and I were fast friends with Ana, his partner. Between the four of us, we made up a great unit, with empathy and affection galore."

The relationship between Liber and Octavio in France continued, especially with regard to solidarity with Bolivian victims of reprisals, until Liber and his partner were able to return to Bolivia following the coup d'état mounted by Alberto Natusch Busch on November 1, 1979. That coup was then snuffed out by a popular uprising led by the COB (Central Obrera Boliviana/Bolivian Labor Center), which forced the coup makers to hand power back to Congress, which then appointed Lidia Gueiler president—the first woman president in Bolivian history. Her civilian presidency lasted less than a year because, in July 1980, came Luis García Meza's bloody coup. This latest coup forced Octavio and Ariane to start contacting aid connections in France again. On that occasion, there was crucial assistance received from the CFDT, especially from Pepe Justiniano, one of the leaders of the Bolivian Labor Center (COB).[24] Thanks to their efforts, the French government was prompted to grant right of asylum to four members of the COB who had been arrested in Bolivia, among them Liber, who turned up at Orly-Sud airport before the year was over with Juan Lechín, Noel Vásquez, and Simón Reyes in tow. There was a quaint aside when a delegation from the CGT showed up to ferry Simón Reyes away, he being the only communist among the four of them. Through Liber Forti, Octavio established quite close connections with the COB and especially with Juan Lechín, its most important representative at the time. Liber was cultural advisor to the COB and organized miners' radio stations.

Inside the COB, there was a small group described as the "independents group" and it had definite libertarian leanings. Lechín, whose background was Marxist—but not orthodox Marxism—relied on its support in counteracting the orthodox faction. Lechín served as Bolivian vice president in 1952 in the Víctor Paz Estenssoro government.

"What was Juan Lechín like, Octavio?"

"I became very close to him and his children during their exile in France. Later, on the odd trip to Bolivia, I visited his home with Ariane. I had very close dealings with him, almost on a par with Liber. Lechín was still obsessed about becoming Bolivia's president, which he never did. We never had any political ties, just solidarity: we used to cook together and were like one big family, which is the essential relationship and the one that matters, despite all our bickering about ideology and social struggle."

The Trial

OCTAVIO'S ROUTINE EXISTENCE TOOK an unexpected turn in 1981. The French state finally made up its mind to try him alongside the eleven people indicted in connection with the kidnapping of the Banco de Bilbao director some seven years earlier. The approaching trial required the considered preparation of a defense, individual as well as collective. This was no easy undertaking because some of the accused were in fear of very heavy sentences and therefore could not see beyond the judicial aspect of the case and disregarded the political aspect to it. Furthermore, some of the lawyers were out for their own financial benefit alone, in contrast to the strategy of the other lawyers who declined payment for ideological reasons. Such was the case of Yves Dechezelles, Octavio's counsel, who had no hesitation in adopting a political approach to the trial. This created some misgivings and some friction among the eleven accused—and their respective counsels. Some of the accused even considered the possibility of going on the run, leaving the country, in order to wriggle out of the trial. Several meetings were therefore held to hash out a consensus on strategy, and this was reached at a general meeting with members of the support committee, the lawyers, the accused, family, and friends. That meeting was held at a large premises, and turned into a public rally, with upwards of three hundred people in attendance. There, it was determined that the accused would all show up for trial, would deny direct involvement in the kidnapping, and, at the same time, would express their political solidarity with those who had mounted the action against the Francoist banker.

The proceedings began on March 19 and lasted until March 31. It attracted a lot of media attention, which was only reasonable, since—six years after Franco's death—there was something anachronistic about holding in France a trial regarding anti-Francoist activities back in 1974. But also because no one knew what the Criminal Court's determination would be. In the end, the jury decided to acquit, on every count, the eleven accused.

"From what you were saying earlier, you had made reasonable preparations for the case and had a lot of influential people on your side."

"Sure. Hence the significance of my having been able to rely in the trial
upon the support of the EHESS lecturers and other French intellectuals of renown. My defense was that the act had been political and that there was much
more to be gained by it than to be lost. On the night before the trial, we had
to sleep in jail and attend the proceedings in handcuffs. This made the trial—
meaningless after all those years had gone by—that much more ridiculous.
Nevertheless, on the opening day of the trial, our lawyer tabled a request asking for the police handling of us to be ended, even though it was in accordance
with regulations. The judge agreed to this, in view of the accused being of little
danger and, luckily, the handcuffs were removed immediately."

"And how did the trial fare?"

"Since they hadn't found a single thing at the time—not the location
where the abductee was held, nor any weapons used nor anything else that
might have incriminated us—they had a really hard time proving our guilt. I
was accused of having orchestrated the whole thing, of being the mastermind.
I accused the French state of conniving with the previous fascist Spanish government in arresting and charging me. There was evidence that the French
police worked hand in hand with the erstwhile Spanish BPS and allowed the
man who was their 'plant' in our ranks, Inocencio Martínez, to slip away. Ever
since we were arrested his whereabouts had been unknown. Our counsel was
able to show this because there was a telegram included in the prosecution file
showing the French police's connivance with the 'evaporation' of Inocencio
Martínez."

In the January 10, 1981 edition of *El País*, one journalist wrote:

It looks as if Michel Poniatowski (the French minister of the Interior in
1974, the year of the abduction) summoned Spain's ambassador José María
de Lojendio to show him a photograph in which someone could be seen
picking up the three million franc ransom. De Lojendio stated that he was
unable to identify the individual in the photograph, and Poniatowski then
produced the corresponding identification file: it belonged to a Spanish
police officer and, naturally, no one had been able to show whether he was
the one who handed Alberola the three million and set up the kidnapping.

The article then went on to conclude that, at the time of the trial, there was some friction between France and Spain and this had impacted the verdict. That had to do with there being OAS personnel in Spain out to kill De Gaulle for having recently awarded Algeria its independence. France complained that the Spaniards had failed to extradite the OAS terrorists and had allowed them to operate freely on Spanish soil.

"What support did you have for your case?"

"Well, to explain that I must first tell you a story about Régis Debray. He asked me to draft a text for intellectuals to add their signatures to. I did so and brought it to his home for him to sign, so that he could see that it had been written for him. That was shortly before the elections in which Mitterrand stood, with Régis's backing. Actually, Regis subsequently became the Mitterrand government's advisor on Latin America. Régis endorsed the manifesto and, with his name on the document, celebrities such as Michel Foucault, Félix Guattari, Max Gallo, and Yves Montand supported us in the trial. Régis carried a lot of weight in French intellectual circles at the time.

"The Catalan anti-Francoist priest Lluis Maria Xirinacs also showed up at the trial, having come down from Brussels for that very purpose to act as a 'character' witness for the accused. Our lawyer thought it might be interesting to have him testify on my behalf as an anti-Franco fighter."

"Xirinacs is an interesting case from the Christian anti-Francoist resistance. To this day he is greatly respected in many different quarters in Catalonia."

"He is an odd bird, this Xirinacs. When he spoke at the trial he mentioned that he had met me some time back as part of the anti-Francoist cause, which was false, as this was the very first time I had set eyes on him. Later we were all having a coffee with our counsel, and Xirinacs explained the lie away in terms of, I cannot quite recall, some rhetorical ploy that he had been using in his remarks. Being a priest, it was very important to him that he not lie. He had some very sound Christian principles. Small wonder that he is respected far beyond his political beliefs. But I never did find out why he had come or who had invited him to testify."

"Your lawyers performed very well."

"Oh, yes. Our lawyers' strategy was very important. We were advised by Yves Dechezelles, Thierry Lévy, and Henri Leclerc, who were famous because of their defense of wanted men who had campaigned for decolonization in

Algeria and elsewhere in former French Africa. We should also highlight the role played by Liber Forti's statements to the court, confirming the internationalist character of our solidarity actions. It was thanks to this mobilization and the trial itself being such an anachronism by then, that the jury acquitted us. It ended my 'house arrest' and my semi-clandestine movements around the country.

"There is no question that the verdict was swayed by the dealings we had been having with movements exposing and opposing French repressive agencies at the time. Especially with the Félix Guattari-led campaign against prisons and psychiatric centers."

"Which resulted in Ariane's book."

"Her book mirrors her experiences as an inmate in 1974. *Prisons de femmes* (Women's Prisons) was written in partnership with prison visitor Natacha Duché and had a foreword by Claude Mauricac.[25] I remember that shortly afterwards Ariane and Natacha were interviewed by Bernard Pivot, the celebrated presenter of the book review TV show *Apostrophes*."

"And how did Irene react to the news of the trial?"

"I can't quite remember if it was then or after the trial that Irene showed up to visit us."

"So now you were able to find work and were free to leave the country."

"In that respect, François Mitterrand's election victory that May was the tipping-point. Shortly after that, and after he took up the presidency, I secured the repeal of the 1968 order expelling me from France. That was thanks to the intervention of Régis Debray, who by then was Mitterrand's advisor on Latin American matters. From that point on I was at last free to leave France legally."

"Meaning that you could, say, have gone to Spain. After all those years of struggle against the dictatorship, you were able to enter the country lawfully for the first time since 1939."

"That's the truth. But that wasn't my priority. Being able to leave France meant that we were better placed to launch our scheme to safeguard the archives of Latin America social movements. A lot of them had gone missing or been destroyed by the military in the course of their coups. We had launched the scheme in response to a request received from Juan Lechín and Víctor López, on the advice of Liber Forti, during our time in exile in France."

"Plus, Spain was in some regards not yet fully democratic. Crossing the border might not have been all that safe.

"In that respect, a month before the trial concluded, there had been an attempted coup d'état mounted in Spain on February 23 (referred to as 23F), spearheaded by Tejero. Shortly before that, Ramón Chao (Manu Chao's father), a journalist with RFI and correspondent for the Spanish weekly *Triunfo*, had conducted an interview with me and, in answer to one of his questions, I had stated 'that I could not go to Spain as I had a trial still pending in France; but then again, I didn't think that the political situation was all that stable.'"

"Had you got wind of something, or was that just intuition?"

"I can't remember. Shortly after 23F, Chao asked me if I had known that the coup was being hatched. Like you, he had been taken aback by the premonition."

The "Normality" of the Normal Guys

Like a skipping brook

I want you free
As a brook
Skipping from rock to rock.
But not my own.
I want you great
Like a hilltop
With the promise of spring,
But not my own.
I want you fine
Like bread unaware
Of its doughy goodness.
But not my own.
I want you tall
Like a poplar
Stretching into the sky.
But not my own.
I want you white
Like orange-blossom
On the ground.
But not my own.
But not my own
Nor God's nor anyone else's
Nor even your own.

AGUSTÍN GARCÍA CALVO

ON MORE THAN ONE occasion Octavio had remarked that the Agustín García Calvo poem above largely mirrored his own approach to life. But he was referring, not to the simple things cited therein, such as ownership of something and a self-conscious non-ownership. Nor even those closing, unmistakably anarchist lines reminiscent of the "Neither God Nor Master" watchword of the Paris Communards. No, what the poem conveys and what it reflects of Octavio's life is the tenacity, the striving to cling to such principles, the need and the staunch belief that one has to stay alert and be deliberate in one's actions. Which is what the "labor" of not being authoritarian is all about.

The García Calvo poem dates from 1976 and reflects Octavio's stance after acquiring a brand-new status, in terms of his civic life. Now, he was just one among his peers. That simple notion was not so straightforward to his way of thinking, in that implicit in it was the embracing of a way of life and, in a sea of contradictions, acting in a manner congruent with what you aspire to be.

The poem is relevant because, at the time it was written, Octavio and Agustín were very close friends. It was an unrepeatable time of affection and intellectual intercourse between them and this extended to the "family," that is, to Ariane and Isabel too. "*I want you free*," Octavio said, "encapsulates a lot of things that are as much mine as Agustín's," but he did not offer any further explanation.

Beyond Octavio's approach to life, we come now to the 1980s which closed out the twentieth century, economically and ideologically. The Soviet Union fell apart, opening up space for a new world in which the huge victory of neoliberalism, which has endured into our own day was in the making. Back in the day, there was the pompous championing of Francis Fukuyama, that great liberal paladin, by Ronald Reagan and Margaret Thatcher. They promoted the political scientist's notions; he provided justification for their policies by telling us all that we (the whole of humankind) were witnessing the "end of history," as if he was some sort of a philosophical giant. And so they steered their neoliberal policies in the direction of globalization.

"Octavio, why have we fallen into the neoliberal trap?"

"Well, there is something that always gets forgotten when it comes to defining the great change that arrived in the 1980s. I am talking about the experience of actual socialism implicit in the Soviet Union, which by then was what is today—Russia—and which proved to be nothing more or less than just another capitalist country like all the rest. The anticapitalist failure of real socialism, meaning the alleged implementation of socialism in practice, proved a failure since such 'socialism' turned out to be nothing short of state capitalism. This paved the way for the success of neoliberalism. Real socialism held out the prospect of progress, but not of freedom for the individual. It turned out to be a lot worse than capitalism, in terms of the prospect of progress, or at any rate apparently so. Capitalism was more practical and, in addition, it held out the prospect of freedom offered by democracy. Capitalism is unfair and noxious, it is stained with blood and represents an ecological threat, but with its pragmatic approach, it rode roughshod over the experiment in actual socialism, which was itself yet another bloodstained caricature of capitalism. Thus, from the 1980s onwards, capitalism was everything. In the media, there were only two opportunities for criticism: targeting capitalism, if you were against it, or targeting actual socialism, which was pretty much the same thing. That is all there was and there was no room for any other sort of critique. And the media steer public opinion.

"The issue of power which left such a deep impression on us in the 1980s and is still as cogent as ever came later. To the extent that you agree to wield power and find yourself being challenged, you will resort to violence, repression, or censorship in order to cling to that same power. This is what is going on in the new, current model of democracy we are witnessing in Turkey, Venezuela, or in China."

"Let's talk about 'normality.' With your brand-new status under the law, you had become 'a regular guy,' by which I mean, pretty much like everybody else. Which is something that had been of great concern for you for quite some time. What is a 'regular' citizen, as you see it?"

"A regular citizen is one who enjoys a freedom that is, in every sense, monitored and he is unaware of this because he has the feeling that he is free. It was a complicated business, my adapting to that status. It was different before, because, being clandestine or under house arrest, I felt like an outsider, even though I was in many regards living and behaving like everyone else. The situation of outlawry was the 'excuse' for being obliged to accept normal things. Clearly, by stepping inside the law and being just one of the guys, I had no excuse left. And it was then that I became sensible to and more consciously lived out the contradiction of agreeing to be 'a regular guy.'"

"I am struck by the importance you give to being law abiding, meaning finding yourself obliged to accept the rules laid down by the state."

"It's hard to understand, right?," Octavio replied. "To the extent that you embrace legality, everything else falls into place. You set boundaries for yourself. I had to agree to live within the law and see how far I could go in overcoming the contradiction in that."

"How did you describe yourself at that time?"

"How did I describe myself?," Octavio paused to reflect. "I don't think I have ever defined myself. I cannot claim that what I think is what is actually construed, or whether it needs interpreting. I'd say that it matters more to me that I am heard and people decide for themselves."

"I see a contradiction between what you are saying and your efforts to be spontaneous, which you undoubtedly were."

"No. I see no contradiction," Octavio blithely answered. "Because, as analyzed, to a materialist determinist who thinks he is one, like me, spontaneism does not have a lot of meaning. There is no such thing as a spontaneous act. But, spontaneity does have a meaning against the backdrop of society. Because it is what we term 'trial and error', meaning, not sticking at all times to some set line in what you do and trying to sample different experiences. In Mexico, I was responding to circumstances rather than according to some predetermined program. We have to be 'flexible' spontaneists. But in my own opinion, being spontaneous should not be a modus operandi or some unbending, singular modus vivendi. As I see it, spontaneity is all about steering clear of dogma."

"That is what I can see during the period we are speaking of: In the 1980s and 1990s you had absolute freedom to choose what to do and with whom."

"Naturally, the circumstances made that possible," Octavio said, warming to the thought. "But, as I mentioned to you, while living under the radar, I shied away from a heap of personal pursuits. I was obliged to pose as something that I was not. I even changed the way I talked, for safety reasons. Being a 'regular guy', I could do everything that had previously been off-limits to me, such as making the acquaintances of lots of people that I, as an outlaw, would never have been able to rub shoulders with. Prior to the trial, as well as after, I regarded being legal as crucial. Because circumstances are decisive, albeit that the genes are too, of course. But one's persona is a cultural construct and, in a way, an auto-construct. And the essential point about the 'construction' of the persona is the links you establish with other people or contexts; links that allow us to be, and through which the individual can access a conscious

existence. And since those links can only be established by means of relationships, these were and are very important to me.

"It wasn't that my brand-new 'legality' had made any radical alteration to
my behavior in political or affectionate terms, but I was striving to be more authentic, more consistent with my way of thinking and being. Not that I think
there was a before and an after attached to this 'change,' but, relieved now
from the psychological and moral pressures of the duty or 'excuse' of fighting
Francoism, action and my dealings with others were embedded in new, different and 'freer' conditions that allowed me to be or to strive to become the free
man I wanted to be."

"So, what did that 'change' consist of?," I probed, not quite grasping
where Octavio was going with this.

"Well, what changed was that I had more time and resources at my dis-
posal in order to arrive at conclusions, after subjecting myself to the test of
'experience,' to experiences married to reflection and their impact upon the
human being, individually and collectively. Experiences primarily of involvement in or intercourse with particular ideological factions and specific practices, confined to a single location. Experiences that had this in common, an
aspiration to a more ecological, more solidary planetary community."

"All of these novel experiences had already begun when you returned
to education. I think Paris was an ideal location for you, because there were
always people passing through, intellectuals, debates, and solidarity activity.
How many years did you live in Paris?"

"Taken together with the almost seven years spent under 'house arrest,' it
must be over thirty years."

With his newly granted lawful status as a "free man," Octavio started out
on his new life, with a passport made out in his own name, traveling wherever
he felt like. Activism, research, opinion ... He drifted through a lot of places
over those years. His circle of comrades and friends widened as old and new
personal relationships from a wide variety of origins flowed into one another.
After many years of mixed fortunes and living on the edge, his finances were
stabilized thanks to a job with *Le Quotidien du Médecin* where, working half
days or on and off, Octavio worked right up until he retired in 1996 at the age
of sixty seven.

"Though you were still living in France, I sometimes think you were
more of a South American than ever. I don't mean in terms of any sense of

national belonging but given where you felt most comfortable in terms of your experiences."

"Liber Forti was make-or-break here. Liber and the city of Paris brought me back to Latin America. But I never looked upon it as an obligation. People from there always aroused my curiosity, solidarity, and sympathy. In late 1981 we mounted the First Latin American Libertarians' Get-Together in Paris, involving Chilean, Bolivian, Argentinean, and Uruguayan comrades living in exile in France and elsewhere in Europe. Then, in 1982, I went with the comrades from the Bolivian COB to a solidarity rally organized by the French trade union confederation, the CFDT. In reality, the rally had to do with supporting the strikes in Poland. Lech Walesa took part in it, having traveled from Poland for that express purpose. Also there was Genaro Flores from the Bolivian Peasants' Central. I acted as interpreter when they introduced him to Walesa. Genaro was granted asylum in France where he was able to receive medical treatment at the Garges Hospital, as his legs were paralyzed by a bullet that had pierced his spinal column in the course of the military's raid on the COB headquarters in La Paz, right at the start of the García Meza coup in 1980."

"Lech Walesa was the Great White Hope for Polish freedom, or the western media marketed him as such. The Polish Pope, Wojtyla, has something to do with that."

"Remember that he was just launching his struggle when he took part in the rally. Walesa was a dissident in terms of really existing socialism, he championed the workers and had not yet turned into the Walesa he later became, an alcoholic Christian."

"According to the CIA, they were funding him."

"Yes, and, again according to the CIA the Chinese were funding the First of May Group. What they say has to be taken with a grain of salt. Look at the coincidence: even as the repression in Latin America was ferocious, it was the same in Poland, and both of these facts came together in Paris in one solidarity rally. And there was I, taking part! I only ever saw Walesa at the rally. I remember there was an exchange of gifts with Genaro Flores and that the Bolivians presented him with a very fine vicuña hair scarf. Somewhere, I have some snaps of that 'moment in history.'

"Back then, the South American element was everywhere. I can remember the broadcasts on 'Tribuna Latioamericana,' a show on the Paris-based Radio Libertaire in which we interviewed those involved in South American social struggles who happened to be passing through Paris. That is where we ran into the Chilean Néstor Vega and screenwriter Lise Bouzidi. Such connections afforded us access to Domitila Barrios de Chungara and Rigoberta Menchú."

"Both of those women very prominent in the history of the Indigenous peoples and social struggles."

"I struck up a friendship with Bolivian-born Domitila. We had quite a few dealings with her as she was in exile in Sweden, which is where we met her. Later on, some people held her accountable for having lined her pockets through her activism, but I'm not too clear about that. Domitila was unaffected and had little in the way of education, but she was a free spirit and very much up for a fight. She was a reference-point in Bolivian miners' struggles. There was more of a question over Menchú, however, as champion of the Indigenous peoples, given her own Mayan origins. When I met her through Elizabeth Burgos, Rigoberta was co-writing her book *Me llamo Rigoberta Menchú y así me nació la conciencia* (*My Name is Rigoberta Menchú, and This is How My Conscience Was Born*)[26] with Elizabeth. In fact, Elizabeth wrote the book, basing it on Menchú's life story. Over the years and after winning the Nobel Prize, Rigoberta turned into a sort of a transnational trading in the demands of the Mayas of Guatemala."

There was one essential thing that left its mark on Octavio back then. Both he and Ariane had developed an interest in preserving the original archives of the right and long-standing labor struggles of the various countries of South America. Yet again, the idea originated with Liber Forti and the trade unionists Juan Lechín and Víctor López.

In Bolivia, as well as in Peru, Argentina, and elsewhere, the labor struggles of the twentieth century had left in their wake trade union, anarchist, and other archives that needed to be preserved. Because of the precarious situation in those countries, the testimonies of workers were being destroyed every time a coup d'état came along.

Octavio and Ariane worked on the complicated task of putting workers' bodies in touch with interested French foundations and/or archival collections possessed of finance and technical expertise. Also involved alongside them was the French sociologist Yvon Le Bot, and the upshot of their endeavors was the foundation in France of the Center For Preservation of Popular Memory in Latin America (CESAME). The first order of business was to rescue and microfilm the originals of the Argentinean anarchist newspaper *La Protesta*, covering the years 1922–1930. The idea arose because, at the university that he was attending, Octavio had met Argentinean Edgardo Bilsky, who had links with the Bibliothèque de Documentation Internationale Contemporaine (BDIC/Library of Contemporary International Documentation). Together with Bilsky and Eduardo Colombo, they reestablished contacts inside Argentina. However, Octavio acknowledges that, in salvaging the newspapers, Geneviève Dreyfus, whom he had known since the EHESS, was crucial. She was head of the Iberian and Latin American Department at the BDIC. Interest in these archival endeavors grew, and other bodies showed an interest in cooperating with and extending the scheme by retrieving and preserving original documentation from Bolivia, Peru, etc. Retrieving the archives was a complicated business. In the case of Argentina, given that the BDIC is a state body, no travel was required and a diplomatic bag brought over the newspapers. But Bolivia was a different beast. The archives of the miners' unions that had been destroyed in the wake of the García Meza coup d'état had to be gleaned and tracked down to the mines or in their places of origin.

"Did you ever travel to Bolivia, Octavio?"

"I made one trip there at the outset so as to organize everything, but Ariane was the one who handled the field work. She traveled all over the place in search of materials. I stayed behind in Paris to help Geneviève Dreyfus coordinate the delivery of materials and handled administration at the CESAME. The advantage we had was that, being independents, the various political factions within the unions raised no objection to handing over materials. Ariane made lots of trips to Bolivia at the rate of almost one a year up until 2000. I was in no position to quit work at the paper, since we were dependent on it for our survival. The last material she brought over was an unbelievable archive, a whole trunkful, containing the names of all the military and paramilitaries involved in Plan Condor in Bolivia: files complete with photos of every single one of them! A complete fluke of a find, obtained through a lawyer who had stumbled upon them during the short-lived presidency of Lidia Gueiler. They had been held at the Interior Ministry, and the serving minister had pinched them and they were later passed on to the lawyer. Documents too dangerous for one person to hold onto and they can now be found at the BDIC. Ariane did formidable field work.

"Little by little the efforts made were bringing in more and more materials and growing international interest. Thus, bodies such as the International

Institute for Social History in Amsterdam, the Feltrinelli Foundation in Milan, and the Spanish Ministry of Culture's Centre for Archival Documentary Information got involved and signed cooperative protocols. Thanks to this, there is a significant archive from the Bolivian COB and MNR (Movimiento Nacionalista Revolucionario/Revolutionary Nationalist Movement) at those institutions and in Bolivia itself. Everything was microfilmed and the originals returned with an additional copy."

One benefit of the project was that, through Liber Forti, Octavio and Ariane, the Bolivian Miners' Federation came into contact with the Ateliers Varan in Paris.²⁷ The idea was to train young miners in the production and shooting of documentary films on life in the mining areas. There was very close cooperation in Bolivia as well as in Paris, especially with the director at Ateliers Varan, Jacques d'Arthuys.

"There's something else I think we should talk about," I said, changing the subject. "The schedule of antiauthoritarian events that you organized in Paris. Something directly traceable to the May '68 experience."

"Since May '68 there had been a sort of ebb tide away from what happened then, albeit that the people who had taken part in the events fell back into their routines. Thus, the Trotskyists, Maoists, anarchists, and other currents opposed to the system reverted to their cant, each faction criticizing the rest, rather than trying to build bridges and keep the experiences of '68 going. In order to rebuild some sort of a connection, a group of us, made up of Trotskyists, Maoists, and libertarians, decided to organize a schedule of events to encourage rapprochement and reflection by a wide range of antiauthoritarian currents under the designation of the COJRA (Anti-Authoritarian Reflection Events Organizing Commission); ecology movements also took part, and there was a turnout of upwards of five hundred people. It proved a very useful and enriching experience that helped build bridges between the various partner organizations, and created more fraternal relations with a shared premises complete with library, etc. It survived until 1989, at which point we decided that it had served its purpose as we could detect a greater openness in dealings between the antiauthoritarian activists from all those organizations and in the planning of joint ventures. It was a useful experiment because it banished the sectarianism between the differing currents and conjured up brand new connections. Sustaining the 'Augustinian' (Agustín García Calvo) notion of 'I want you free.' Everything was up for discussion: couple-dom, life, activism, that is to say, one's whole approach to life. We also took part in a few of the self-managing high-school experiments encouraged by Gaby Cohn-Bendit, Danny the Red's older brother."

From 1984 onwards, Octavio was involved in many debates, working parties, and congresses. He traveled to Italy to participate in the International Anarchist Congress in Venice. Octavio remembers that he had an odd feeling during the trip. "Being able to travel and chat, without fear of discovery and arrest was a strange sensation. As if what I was doing was no longer of the same value, the same significance," he told me.

At the Venice Congress, Octavio tackled a controversial subject: he spoke of the decline of anarchosyndicalism, especially the Spanish variety. On the basis of the history of Spanish anarchosyndicalism, Octavio asked why the workers' movement was gradually jettisoning its first and most essential revolutionary aim: emancipating the working class from all forms of exploitation and domination.

His part in the 1986 symposium, organized by the Lyon-based Atelier de Création Libertaire (Libertarian Creativity Workshop), was also remarkable. Octavio and Fernando Aguirre submitted a text in which they argued that:

"If the real issue in Democracy is perversion of representative democracy by means of universal suffrage," it was a nonsense to want to preempt such "perversion" by querying "democratic rules without querying the ideological mechanisms that produce them." Which is why it strikes us that there is a need "to combat the thousand paths of voluntary servitude, beginning with combating them within our own selves."

They closed by urging libertarians not to accept submission, not to be sectarian or authoritarian if they were going to be authentically anarchist. Their paper was later included in the book *Au-delà de la démocratie* (Beyond Democracy), published by the ACL that same year.

Trips and Expositions

IT'S HARD TO PICTURE Octavio as a cultural manager, an area of work connected with bureaucratic-style organization such as museums, libraries, or cultural centers, with all of the orchestration and arrangements that goes with these. But he and Ariane made up a team that organized a number of exhibitions in 1982. There was *The French Revolution, the Iberian Peninsula, and Latin America* at the Richelieu Chapel at the Sorbonne in Paris; and in 1992 there was *1492–1992: The Europeans and Latin America—Five Centuries of Remembering and Forgetting. From Humanism to the Rights of Man*, initially at the IHEAL and later at the BDIC Contemporary History Museum at the Palais des Invalides in Paris.

"Octavio, what was behind those two expositions?"

"Well, Geneviève Dreyfus and Mona Huertas, who worked in bodies that carried some institutional clout were decisive. They both had a certain affinity with the work that we were doing with the CESAME in the Latin America context and, thinking that it might be a good idea to give it a bit of a boost, they suggested that we take on something new. Our purpose was to lay out the influence of the French Revolution, seizing upon the bicentenary year, in the revolutionary process that culminated in independence for the countries of Latin America. We spelled out the idea at the International Congress of Americanists in Amsterdam and it generated some interest. It struck me that it might be a good challenge for me 'as a former terrorist' and supervisor of the exposition, to tackle the history of South America from an institutional, cultural angle. It also has to be said that it carried a very welcome salary and we had a free hand in terms of how the topic should be tackled. It was a very stimulating experience. Specialist historians oversaw our efforts through a scientific committee chaired by the historian François-Xavier Guerra. The exposition had the backing of the Fifth Centenary Committee, which was overseeing the 1992 preparations in Spain for marking the discovery of the Americas; it decided that the exhibition should be staged simultaneously in Madrid.

"The launch in Paris was a big deal because it was attended by ministers from the Mitterrand government and indeed from the Spanish government. The exposition in Madrid was staged at the National Library with documents borrowed from our exhibition and some brand new Spanish documentation. We did not attend that launch. Ariane and I refused to attend the official banquet with the ministers because we were the only two to have been invited in our capacities as exposition supervisors, rather than everyone who had helped create it. It was stated that we would not be attending for work reasons. The historian François-Xavier Guerra, BDIC director Joseph Hüe, and Geneviève Dreyfus attended in my place."

"And what about the Fifth Centenary exposition?"

"That exposition grew out of the success of its predecessor. The same panel of French institutions suggested to us that we organize it in 1992 by way of a commemoration of the fifth centenary of the 'discovery' of America. We agreed and planned to make its focal point the struggles for human rights in the Americas over those five centuries. There too we were overseen by a committee of historians, but there were certain frictions with one Argentinean historian by the name of Diana Quattrocchi-Woisson. She being a Guevarist, she did not take to our assessment of Ernesto Guevara. Apparently, it didn't sit well with her that we touched upon certain authoritarian aspects of his personality and, as we saw it, in the purpose behind his struggle. She took an uncritical view of him, regarding him as some sort of a hero. In the end, our more historical and less political view prevailed."

Those were busy years, with Octavio delving into lots of fields. There is no need for us to catalog everything he got up to and it would make for a long list, but, as an example, we need only mention various trips to Peru and Bolivia, where he met people with whom he has since stayed in contact. He also took part in many events, including one held in 1988 at Barcelona University on the subject of "Future Modeling, New Technologies and Cultural Tradition." In his paper, Octavio proposed "reintroducing into groups that purport to be antiauthoritarian and revolutionary, the practice of daily criticism and self-criticism, free of discrimination or anathema, setting aside petulant paternalism and slick ideological denunciation of the State, Capital, Religion,

Parties, etc.," in an effort to "understand the allure of the authoritarian temptation" and why "authoritarianism continues to gain such huge numbers of recruits, and resurfaces even within discourses and behaviors (individual as well as collective) intent upon denying and combating it." He concluded by saying that we have to say no "to the mirage of radiant tomorrows; as well as to ethical pragmatism, resignation, and acceptance of the Present." And say yes to "freedom and equality in what we do" in order to defend the right "to difference, autonomy, and unfettered experimentation by all at every level and in every aspect of our day-to-day- lives."

That same year, Octavio met Jorge Masetti, junior. Together with Gabriel García Márquez, Jorge's father had cofounded the Prensa Latina news agency back in 1959, before vanishing in 1964 into northern Argentina in the earliest attempt to conjure up a Castroite guerrilla campaign in the country. As for Masetti junior, the Internet holds a huge number of vilifications of his person. There is abuse and allegations that he was a CIA agent, a traitor to Fidel Castro, somebody who abandoned the Cuban ship, etc. There is a sort of an open warfare being waged against him.

"Until the day he dies," Octavio says, referring to Masetti's son, "Jorge will always be 'the traitor,' the hero's son who betrayed his own father."

"How did you come to be friendly with Jorge Masetti, junior?"

"Jorge and his partner, Ileana, arrived in Paris in 1991. Ileana was the daughter of Colonel Toni de la Guardia who, in 1989, was shot along with General Ochoa in Havana following a trial chaired by the Castro brothers. The Castroists had insisted that Jorge blacken the character of Toni de la Guardia, his own father-in-law. Jorge refused to play along and that is why he was represented as a Judas and had to leave Cuba.

"He contacted us through Elisabeth Burgos who, at the time, was head of the French Cultural Institute in Seville and who had lent them her Paris apartment. Ileana and Jorge had had no option but to come to France as they had not been able to secure rights of asylum in Spain, which was under the government of the 'socialist' Felipe González at the time. They contacted us to help Jorge locate historical documentation at the BDIC for the memoirs he was writing about his earlier career as a revolutionary activist in the service of the Cuban state. My dealings with Jorge and Ileana drew me more actively into the company of the Cuban dissidents who were calling for the release of political prisoners and for freedom of expression in Cuba. With them, I had a hand in publishing the bulletin *Sin Visa*, which was issued by a bunch of Cuban dissidents living in exile in Paris.

"In 1996, the arrival in Paris of Daniel Alarcón Ramírez, aka Benigno—one of the three Cubans who outlived the tragic finale to Che's guerrilla campaign in Bolivia—also helped keep me in touch with the activities mounted by the Cuban exiles in France in solidarity with political prisoners back in Cuba. Shortly after that, we interviewed him on Radio Libertaire along with a well-known Trotskyist activist, Daniel Bensaïd, who was also supportive of the Cuban dissidents."

"Why is it such a mortal sin to acknowledge that what happened in the USSR was a failed experiment? How does the Castro you knew back in Mexico in 1965 measure up against the dictator in his classic phase?"

"Well, as you already know, the left falls into two camps. There's a sizable section of the left that acknowledges what you are saying. These days I think there can be no justification at all for there being factions on the left who regard the Castros as socialists or classify what we have in China as 'communism.' One would need to be really stupid to not see what Cuba and China are at present.

"What happens is that, faced with the neoliberal dominion over the world, certain factions will forgive anything, just as long as it 'opposes' the Americans, say. I classify this as an irrational psychological phenomenon. There are even libertarians who give the glad eye to calamitous characters like Chavez or Maduro just because they 'oppose' big capital as represented by the United States. And the worst thing is that, if you expose them, the first thing such leftists do is blacken your name. They accuse you straight out of being a CIA agent or in the service of capitalism.

"Something of the sort happened with Masetti and Ileana. They were shunned for their refusal to lie. Initially they were in such difficulty that we even had to help them out financially in Paris. They were allegedly awash with CIA dollars, according to their opponents. But the plain fact is that they were supported by no one, not on the right nor on the left, just by those of us who refused to believe such nonsense and who witnessed their precarious situation for ourselves. To this day, they drop in on us in Perpignan from time to time."

"And so time rolled on, and Alberola retired," I said, half in jest, changing the subject.

"Ah, *oui, oui*, that was in late 1996. I retired at the age of sixty-seven; I needed three more years than normal because I was a late starter when it came to Social Security payments."

"So far we've been talking about intellectual activist pursuits..."

"I see where you're going here," Octavio interjected, laughing. "On the emotional side of things, I remember that throughout those years, in addition to my relationship with Irene and my kinds, I also had interesting dealings with people outside of the circles of my cultural or ideological activities, with whom I became great friends, even to the extent of intimate feelings; always, on my part anyway, on a basis of affection freely given."

"What does that mean?"

"Well," Octavio laughed, "ever since I got out of jail, as we were saying earlier, I have had a wide variety of connections; like the ones I mentioned whom Ariane knew and who became part of our life. In terms of human relations, when affection reaches a certain pitch, the physical side of things kicks over the traces of convention. The same goes for other surroundings and relationships, in my own case as well as in Ariane's. We have never had any problems in that area, since we never set ourselves up as a couple in the classical social meaning of the term. It was just something very natural and coherent, to the extent that you think one way and you put your thoughts into practice with other likeminded individuals. But that is not to say that everybody lives the same way. Sometimes there were situations requiring a lot of thought and explanation. Because we are human and there are a lot of factors at play."

"Only to be expected, given that your practice with regard to society's cornerstone is slightly different."

"We were questioning the whole concept of 'family.' Starting with Ariane who never wanted to formalize her relationship with me."

"Do you think the notion of 'family' is founded upon a certain sense of ownership over the opposite sex?"

"Not merely the sex but ownership of the other person's body. We were questioning body ownership. This was one of the many issues we had. But it wasn't a fad; it was the natural outcome of the way we were. It was quite spontaneous. We weren't questioning the fact that there are couples that don't feel any need for anybody else. We had no doubt about that. But we were questioning the institutionalization of it. The claim that two people cannot live in monogamous coupledom, also strikes me as nonsense. It is a matter of choice.

At the same time, Ariane and I were living, in some people's eyes, as a couple. They said to us 'but you are always going around together,' to which our answer was that we were a couple because it worked for us, but that it didn't mean that we shied away from loving relationships with other people. And look at how many years Ariane and I have been together.

"Human relationships are complicated. We all have our caprices, jealousies, and human failings. We debated lots of things but at no time did we ever raise doubts about free relationships."

"You mentioned jealousies there..."

"Jealousy is a very strange business. No harm to the psychoanalysts, but we realized that jealousies are the manifestation of looking upon other people as property. It was a battle with ourselves because we were aware of being under the sway of a certain brand of social education."

"And what was going on with the family in Mexico?"

"I was in contact with Irene and my kids by letter throughout this time. Helie came over to see us in 1983 with her Mexican girlfriend Gaby and came back again in December 1995, by which point she was living in the United States with her husband, an American, and her first-born daughter, Krizia. My son Octavio corresponded with me, and by 1996 he'd relocated to Andorra. My connection with Aldo was looser: but he came over to see me in 1996 with his Mexican partner, Mercedes. That was before his son, Oto, was born.

"And, turning to my 'other family,' the circumstances of Catherine, Ariane's friend from her prison days, ensured that we were the ones who often looked after her daughter Virginie who was born in 1975, and after her son, Sébastien, born in 1978 of a different father. Nini and Sebas lived with us for several months until their mother got over her depression and was able to take care of them again. And then there was Kata, who came to us via Jacques d'Arthuys. The Varan project in Bolivia introduced us to Catalina Villar (aka, Kata) in 1987; she was involved in moviemaking circles. With Kata we developed very close ties of affection, almost as if we were substitutes for her biological parents. Especially following the 1988 arrest of Jacques d'Arthuys in Peru in a police frame-up regarding 'alleged drug smuggling.' And, lastly, let me mention Violeta Nazar de Pango, whom we first met in 1990 and who was from Peru. Her six year-old daughter, Tania, was suffering from hepatitis and, shortly after we met, she underwent a kidney transplant operation, one of the very first in France and around the world. We helped them out when they arrived in France and every time that Violeta had to leave Tania behind in Paris, we would look after her. In short, between 1981 and 1996, Ariane and I had Nini, Kata, and Tania as foster daughters."

"You're always saying what great friends you were with Antonio Téllez and Alicia Mur. They both had long careers as activists."

"As you know, Téllez was a well-known writer and member of the CNT. My connection with him was long standing, dating back to the DI. In the 1980s, Téllez was working as a Latin America correspondent for France Press and that brought us into closer contact. He had a strong personality and could be a handful. But we respected each other and we were able to sustain a rather close relationship with him and with his partner, Armonía Pérez, as they had settled in Perpignan. On occasion we availed of the chance also to meet up with Alicia Mur who lives in Barcelona and with whom we are still fast friends."

Memory

AT THE BEGINNING OF the 1990s a campaign was beginning to take shape, which would take Octavio down different byways. Spain had been in democratic transition for fifteen years by then and there were inklings that there might be a chance of raising the issue of remembrance. Unease had grown up regarding matters that the official discourse (no matter which party in government) appeared to have written off. Attempts to overhaul what had happened over the forty years of the dictatorship was something that was forever being cut short—by the right, the center, and the left—with the cliché "off-limits right now." As the heirs to Francoism, the right never raised the issue, any more than the political center did, but was it not necessary, with all those victims of reprisals, all those dead, and all those injustices, that the self-styled "left" should engage? This was one of the most painful aspects of the Transition. When it came to the need to set right, say, the court martial verdicts passed on Salvador Puig Antich, Joan Peiró, Lluís Companys, and Joaquín Delgado and Francisco Granado, all of whom had been executed by the fascists, the left in government spectacularly failed to act. No one even ventured to acknowledge the injustice committed or to amend the laws that the dictatorship had signed and sealed. The need to deliver justice and social rehabilitation to the affected parties is still outstanding. The stubbornness displayed by successive Spanish governments in refusing to acknowledge the victims, their reluctance to acknowledge the victims of the dictatorship's reprisals and those executed who are still being held culpable under that law and whose legal standing under the democracy has yet to be redefined, has been surprising. What we have here is a useless democracy, incapable of overturning the old fascist politics and delivering justice.

"What do you make of this negation or forgetfulness where the past is concerned?"

"For a start, I think that institutional history always strives to justify whatever suits the powers-that-be. As I see it, history is not what the institutions preserve or what states want, but what emerges from all of the research conducted within and without the institutions. History is everything that can be borne in mind about the past and it is important that every generation can reach for it as the need arises. Everything that helps show the past in the most objective light possible strikes me as useful. But we need to be clear about the institutions having no interest in turning a light on everything that happened, and they will throw a wrench in the works as it suits them. From that point of view, I am not a believer in institutional memory. History is the handiwork of the people and of what they quested after in the past. Thus, I have never contributed and will never contribute to institutional history and have always done my bit on behalf of memory, to the extent that the latter can be added to. Because whereas institutions cover up facts from the past, it seems to me that we have a duty to expose this. I felt it was our duty to have done all in our power to ensure that what was done under Francoism was made known, as it also is to force institutions to acknowledge the injustices of the past. Besides, I thought it very important to highlight the reasons why an attempt was made to cover up everything that had happened."

"How far back does your involvement with this matter go?"

"It has always been in my head. It was remembrance that in Mexico drew me into what happened in the Civil War. But I imagine that you are referring to the TV documentary *Granado y Delgado, un crimen legal.*[28] You see, back in 1995, after the screening of the documentary *Objetivo: matar a Franco*, produced by Televisión Española and directed by the journalist Llùcia Oliva, in which my testimony was included, the Catalan producers Xavier Montanyà and Lala Gomà got in touch with me. They wanted me to take part in a documentary they had in mind about the case of Francisco Granado and Joaquín Delgado who were executed in Madrid in 1963. I had a particular interest because Montanyà, who had earlier spoken to Luis Andrés Edo in Barcelona, told me that Edo had assured him that, if only I would agree to take part, he could talk Sergio Hernández and Antonio Martín (the actual perpetrators of the DI's Madrid bomb attacks for which Granado and Delgado had been convicted and executed) into taking part too. They would publicly take responsibility on camera. I agreed and Edo came to see me in Paris shortly after that with the two producers and the film crew.

"The documentary was made by the European ARTE channel. Neither Catalan nor Spanish television dared either make it or screen it, to begin with.

In France, it was broadcast on December 4, 1996 and it was only shown in Spain a year later.

"They were reluctant to focus on memory."

"Well, they are 'news' media dependent on the politicians. Which brings us back to what we were saying about what is institutional and whether that is appropriate or not. The documentary covered a little-known incident and exposed the fact that the Francoist verdicts have yet to be repealed. Currently, there are some parties, like the Socialist Party, the former Communist Party, and indeed the Catalanist parties who embraced the forgetfulness, the betrayals, and everything that the Transition stood for. Don't forget that Tarradellas welcomed the home rule he was granted and indeed accepted the title of 'marques.' A lot of people are implicated in this and none of them has any interest in the past becoming known. Which is why I got involved, because this was a battle against non-remembrance and to bring that non-remembrance to an end.

"The documentary was a pebble in the shoes of the politicians, which is why it was hard to get a screening for it. Later, come prime minister Zapatero's craven Historical Memory Law, nobody remembered the seventeen years of Socialist rule under González, when nobody could remember a thing. It is those people, those cowards who are keeping the past unknown to this day."

"Aside from the documentary, what did you get up to in respect of the campaign for remembrance?"

"I gave talks at the Fundación Salvador Seguí in Madrid and in other cultural centers in various cities. In order to promote the documentary in Spain, we had to persuade ARTE's head of documentaries to hold a press conference in Barcelona. Apparently, the fellow was taken aback by Televisión Española's reluctance to broadcast the documentary. In the end, *Granado y Delgado, un crimen legal* was aired on November 7, 1997... In a midnight slot.

"Despite its time slot, somebody must have seen it because the journalist Carlos Fonseca, who was working for the magazine *Tiempo* in Madrid, got in contact and interviewed me. He wanted to mount an exhaustive piece of investigative journalism into the Granado-Delgado case and the role played by Jacinto Guerrero, aka El Peque, a BPS informer whom the press at the time was linking with Vera and Barrionuevo, with the GAL and the 'sewers' of the Interior Ministry. All of these factors facilitated a get-together of all of us libertarians who had been involved in the 1963 operations, along with the family members of the two comrades murdered by the Francoists. It was there that the idea germinated that we should submit an application for the review of the verdicts to the Supreme Court. Our contention was that the statements made by Sergio Hernández and Antonio Martín constituted fresh evidence and, in any state of law, that was grounds enough for the opening of a fresh investigation and a review of the trial."

The Delgado-Granado case is only one of the many awful things that happened during the late Francoist years and that scandalously expose the dictatorship's injustice. There was obvious evidence to show that the executed pair had had nothing to do with the offense charged against them. In order to sum up the labyrinthine legal process, we ought to highlight the fact that the lawyers and the panel headed by Octavio and the families of the murdered men forced a reopening of the case in February 1998. Their efforts had the backing of the CGT and were pursued through court prosecutor Ana Lobera Argüelles. The case for a reopening was made by lawyer Paco García Cediel, based on the confessions made by the men who actually had committed the offense. The availability of Octavio Alberola, Luis Andrés Edo, and Vicente Martí (DI activists back in the day) who confirmed the truthfulness of the confessions underpinned this, as did the willingness of one and all to ratify this in front of the Supreme Court.

The Supreme Court granted the application and summoned the two real perpetrators to give evidence, leaving out everybody else. But this aroused media interest and Octavio turned up on the back page of *El País* newspaper on November 9, 1998 and was interviewed by Julia Otera for Telecinco.

Despite lobbying by certain media, and demonstrations calling for rehabilitation of the two anarchists lynched by the Francoists, the Supreme Court, twenty years after the fascist verdict was handed down, rejected the application for review, arguing that the verdict had been delivered "in accordance with the prevailing legality."

But the door was left open for an appeal and, capitalizing on the political circumstances at the time, Octavio met up with the sisters of Salvador Puig Antich in Barcelona. They, along with the Parliament of Catalonia, submitted an appeal asking for the case of their brother (who had been sentenced to death in 1974) to be reopened. Simultaneously, the "Group for Review of the Granado-Delgado Trial" hit back by tabling an appeal against the verdict delivered by the Supreme Court. To step up the pressure, a document detailing the case and the submission was issued to every deputy and senator and a range of personalities (the Ombudsman, the political parties, trade union organizations, all the media, and groups and activists from social movements). An international campaign to expose the blatant absence of justice from Francoist trials was also launched.

At this point in the story an unusual opportunity presented itself. Prime minister Aznar and the Spanish king traveled to Cuba to attend the XI Ibero-American Summit of Heads of States in Havana. Jorge Masetti put Octavio in touch with members of a Cuban ex-prisoners' group known as "Los Plantados," who had requested help in highlighting the predicament of political prisoners in Cuba. Los Plantados's plans were for the wives of political prisoners to mount a demonstration, taking advantage of the heads of state summit and on a foreign VIP witnessing the dispersion of the demonstration, thereby triggering a media sensation with international repercussions. Octavio's task was to lay the groundwork for a get-together between the demonstrators and the foreign VIP in a square in Havana. Initially that VIP was going to be the French writer Bernard Henry-Lévy, but his place was taken by Eurodeputy Alain Medellin, a member of the European Parliament's Human Rights commission. Finally, Octavio agreed to make the trip when Edwy Plenel, editor-in-chief of *Le Monde*, assured him that, in the event of his being arrested, the paper would make it public that his mission had been to denounce King Juan Carlos and Prime Minister Aznar for upholding Francoist jurisprudence in Spain and standing in the way of the repeal of the sentences handed down by the dictatorship's courts.

In November 1999, Octavio traveled to Havana for two purposes. The first, to put the center-right Eurodeputy Alain Medellin in touch with the families of Cuban political prisoners, and, second, to publicize the cause of historical justice in Spain. The Granado-Delgado case was denounced in the form of a letter from the Granado-Delgado Trial Review Group, sent out in advance to all the delegations attending the summit and hand delivered to the staff of the Spanish Embassy in Havana for forwarding to King Juan Carlos and Aznar (just a few hours prior to the flight back to Spain).Octavio was arrested at the airport and held for an hour by Cuban intelligence services personnel for—as they put it—a "chat" and so they could warn him that they had been monitoring his movements. At the end of the "chat" they declared that there were very well aware of who he was and said that he was free to leave.

They did suggest that he should avoid returning to the island. Octavio thinks that they were under orders to avoid scandal during the Summit.

The story of the Granado-Delgado case is a long and lingering one. In 2001, following much persistence and lots of protest meetings, the Izquierda Unida parliamentary group, on its own, tabled a proposal in both houses for a law rehabilitating victims of Francoism and compensation for their families. This Izquierda Unida initiative was backed by every other parliamentary group except for the PP (Partido Popular), which once again rejected pleas for justice and the compensation awarded by the Community of Madrid to Francoism's ex-prisoners. Following the claim submitted in the name of Granado's widow the PP acknowledged that this was an injustice, but insisted that it fell under the remit of the State Parliament, which is to say, the chamber that had already rejected the submission.

In addition, there was a number of other campaigns, such as the one mounted by José Antonio Labordeta Subías, a deputy serving on the Chunta Aragonesa (Aragonese Council), who questioned the government in the Congress of Deputies regarding compensation for the relatives of victims of Franco's repression. At a subsequent sitting, he issued a reminder that, after the Amnesty Law of October 15, 1977 "those who suffered imprisonment under Francoism were invited to apply for state compensation and Francisco Granado's widow was unable to access this because the Exchequer has taken the view that her husband, executed seventeen days after he was arrested, fails to meet the criteria set out in that law." Labordeta then reframed the issue as follows: "Has the government any intention of amending its decision so that the Granado and Delgado families may qualify for financial compensation, given that they were unjustly executed in August 1963?"

Undaunted, the Granado-Delgado Trial Review Group issued a letter to all deputies asking them to introduce a non-legislative proposal that these cases be dealt with. This time, the Socialist Party picked up the gauntlet and tabled a non-legislative proposal designed to resolve the cases of the widows or widowers of anti-Francoists executed during the dictatorship. That submission was rejected because, although it had backing from every other group, the PP opposed it, despite stating, for the very first time, "its unqualified moral acknowledgment of all the males and females victimized by Francoist repression for having championed freedom and having subscribed to democratic beliefs."

And so it was that Spanish politics, the courts, and other agencies carried on toying with the tragedy inflicted upon thousands under the fascist yoke. The conspiracy of silence held firm and adamantine as part of what had been agreed with the dictatorship's heirs during Spain's so-called "transition."

The Granado-Delgado Trial Review Group fought on, using whatever weapons came to hand. Protest meetings were held all over Spain, a letter (bearing the signatures of ex-prisoners of Francoism) was issued to all the parliamentary factions urging them to come to an accommodation and introduce a proposal for final resolution of the cases of the widows and widowers of those executed by the Francoists and for the rehabilitation of all victims.

Within days, on a symbolic November 20, every one of the parliamentary groups in the Congress of Deputies passed a resolution (described as "historic"), in which the PP for the very first time agreed to condemn "the army revolt of 1936." This was tantamount to acknowledgment of a "moral debt owed to all those men and women who were victims of the Spanish Civil War and all who subsequently endured the Francoist dictatorship's repression." There was also a call for "recognition and financial and social protection for Civil War exiles and war children." That resolution was a landmark in the battle for remembrance in Spain.

But the Francoist verdicts were left to stand and the matter of compensation for Granado's widow, Pilar Vaquerizo, was still unresolved. The frightening haste of the fascists' execution of Granado meant that, according to the law, he was not to be considered as having been in "custody." So, the fight was still on, time was passing, and the non-legislative proposals continued to be tabled, as did the pressure for the identification of common graves, shootings, and other criminal acts. Some progress was made, such the consensus shared by a range of political parties calling for "the rescinding of all summary trials" held during the Francoist era.

Some time later, a number of Catalan parliamentary groups (the CIU, PSC, ICV, and ERC) put to the Catalan Parliament a non-legislative proposal "to review and descend the verdicts handed down during the Civil War and dictatorship on political, social, or ideological grounds."

On March 14, 2004, Zapatero won the elections, and on July 13, the Constitutional Court overturned the Supreme Court determination of March 3, 1999, which had refused a review of the 1963 council of war that had passed the death sentences on Francisco Granado and Joaquín Delgado. This was a historic decision; it was the first time the Constitutional Court had contradicted the Supreme Court.

Now it all began afresh—the relevant appeals, the lack of political interest and the passage of time, the timeless years on which the official courts always rely, dragged on until 2006, at which point the Supreme Court once again rejected any rescinding of the summary trial of Delgado and Granado, despite its having been obliged to hear Octavio's evidence only a few months before.

Under pressure, Zapatero tabled a draft of what was to become the Historical Memory Law, which was finally passed in late December 2007. That law did not rescind the verdicts handed down by Francoist courts, and as a result, it failed to do right by the victims of Francoist repression. With regard to compensation for the families of those executed by Francoism, it introduced a despicable distinction between those executed prior to January 1, 1968 and those executed between that date and October 1977. The former were entitled to compensation to the tune of 9,616 euros and the latter of 135,000 euros. Why the 1968 watershed?

Octavio asked Granado's widow if he should carry on with the legal campaign, since the likelihood was that eventually the case could be won, but the woman could take no more and let it drop. Ten years in the courts were more than she could face.

"The Historical Memory Law infuriates me," I remarked to Octavio, unable to be any less blunt about it.

"Getting angry is pointless. But that's how it was. We were fed up and she and her daughter agreed. I railed about the discriminatory nature of the Zapatero law, but everybody had agreed to it, even the '*memorialistas*' who are still fighting to have certain streets renamed or monuments removed. Streets and statues are nothing when set beside such atrocious discrimination. The Granado-Delgado case is not closed, but I hadn't the energy to carry on."

"And yet, in legal terms, the injustice of it has been acknowledged."

"I wasn't looking to the official courts for justice, because I have no belief in them. I was out to force the politicians and judges to rehabilitate and compensate the families. There is no such thing as official, universal justice.

"Because, if those courts lay down a precedent, that is the start of a political issue. As in the cases of things like the dirty war in Europe, with the Red Brigades in Italy and the RAF in Germany... take the Feltrinelli or Ulrike Meinhof cases, say. The state claimed victims itself, and in both Italy and

Germany, there is no way that those cases are going to come up for review. Any more than in the cases of those French who collaborated with the Nazis in the deportations. Justice has not been delivered there either.

"Why, just the other day, Emmanuel Macron acknowledged collaborationism," Octavio laughed. "I place very little store by this whole 'official recognition' business. Nevertheless, such campaigns to expose the lies of some government or a state, measured in terms of its own notions of justice, do strike me as interesting. But I see a contradiction in looking for official acknowledgment, and, besides, there is nothing definitive about it, since years afterward the acknowledgment is allowed to drop by opposition politicians, whereas we are what we are."

"I still think that the French state's acknowledging what happened can do a French Jewish family some good," I said, as I was not in very much agreement with Octavio here.

"In some cases, yes, in others, no. In my own case, I don't think it's important. I agree that there might be some use in a state's acknowledging its responsibilities, but I place no great store by that. I only do that if it helps demonstrate the reason why the state didn't budge.

"Justice is meted out piecemeal. Reading over the Delgado-Granado case, there were various courts, judges, bureaucrats, etc., involved. And the distinction between 'legislative' and 'non-legislative' I find laughable.

"The purpose of it all is to uphold the prevailing status quo. Such bodies shift according to interests. Whenever one of these apparatuses ceases to be of use, change comes in. For instance, when I testified before the Supreme Court regarding the Delgado-Granado case... I am not a believer in that court, but we had forced them to take my statement. In terms of 'their' jurisprudence, I was delighted to force them to hear me out and to be able to denounce what had gone on under Francoism. Even though it was all a farce, because there were three conservative judges and two 'progressive' ones. Three against two, the three always have right on their side, as indeed proved the case. It is not justice that prompts the passing of a verdict, it's politicking and interests.

"After twenty-five years of un-remembering the self-styled 'leftist' parties had yet to address the matter of Francoist repression and were compelled to grapple with it. Something did happen: victory for the demands being made by the *agrupaciones* (such as the one we set up). Now the Socialists boast about the law's being a political feather in their cap. That was the great farce that was the Zapatero law.'"

Alongside this whole campaign to rescue remembrance, Octavio kept up his connections with South America. Various activities caught his attention, such as the anti-Castro Cuban dissidents or the Zapatista movement back in Mexico. The latter forwarded to Octavio a letter from Subcomandante Marcos. The Zapatitas wanted to place the wide-ranging film archives they possessed in safe keeping. Along with Yvon Le Bot and Régis Debray, Octavio tried to secure funding from Education minister Jack Lang who showed interest in the matter, but nothing came of that as Lang left the ministry in May 2002.

In the specific instance of Cuba, Octavio worked to promote the little-known dissident anarchist movement. This was a delicate matter, since, a far as many people are concerned, especially progressives, anything other than Castro is a *gusano* (worm), which is to say, every Cuban dissident is in the pay of the CIA. In fact, few people realize that there was a rich anarchist tradition over there in early twentieth century Cuba and that it survives to this day on the island, as reflected in the *Observatorio crítico*, a sort of a digital forum, which, though not anarchist, does have some anarchist contributors.[29] Throughout the entire Castro period, Cuban anarchist trade unionists were forced into exile and they set up the Movimiento Libertario Cubano (Cuban Libertarian Movement/MLC). In 2003, Octavio worked with them on a bulletin entitled *Cuba Libertaria*. But Octavio's cooperation with the Cuban dissidents had to do with the documentary that Jorge Masetti made about the history of trade unionism in Cuba, a film funded by the Swedish anarchosyndicalists of the SAC.

The most telling political visitor, as "coincidence" had it was Canek Sánchez Guevara, grandson of Che Guevara. Despite the great age gap between them, he and Octavio really hit it off.

"You're always mentioning the names of Canek and Masetti, Octavio."

"Because those are two cases that bear witness to the hope of rebellion in human history. Exemplifying the fact that rebellion can be sustained and can triumph over a legacy and a political-cum-family environment that were invitations to the easy life and docility. The rebel is always going to be, or will always end up as an anarchist."

Canek Sánchez Guevara's life was tragically short. Regrettably, he died of complications following a heart operation in his forties. But in order to understand who Octavio is talking about, this is something Canek said, which I believe sums him up:

> Let us understand one another, I didn't know a damn thing about the revolution, other than intuitively understanding that it was at the core of our lives (the life I had been leading with my family) and that it was something one only spoke of in trusted company. Indeed, my family connection to Ernesto Guevara is that I was born in Cuba and inevitably I was dubbed "Che's Grandson" from the age of twelve onwards [...] Being "Che's Grandson" was extremely hard: I was used to just being me, full stop, and people were soon cropping up and telling me how I ought to be behaving, what I ought to be doing and not doing, what I ought to be saying and what I ought never to say. You can imagine that that was too much for a pre-anarchist like me. Naturally, I made it my business to do the very opposite.[30]

Perpignan-Bound

IN 1999, OCTAVIO LOST his friend Fernando Aguirre. Pancreatic cancer snatched Fernando away before anything could be done to help him. 1999 was also a year of relocations. Octavio and Ariane moved into Ariane's mother's house, as she was becoming more dependent by the day and was showing indications of Alzheimer's. Soon, the disease left her completely paralyzed and she needed the care of specialist staff. And the string of disasters continued when Ariane underwent an operation for breast cancer. Luckily, following a year of intensive care and routine check-ups, she was discharged.

But the most telling and extraordinary incident came in 2005. Octavio received a message at *Cuba Libertaria* from someone who signed themself Livia Alberola. He was stunned with surprise and emotion, and, following that initial contact, Livia explained that she had been trying to track Octavio down using the Internet for some time.

"We haven't mentioned the daughter you had by Gloria since you told me that Gloria had asked you to go back to Mexico. And, if memory serves, when you got the letter in question you were approaching eighty years of age."

"It came as quite a surprise, out of the blue! I had always wanted to find out about her, but I had no desire to meddle in their lives, especially following my alienation from Gloria. Later, I spent a lot of time mulling over my past. I was curious, perhaps sentimentally so, to find out about them. So it came as a great surprise, a great gift, when Livia turned up in my life. Some months later, Livia came to Paris with her son, Alejandro, and her daughter, Montserrat. For the first time I was meeting the daughter I had had with Gloria. The oddest thing is that it was all very natural and unforced. There was no formality. We had been communicating over the Internet quite a bit before that and when we set eyes on one another it was all very natural.

"I had occasion to speak with Livia about our lives over those forty-odd years. She confessed to me that she had been afraid that I might not want to see her. And she expressed the wish to meet my other three kids, her half-siblings, and, immediately I gave her their addresses."

"And Gloria?"

"I gave Livia my side of the story and found out that Gloria had not taken kindly to what I had told her back in 1974, that she should get on with living her life, given the painful prospect of imprisonment that I thought lay ahead of me. She felt rebuffed and it hurt her. Livia had a difficult relationship with her mother, but from what she said, Gloria was all for this renewed contact between us. However, I never wrote to Gloria again."

"And did Livia meet her siblings?"

"Yes. I wrote to Helie, Octavio, and Aldo filling them in on the reunion with Livia, her visit to Paris, and her eagerness to meet them. When Livia went back to Mexico she met up with Helie and Aldo and started emailing Octavio. They have been in contact ever since and meet up from time to time. The odd thing is that, even though they had never met before, they hit it off with one another. I correspond with all my kids and it's a joy. I am delighted that we have met up and that my children respect what I have been all my life."

"And then one day you took a notion to move to Perpignan. You were around eighty then."

"To understand it you have to bear in mind that Ariane's mother passed away in 2005. So, from 2006 on, we started to prepare to relocate to Perpignan. As luck would have it, Nicole—Ariane's sister who lives in England—decided to sell the house she had bought in Saint-Laurent de la Salanque and suggested that Ariane use the money to buy an apartment in Perpignan that we could move into, while Ariane put the Paris apartment on the market. Towards the end of 2006, with help from some comrades from Paris and Perpignan, we began the move. And by the end of 2007, we had settled once and for all in Perpignan."

"Yes, of course, but I had other reasons for asking you."

"Well, life in Paris was no longer what it had been. We had lots of acquaintances, like Téllez, say, in the Perpignan area. Besides, living was cheaper here, it is close to Barcelona where I was still visiting as part of the campaign of remembrance we were talking about earlier. It was handier and the climate was better for somebody getting on in years."

"You do realize that we are coming to the completion of the edifice you were building over all those years? We have just one story left."

"Plus the roof. Don't forget the roof," Octavio replied with blithe vigor.

AT THE CENTER OF THE WORLD

The World Viewed from Perpignan Railway Station

ONE OF SALVADOR DALÍ'S oddest paintings, painted when he was at the height of his career and already famous worldwide, bears the modest title *Gala looking at Dalí in a state of anti-gravitation in his work of art "Pop-Op-Yes-Yes-Pompier" in which one can contemplate the two anguishing characters in Millet's Angelus in the state of atavic hibernation standing out of a sky which can suddenly burst into a gigantic Maltese cross right in the heart of the Peripignan railway station where the whole universe must converge*, which he himself referred to, in shortened form as *Perpignan Train Station*. In it Dali defined Perpignan station as the center of the world. The painter said that, for a few moments, he "understood" the universe as he pondered sunlight playing on Perpignan train station and, after some mystico-physical theories according to which he was able to "see" in three possible dimensions, he hinted that his painting was a great work of art summarizing his whole universe and the real and human universe in total.

On the far side of the world, the Tzotzil Mayas of San Juan Chamula have been arguing for millennia that that little town in Chiapas is the navel of the world, the center via which one moves from the world of the living to the underworld of the dead.

None of this has anything to do with the worldview and view of the human intellect to which Octavio subscribes, but in any case, setting to one side the painter's egocentric needs and the mystical urgency of the indigenous community, Perpignan is, in a way, a reference-point, a central core in respect to wartime Spain and the era after the dictatorship. Thousands of exiles passed that way with small children in tow during the unforgiving winter of 1939; children such as Octavio who, to this day, carries in his heart of hearts the

picture of the place and his transit through the concentration can
mistically described as "refugee" camps. Some of those children are
and now in their eighties, living in and around Perpignan. These are
styled "Perpignan *communards*." I will never forget attending the get-to
held on Sundays in Saint-Laurent de Salanque. A lot of the attendees cr
the border as children, fleeing with their parents from the Spain that wa
more, and they didn't go back to live in the Spain that the dictator left beh
him. A lot of them spent much of their lives elsewhere in France but, as the
aged, and for a variety of other reasons, they converged on Perpignan over the
years that followed.

The Perpignan *communards* normally meet up at the home of José Morato, who has been a comrade and friend of Octavio and Ariane's since the 1960s. Jose and his partner, Montse Turtós, were two of those who crossed the border back in 1939, at a very young age, in the course of the republicans' retreat. But so too was Valia "Germania" Doval, one of the so-called "Russia girls" (in a desperate attempt to save their children, some republicans shipped them off to Russia), whose life story would make a good book. Those Sunday lunches are an excuse for a get-together and for others—as in my own case—to get the chance to meet them and share in their experiences.

When Octavio arrived in Perpignan, he was seventy-nine years of age and very eager to carry on with his active life, far from the pressures of gainful employment.

"You speak of the center of the world. Is Perpignan the center of the world?" I asked Octavio by Skype.

"Well, it takes a bit of explaining. Little wonder that the years spent living in Perpignan have prompted me to think that wherever one is is the 'center of the world.' It's an idea that might, at first glance, seem somewhat whimsical and indeed folksy. In fact, where one is, is always the outcome of a subjective impression produced by the objective 'reality' of our perception; the physical-spatial of the horizon we observe as we move around and the psychic-affective influence of the horizon marked out by our dealings with others."

"Meaning that reality is oneself."

"Man, and more specifically his brain, is the center of the reality that he thinks, lives, and describes. Every human being qualifies for that description because he or she has the capacity for thought and is conscious of the fact. It is not merely a case of 'I think therefore I am' but also of 'I think because what

ps euphe-
still alive
he self-
gether
ossed
no
nd
y

...ainly, that Cartesian intuition, while it
...on, the way every certainty is; but, even
... by means of our thinking, which is what
...stence and of 'conjuring up' everything that

...ther way of staking a claim to be the center of

...nat may. How could one fail to feel that one is the center
...believe that one is? How is this to be avoided if everything
...nly happens for each and every one of us because our brain is
...the capacity to think it? Which is why every recollection, and I
...eferring to received memories here, is different. It even varies accord-
...mindset and time. When I speak of memories, it is always in a relative
...se because they possess relative meaning and value."

"It was your thinking that brought me to the Dalí painting. Dalí really was his own hub, magnified by the huge lens of his extraordinary ego."

"*Oui, oui*, but the business about Perpignan being a center was more than just an egocentric whimsy of Dalí's. And it wasn't that for me either through all the years I have been living here; because, although I may not advertise the fact, 'center of the world' means that, thanks to the Internet, I have been in communication *urbi et orbi*, as Ariane says, when I settle down in front of my computer. Besides, when it comes to the Paris–Madrid or Madrid–Paris rail line, Perpignan train station sits almost at the halfway point and so our friends can use it to come and see us."

"The Internet we all have, shall we say? But we do not always have a train station bringing friends to our homes or from which we can wave them off."

"Well, joking aside. This privileged position is something akin to the 'I' that remembers of being at the 'center of the world.' It has been a great asset to a lot of the visits we have received over recent years. It also allowed us to concentrate on ourselves for a little longer because, whether it was being in Perpignan or because of our leading a less exhausting life, and having more recent memories of this period, closer in time, they strike me as more personal, livelier, and more authentic."

"Do you think that the closer they are to the present the sharper memories become?," I asked, none too convinced.

"Can't say for sure. But it would be something along the lines of the 'I' that

remembers them being a more real, more Cartesian 'I.' Meaning that the awareness of existence is articulated through thought and language; but there is also
an awareness that we do not pick our point of departure, that we are born into
a culture and with a body and that if one is to be able to see 'the other,' one
must first be 'one,' which is to say, whatever one thinks oneself to be.

"My Perpignan memories are sharper because I think along more leisurely
lines and my mental analysis is less fraught. In Paris, I was prey to various
strains. Here, my thoughts are more considered and rational. But, getting back
to what we were talking about at the beginning of this book, memories are a
personal reality and nothing more. And never forget that they are relative."

"Yet you are now devoting quite a bit more of your time to remembering."

"Well, that's because of my circumstances. Historians and journalists have
'forced' me into remembering. And, given my age, my physical condition allows me to get more brain work done than physical labor. So, I remember and
it stops the machinery of the mind from gathering dust."

"In order to draw conclusions, you speak of 'one' and of 'the other.' Sometimes the dividing-lines are hazy. Because, as an individual, you also construct
'the other.' Think of those anarchist avengers who thought that by doing away
with 'the other,' reality would be altered. You remarked there that 'the other,'
in those instances, is replaced, because what is not killed off is the idea that
that 'other' stands for. Is the construct of the 'other' heavily dependent on
whatever has gone into the construct of 'one'?"

"Yes, although the dividing-lines between the two notions are hazy. Getting back to the avengers and setting aside the historical context in which they
were operating, I think that was a misstep because, just as human situations are
so complex, tinkering with one tiny element—meaning, eliminating one person—does not change everything. Even though things may not change, something changes. The matter of the avengers is a complex one and, as you can
see from my reply, an ambiguous one. Had we managed to bump off Franco,
things in Spain would assuredly be different. There is always the lingering possibility that this small change has some impact.

"As for your remark about the construct of the 'other,' one pictures him
somewhat the way one is oneself, that is to say, you transfer whatever you are
into the construct of the 'other.' It happens to us all and there is no avoiding
it. All we can do is strive not to portray the construct in absolute colors. Leaving some room for doubt. Leaving that door always open. Over time, you see

people differently. Down through the years, experience sets us to constructing 'the other' differently; that is, you learn to leave room for *nuance*, as the
French say; for different shades. Over time you see more nuances."

"I reckon that the more one has based oneself on permanent questioning
and considered thought, the richer and more complex the construct of what
you have in front of you will be."

"*Oui, oui*, but you also run the risk that, over time, interests will intervene
between 'one' and 'the other' and that these will run counter to your interests.
There is an ongoing friction there. I insist that one must abide by a relative notion of things rather than construct hard and fast realities. It is nonsensical to
be absolute in your beliefs, and the belief that you think in absolute terms, and
that yours is the only truth is a nonsense."

"And what of the relationship between 'one' and 'the other'?"

"Let us be clearer here: the 'one' and 'the other' are shaped by the ongoing dialogue or clash between civilizations and eras: it is not a case of 'this
way alone' as the current saying in Mexico has it. Because we don't even get to
choose where we go, as I have never wearied of reminding participants in the
debates at the Perpignan People's University (UPP)."

"Tell me, what was it like, moving to Perpignan?," I asked, changing the
subject.

"I remember how, without waiting for us to settle in properly, Ariane
quickly put together a dinner with the comrades who had given us a helping
hand and some local comrades. Which is to say that neither in Paris nor in
Perpignan were we on our own."

On the Move, Forever on the Move

THE YEARS WENT BY and friends were making their way to the "center of the world." A list of all those who visited Octavio and Ariane would be endless. Many of those who crop up in this book—and who were still healthy enough to travel—turned up at Perpignan train station to see Octavio and Ariane and others whom we haven't named. All of these people are the fruits of a life of activism, ups and downs, and the drive to construct a liberated self, Octavio's lifelong ambition.

But as to the activities in which Octavio engaged and still engages at the age of ninety-one, it is interesting to note a few, such as the huge number of texts, visits to congresses, interviews, and films in which he has had a hand.

Together with Granado's widow, Octavio pursued shrewd action to push the demand for historic justice and to expose the wretched law with which the Zapatero government tried to end all the claims of injustice leveled at the dictatorship—to "tie them up with no loose ends" as Octavio puts it. One way of pressing the claim and placing on record everything done, with regard to historical memory, was the suggestion that Octavio suggest to his cousin, the historian Félix Villagrasa, that they co-author something about the historical process and the gestation of the Historical Memory Law introduced by the Zapatero government, which Octavio denounced as cowardly, faint-hearted, and iniquitous. That book, *Miedo a la Memoria. Historia de la ley de reconciliación y concordia* (*Fear of Remembering: A History of the Reconciliation and Concord Law*) was published by Barcelona's Flor del Viento Ediciones in 2008. It was one way of drawing a line under all those years of politico-legal effort and wrangles seeking to rehabilitate the memory of Francoism's victims. The historian Pelai Pagès, who met Octavio in 2007 at the Gorizia History Festival, helped with the book's launch.

That done, Octavio thought that his duty of solidarity had been fulfilled and, given the essentially legal nature of the campaigns surrounding historical memory, the members of the Granado-Delgado Trial Review Group withdrew from active engagement in the field. That withdrawal, though, did not imply their ceasing to contribute crimes in the form of press and Internet articles to the debates on historical memory and the impunity of Francoists. To give one example, in May 2008, the Catalan review *El Triangle* carried an interview with Octavio under the by-line of the journalist Dionisio Giménez, dealing with the Transition and the Historical Memory Law.

Meanwhile, in Perpignan, Octavio attended and encouraged courses at the Perpignan People's University (UPP), which was launched in 2006 by the Perpignan intellectuals Henri Solans, Dominique Sistach, and Jordi Vidal. The UPP's purpose was, and remains to this day, to offer courses to "pass on knowledge and share critical thinking," following the example set by the people's university launched by Michel Onfray a few years earlier in the city of Caen in Normandy.

"It's a forum for considered thought and it reminds me of a similar attempt to conjure up an alternative to the state education system," I said to Octavio, regarding the UPP.

"No, not in the least," Octavio replied, emphatically. "Not at all. Nothing to do with institutional education. What was and still is clear in that instance is that there is no definitive learning and that there are no experts when it comes to knowledge. Far from it. Knowledge is always open to question. In the universities, some lecturers purport to have a teaching method for passing on what they know on the basis of master classes where they talk and talk and the other guy shuts up and listens. Initially, at the UPP, they open with an exposition and later a discussion is thrown open. What counts is the intercourse as a way of encouraging considered thought. Knowledge is passed on when exposition of it generates discussion. Debates are created because the ideas articulated clash with one another. The work of the people's universities established after the pattern of Michel Onfray's idea operates like that."

"So it's all about passing on knowledge..."

"No, I don't think there is any mechanical passing on of knowledge. There is discovery learning as the knowledge is built up. Each person builds it up as a result of the knowledge put before him and whatever conclusions he draws from it. The real learning is in those conclusions, rather than the information being presented.

"In an institutional setting, knowledge is information accepted as received wisdom and if, in addition, it has been edited and endorsed by some prestigious celebrity it is taken for granted that it is truth and is passed on as truth rather than as data. Knowledge is information, not truth. Truth is an ongoing creation of accumulated knowledge that has been thought through. Truth isn't a fixed process, it is a dynamic one."

"And pedagogy, what remains of that in everything we have been talking about?"

"Pedagogy, as you know, is a word, a concept the very etymology of which refers to 'leading,' 'bringing,' about a pathway, to accompanying the 'child,' and therefore also the adult, along his path. Therefore, pedagogy is the transmission of knowledge in a manner that does not amount to imposition and where knowledge has not been pre-chewed so as to steer it in a predetermined direction. Which is why we should be talking about 'pedagogies': some of which invite acceptance and others of which invite questioning. 'Libertarian pedagogy' is one of the latter insofar as received wisdom is called into question, but it doesn't end at mere questioning per se, but at questioning for the purpose of intellectual reflection, and the child or adult recipient of the knowledge can go back and re-order what he has received. In that sense, I think that if the pupil receives his knowledge through first-hand experience, that pathway is even better and his considered thoughts will be better."

"So you still believe in the old anarchist adage about education as the only thing that can set men free?"

"In the sense that education is not an imposition but an experiment carried out by the individual, yes. Education should not be for the purpose of turning you into whatever the educator may want you to be, but rather so that the educated can be self-made, so that they can become self-made."

"Capitalism is a believer in education."

"Sure, so that the individual, through such education, will embrace and believe in the system. The purpose of creating brand new experts and technicians is to render capital profitable. Such education leads the educated in the direction of a specific, closed model that lacks openness. Nevertheless, these days the stance of being mere recipients no longer works the way it used to. There are changes that make subtle alterations to capitalist education on the basis of inevitable questioning of their lives coming from individuals. Consider ecology. Thirty years ago, it was inconceivable that capitalism would give it the time of day. It wasn't invented by capitalist education, but is the upshot of the noxious impact of capitalist development. Capitalism reluctantly adapts because that is what is required of it."

Over the past ten years, which is to say ever since Octavio moved to Perpignan, he has written and spoken in lots of media and in various forms about what he thinks on a wide variety of topics. Since I cannot go into everything that he has been up to lately, allow me to quote just a few examples.

In 2010, Octavio took part in a schedule of libertarian events held by the CNT in Córdoba. They were the lead-in to the tenth congress of that historic organization. Looking past the topic he dealt with, the remarkable point is that for the first time since the 1960s, Octavio was taking part in a CNT event. As a veteran activist, it must have mattered to the CNT back then that Alberola should park their differences and take up a formal invitation issued by the Confederation.

"Why did you accept the invitation to take part in the CNT events in Córdoba?"

"Well, I agreed to attend for no particular reason. What happened was that the CNT had not previously invited me to anything. They invited me that time and that was that. I was aware of the many silly internal splits within the CNT and was not in agreement, but I decided to go because of the interest. They were the ones who had invited me and I detected a certain shift due to the departure of the orthodoxes and sectarians. These were young people, fresh blood and that was interesting. Two years before, there was a rally in Barcelona, in Montjuich, that I had attended at the invitation of libertarians from the city. Meaning that there had been earlier contacts."

"And what is your relationship with the current CNT?"

"There's been a change of stance inside both the CNT and the FAI. Although they are still at odds with the CGT from time to time. My relationship is fine; I collaborate with them by writing articles and, insofar as my physical condition allows, I collaborate with festivals and other events."

In 2010, Octavio also took part in activities in European countries other than France or Spain. In the eyes of many—especially young libertarians in countries such as Holland, Sweden, and Germany—Octavio is a prominent personality and his voice is regarded as important. To cite a few of his international activities, we might mention the anthology *Von Jakarta bis Johannesburg. Anarchismus weltweit* (From Jakarta to Johannesburg: Anarchism Worldwide) on anarchism as an ideal, published in German by the Unrast

Verlag imprint. Octavio suggested the original idea to the philosopher Gabriel Kuhn and wrote an essay on his vision and the future of the anarchist movement.

Other countries looked to him for his opinions on universal notions like anarchy, revolution, and man in the round. What the curious, academics and present-day movements, and left-wing activists find most attractive about Octavio is his tremendously lively outlook on life; his belief that, despite all the disappointments, empires, and tyranny, man—his notion of man free, and of a society free as well—will gain ground.

"You are always engaging in what is new: the Internet, new youth trends, philosophers under thirty years of age."

"Well, I live in today's world and I'm still curious. There is nothing to hinder me from wanting to find out what is going on in the world. Besides, I am open to anything that grabs my attention. Since I have a predisposition vis-à-vis the other guy, and bringing him into a sort of a 'universal family,' I am forever doing things. I find contact with different people enriches me. Thinking is a forever apprenticeship."

"Like taking part in the Anti-Fascist Mayday Festival held in Prague in 2011. I had a look at the promotion for the event on YouTube at the time and could not help but smile at the sight of you surrounded by rock musicians, rappers, and young people who had come to the festival from all over Europe. And there you were, eighty-three years of age."

"Yes, I remember the event of course. Thousands of youngsters from all over Europe attended. I spoke after the English philosopher Alan Carter and the Irish sociologist John Holloway, on antiauthoritarian struggles in the world today. As I concluded my address I was approached by two young women from Madrid who wanted to congratulate me for my optimistic outlook on the prospects for antiauthoritarian revolts. At the time, they were highly pessimistic as to Spanish youth's ability to hit back. The curious thing is that Spain's 15-M Movement started in Madrid a few days later."

In 2011, Octavio wrote a piece on the ideological and social trajectory of Spanish anarchism and the CNT for the Dutch anarchist review *DE AS*, contributors to which included Rudolf de Jong, Hanneke Willemse, and Jan Groen. That same year, however, Octavio took part in the documentary *Les caixes d'Amsterdam* (The Amsterdam Crates), acting as a special historical advisor in the making of Catalan producer Felip Solé's film. That film, produced

and broadcast by TV3, tackles the history of the international anarchist movement since the evacuation to France of the crated archives of the Spanish Libertarian Movement and the CNT, which were removed from Barcelona on
January 26, 1939, just a few hours ahead of the entry of Franco's troops. Apart
from Octavio, there were also interviews with Noam Chomsky and Michel
Onfray included.

Getting back to the Perpignan People's University, Octavio set out his
ideas—on the basis of texts submitted by the philosopher Michel Tozzi—
regarding "the complexity issue." He spelled out what he understands by
the term "complex thinking" and his own view of philosopher Edgar Mori's
attempt to turn it into a brand new paradigm in contrast to the "laws" of
mechanics-based paradigm of current science.

"Why such interest in the issue of complex thinking?"

"Not just because of the epistemological consideration, but also because I
think that the operation of our society is incontrovertibly becoming increasingly complex. Hence it is vital that we not succumb to fads about 'simplistic
thinking,' guesswork, preferences, and belief. We have to embrace 'complex
thinking,' which consists of putting forward hypotheses, building relationships, looking for yardsticks, relying on sound argument, making corrections,
etc., and also remain being mindful of the need for systematic learning, a
method, and not forgetting the environment."

"Do you agree with Hannah Arendt's complaint that the system has a ten-
dency to render society's grave problems banal?"

"Well, the 'banality of evil,' to quote Hannah Arendt, in the case of Hitler
is more than self-evident and I agree with that. Simplification is a way of evad-
ing considered thought."

"Back in the 1960s, the left also rendered ideas banal and simplistic."

"Of course. Just look at the grossest simplification involved in the talk of
capitalism versus socialism."

"Yes, but I am not thinking merely of abstractions but of simplification
turned on actual individuals. Writing some people off as 'petit bourgeois,' for
instance. There has always been room for reductionism in the thinking of the
left."

"And the worst thing is that it still prevails. Take what is going on in Venezuela right now, for instance. Some on the so-called left make excuses for state
repression because it is coming from what they consider 'their own.' And then,

elsewhere, you denounce state terror simply because the government's colors are not your own. Take another example: In Argentina the present government is lashing out and that makes it a bad one. But whenever the blows were coming from the previous government, what you thought was 'your' government, then they were justifiable. Just the other day I heard somebody who regards himself as a leftist saying of Venezuela that 'the machinery of repression was on the right side.'"

"I think that technology has also been great help in reductionism in ideas. And simplistic discourse. To condensing ideas into two lines, the way Twitter does."

"It's just a way of separating things into 'suits me or doesn't suit me.' But don't forget that technology also allows us to express ourselves. You can write or read lengthy expositions on the Internet."

"You've also written about progress, something upon which you are constantly pondering. 'Progress is capitalism's great gimmick,' 'the greatest human and ecological aberrations have been committed in the name of progress.' However, there are those like yourself who look to a measure of progress as a driver of human change."

"Well, I wrote a piece about this subject, 'La ilusion capitalista' and 'La "generación" Internet" ('The Capitalist Dream and the "Internet Generation"'),[31] in response to an article about innovation by the French writer and philosopher Roger-Pol Droit and the book *Petite Poucette* by Michel Serres,[32] which champions an optimistic outlook on the digital world and upcoming generations. In those two texts I tried to explain why I too had the impression that technological innovation might contribute to triggering the feeling of the 'utopia of us all living freely connected and together' as heralded by Michel Serres."

"Right. Here you are getting on to the thorny issue of the Internet, the society of the spectacle, fashion, virtually everything. The market has its interests too."

"Everything is bound up with the dominant system. Fashion is a tool for the continued generation of surplus value. You have to be constantly innovating so that the masses can embrace and crave it and thereby generate merchandise. It has nothing to do with originality or creativity. It is advertising and propaganda that depict everything as something new. Occasionally there are innovations that actually are of use in our social lives, but, since they are commercially damaging to certain industrial or financial interests, they are not rendered universal by means of fashion, and are cast aside or else the discovery is covered up. Fashion is a device for boosting consumption."

"Where do you stand on the 'success and failure' of the individual?"

"Those are ghastly, nonsensical terms since 'success' of the one requires that some other person or people fails. These terms are rarely used consciously. They hold no interest for me ... The word 'failure' can be used to reflect a situation that was not necessarily a failure but represented change. When there is talk of the 'failure of socialism,' for instance, the fact is that the desired outcome, socialism, was not achieved, but the experiment has taught us things that previously we had not known. So it was not a failure but an experience useful in the avoidance of errors. But the cliché exists. In my view it is part and partial of simplistic language."

In 2013, Octavio brought out two books, one in French, *Penser l'utopie—À l'Université Populaire de Perpignan* (*Thinking Utopia: At the Perpignan People's University*),[33] an anthology of texts he had written up that point for debates in UPP workshops, and the other in Spanish, *Pensar la utopía en la acción. Trazas de un anarquista heterodoxo* (*Thinking Utopia in Action: Traces of a Maverick Anarchist*),[34] a collection of articles he had written since the 1950s and which he had managed to retrieve thanks to the Internet.

Interestingly, a lot of this stuff was typewritten, and anonymous individuals around the globe, attracted by Octavio's thinking and considerations, had been uploading them to the Internet in recent years.

That same year, Tomás Ibáñez's book, *Anarquismo es movimiento* (Anarchism is Movement),[35] was launched at the Torcatis bookshop in Perpignan. The matters set out in the text provided Octavio, who launched the book, with an opportunity later to develop his thoughts about post-Marxism, neo-anarchism, and post-anarchism as "new" liberating ideas.

"Why this need to redefine the concepts?"

"These notions of Marxism and anarchism have shown themselves not to be serviceable enough, as circumstances have changed and so they need reelaborating, amplification, or amendment. A lot of theories mirror historical circumstances though the position today has changed greatly. An update is an acknowledgment that what you are looking for has to start from current reality. In my articles, I try to not let myself get locked inside ideologies or orthodoxies. In that sense, I subscribe to Agustín García Calvo's idea when he asserted that he was opposed to an idea as anything definitive. An idea has to be forever evolving and must change."

"Is there anything fixed within this ceaseless swirl of movement?"

"I'd say that the only thing that does not change is the need to exist and to press ahead with the movement. This need to exist and continue through time is what conjures up the notion, the concept of freedom on the basis of what works in favor of life and what does not, and hence the notion of ethics raises its head too. These tensions between these two concepts or situations, these two great imaginary meanings, is what drives human history, nurtures ideals, and is the font of thought in general. Obviously, when one talks about the notion of freedom one is also talking about the notion of authority; two contrasting notions that are to all intents present in all rational human thinking. Even in the thinking of modernity, which has found itself obliged to take on board the ecological consequences of human activity, since freedom and autonomy must now be aware of the harmful, ecocidal effects of having become the rule of reason in the world.

"For a long time, too long now, even progressive views of history have thought that freedom was inseparable from reason's dominion over nature in the liberation of men. Today we know that such dominion is a menace to our own autonomy. Especially the odd way in which autonomy and freedom are construed by capitalism as 'entrepreneurial freedom.'"

"Is capitalism redefining itself?"

"Capitalism changes and adapts to circumstances in order to cling to its aim, which is to grow capital. But the fact that it remains the main system of production and the main way of organizing social coexistence today does not mean to say that it will be the same tomorrow. At certain points there were internal squabbles between free marketeers and those who think that capital has to be curtailed by means of borders. Those squabbles rumble on. Notionally, as well as in practice, it is still capitalism, but it is evolving due to its internal contradictions."

"The simplistic capitalist discourse is hard to grapple with. A present-day soccer superstar is an alluring and simplistic topic of discussion that casts a huge shadow over richer and more complex discourses."

"Because it is easier and handier to obey rather than reflect and rebel. If you place an individual in a position where she has to strive to think about what is happening, it is a burden to her. Obedience and acceptance are a lot easier. Thinking is wearisome and exhausting. However, embracing obedience does not deliver paradise and turns into frustration and, with that, comes protest. Fortunately, the system's own contradictions trigger the response: struggle."

"Meaning that if all the soldiers in a war were to stop obeying and paused for thought, the war would be over."

"Which has happened. Not sufficiently to halt the war, but in, say, France in the 1914 war, there were a lot of soldiers who wearied of the war and refused to go to the front, and were shot for it. And it happened on the German side too. The French and German military do not like to be reminded of this."

"Getting back, to your activities, there was a German documentary made about you, wasn't there?"

"In early April 2013, two German journalists—Daniel Guthmann and Joachim Palutzki—contacted me. For the German ZDF-Info television channel, they were planning a documentary about the attempts to assassinate Franco. The point about the shoot is that I had had a fall the night before they showed up and not only had a scrape on my nose and forehead but I had my head bandaged, so when they came to film me in those conditions they had to hide the bandages underneath a beret pulled down over my eyebrows."

"Octavio, I've read a large number of obituaries and vignettes that you've written. I can see that you have compulsion to write such stuff. The list is a lengthy one and can be read on the Internet."

"Right. I've written about ten obituaries. Not all for the same reasons. For instance, in January 2015 I had a phone call from Jorge Masetti informing me that Canek Sánchez Guevara had died in Mexico. I penned an obituary in memory of my cherished and brief relationship with 'Che's anarchist grandson,' as the press used to refer to him. Others were commissioned and still others were written because I felt the need to do so, as in Agustín García Calvo's case. I felt a need to talk about him. Over the last three years I have been relentlessly writing obituaries about some very close comrades and friends: Domitila Chungará and Agustín García Calvo in 2012, David Antona in 2013, Moisés Martín, Paul Denais, Antonio Martín, Salvador Gurrucharri, and Floreal Ocaña Sánchez in 2014. In 2015, it was Liber Forti's turn. News of his death arrived two weeks after I had completed and sent off to his partner the introduction I had been asked to write for the book she was finishing, based on the conversations she had had during the last two years of Liber's life. That book, *En LIBERtad. Charlas con aquel que está aquí,* was published by Ediciones El Cuervo in La Paz, Bolivia, in April 2015.

"I remember beginning the obituary like this: 'Liber Forti, libertarian and solidary.' Not merely because he had been but also because, as far as he and I were concerned, being libertarian necessarily implies solidarity. When they were working on the book, Liber told Gisela plainly: 'I've said it to you lots of times and I'm telling you again that showing solidarity is a feature of the anarchos ... You see someone who shows solidarity and you are looking at an anarcho, who may well not even know that he is an anarcho.'

"But writing obituaries is not some personal compulsion of mine. I don't enjoy doing it, as you might imagine. But that's how it is. People depart."

Facing the Imponderable and the Inescapable

RECENT YEARS HAVE BEEN hard for Octavio. Hard times because the passage of the years impacts mostly the body, and particularly tough because this is true also of his life companions, such as Ariane. Ariane went through a period of severe depression, added to the nervous ailment that has erased her short-term memory. Which represents a huge burden for somebody of Octavio's years. Since 2015, at the age of eighty-five, he has been managing their affairs, given Ariane's utter vulnerability in day-to-day life. Fortunately, for the last two years Ariane's depression has been under control, as a result of which, to borrow Octavio's words, "her behavior has been almost normal," so much so that she can tackle certain intellectual tasks together with him.

"I don't know how to broach the topics you have chosen for the ending of the book," I told Octavio as he gazed at me intently, sitting directly opposite me. The room was unchanged since my last time in his home, albeit that the cat must have been out in the garden as he did not come out to greet us.

"Well, you know, this is the position in which I find myself and how I operate in terms of my thought processes and lifestyle. Everything in my life is now more thoughtful than before."

"In rounding off the book we are doing about your life, I feel it is important that you speak about death."

"It's hard to ponder my condition and the proximity of the end. I cannot boil down into a single sentence everything I feel because that would not sit well. I often mull over why I have come to reflections of this sort and why I have articulated them. The conclusion I have come to is that, in doing the work we have about my passage through life, the thing to be valued is that I have been able to reflect upon my current position. And have an enhanced awareness of the position that I am in."

"Then I shall leave it you speak precisely as you chose to write down your words."

"Spot on."

Of course, Ariane's problem being what it still is, our day-to-day life is not entirely normal, any more than my relationship with her and hers with others; but, compared with the recent past, things can be construed as having improved.

The issue now is that the continuation of that "normality" is dependent more than it used to be upon a different "normality" that is precarious and provisional; that of my great age and the ineluctable aging of my body. Within a few months, I shall turn ninety years of age and the body starts to turn more and more into a prison and a torture machine. Especially during the night hours, which ought normally to allow me to get some rest ... by sleeping. I can only get some rest in fits and starts because aches keep waking me up; I have to get up every two hours or hour and a half and walk around for a bit to ease the ache before I can go back to bed.

This situation dictates my day-to-day routine and it is hard to avoid the impact on my frame of mind of the circumstances in which I am presently living. The most serious point is that my aging shows itself in increasingly tiresome everyday demands upon my waking hours and these sit at the heart of my present worries.

Up until a short time ago, plans occupied a central part in my purposes and I use to spend most of my time on them. Even doing some physical exercise by playing tennis once a week with Corine in Gruisan. But, since the imponderable and inescapable have made themselves such a presence in my daily routine, I find myself obliged to spend less time on intellectual schemes and push them into second place. I have even had to suspend outings to Gruisan. I am fully aware of this; but even though I accept it and adapt myself to the inevitable character of such a prospect, I cannot avoid feeling frustrated and bitter at having to resign myself this way.

"But, no matter what you may say, you are active," I added, after reading that text aloud. Octavio looked at me, impassive, as if listening to his own written words.

"Yes. But with a degree of frustration. Because I can see that whatever time I have left is short and that my physical capabilities are few. I accept this serenely because what is happening to me is only normal."

"That's a brand-new feeling in your life. Inevitability."

"Right. It's new to me, but the inevitable imminence of the dénouement does not leave me depressed. Instead, even though I have been conscious from a very young age of death's inevitability, Camus's paradox of the absurdity of life in the face of death, consciousness of the pointlessness of rebelling against it, reaffirms my belief that the only way out of absurdity is to rebel, and to hold oneself in a state of ongoing rebellion against imposition and domination in any form.

"My most important concern now is not what we do, it is, regrettably, everyday things. What condition I am going to be in tomorrow. I think that what we have done and the point of doing it was to reflect upon the past. It is the little that we can do in the face of the facts."

"Throughout the book you have talked about anarchism, the movement to which you subscribe. What future do you see for it?"

"First off, anarchism is not an ideology. Which is why it possesses neither a present nor a past nor a future. Anarchist is a stance vis-à-vis authority. If there were no authority in life, the notion of freedom would not exist, since there would be no need for it. But since authority does exist, lo and behold the notion of anarchy.

"It is hard to picture what anarchism will be. For once and for all, perhaps, it will cease being a concept and turn into a natural practice since, from my point of view, it represents the only avenue to coexistence. In any case, by talking about it, I am indulging in a little science fiction," Octavio rounded off, with a barely perceptible grin.

"On another occasion you were talking about the matter of power. Doing away with power. But power can be found nearly everywhere. Except perhaps in the case of madness, where the individual has no capacity for power since he is not governed by the norms all around him. But what of the power to, say, end one's own life?"

"This wielding of power over oneself, suicide, is a decision made when one finds oneself incapable of going on. In the case of a terminally ill person, say, it is different. When life runs out, when you come to the end of your tether and derive no satisfaction from life, you may feel the need to bring it to an end."

"So it is a right vested in the individual?"

"Sure. Being able to carry it through is quite another matter. Because, as you know, socially, they make it hard for you." Octavio completed the sentence and lapsed into a thoughtful silence. After a while he continued, "I haven't ended, haven't finished my life because I still believe that I have a use for it, and my body is not as much of a torment to me as it might be. I have thought about it a few times, deliberately ending my life. I have no problem mulling over the possibility of voluntarily ending my own life. Who am I to tell anybody who decides to take his own life not to do so?"

"Alexander Berkman, for instance, took his own life."[36]

"I have a number of comrades who did so."

"In many cases on the left, suicide is taboo. Covered up or nonsensical arguments put forward. There is even lying about it. A comrade does not commit suicide."

"Well, it is my belief that that does not go on in libertarian circles. Many a comrade has taken his own life. It is part of the right to decide. Look, the guy in this photo," said Octavio, pointing, "is Fernando Aguirre. He fell ill at a very young age, forty, with incurable cancer and went through agony. In hospital he told me that he wanted to die, to end his life, and that he would do something, and would I help him. Obviously, he was in no position to do it on his own. I had a word with the doctors and informed them of his wishes. He died two days later. I think humankind's scruples about assisted dying are silly."

"Let me put this niggling thought to you," I said to Octavio, changing the subject again. "I should like you to go on. For some time, I have been mulling over the discoveries made regarding comets. Surprisingly, they hold large quantities of water, water created and traveling through time and space ever since the big bang of creation. Meaning that their water is the oldest in the universe. And the most surprising thing to me was that we are made up of water—70 percent. We are, literally, immemorial water become conscious. In a way, the water created in the big bang has come around to expressing itself and, say, trading ideas the way we are now doing. This notion of intelligent water confuses and perturbs me."

"Well, there is a poetry to what you say," Octavio answered. "For life to exist there has to be water. Where none exists, there is no life and there is no explanation for that. Thanks to water, we have the production of more complex factors such as the organs that make us up. I have no answer to that. Nobody does. What's the sense of applying a poetic outlook to the phenomenon? Well, I get a real kick out of drinking water. A fetus, life itself comes from a watery setting. Water is matter, electrons, particles, etc. What can we deduce from that? There is an essential value to this harmony because it is part of our makeup. Starting from there, I like and love the poetic, and the preservation of it is a natural follow through. I am against the destruction of this poetic fact that you describe."

"Is there still room for the poetic in human makeup?"

"Would poetry exist where there is no human makeup? A poem needs someone to write it and is meaningless unless there is somebody to read or listen to its being recited. One of the important preconditions for the preservation of life is words and, regrettably, words sometimes come heavily loaded with crap. I have an essential interest in stripping the crap away from words in order to get back to the essence of terms in the preservation of life.

"Just to give you an example, I once defined anarchy as a far cry from being an ideology, and the anarchists on the editorial staff of the *Tierra y Libertad* newspaper refused to publish that article of mine because they did not see eye-to-eye with anarchism's being mentioned as anything other than an ideology or a doctrine. In their eyes, treating it as an ideology or doctrine mattered if there was to be any added value to the term. The fetishism of words! Who's in charge of words and their definition? Language is a construct and we have to protect it and use it for what it is, rather than as a weapon of confrontation."

"As Orwell had it, we have to fight against the manipulation of meanings," I added, mindful of the Ministry of Love (love=war) in *1984*. "Spain's current prime minister speaks in the name of common sense, freedom, etc., but his definitions are a far cry from those notions, and he perverts them."

"Agustín García Calvo, for instance used to sign his writing between question marks. Agustín was querying the very meaning of his own name. A whole statement of principles."

"Octavio, our exchange has covered pretty much every subject. And I think we ought to let your own words act as the finale to the story of your life."

"Fine by me."

It is my absolute conviction that rebellion is the only meaning that life has in the face of the absurdity of existence (to borrow Camus's terms) and that rebellion affords us access to freedom; rebellion, defined as one of the universal values underpinning and manifesting human existence in the sense of the instinct of survival in action. Rebellion, from even prior to birth and later when we share in the life of society with other people—not just in making our own decisions and living to the full, but also in the search for and investment of meaning into our lives and into human society, so that it may be universally accessible to all.

This is the utopia that keeps us on the move and moving forward—knowingly or otherwise—down the byways that crisscross our lives, relentlessly, in spite of any weariness and setbacks. In my case, these are the byways I have been tramping to this very day ever since my youth, when, being exiled in Mexico, I started to rebel.

A rebellion, therefore, against all the forms of dominion, against Capital, the State, and Religion, but also against all instances and institutions that allow that trio to consolidate their dominance and perpetuate themselves within human societies. Among those, of course, there is the nuclear family (father, mother, children), which Capital, the State, and institutional religions portray as the "natural, universal, fundamental building block of society," in either its patriarchal or matriarchal form—plus other social institutions that mold disciplined citizens obedient to the established powers-that-be. There is a logic therefore behind my striving to espouse such a policy of behavior as my own. Whether I have pulled it off I cannot say, but I have always been coherent and consistent in this yearning for freedom; that "I want you free" was a constant in my performance or merely a form of words more or less demagogically articulating a yearning that, at present, at any rate, is beyond my reach.

I think I have been consistent in my behavior vis-à-vis all the people with whom circumstances have brought me into sentimental (affectionate, sexual) or affective relationships, whether in respect of my antiproprietorial stance or in the sense in which it should be a priority in every human relationship. I think I have been coherent in my dealings, in Mexico, living as a clandestine and right up to the present day. Coherent and transparent; as I have never made any secret of my mindset and modus vivendi with others.

Not that I have always been understood and accepted; but I do not mean by this that others were under some obligation to understand and accept me, that they had no right to wait for something else to come along, and that the failure to achieve has not left them frustrated. All I can say on this count is that I was aware of this and I faced up to the consequences. Not only of not being understood but also of being judged.

With regard to and insofar as circumstances have allowed, the exercise of freedom did not end any of the sentimental or affective relationships that circumstances have allowed me to establish, from my youth through to my present age, which is now threatening to interrupt them once and for all.

So how could I not have fond memories of those relationships when they are not only part and parcel of my life but also when it was through them that I was able to act upon my yearning or entitlement to be free? All the more so now, when age and the state of my health have whittled down my life to the simplest most essential features of human existence and to memories.

I continue to think about and yearn to be free as much as or more than ever. Because I believe human relationships should always to be the result of a freely made decision and should be freely sustained. As a result, this is also the manner, the path by which we shall someday see a free humanity.

Frustration and bitterness at my having to resign myself to bodily circumstances and the inevitable end do not depress me and do not alter my belief in continuing to rebel against the imponderable and the inescapable. It is that, which even today keeps me upright and walking, despite the aging of my body and the lack of stimulus in today's world. I'm still waiting for a world where the Spanish dictator is "tied up, with no loose ends" forty-two years on from his death.

Starting right now, in the late August of 2017, the imponderable and inescapable will have an increasing say in my life and, thus, in my rebellion which is more tokenistic now, and my dealings with those who are still around and still in touch with me, this "family" that circumstances have allowed us to build. Cognizant of this, the only thing that I can bequeath to them is whatever store they place by these recollections, which bear witness to our affection and to what my passage through this world was all about.

OCTAVIO ALBEROLA, Perpignan, late August 2017

Open Letter to Pedro Sánchez

Sr. Pedro Sánchez
Prime Minister

Being one of the Spaniards who crossed the Pyrenees on foot in 1939 seeking refuge in France, I felt that your tribute to Manuel Azaña and Antonio Machado spoke to me. Those two individuals also "found themselves compelled to leave Spain" and had to perish—like many another—in exile.

I was eleven years old back then and am now ninety-one years of age and, since 2007, following the promulgation of the Historical Memory Law, I have never stopped my denunciation of the unfathomable cravenness of a law which, though purporting to do right by the victims of Francoist repression, fails to rescind the verdicts handed down by the Francoist courts and, furthermore, perpetrates the victims' infamy—in its Article 10—in which they are divided into two categories, depending on the date of their executions, without a word of justification or explanation.

You will not, therefore, be surprised if I ask you once again to end this cravenness and this infamy. Not just because this can feasibly be done this day by decree, but also because it would be truly shameful if you were not to do so, having asked the exiles for "pardon" for Spain's not having done so "long ago."

The truth is that "exile is always an abomination," but the Francoist repression was even more abominable. Which is why it is infamy to retain the article of that law which draws a distinction between the individuals who, for fighting for the democratic freedoms that everybody in the world today purports to uphold, were deprived of their lives by Francoism.

Precisely because "it is late, very late," there should be no further delay ...

February 25, 2019

Notes

1. A Velázquez Hernández "El exilio español impulso económico para México? La experiencia empresarial del CTARE en 1939," in A. Mateos López and A. Sánchez Andrés (editors) *Ruptura y transición. España y Mexico, 1939* (Madrid, Spain: Eneida, 2011), 227–50.

2. Raúl "Carballeira" Lacunza (1918–1948), Argentinean-born maquis. After the Spanish Civil War, he fought in the French Resistance against the Nazis. Come the end of the Second World War, he switched to the anarchist resistance to Franco on behalf of which he mounted a number of incursions into Catalonia. He was gunned down by members of the BPS on the grounds of Montjuic in Barcelona.

3. The so-called Causa General was the process whereby Francoism investigated and purged anybody on the basis of what was described as "criminal acts carried out anywhere in the territory of the nation during Red rule."

4. DI were the initials of Defensa Interior, an armed agency set up by anarchists for the purpose of "chastising" the Franco regime; it was active from 1962 to 1965.

5. Juan García Oliver, *El eco de los pasos* (Paris: Éditions Ruedo Ibérico, 1978).

6. The Inter-Continental Secretariat was a body within the CNT, designed to ensure cohesion between the organization's structures in the various areas where the anarchist exile community resided (France, England, North Africa, Mexico, Venezuela, and Argentina).

7. The Iberian Revolutionary Liberation Directory (DRIL) was a Galician-Portuguese revolutionary group fighting against the Salazar and Franco dictatorships. Launched in 1959, it mounted sustained activities, complete with bomb attacks, from 1960 to 1964 when it mounted its last known operation.

8. Agustí Pons, *Converses amb Frederica Montseny* (Barcelona: Laia, 1977).

9. Federico Urales (real name Juan Montseny y Carret, 1864–1943). Trade unionist and anarchist born in Reus, he was a prominent publisher and director of *La Revista Blanca*. He wrote many articles and books and was highly regarded as an anarchist intellectual inside and outside the movement.

10. For the Delgado-Granado case, see C. Fonseca, *Garrote vil para dos inocentes* (Madrid: Temas de hoy, 1998) and E. Gomà Presas and X. Montanyà Atoche, directors, *Granados y Delgado, un crime légal* (documentary), France-Spain, Point du Jour, La Sept ARTE, Ovideo TV, 1996.

11. The "reserved sitting" was a meeting held privately at the congress in order to protect the security of participants. Not all congress participants were given prior notice, and security was very tight in order to preempt potential informers or indeed the police, who were aware of the congress.

12. Of student origin, the Dutch Provo movement was set up sometime around 1965. They organized *happenings* and all manner of countercultural events designed to grab attention by peaceful means, employing humor and creativity. They ceased operations around 1968.

13. *Cincopuntismo* was the name given by anarchists to overtures designed to arrive at an accommodation between the so-called Vertica Syndicates, meaning the Franco regime's Spanish Syndicalist Organization (OSE) and the CNT. After winning the civil war, the regime had set up a single trade union body, which lasted from 1940 until 1977; membership was compulsory, for workers and employers alike. The older Spanish trade unions, such as the CNT or the UGT, were outlawed.

14. The Public Order Court (Tribunal de Orden Público/TOP) was a judicial body in late-Francoist Spain. Essentially, it dealt with crackdowns on dissent or what the regime deemed political offenses.

15. The Industrial Workers of the World, founded in 1905, was a federation of internationalist-minded American trade unions. Though, as an organization, it has never defined itself, its ideology is akin to anarchosyndicalism.

16. See Stuart Christie (2005) *Franco Made Me a Terrorist*, and F. McHarg (2005) *Pistoleros! 3: 1920–1924*, Hastings, United Kingdom, both ChristieBooks.

17. Ñancahuazu was name given to the guerrilla war in the part of Bolivia under the command of Ernesto "Che" Guevara.

18. Giangiacomo Feltrinelli (1926–1972) was an Italian publisher and activist and founder of the GAP paramilitary group, which, together with the Red Brigades, were two instances of armed guerrillas in 1970s Italy. At the same time, Feltrinelli was a publisher of some note. He died following the accidental detonation of explosives that he was planting below an electricity pylon in Segrate near Milan.

19. Jean-Jacques Servan Schreiber (1924–2006), French journalist, essayist, and author. A writer of some vehemence, he normally focused on polemics about politics in the daily press. He was the founder of *L'Express*, which brought together articles by great French authors such as Camus, Sartre, and Malraux. Servan Schreiber subscribed to views close, politically, to those of his friend Francois Mitterrand and he earned some notoriety for his essay *The American Challenge* (1967). In all likelihood, Servan Schreiber was giving talks on that book during his visit to Spain.

20. Guy Debord (1931–1994) was the main driving force behind Situationism.

21. A Nansen passport was a personal document recognized by the UN; it had been devised by Fridtjof Nansen and helped identify political refugees during the twentieth century.

22. L. A. Edo, *La CNT en la encrucijada, Aventuras de un heterodoxo* (Barcelona: Flor del Viento, 2006).

23. Federación Obrera Regional Argentina (Argentinean Regional Workers' Federation) was the main Argentinean anarchist union organization. It was very prominent from the beginning of the twentieth century through to the early 1930s, when it went into decline with the advent of Peronist trade unionism.

24. The CFDT (Confédération Française Démocratique du Travail/French Democratic Labor Confederation) was one of several trade union confederations in France. It was organized on the basis of assemblies.

25. Natacha Duché and Ariane Gransac, *Prisons de femmes* (Paris: Editions Denoël, 1982).

26. R. Menchú and E. Burgos (1983) *Me llamo Rigoberta Menchu y así me nació la conciencia*, Havana, Cuba, Casa de las Américas.

27. Ateliers Varan was a training school for documentary filmmakers. It was founded by Jean Rouch and Jacques d'Arthuys.

28. E. Gomà Presas and X. Montanyà Atoche (directors), *Granado y Delgado, un crimen legal*, 1996.

29. See https://observatoriocriticocuba.org.

30. Tania Quintero, "'Me aburre ser nieto del Che' me dijo un día Canek Sánchez Guevara," October 8, 2017. https://www.radiotelevisionmarti.com/a/me-aburre-ser-nieto-del-che-me-dijo-canek-sanchez-guevara/154245.html.

31. Octavio Alberola, "La ilusión capitalista y la 'generación Internet,' July 26, 2012. http://www.alasbarricadas.org/noticias/node/21606. Octavio Alberola 'L'illusion capitaliste et la petite poucette,' July 23, 2012. http://lesoufflecesmavie.unbog.fr/2012/07/23/lillusion-capitaliste-et-la-petite-poucette-octavio-alberola.

32. Michel Serres, *Petite poucette* (Paris: Pommier, 2012).

33. Octavio Alberola, *Penser l'utopie—À l'Université Populaire de Perpignan* (Lavern, Spain: Bombarda Edicions, 2013).

34. Octavio Alberola, *Pensar la utopía en la acción—Trazas de un anarquista heterodoxo* (Lavern, Spain: Vombard Edicions, 2013).

35. Tomás Ibáñez, *Anarquismo en movimiento* (Barcelona: Virus Editorial, 2014).

36. Alexander Berkman (November 21, 1876 [Vilna, Lithuania]–June 28, 1936 [Nice, France]) was an anarchist writer and activist, and lover of the Russia activist Emma Goldman. After spending many years in prison, with his health fragile and disappointed with Soviet policy, he took his own life at the age of sixty-five.

AK PRESS is small, in terms of staff and resources, but we also manage to be one of the world's most productive anarchist publishing houses. We publish close to twenty books every year, and distribute thousands of other titles published by like-minded independent presses and projects from around the globe. We're entirely worker run and democratically managed. We operate without a corporate structure—no boss, no managers, no bullshit.

The **FRIENDS OF AK PRESS** program is a way you can directly contribute to the continued existence of AK Press, and ensure that we're able to keep publishing books like this one! Friends pay $25 a month directly into our publishing account ($30 for Canada, $35 for international), and receive a copy of every book AK Press publishes for the duration of their membership! Friends also receive a discount on anything they order from our website or buy at a table: 50% on AK titles, and 30% on everything else. We have a Friends of AK ebook program as well: $15 a month gets you an electronic copy of every book we publish for the duration of your membership. *You can even sponsor a very discounted membership for someone in prison.*

Email **friendsofak@akpress.org** for more info, or visit the website: **https://www.akpress.org/friends.html**.

There are always great book projects in the works—so sign up now to become a Friend of AK Press, and let the presses roll!